CENTENARY OF THE BOROUGH OF DOUGLAS 1896 - 1996

A CELEBRATION

compiled by

GORDON N. KNIVETON
ROBERT E. FORSTER, B.A.
ROBERT KELLY
STUART SLACK
FRANK COWIN, F.R.I.C.S.

The Corporate Common Seal of the Borough, which is the Borough Arms,
was adopted and approved at the first statutory meeting of the Town
Council on Monday, 2nd March 1896. The design was prepared by T. G.
Taylor, the then Borough Surveyor, and is in the form of a shield, the four
quarters of which are designed as follows: In what is known and
described in heraldry as the dexter chief corner, the old Viking Ship is
placed; in the adjoining quarter, the Eagle and Child, representing the
Arms of the Derby family who were rulers of the Isle of Man for four
centuries.

Immediately under the Viking Ship is placed a Lion Rampant, representing the Arms of the Athol family, successors to the Derby family; and in
the quarter adjoining, the Three Legs of Man ungartered; the whole being
surmounted by the Monarchial Crown of Her Majesty the Queen, as Lord
of Man.

Underneath is a scroll with the words "Borough of Douglas", and
another scroll containing the words in Manx *"Kiannoortys cheusthie
jeh Kiannoortys"* which, in English, means "Government within a
Government", the Latin being "Imperium in Imperio".

*A Douglas "logo", or emblem, to be used in conjunction with
the Borough Arms, was approved by the Council in 1993 in
preparation for the Douglas Corporation Centenary. This
emblem is to be used on street furniture, letterheads and other
applications where a symbol less formal than the Common
Seal is appropriate.*

ISBN 1 873120 20 6 (Soft Back) 1 873120 21 4 (Hard Back)

FOREWORD
by
The Worshipful Mayor of Douglas
Councillor W. J. Corkish, J.P.

IN this Centenary Year we celebrate the achievements of the men and women, members, officers and employees of the Corporation who have, over the past hundred years, been responsible for many remarkable achievements. In the forefront of our minds must be the Corporation's water, transport and electricity undertakings, and in the area of housing and public health, not to mention the provision of entertainment for Islanders and visitors at the Villa Marina and the Summerland Leisure Complex. The extent, variety and quality of the Corporation's pioneering achievements in these areas is a standing tribute about which the people of Douglas can be justly proud.

Over the years the benefit of much of this early investment by the Corporation has passed to the Isle of Man Government thereby benefiting the Island as a whole. Further considerable gifts of land by the Corporation for Departmental projects have furthered that partnership, the Corporation along with other Local Authorities on the Island, now looking to the Department of Local Government and the Environment to provide the leadership and support that is necessary to enable the Island's Local Authorities to meet new needs in the twenty-first century.

Much of the rest of this decade will inevitably be spent with Government in providing the money needed if the Douglas infrastructure and buildings are to be fit for Douglas in the years ahead. A number of important projects form part of the Corporation's Centenary celebrations and further projected plans. In the forefront of these is the Villa Marina development, the renewal of the sewerage infrastructure, the refurbishment of the Town Hall, Jubilee Clock and horse tram stables as a working museum. Significant provision has already been made by the Corporation as agents for Government in providing advanced sheltered accommodation at Waverley Court and the attractive new Donkey Fields housing estate, known as Lheannag Park.

All of these new projects are the result of considerable unsung work on the part of the members and the officers of the Corporation who wish to play their part today in commemorating those early pioneers who have left their mark on the Island's capital and shaped it for the future. What better way to commemorate those achievements than looking forward with Government and the private sector to the development of Douglas in the years ahead and in furthering its devlopment as an international financial and banking centre and as the capital of the Isle of Man. We look forward to the vision of Douglas 2000 being realised together.

What then lies in the years ahead when the immediate festivities of the Corporation's Centenary are passed? The answer to this must lie above all in the readiness of the Corporation to adapt to a new partnership role guided by Government and in partnership both with Government and with private and voluntary sectors. In short, in order to have an effective and viable rôle in the future, the Corporation will need to be as much an agency for change and development as in exercising its traditional rôle as direct provider of services to the public. The search for greater effectiveness and value for money will need to reflect and sometimes challenge the best achievements of the private sector.

The Corporation's motto over the past one hundred years - *Kiannoortys Cheusthie-Jeh Kiannoortys* - Government within Government - is in need of modification or addition. That is why our pledge for the future must be Government within Government - diversity in provision.

We are fortunate in not celebrating our Centenary alone but together with the representatives from other associated areas with whom the Corporation has developed links - Dun Laoghaire, Wyre and Victor Harbor, Australia, the last of which runs a parallel but year-round tram service in the Southern hemisphere. A hundred years ago such an association would have been unthinkable if not impossible - what will the position be in one hundred years from now? I hope that a number of changes may reflect a rounding of the circle of values rather than ever-increasing change for change's sake, and that the traditional symbol and flagship of the Douglas Corporation, the horse trams, will still continue to operate in some form or another.

I hope that the people of Douglas will find something in the planned programme for the Centenary year which they might enjoy and share as a tribute to this great town of Douglas, past, present and future.

W J Corkish

CONTENTS

PART ONE: 1896-1918

PART TWO: 1919-1945

PART THREE: 1946-1996

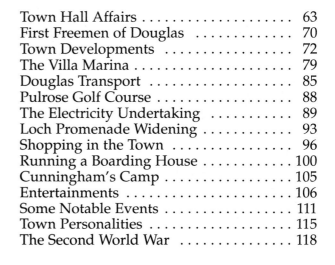

APPENDICES

THE BEGINNINGS

IN 1896 The Municipal Borough of Douglas came into being as a result of Tynwald's approval, granted the previous year, of the The Douglas Municipal Corporation Act. The Act, in effect, entrusted 18 Councillors drawn from 6 wards, 6 Aldermen and a Mayor with the task of seeing Douglas into an exciting new century. It was undoubtedly the century which proved to be the most innovative, scientifically progressive, and even catastrophic, in Manx history.

Like the other Manx river settlements, Douglas had started its life as a humble fishing village, its tiny houses clustered on the river bank, the fishing boats drawn up in the shelter afforded. There can be little doubt that the Vikings found the bay and sailed their longboats up river, but thereafter the little village remained comparatively quiet and undisturbed for several centuries.

In the seventeenth century the then Lord of Mann remarked that the Island would remain poverty stricken until 'there trading be'. But if there was to be trading, where to and where from? And if there was a good harbour then the 'where' would be identified the more readily. In the mid-seventeenth century Chaloner, the Island's Governor during the Commonwealth period, described Douglas as 'the safest harbour'; in 1681 the harbour was 'commodious' and 'a safe road for ships'. By this time, too, the discovery and settlement of the New World had resulted in the rapid development of ports on the west coast of Britain, one of the most famous being Liverpool which was handily placed for Douglas. Indeed, by 1726 the historian Waldron was able to describe Douglas as 'the town of most trade' and throughout the century the town developed as its trade increased hand over fist.

The great Manx merchants of the eighteenth century - such as the Murreys, the Moores and the Bacons - presided over what today could well be described as a boom town. The population increased by 800 or so in 1710; and by almost 2,500 in 1784; the number of houses increased, and the wealth of the town increased. It was a town built and maintained by trade, especially the euphemistically named 'Running Trade'. Smuggling had been the most lucrative pursuit of the Manx for many years and Douglas played its full part in it. Naturally, the 'commodious' harbour had to be improved to cater for such busy shipping. Quays had to be built; piers to provide shelter; and bridges, even when quarrelled over so bitterly by such as Moore and Heywood, constructed. Such harbour schemes were capped by the start in 1793 of the construction of the Red Pier.

THE NINETEENTH CENTURY

The expansion of the town became more rapid with the onset of the new century. The general demographic trend in the United Kingdom with people moving from the country to the towns was reflected here as rural distress bit deep. However, this movement paled into insignificance when from virtually the beginning of the nineteenth century the fashion of sea-bathing, of a bracing seaside holiday took hold. Douglas with its magnificent shore and the unparalleled sweep of its superb bay was ideally placed to exploit this new custom. Its geographical situation and its connections with Liverpool and the vast potential market of an increasingly industrialised North of England guaranteed the successful development of Douglas as one of the new fangled holiday resorts.

The effects of all this was cataclysmic. The narrow lanes enclosed by desperately small insanitary dwellings - the 'rookeries' - twisted and turned in

This earliest pictorial representation of Douglas is one of a series of drawings by Daniel King who visited the Island in the middle of the seventeenth century. The sheltered harbour led to the tiny fishing village of Douglas developing into a small town. (Manx National Heritage)

greater numbers. The middens, the open sewers, the stench of the harbour at low tide cast a noxious cloud over the town. Names that became familiar - such as Fairy Ground, Fancy Street, the Happy City and New Bond Street - could not disguise the fact that such conditions were no longer acceptable, although the new Duke Street and Strand Street did a little to improve things. Nor were harbour facilities suitable for seamen acceptable for holiday makers. Things had to improve. By 1829 the first oil lamps were seen on the streets; a few years later gas lamps appeared. A hospital in Fort Street had joined the Dispensary by 1850. Earlier, in 1837, the House of Industry had begun to address the problem of the destitute. Problems still existed - epidemics raged and cholera continued to strike down its victims. But through the first half of the century Douglas struggled to tackle the problems of its growing size and increasing success.

The major difficulty was perhaps the government of the towns. The old system of Town Captains had long been replaced by the rule of the Town High Bailiffs. But this system was finding it increasingly difficult to cope with the complexity of the town's problems. Yet, what to replace it? In 1844 the townsfolk at a public meeting had rejected a proposal to elect a Town Council. This was followed by a series of public meetings at which time after time it was stated that 'in sewering, paving, lighting and cleansing this town is far behind'. But

when the Town Bill, with its optional clauses, was passed by Tynwald in 1852 and the good citizens of Douglas were asked if they wanted to see it applied to Douglas, they voted 848 to 79 against!

However, public opinion slowly hardened throughout the decade as it became more and more obvious that something had to be done. By the end of the decade it was clear that the town's ratepayers increasingly believed that they should have the power to assess themselves and to elect their own commissioners to control their money. A new Town Bill, remarkably similar but without the optional clauses of the 1852 Bill, was introduced and accepted. In 1860, on Tuesday, 24th July, the first election of the Douglas Town Commissioners was held. The Court House doors in Athol Street opened at 9 a.m. and the crowd rapidly built up. Thirty candidates were nominated for the nine seats. At the end of the day it was announced that 3,467 votes had been cast and Samuel Harris with 388 votes and Richard Sherwood with 344 had topped the poll. Both were advocates and the remaining Commissioners included two builders, two grocers, one tailor, a printer and an agent. Seven days later at their first meeting Samuel Harris was elected Chairman.

THE TOWN COMMISSIONERS

The new structure was thus firmly established and Douglas Town Commissioners became responsible

One of Thomas Keig's classic views from the top of the harbour as it was in the mid 1890s. One of the Steam Packet paddlers is at its winter moorings by the Tongue, the jetty which was built on the tongue of land between the mouth of the Douglas river and the tidal seawater of the harbour. On the right stand the offices, chimney and gasometer of the Douglas Gas Light Company, while further down the South Quay can be seen the chimney of a former brewery. (Keig Collection)

for the development of the town in one of the most important periods in its history, recognised in 1869 when the status of Capital was conferred. Four years after its conception the Commission was empowered to enact bye-laws and later still given unlimited rating powers and the right to borrow funds.

With commendable speed the sewerage problem had been tackled by 1869 but if the proper development of the town as a major holiday resort were to occur then there would have to be better harbour facilities for the ever increasing visitors. Just as important, there had to be accommodation for them in areas of the town more salubrious than the smelly jumble of narrow insanitary lanes of the old fishing and trading port. Such more pleasant areas would need to be more accessible and this in turn meant new streets.

Fortunately, these demands coincided with the governorship of Henry Loch whose energy and vision were of inestimable value to the Island in those crucial years, and to Douglas in particular. By 1867 the magnificent new pier, to be called the Victoria Pier, had been started followed in 1879 by the Battery Pier. Douglas Harbour had been transformed. The driving of the new broad thoroughfare of Victoria Street through some of the old town enabled the holiday-maker to have a comfortable passage from the boats to the upper and newer terraces. A little later, in 1878, enclosure of a large area of the foreshore and its division into building plots enabled the construction of the Loch Promenade. This was of particular significance as it ensured the reorientation of the town, started by the construction of the Castle Mona, from one looking to the harbour as its main concern to one looking out to the bay.

In 1870 60,000 visitors came and this figure increased annually with 182,000 arriving in 1884. Queen Victoria's Jubilee in 1887 saw 310,916 visitors landing at Douglas. These were almost phenomenal increases and just as half a century earlier great pressure had been put on the structure of the town's government, so once again thought started to be given to further progress in that area. By 1891, too, the percentage of the Manx population living in Douglas had leapt to 35%

The Commissioners themselves were well aware of the need. They recognised that the 'existing system' should give way to a system 'which will undoubtedly lend more dignity and eclat'. They were especially keen that Douglas should be placed on an equal footing with its 'English competitors and Rivals'. Nor were they unaware of the Municipal Corporations Act that had been passed in the United Kingdom in 1882.

Early in 1895 a Bill to provide for the Municipal Incorporation of Douglas was circulated amongst Members of the House of Keys. By the autumn the Town Clerk, Thomas Nesbitt, had produced an erudite and comprehensive report on the topic in which he emphasised he saw 'no additional cost being incurred as the direct result of incorporation' - a matter dear to the heart of ratepayers.

DOUGLAS CORPORATION

The Douglas Municipal Corporation Act of that year provided for the election of 18 Councillors from the six wards already in existence, three from each ward; and the further election by them of six Aldermen and a Mayor. This new body would exercise all the powers the Town Commissioners already possessed plus others particularised in the Incorporation Act.

The new development caught the imagination of the burgesses. The election was fixed for 20th February, 1896, and the newspapers reported that it was 'agitating the minds of everyone'. The main issues soon emerged: Drainage of the Town; Douglas Water Supply; Market Accommodation; Public Baths; Tramways, Lighting and 'resistance to any unnecessary increase in administrative costs'. Public meetings were held in all six wards, and stormy meetings they often were. Chairmen appealed sometimes unavailingly for order; loud

A Keig view along the North Quay. The harbour was a busy scene as sailing ships from many parts brought in coal and timber, together with supplies for the hotels and visiting industry. Note the gas lamp, supplied from Gelling's Foundry on the South Quay. These gas lamps were the first public gas lamps in the Island and were provided by the Harbour Commissioners. (Keig Collection)

THE TOWN COMMISSIONERS MAKE A START

The eventual passing of the Douglas Town Act of 1860 resulted in nine Commissioners being elected as representatives of the townsfolk. Mr Samuel Harris of Marathon House was elected the first Chairman. Early meetings were held in the Court House but subsequently moved to the old Seneschal Office owned by Mr Harris. George William Dumbell was appointed Treasurer to the Commissioners and Mr William Clifford was appointed Clerk, Surveyor, Overseer and Collector at £85 per annum. With considerable dedication these first Commissioners began to tackle in earnest the inherent problems confronting them - drainage, water supply, street lighting and paving to mention but a few. One of their first acts was to employ six scavengers to clean up the streets and remove the ubiquitous midden heaps. Other matters included the extension of the limited boundaries and the levying of the stipulated rate of one shilling which included the cost of evaluation.

The Commissioners, however, soon found that they were inhibited by their statutory powers and gradually the Douglas Town Amendment Bill was formulated and presented to the Keys early in 1864. It was rejected, the self-elected Keys, mainly the landed gentry from outside the town, being reluctant to divest further powers to the Commissioners who, as one member put it, were 'mere tradesmen' wishing to be treated as kings. Feelings ran high and Mr George Brown, editor of the Isle of Man Weekly Times, was gaoled at Castle Rushen after being found guilty of contempt by the Keys following his refusal to apologise for his writings. The Bill, however, was quickly re-introduced and, with certain amendments, was finally promulgated in May of that year.

The Amendment Bill gave the Commissioners many additional and increased powers, in particular relating to bye-laws, building requirements, fire fighting, slaughter houses, sanitary provisions etc.; but probably the most important were the powers to fix their own rate and to borrow money on mortgage of the rates for a sum not exceeding £6,000 for Drainage and Sewerage. It was the latter which was by far the most pressing problem. In the older part of the town the open channels led into the harbour or direct onto the shore. In the heat of summer the obnoxious stench increased and could be detected far beyond the town limits. Cholera was a constant threat and the town had a higher death rate than anywhere in England. Nor was this tolerable for the ever increasing number of summer visitors.

In September, 1865, Mr G W Stephenson, borough engineer of Halifax, was engaged to draw up plans for a drainage and sewerage system for the town. Work commenced the following year. The system began opposite the Castle Mona from which point a main intercepting sewer, 15 inches in diameter, ran along the shore road to Broadway. At this point the secondary drains from the higher parts of the town, in the neighbourhood of Victoria Road and Derby Road, were connected with the main drain

Originally built as the Registry Office in the time of the Duke of Athol, this building was adopted as the Town Hall in 1860. Later the building was considerably enlarged and was known as Seneschal House. In the background can be seen the lofty nave of St. Barnabas Church. (Keig Collection)

which was now increased to a diameter of 24 inches. Proceeding along the Shore Road to Castle Street, it there received the drains from the districts lying to the west, including Wellington Square, Finch Road and other parts and then, further enlarged to a diameter of 30 inches, it turned on to the shore along which it ran, receiving subsidiary drains at the different 'slips' or openings on to the shore. Opposite Drumgold Street it was again enlarged to 36 inches, and, crossing the sands to the Pollock rocks, it joined the main outlet, which was 42 inches in diameter.

The south part of the town, between Drumgold Street and the harbour, was provided with a second intercepting sewer, with subsidiary drains running into it, along the North Quay and through the adjoining districts, joining the main outlet at the Pollock rocks. The outfall was carried along a natural slope through these rocks to below sea level where it discharged the sewage matter into the sea. The system was completed in 1869 and, with modifications, extensions and maintenance, continues to serve to the present time. It was the first major capital work of the Commissioners to be followed in the next thirty years or so by many developments and improvements to the town.

This design for a seal and for use as a heading for letters was adopted by the Town Commissioners in 1863. The same design was carved on the Chairman's chair which is still in use by chairmen of Committees of the Town Council.

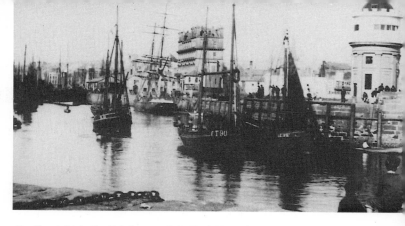

A busy market scene on the North Quay with the original British Hotel overlooking the market square. It was here that the Corporation built the market halls of today, these being officially opened in 1900. (Keig Collection)

On the right is the lighthouse of the Red Pier which was opened in 1801 to receive passenger ships. The tall building in the centre is Imperial Buildings, once the headquarters of the Steam Packet Company, which was originally built as the Imperial Hotel in the 1860s. (Keig Collection)

cries of 'put him out' were heard. 'Offensive dog-gerel verses' appeared on handbills. Indeed, one newspaper felt obliged to comment: 'All candidates as a result of the dirty missile (mud slinging) are plentiful bespattered'. It added ominously that whatever the outcome of the election the candidates could rest assured of one thing - 'the mud will stick for a long time'.

The situation soon became clear. Of the six wards there would be no contest in Numbers 5 and 6, three candidates coming forward in each. In the other wards the most hotly contested was Number 3 with six contestants. Voting day proved inclement but exciting. The public houses in fact reported a roaring trade but by 9.30 p.m. the votes had been counted and the results declared from the balcony of the Court House in Athol Street. The three successful candidates in each of the four contested wards were announced. A total of 4,491 votes had been cast and there had been a 66% turn-out. On 2nd March the first meeting of the new Council was held in the Town Hall in Fort Street, first used by the Town Commissioners. Mr Thomas Keig, photographer, who had been returned in No.2 Ward was unanimously elected as the first Mayor. The six Aldermen were then elected, occasioning by-elections in Wards 2, 4, 5 and 6 some fourteen days later. The new institution composed itself, dealt with the seating positions of the new Councillors - one suggestion was that they should work round according to the sun - decided the motto of the new borough should be in Manx, and then began to tackle the issues on which they had been elected.

It was soon clear that the urgency with which the several issues had been discussed was well merited. The increase in holiday-makers continued, reaching over 351,000 in 1900 with the new boarding houses in the upper town and along the bay proving increasingly attractive.

Further areas of the old town were dealt with immediately. Between 1895 and 1899 the James Street, King Street and Lord Street areas were cleared and rebuilt. In 1899 the Borough Cemetery was established. The Cable Trams were operating by 1896 and in 1900, as a recognition of the new status of the town, the new Town Hall and Public Library, built at a cost of £25,078, was in use. The new century was starting and the Borough of Douglas had the new government structure necessary to cope with the challenges that lay ahead.

INTO THE TWENTIETH CENTURY

With visitors arriving each summer in their hundreds of thousands, with building going on apace, new streets, roads and avenues appearing in rapid succession, the Town Council were entitled to look forward with confidence. Douglas really was booming and all speculative ventures seemed blessed with success. Until 3rd February, 1900, that is. On that day Dumbell's Bank failed and its effects were quite simply catastrophic. Shops closed, businesses collapsed and many in all walks of life were ruined. Yet perhaps the greatest blow of all was to the confidence of the townsfolk. The almost arrogant optimism of recent years vanished never to return and the businesses of the Island, and Douglas in particular, while picking up the pieces with remarkable speed, now found an element of caution in their plans.

No doubt Douglas Town Council reacted similarly but it held its nerve and in the first decade embarked on a series of developments that were to serve the town virtually for the rest of the century. In 1900 the Baldwin Reservoir was started, being completed in 1905, a project of incalculable importance to the future of the town. The Public Markets were opened in 1900 at a cost of some £16,000. By 1902 the Tramways Undertaking had been bought for £50,000 and new Tramway bye-laws published; and the extension to Victoria Pier completed. Two years later the town boundaries were extended followed by the first of the benefactions of Henry Bloom Noble with the building of Noble's Baths with detailed bye-laws for its use. Males over eight years, for example, were expressly forbidden from entering the baths for females.

In 1909 Noble's Park was given by the Trustees of the H.B. Noble Estate for the recreation of the townsfolk. As a result of the 1910 Villa Marina Act, the Villa Marina and its grounds were purchased from the Noble's Trustees for £60,000. The Royal Hall and the Villa Marina complex, then known as the Kursaal, was opened on the 19th July, 1913, the year in which the total of visitor arrivals to the Island peaked at 615,726. Then Europe was plunged into the First World War.

BOUNDARIES AND WARDS

Under the Douglas Town Act of 1860 the Commissioners were empowered to make application to extend the boundaries under their jurisdiction. This was one of the first matters to be discussed and by November, 1860 the boundary had been fixed as follows: From the boundary wall of Harold Tower up to above the road leading to Douglas Head and thence above the quarry behind Taubman Terrace and the Gas Works before dropping to the west side of the bridge at the top of the harbour; across the river to the Lake and across Peel Road just below the Brown Bobby Inn; across the Hills estate north to Eastfield thence to Woodbourne Road (about to be laid out for building) opposite the end of Woodside Terrace. The line then proceeded to the top end of Stanley Terrace and then north to Victoria Road behind Marathon House. From Victoria Road the line led to the upper Lodge of Falcon Cliff and then to the summit of the Crescent and above the quarry at the foot of Burnt Mill Hill (Summerhill) to a point beyond the reservoir of the Water Works Company. From there it crossed the Burnt Mill Road then turned east above Strathallan Crescent and dropped steeply to beyond Pollock Castle to the low water mark; then easterly along the foreshore to the Pierhead and across to the point below Harold Tower.

In 1867 the Douglas Foreshore was purchased from the Crown for £764; and in 1892, as a result of the Howstrake Act of that year, Port Jack Glen and the Brows from Derby Castle (formerly Pollock Castle) to Onchan Harbour were vested in the Town Commissioners. The Commissioners successfully made extensions on five occasions to include areas where residents earned their living by working in the town. By this means the town population was increased by 2,000 and, in return for the payment of rates, the new burgesses benefited by connection to water mains, the sewerage system and having the streets cleaned and lighted.

The extension of boundaries was taken up by the Town Council whose Boundary Committee had ambitious ideas. In 1903 approaches were made to Tynwald to extend the town's influence by taking in the huge Ballaquayle Estate, Onchan Village and the Howstrake Estate. Strong opposition from the Onchan Commissioners was accepted by the Tynwald Court Committee now presided over by the newly-appointed Lord Raglan. Negotiations then concentrated on the Ballaquayle estate and its inclusion within the town boundary meant that Douglas almost doubled in size and its rateable value increased to £123,000. Thus began the spread of the town into Upper Douglas and it was estimated a 1.5 penny rate would be required to bring the roads, sewers and water mains of the new area into line with the rest of the town.

The inclusion of the Ballaquayle estate came into effect in 1904 and, with Town Council elections at the end of that year, a revision of the six wards was undertaken. At the same time it was decided to refer to each ward by name rather than by number.

The names were chosen because of their historical connections with the town, especially those of the Derby family and their successors, the Athols and Murray's. Thus the wards were named as follows : 1 - St. George's; 2 - Victoria; 3 - Hills; 4 - Derby; 5 - Murray's (in preference to Woodbourne) and 6 - Athol (in preference to Crescent). These names are still in use today though over the years adjustments have been made to equalise the number of burgesses

A view of the outer harbour at the turn of the century when steam cargo ships were taking over from the sailing ships. The photograph also shows the swing bridge built by the Harbour Commissioners and opened in 1896 to connect the North and South Quays and give easier access to Douglas Head.

NINETEENTH CENTURY TOWN DEVELOPMENTS

It was not until the 1870s that Douglas made use of its magnificent bay which enabled the more flamboyant writers to refer to it as the 'Naples of the North.' This was the result of the efforts and foresight of Governor Loch who pushed forward schemes which led to the decade seeing a fine new pier and a wide street linking it to the developing upper part of the town, both of which were named after the reigning Queen Victoria. Part of the Governor's great plan also included a new promenade which still bears his name.

Prior to that period which really heralded the visiting industry, the town huddled around its commercial centre - the harbour - while the waters of the bay swirled around the rear of the houses in Strand Street (formerly Sand Street) and Fort Street. The earliest records show the town in the form of a triangle and at the commencement of the eighteenth century it is estimated to have been bounded by the modern Parade Street, Fort Street, Wellington Street, Nelson Street, Barrack Street, Queen Street and the Quay. The harbour extended as far as the point of the Tongue, and the area above that encompassing the upper harbour, railway station and the timber yards was a swampy waste known as the Nunnery Lake, hence Lake Road.

The houses on the north side of Queen Street and the south west side of Fort Street looked onto the Lake and Bay respectively, and it was the completion of these streets that could be said to be the first 'filling out' of the town. The east side of the Parade, now Parade Street, was a beach and it was only by continuous repair of a bulwark, known as the 'ffence', that the town was not flooded more frequently than it actually was.

The mid-eighteenth century saw the Ballakermeen quarterland, which formed the backcloth to the town, changing hands and parts of it bordering the Sandside, which later became Strand Street, being sold off. A bridge was built across the harbour amid much controversy, and this led to the development of the South Quay mainly to the benefit of Captain Thomas Heywood of the Nunnery who owned all the land south of the river and who sponsored the bridge.

Heywood's bridge crossed the harbour at its narrowest point between the modern Ridgeway Street and the Gas Works, and it supplemented the existing bridge which was at the top of Leigh Terrace and which continued across the Lake by means of a causeway as far as the Big Well which gave its name to what is now part of Lord Street. The new bridge lasted but twenty years before necessary expansion of the harbour led to its demolition and the replacement of both bridges by the two-arched Stone Bridge on the site of the present concrete structure which was updated in 1936.

It was later in the eighteenth century that large parcels of the massive Ballaquayle quarterland came on the market, eventually coming into the

This historic photograph dates from the 1860s. Bottom right can be seen the remains of the Douglas fort standing on Pollock Rock and which gave its name to Fort Street. At that time there was little protection from the sea. The ramshackle layout of the older part of the town is in contrast with the stately terraces appearing on the slopes above the seafront. (Manx National Heritage)

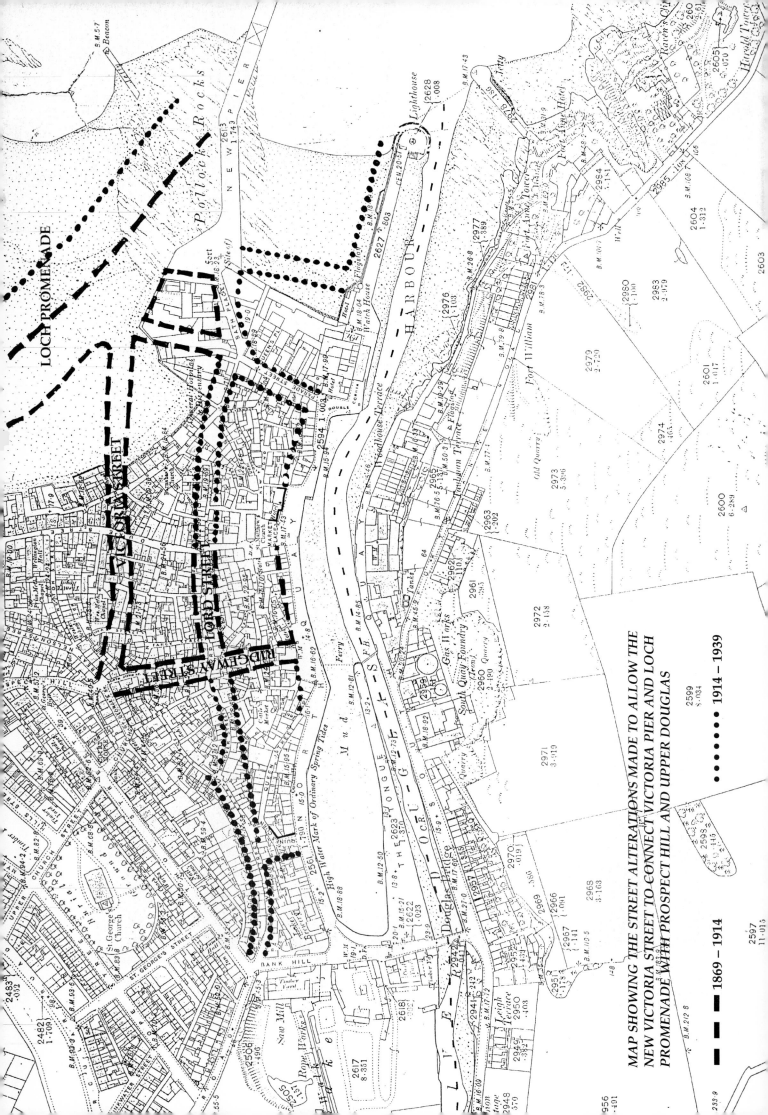

MAP SHOWING THE STREET ALTERATIONS MADE TO ALLOW THE
NEW VICTORIA STREET TO CONNECT VICTORIA PIER AND LOCH
PROMENADE WITH PROSPECT HILL AND UPPER DOUGLAS

— — — 1869 – 1914

●●●●● 1914 – 1939

The first residences of Athol Street appeared in 1811 and later it was described as 'the best built street in town'. However there were many complaints about the state of the street caused by builders conveying materials to Finch Road and by farmers carting seaweed for manure. The situation was somewhat remedied in 1839 when the street was one of the first to be macadamised. The photograph shows the street's welcome to Governor Pigott in 1861. (Manx National Heritage)

Collister's coaches being made ready in St. George's Street for the arrival of Governor Loch, 17th February, 1863. The bank premises on the left are those of The Isle of Man Bank for Savings, more popularly known as 'The Penny Bank', which later moved into Athol Street. (Manx National Heritage)

hands of the Fourth Duke of Athol by a series of strategic purchases. Ballaquayle covered the area on which much of the upper part of the town is now laid out and stretched from the seafront between Broadway and Palace Terrace in a wide swathe across Ballaquayle Road and Bray Hill to the River Glass between Quarter Bridge and Tromode weirs. By the time the Duke built the Castle Mona in 1804 he had also acquired parts of the Glencrutchery and Bemahague quarterlands on which he erected in 1824 the first four holiday villas on what became Strathallan Crescent. The Duke thus owned the margin of the bay from Broadway to Derby Castle.

Meanwhile there was still a reluctance to extend the town up onto the banks above Nelson Street and Barrack Street and although St. Georges's Church had been completed in 1780, it was still 'in the country' until 1809 when Athol Street was laid out, providing plots for some fine late-Regency style residences. The town continued to grow along the line of Strand Street and Market Street and the first major development was in the area known as the Big Garden which later became Wellington

Square and which is now the site of the Chester Street car park.

The earliest street name dates from 1787 when part of John Mylwrath's (pronounced Mucklewrath) property known as Muckle's Gate was mentioned in a deed of sale. The thoroughfare still exists as the service lane alongside the Co-op building in Duke Street/Lord Street. Other street names had followed by the end of the eighteenth century including Strand Street, Church Street, Big Well Street and Duke Street.

An important purchase in 1805 was that of the Marine estate by George Steuart, architect of the Red Pier and Castle Mona; it was on this land that Villa Marina, Derby Square and the Windsor Park properties were eventually constructed. The 1830s saw much change with Castle Mona becoming a hotel following the death of the Duke, Prospect Hill being opened out and Finch Road being laid out, the latter, in effect, forming a by-pass between the lower town and the developments beyond Broadway in order to avoid the narrow roadway and tight bends of Strand Street.

That decade also saw the development of Stanley Terrace and Victoria Road on part of the now available Castle Mona grounds. In the following years the prestigious terraces of Clarence and Esplanade were laid out on the Castle lawns. By 1850 the area

This eyesore of a building, plastered with advertisements, stood on the corner of Athol Street and Prospect Hill. It was demolished to make way for the head office of the Isle of Man Bank. (Manx National Heritage)

The prestigious head office of the Isle of Man Banking Company Ltd. was completed in 1902. Using light grey granite from Aberdeen it was designed in the style of the Italian Renaissance.

Typical of the streets of old Douglas was Fancy Street whose name did little to hide the squalid housing conditions. This photograph is dated 1895 when the street was one of those demolished for town improvement projects, in this case for the creation of Ridgeway Street. (Manx National Heritage)

This well-known feature of Strand Street, sometimes known as Arch Lane, but more correctly as Guttery Gable, led to a small square and Market Street. It survived when the Strand Cinema was built in 1913. (Manx National Heritage)

around Prospect Terrace was taking shape as were the terraces on Douglas Head, while three or four years later parts of Finch Hill were sold off by the Christian family to form Albert Street, Christian Road and the adjoining roads. Hope Street dates from this period followed by Circular Road and the streets on Harrison's Woodbourne estate - Sydney, Brisbane and Oxford.

By this time, 1860, the first Town Commissioners had been elected and the town continued to expand along Woodbourne Road and on to the Murrays estate, with fill-ins in the block between Tynwald Street and Allan Street.

Despite clashes between the first popularly elected Keys in 1867 and Governor Loch, who had taken office four years earlier, plans were pushed forward to create the Victoria Pier and provide, for the first time, a satisfactory low water landing facility. This was formally opened in 1872 and immediately the problem of access through the narrow streets of the town became apparent. Samuel Harris, now High Bailiff of Douglas, had demonstrated the advantages of a promenade having constructed, with public subscription, the one which now bears his name. Plans were laid to form an embankment from Harris Promenade to the new pier and this was eventually linked with a scheme to thrust what

was to become Victoria Street across the old streets to join the pier with Prospect Hill, thus creating access to all parts of the town.

Arrangements were made for part of the foreshore to be purchased from the British Government, and despite considerable dispute, details of which would fill another volume of this size, both Loch Promenade and Victoria Street were completed in 1875 - a tribute to Governor Loch's great pertinacity. Building plots both in Victoria Street and on the new promenade were much sought after and their sale went a long way to defraying the construction costs.

The 1880s saw the Farrants' part of Ballaquayle being sold off which resulted in the laying out of the land around Hawarden Avenue, Queen's Gardens and Selborne Drive; and the appearance of Hutchinson Square, Little Switzerland and the promenade Drives - Empress, Mona and Castle. Walpole Avenue was pushed through Twemlows shipyard and, in 1894, another major construction took place with the building of Ridgeway Street, just in time for the incorporation of the town and the erection of new municipal offices there.

ARTISANS' DWELLINGS

Under the Town Improvement Acts the town authorities were empowered to purchase and demolish older properties which were barely fit for habitation and provide new accommodation for the displaced persons. This was a formidable task

For nearly two centuries old St. Matthew's overlooked the comings and goings of the busy market square. But the scene changed when the church was demolished to make way for the market halls opened in 1900. (Manx National Heritage)

as the old part of the town abounded with such primitive housing. A start was made in 1895 by the Town Commissioners and by 1899 artisan dwellings, as they were then called, were completed in King Street and James Street. Attention then focussed on Lord Street which then extended between Duke Street and the newly-created Ridgeway Street. This was valuable land and a petition was made to Tynwald for the Corporation to sell the land for private development. Such were social attitudes that there were some Councillors who questioned the wisdom of providing housing for the poorer classes who were hardly worthy of modern accommodation when they were barely able to afford the cheapest private housing. On the other hand, there were those who said that many artisans were respectable hard working people who deserved their support. The arguments raged on and it was not until 1911 that Lord Street was finally built as 'Council' houses with satisfactory sanitary conditions.

MARKET HALLS

The open Market Place with stalls spreading on to the quayside was the centre of much of the commercial life of the town and it was here that the great majority of people of the town and the surrounding countryside obtained their provisions or attended to personal business in nearby offices. Overlooking the busy scene was Dixon's British Hotel from where coaches departed to all parts of the Island. The stalls were open to all weathers and cleanliness left a lot to be desired. One of the first acts of the Corporation was to rectify this and steps were taken to clear an area large enough to build substantial market halls. The clearance operation saw the demolition of the British Hotel together with old St. Matthew's Church which had stood by the Market Place for nearly two centuries since being built as a Chapel of Ease for Kirk Braddan in 1708.

The cleared site was used to build two Market Halls, one as the Butchers' Market and the other as the Fish, Butter and Vegetable Market. The latter, costing £3,000, was built entirely of iron and could be kept open in summer and closed in winter with the exception of the main entrances. The Fish Market was separated by a white glazed brick wall running the full height of the building. Being close to the quayside it was convenient for the fishing boats. Lavatories were provided and a boiler installed for the provision of hot water for washing the stalls and fittings.

The Market Halls were opened in 1900 and the Corporation issued Bye-laws which were strictly enforced by the Market Inspector. Summer hours for opening were from 7.00 a.m. to 10.00 p.m. Mondays to Fridays, with longer hours on Saturdays when the Markets opened at 6.30 a.m. and remained open until 11.30 p.m. Slightly reduced hours applied to the winter months.

THE TOWN HALL

Now that the town had been incorporated as a borough the Corporation took steps to build a

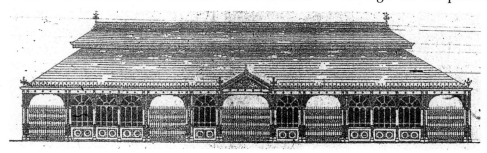

Douglas Fish, Butter and Vegetable Market. It was designed by Borough Surveyor Mr A.E. Prescott and opened in 1900.

Town Hall and Public Library worthy of its new status. A convenient site was reserved in Ridgeway Street which had been named after the Governor of the day. Entrusted with the design of the building was Mr Ardron F.R.I.B.A. of Messrs Ardron and Dawson, Westminster. The main building contractor was Messrs Gradwell and Co. of Barrow in Furness. The style adopted was 'Renaissance' and the aim of the design was to combine lasting strength with lightness and elegance. Dressed rubble stone from local quarries was used with Bath stone dressed facings.

The following description of the interior of the building is based on a feature in the Mona's Herald of March, 1900:

'The principal entrance is in John Street leading to a spacious corridor, with floors of marble Mosaic, containing the main staircase. On the left of the main corridor are placed the Municipal Offices - the Town Clerk's Office, Enquiry Office, Public and Rates Office and the Accountant's Office. To the right of the main corridor is the Water Office and along the John Street side of the building are the Borough Surveyor's Offices - Enquiry Office, Drawing Office, Building Inspector's Office and the Car and Sanitary Inspectors' Office.

'Ascend the main staircase and we reach the floor on which the Council Chamber and Committee Rooms are situated. The Chamber itself is a magnificent room, 47 feet by 32 feet, which has an arched roof with panelled ceiling. The floor is laid in oak which is also used for the wainscotting and the Ardron mantelpiece. Overlooking the Chamber at the Church Street end is the public gallery. A desk and chair is provided for each Councillor arranged in horse shoe style. A handsome bench is provided for the Mayor and Aldermen along the Ridgeway Street end. On the bench is also provision for the Town Clerk, Borough Surveyor, Staff and representatives of the press. The furniture upholstery is in Morocco leather.

'The Mayor's Parlour adjoins the Council Chamber and the Committee Rooms, waiting rooms, cloakroom and lavatory are also on the same floor. The furniture for the Mayor's Parlour and the Offices has been supplied by Messrs Spence Bros. of Athol Street who have a steam cabinet works on Shaw's Brow. The floor above is given over for the accommodation of the Caretaker and his family.

'The whole of the Basement is excavated and on the front is a large room utilised as a book store in connection with the Town Clerk's Department. Spacious cellars are occupied by the Water Department as a store, with provision for the heating apparatus by which the buildings are being heated by low pressure wall radiators. Also in the Basement is the Strong Room which is entered from a staircase from the Accountant's Office.

'Adjoining the building in John Street provision has been made for the town Fire Brigade. A large room houses the (horse-drawn) manually operated fire engine and appliances. There is also a tower for drying the hoses plus a large Assembly Room for use of the men.'

The new Town Hall was ready for the official opening in March, 1900, the total cost amounting to over £25,000 including all the furniture and fittings, illumination being by gas. Unfortunately the Mayor, Alderman Webb was ill, so the grand opening had to be postponed until 3rd May. But the first Council Meeting was held on 14th March and all assembled expressed great satisfaction with the new Municipal Building and much gratitude to all who had been involved in its construction. Councillor Cubbon presented a handsome brass shield containing the names of Councillors and officials to commemorate the opening of the Town Hall. By now Mr Alexander Robertson had been appointed Town Clerk in succession to Mr Thomas Nesbitt who, as Clerk to the Town Commissioners, had worked tirelessly to prepare for the incorporation of the Borough. Mr Nesbitt emigrated to Australia and became Town Clerk of Sydney, New South Wales.

THE PUBLIC LIBRARY

For most of the nineteenth century the middle classes had to rely on Subscription Libraries to further their reading. By 1880 the Douglas Penny Library was in existence and for a shilling a quarter poorer people could have access to a library and all the leading newspapers. There were also facilities for billiards, chess and draughts. But there was strong agitation for a free Public Library with both Governors Loch and Walpole lending their support. Samuel Harris, High Bailiff of Douglas,

Nothing was spared in providing a splendid Town Hall now that borough status had been gained. Officially opened by Mayor Sam Webb in May, 1900, the main entrance was, as shown, from John Street though this was altered in the 1920s. On the left , in Ridgeway Street, is the Public Library while on the right, in John Street, accommodation was provided for the Town Fire Brigade.
(R. & L. Kelly Collection)

managed to collect about £1.000 from his fellow directors of the Isle of Man Savings Bank as a contribution. The way was made clear when the Library and Museums Act was promulgated in 1885. This envisaged a site containing both a Library and Museum though the two became separated when it was realised the Library was for Douglas while the Museum was for the whole Island. However, the Town Commissioners were now permitted to levy a penny rate for the purpose of providing a Library and salaried staff. Unsuccessful in their search for a suitable and convenient site, a temporary solution was found in 1866 by renting Athol Hall in Athol Street. The lending, reference and newspaper libraries were all found in a single room and overcrowding soon became a problem.

When plans for the new Municipal Buildings in Ridgeway Street were being considered it was decided that here would be the ideal position for a central public library adjoining the Town Hall. A date above the entrance to the Library suggests that work began on its construction in 1897, two years before the foundations for the Town Hall were laid. The Town Librarian, John Taylor, set out the requirements for three rooms to house lending, reference and newspapers. A newspaper room was considered of prime importance because of its popularity at a time when newspapers were a costly item and because of the cramped conditions of most households.

John Taylor's design has stood the test of time and has remained basically unchanged. The entrance leads to the ground floor which contains the lending library, fitted with a gallery, and the newspaper room. Upstairs are the Reference Library and the Librarian's Office. It could well be that the Library was in use before the completion of the Town Hall. Initially the Library contained 3,000 books which had been donated, but a sub-committee for book selection soon added to the total, so much so that a printed catalogue was required which had to be regularly updated - a costly and tedious business. Such a catalogue was essential because borrowing was only allowed through the 'closed access' system. This meant that readers could not choose books directly from the shelves but had to apply in writing to the Librarian or his assistant. This was the cause of much frustration and the introduction of 'open access' in 1913 was warmly welcomed. A Manx collection was a feature of the Library from its very beginning in 1886 and almost served as a 'national library' until the Manx Museum was opened in 1922.

John Taylor served as Librarian for twenty years, retiring in 1912. Previous to that, and for a similar period, he had been Headmaster of Thomas Street Wesleyan Day Schools. He had also acted as Secretary of the Douglas Penny Library and his experience and enthusiasm was invaluable in establishing the Town Library in its new home. He instigated public lectures within the Library and started a schools' service. He was also a founder member of the Douglas Chess Club and his daughter had the distinction of being the first woman assistant in the Library.

His successor as Librarian was William Cubbon and his appointment was the source of much criticism. He was selected out of 120 applicants, many of whom had library experience while Mr Cubbon's experience was in printing and journalism, though he had a great personal interest in local history. He was working for the *Isle of Man Times* at the time of his appointment and retained his post until 1918 when he resigned to concentrate on being manager of the Isle of Man Labour Bureau. But William Cubbon's main achievements were yet to come. In 1922 the Manx Museum was established in the original building of Noble's Hospital and in that year Mr Cubbon was appointed Secretary and Librarian under the Directorship of P.M.C. Kermode. In 1932 Mr Cubbon himself became Director.

A plaque on the outside wall of the Library commemorates the birth of the distinguished naturalist Edward Forbes F.R.S. who had been born on the site in 1815. He was a brilliant student and became the youngest-ever President of the Geological Society in 1853. The following year he was elected Professor of Natural History at Edinburgh University only to die prematurely later that year while still under forty years of age.

Official Town Hall staff, September, 1900. Seated third from left is a youthful Alexander Robertson who succeeded Thomas Nesbitt in 1898 as Town Clerk. Mr Robertson was at the beginning of a long 'reign' which would last for over thirty years.

(Above) The camera of John Miller Nicholson captures the 'atmosphere' of the shopping thoroughfare of Strand Street during the 1890s.

A later view of Strand Street from a postcard dated about 1910 showing the arrival of the Maypole Dairy Company, on the right, but before the building of the Strand Cinema (R. and L. Kelly Collection)

When Douglas had been established as the capital of the Isle of Man , the search began to provide a suitable building for the House of Keys and Members of Tynwald. It was not until 1879 that an answer was found. In that year the building of the Bank of Mona closed following the collapse of its parent City of Glasgow Bank. The building of 1854, built on the Finch Hill estate, was purchased and adapted to accommodate the House of Keys and Government Offices. This was followed by the completion of the Legislative Buildings in 1894 as seen here.

PROMENADES AND TRAMWAYS

Mr Thomas Lightfoot will long be remembered as the originator of the Douglas Horse Trams. A civil engineer contractor from the Midlands he chose Douglas for his early retirement, settling with his family at Athol House, a seaside villa, the site on which was built the Westlake's Sea Level Hotel. The Lightfoot family arrived about 1870 when exciting plans for the development of the town were being planned. The New Street Board had been instigated by Governor Loch and was charged with creating a new street through the old part of the town to link with a proposed new marine parade or promenade. The first promenade had been completed in 1864 along Colonel's Road fronting the Villa Marina mansion. The paved embankment ran for a thousand feet and was 74 feet wide, allowing space to form a lawn. It soon became popular with residents and visitors alike and had largely been paid for by public subscriptions led by Mr Samuel Harris who was destined to be the last High Bailiff of Douglas. In 1868 he granted the area to the Town Commissioners who renamed it the Harris Promenade. This promenade stopped at the foot of Broadway which was then only 26 feet wide. Beyond Broadway the shore road (Castle Mona Road) led past Clarence, Esplanade and Derby Terraces to the Castle Mona Hotel and its spacious gardens. The shore road then edged inland to form the Crescent with its villas, pavilions and gardens until the bottom of Burnt Mill Hill and Strathallan Crescent were reached.

As Thomas Lightfoot looked from his villa to the newly completed Victoria Pier (1872) he envisaged a horse drawn tramway running the length of the seafront. It would be of great service to the thousands of visitors arriving at the new pier as they made their way to the hotels and boarding houses now being rapidly built. His plans received the support of the Town Commissioners and in the spring of 1876 Tynwald approved the Douglas Tramway Bill. The Act stipulated a three foot gauge track for the horse-drawn cars which after sunset were to display a red light at the front and a green light at the rear. Horses were to be equipped with warning bells. The promoter had to maintain the six foot of paving in which the track was set. The road authority could purchase compulsorily the line and equipment after twenty-one years.

By the end of July the line was complete from the foot of Burnt Mill Hill to the south side of the entrance to the Iron Pier built in 1869 at the bottom of Broadway. In 1865 Mr Lightfoot moved from his villa after purchasing the nearby Crescent Hotel which he renamed Athol House. It had stables for the horses and the walled garden on the seaward side of the shore provided space for a wooden car shed. An official inspection completed, the first passenger services began on Wednesday, 7th August, 1876. The line met with immediate success and work to extend the line as far as the new Peveril Hotel and in close proximity to the Queen Victoria Pier went on during the winter. A passing loop was installed at the Iron Pier and a revised S-bend round the Lifeboat House enabled the New Street Committee to leave space for a pavilion. The Lifeboat House had in 1875 acquired a verandah on three sides to serve as a public shelter. The completed line of just over 1.5 miles opened at the end of January, 1877. Public criticism meant that two horses rather than one should always be used to pull the double deck (open top) cars of which two were in service. The running of the trams was the final touch to the new promenade which had been officially opened in 1875 by Governor Loch, after whom it was named in recognition of the tremendous help and encouragement he had given to the project. In February, 1877, the Loch Promenade was formally handed over to the Town Commissioners. It was 80 feet wide and extended 370 feet to seaward of the 1870 shore line.

The first two double-deck trams are seen here soon after the inaugural day of the horse tram service, 7th August, 1876. This historic photograph was taken on the passing loop positioned by the entrance to the Iron Pier, opposite Broadway. (Manx National Heritage)

The enterprising Mr Lightfoot then became involved with developments in the new Victoria Street where a large plot of ground near the junction with the Loch Promenade had been been bought by the Marine Baths and Aquarium Company, based in Manchester though with many Manx shareholders. The baths were completed to a very high standard in 1877, the famous swimmer Captain Webb being at the official opening. However, the Company was soon in financial difficulties and unable to fulfil its other obligations. The property of the company and the lease of the land were sold by public auction for a bargain price of £8,500. The purchaser was Thomas Lightfoot who proceeded to build the Grand Theatre and the Grand Hotel. It was a costly venture and when obliged to add adequate fire emergency exits to the theatre Mr Lightfoot, too, was in financial trouble. Consequently he was forced to sell his tramway for an estimated £15,000 which was reckoned to be nearly double the original outlay.

The consortium who purchased the tramway in 1882 formed themselves into Isle of Man Tramways Ltd., one of the directors being Major J.S. Goldie-Taubman of the Nunnery who was the first Speaker of the House of Keys and a director of the Isle of Man Railway. With fresh capital available new cars were ordered to add to those, now numbering four, already in use. To use these additional cars it was necessary to add passing loops to the track and accordingly the company made application to the Commissioners for the installation of four such loops. Approval was given to loops near Granville Street and opposite Falcon Cliff where a double Cliff Lift was being installed for the benefit of guests. The two other tramway loops applied for were turned down on the grounds of congestion at Victoria Pier and on the narrow roadway of Castle Terrace, near the Castle Mona. However, an appeal

By the end of January, 1877, a single line extension traversed the newly built Loch Promenade to reach the Victoria Pier. Plenty of opposition to the horse trams was provided by a multitude of landaus seen here queuing for the latest arrivals. (Manx National Heritage)

to Governor Loch resulted in permission being given and the loops were installed in 1885. That year a total of 361,553 passengers were carried, the great majority during the season with 33,284 being carried in one week alone. New terminal buildings were in course of construction at Burnt Mill Hill and the first of the open 'toast rack' trams had arrived, bringing the total fleet to ten.

The future of the Tramway now became closely linked to the many other developments taking place. The Derby Castle Company, formed in 1884, proceeded to double the size of their dance hall; The Falcon Cliff Pavilion Company built a huge glasshouse on the cliff top and the former southern garden of the Castle Mona was used to provide further attractions. As far as other building developments were concerned the land available with the greatest potential was on the Crescent to the north

A view across Douglas Bay about 1878, showing the course of the horse tramway which then traversed about two thirds of the sea front. In the foreground is Castle Mona Road with the tramway close to the seaward wall. In the centre is the 1869 Iron Pier, beyond which can be seen the Lifeboat House positioned at the northern end of the Loch Promenade. (Manx National Heritage)

east of Falcon Cliff. It was here that the Commissioners decided to construct the Queen's Promenade on land between the Crescent Road and the sea. A further extension was to front Strathallan Crescent. Both the Derby Castle and Tramway companies cooperated in conveying land to the Commissioners. In return the tramway company was granted permission to lay a double track along the Loch Promenade and northwards from Falcon Cliff to Burnt Mill Hill. A double-track was also sanctioned from Burnt Mill Hill to reach Derby Castle where the Commissioners negotiated with the Derby Castle company for land on which to build a new tramway depot.

The Douglas Crescent Improvement Act of 1889 resulted in the opening, with great ceremony, of the Queen's Promenade in July, 1890 by the new Governor, Sir Spencer Walpole. He led the entire fleet of 21 loaded tramcars from the 1887 Jubilee Clock to the triumphal arch erected at the southern end of the new promenade. All the visiting bands performed with Blondin being the star attraction at the Palace in the evening, which was rounded off by the illumination of the steamers and of the whole bay.

The horse trams were now handling well over 500,000 passengers annually and were in themselves a pleasure ride along the entire seafront 'the same as taking a carriage'. A double line appeared from Castle Terrace to the Queen's Promenade in 1891 as a result of a wooden seawall being built by the Commissioners to widen the roadway. The tram fleet now totalled 26 and two-thirds of the line was double-tracked. Further progress was impeded by the Lifeboat House on the Harris Promenade, though its days were numbered. It survived until 1895 when it was purchased by the Town Commissioners, following the choice of an alternative site within the confines of the harbour. The Commissioners were now in a position to implement their plans to build a new public shelter on the Harris Promenade while Colonel's Road was widened, thus enabling the horse tram line to be doubled. The grass strip gave way to a promenade which, with the widened roadway, was extended beyond the foot of Broadway, all behind a new sea-wall. The next step was to link up with the new Central Promenade as planned by the Commissioners' Surveyor, T.G. Taylor. The 900 foot long Iron Pier was purchased for demolition in early 1894. It was still in excellent condition and had at one time served as a useful means of sepa-rating male and female swimmers, gentlemen to the south!

Whilst these great works were going on the future of the lucrative horse tramway, with passenger fig-ures approaching a million a year, was under con-sideration as the Commissioners' option to pur-chase in 1897 was approaching. The Isle of Man Tramways, of course, was keen to extend their lease. But there now appeared on the scene the ambitious Alexander Bruce of the coastal electric railway and now Chairman of the newly formed Isle of Man Tramways and Electric Power Company. His vision was to double the remainder of the horse line and electrify it at once in return for a new lease from 1897 together with the right to build other tramways to other parts of the town. While both companies were in negotiation with the Town Commissioners, the Tramways and Electric Power Company also entered into complex negoti-ations to purchase the horse tramway from Isle of Man Tramways. The offer of £38,000 was accepted and on 1st May, 1894, the horse tramway was for-mally handed over to its new owners.

DOUGLAS CABLE TRAMWAY

While the resources of the Town Commissioners were fully stretched, there was considerable agita-tion from residents and traders in the new upper parts of the town for some sort of connecting tramway. Everything seemed to be to the

The Regency style boarding houses of Clarence Terrace and The Esplanade date from about 1840. This Abel Lewis photograph was taken some forty years later and the narrowness of the road meant that the tramlines had to be laid close to the sea wall. The billboards are advertising the attractions of Derby Castle. (Manx National Heritage)

21

On the left is the 1886 car shed and station built at the foot of Burnt Mill Hill by the Isle of Man Tramways Ltd. In 1891 a double track was laid along Strathallan Crescent to reach the entrance to Derby Castle. (Manx National Heritage)

Permission was given to double the single track along the Loch Promenade in 1889 as can be seen in this photograph. In the foreground is the new sea wall of 1875 while vestiges of the original waterfront can still be detected in the lane behind the church and the adjoining row of boarding houses. (Frank Cowin Library)

The construction of the Queen's Promenade in 1890 provided a double track for the horse trams as far as Broadway, though the Central Promenade in permanent form, shown here, was not completed until 1896. (Manx National Heritage)

advantage of those establishments along the promenades which were well served with the horse trams, horse omnibuses and a multitude of horse-drawn carriages. Two companies operating horse buses to the new parts of the town had failed, mainly due to people objecting to the horses having to struggle up Prospect Hill. In April, 1894 the Commissioners had agreed that there should be some sort of tramway linking the lower and upper levels of the town; Surveyor Taylor was instructed to prepare a report. But nothing happened and the agitation increased.

At a public meeting in Tynwald Street School in January, 1895, it was shown that those living in the new terraced houses, built with extra bedrooms to accommodate visitiors, were unable to meet their annual rents of £40. Even when reduced to £25 there were still people being brought to court for non-payment. At the meeting Commissioner R. D. Cowin reasoned that the prosperous bay line should be used to help carry the cost of a tramway to the upper parts of the town. With this in mind a meeting was arranged with the directors of the tramway company, while the Upper Douglas Tramway petition produced signatures of over half the ratepayers affected.

Alexander Bruce was quick to provide further inducements in return for a renewed lease of the horse tramway. Apart from electrifying the horse line he was prepared to extend the line to the railway station; provide free electric lighting for all the promenades and Victoria Street; to supply electricity to the town for general use and, above all, he offered to construct a tramway to Upper Douglas. With the Commissioners apparently in no hurry to make a final decision (there were those who felt strongly that the public tramways should not be privately owned) Mr Bruce offered to meet the Commissioners. The meeting was held at the end of May and this resulted in the Commissioners arriving at a final agreement with Mr Bruce and his fellow directors. In return for a new twenty-one year lease of the horse line, the I.O.M. Tramways and Electric Power Company would double the remainder of the horse line; remove the Burnt Mill Hill horse shed and station to Derby Castle; build an Upper Douglas cable tramway and provide an

interim horse bus service to Upper Douglas. In addition the tramways company would pay the Commissioners 15% of the bay tramway receipts. (Any idea of electrifying the bay tramway was abandoned following the many objections from hoteliers and operators of horse carriages). The Commissioners and the Company joined forces to obtain the necessary approval of Tynwald and the Upper Douglas Tramway Act, setting out the conditions, was passed in November. The haste was the result of all parties being anxious to have the new cable tramway operating by Whitsun, 1896.

The designated route was as follows: from a junction with the Douglas Bay tramway near the Peveril Hotel, past the Jubilee Clock, up Victoria Street and Prospect Hill to Bucks Road, Woodbourne Road and past the top of Murray's Road to the next road (later named York Road) down which the track would continue into Ballaquayle Road and to the foot of Broadway to a junction with the Bay tramway. Apart from the latter section from the top of York Road to Broadway, the line was to be a double track of 3 feet gauge, the nearest rail of which was to be 27 inches from the curbside. It was the latter that caused concern to many traders on Victoria Street and Prospect Hill (which was to be widened) who argued that the passing of trams would be too close to their shop fronts. Mr Bruce complied with their wishes and an Amendment Act was passed in May, 1896, which permitted the Victoria Street - Prospect Hill line to be laid as a centre-of-road double track. There had also been protests about the permitted operating speed of 8 mph and this was, despite the company's objection, reduced to 6 mph on the descents from Hill Street to Thomas Street and from Clifton Terrace to the foot of Broadway. This, of course, had the effect of reducing the speed over the entire system.

Messrs Dick Kerr Co Ltd were appointed contractors. They were the accepted specialists in cable traction and had taken over the patent held by the builders of the San Francisco lines. They worked closely with Surveyor Taylor and by February, 1896 between 200 and 300 men were employed laying the 1.5 mile track and conduit equipped with pulleys to guide the cable to and from the engine

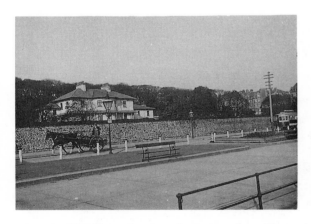

The splendid Villa Marina Mansion became the residence of Henry Bloom Noble by the end of the century. This view dates from about 1890 and shows the famous Colonel's Road along the wall of the Villa Marina estate. In the foreground is Harris Promenade which was further developed, thus allowing the final section of tramline to be doubled in 1897. (Manx National Heritage)

The removal of the Lifeboat House in 1892 allowed the Town Commissioners to provide an ornate public shelter on the Harris Promenade. The difficult S-bend of the tramlines connecting the Loch and Harris Promenades was also eased. By 1895 the Sefton Hotel was completed and during that year its neighbour the Marine Pavilion, forerunner of the Gaiety Theatre, first opened its doors. (Keig Collection)

house. The company bought land opposite Crosby Terrace and at the foot of the future York Road to build a power station and car shed. (The two houses in Laureston Avenue were also purchased by the company and let to their workmen.) The new red brick building was both substantial and pleasing in appearance. A mixture of imported and Ballanard bricks was used, the latter also being used for many of the new housing developments in the upper part of the town. The upper part of the new building was equipped with a transverser to manhandle the cars onto four sets of tracks. The adjoining lower building was occupied by the boiler house with chimney which supplied power for the two 250 hp engines, either of which could be connected to the winding pulley.

The continuous steel cable of over three miles, and weighing 20 tons, arrived early in July, 1896 on two drums because of a 15 ton crane limit in Douglas harbour. The threading of the cable in the conduit was carried out with the help of two traction engines. At the end of this operation an 80 foot splice was required to complete the circuit and on 8th August a car was sent out to test the line. Two grippers were used on each car, one for each direction of travel, which the driver had to combine skilfully with the wheel brakes to ensure that the cable was always doing the pulling and not the car. A slot brake which could grip the slot rails was also available for emergencies. The steepest gradient was 1 in 10.6.

Warning bells were required to be fitted after the official inspection was completed, and on Saturday, 13th August, three cars inaugurated the service, the number of cars in operation soon increasing to twelve as crews were trained, the cars being numbered 71 to 82, leaving 1-70 for the bay tramway. Each car could carry 32 passengers. They were open-sided but the later arrivals, 79 to 82, were enclosed to give more protection, especially in winter. Interior lighting was by oil lamps.

THE CORPORATION CELEBRATES

The completion of the Central Promenade, and the fact that the town now had its longed-for cable tramway, gave great satisfaction to the first Councillors who had been elected in March. Many had been Commissioners and six were appointed Aldermen one of whom, Thomas Keig, photographer, was elected the first Mayor of Douglas, the elderly Samuel Harris declining the honour. Alderman Samuel Webb became Deputy Mayor. Thomas Nesbitt, formerly Clerk to the Commissioners, was appointed the Town Clerk with Mr Alexander Robertson as Deputy Town Clerk. Their many duties at this time included arranging the town's celebrations of the recent innovations, to be held on Wednesday, 26th August.

The celebrations took the form of a lavish two-hour procession with music provided by the Palace, Derby Castle and Foxdale Bands. Starting at the foot of Broadway the procession followed the line of the cable tramway through the town and then along the promenades, now stretching for two miles around the bay, to Derby Castle and then returning to the new promenade fronting the Palace grounds. Here Lt. Governor Lord Henniker and others made speeches in which the Isle of Man

Following the take-over of the horse trams by the Isle of Man Tramways and Electric Power Company in 1894, the old Burnt Mill Hill terminal was demolished and replaced at Derby Castle by a new car shed and passenger facilities with an ornate station building. The new terminus was completed in 1896 and was in close proximity to the entrance to Derby Castle and the electric railway terminus.

Horses, horses, everywhere! To the left of the 1887 Jubilee Clock can be seen the horse buses which made the climb of Prospect Hill and Bucks Road to connect with the upper part of the town. Never successful, they disappeared after the opening of the cable tramway in 1896. (Keig Collection)

The Cable tramway under construction in Victoria Street (above) and on Prospect Hill (below), May, 1896 (Keig Collection)

Tramways and Electric Power Company and Borough Surveyor T.G. Taylor received much praise. The day was fine and both horse and cable cars were gaily decorated for the occasion, which ended with a Pain's firework display from both the small Derby Castle pier and the Tower of Refuge. The following night the tramway contractors, Dick Kerr and Co, provided a lavish dinner for local and Island dignitaries at the Douglas Bay Hotel, the first such building to be illuminated by electricity.

The cable cars settled down to become a familiar part of life in the town with services of ten-minute frequency from 8 am to 11 pm each day, Sundays excepted. Fares were 2d uphill and 1d downhill, but 1d each way during the winter when a slightly reduced service applied. The cars ran smoothly and, apparently, effortlessly and the constant clanging of the bell was necessary to give warning of a car approaching. There was a low hum from the constantly moving cable below ground and children found a new pastime by dropping strips of paper and string down the slot to see them being whisked away; another 'trick' was to place pennies on the line so the wheels would bend them! During 1899 the cable cars had carried 633,624 passengers, with a maximum of nearly 8,000 during one day. That year the horse trams had carried 1,725,155 passengers with the highest day total being recorded as nearly 33,000.

THE DUMBELL BANK CRASH

On Saturday, 3rd February, 1900, came the collapse of the Dumbell Banking Company, its Chairman being none other than Alexander Bruce. In 1892 he had become the town's treasurer and was a Justice of the Peace. Born in Banff, Scotland he served as a junior clerk with the Bank of Glasgow and was then transferred to the Island to become manager of the Ramsey Bank of Mona. He was soon seen to be a man of ambition and charisma and when the Bank of Glasgow collapsed in 1878 the ageing Mr George Willam Dumbell appointed Bruce as General Manager of his banking company. Alexander Bruce was largely held responsible for the demise of the bank in which so much trust had been placed. His borrowings to push the coastal electric railway northwards to Ramsey amounted to £150,000 more than was authorised, and when Parr's Bank in England foreclosed on the loan the result was calamitous. That Saturday morning 500 bewildered customers read the closure notice on the locked door which would spell disaster for over 8,000 businesses and individuals. It also meant disaster for the Isle of Man Tramways and Electric Power Company.

W.H. Walker was appointed as liquidator of the tramways company and the liquidator's book was a masterly work prepared largely by a young advocate, Ramsey B. Moore who later became Attorney General. Offers were invited and the Corporation sought a combined valuation of both horse and cable cars by experts. By August, 1901 an offer of £40,000 had been refused. This offer was increased to £50,000 the following month and accepted by the liquidator, the price being less than half the value of the two lines which appeared in the books of the tramways company. On the other hand the cable cars were, not unexpectedly, losing money, about £1,500 a year. This, however, was more than

(Above) Car 72 passes the premises of the ill-fated Dumbell's Bank at the bottom of Prospect Hill. (Below) Car 73 in Woodbourne Road in 1896 before turning into the then unnamed York Road. (Douglas Corporation)

Above) Car 78 in 1904 following its conversion from open-sided to saloon style. The first houses in York Road have now appeared and the car is on the descent to the depot and winding house shown below. (Douglas Corporation)

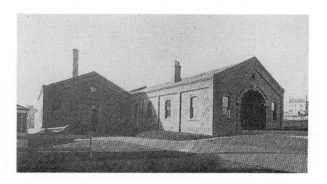

A view of Bucks Road about 1900 showing the cable cars on the kerb-side position above Prospect Hill. (Manx National Heritage)

Woodbourne Road about 1904, showing the kerb-side running of the tramway.

compensated by the receipts from the horse trams.

Early in 1901, the liquidator had stopped cars using the line to and from Broadway. It had been described as 'almost unworkable' by one authority because of the gradients and narrowness of the road. It was said that only two named drivers were permitted to operate on this difficult stretch. This was accepted by the new Tramways Committee and the cable (each of which lasted for 15 months) was foreshortened to turn at Stanley View below York Road. The saving on coal for the boiler house during a 14 hour day was 8 cwt, thus cutting fuel consumption to below 3.5 tons a day. The idea of electrifying the line was considered from time to time but was rejected. Part of the disused track was lifted and relaid to extend the horse tramway on to Victoria Pier and alongside the newly completed triangular Pier Building which provided shelter, shops and a spacious waiting hall. At the same time a car shed was built in Waverley Road to accommodate horse trams for overhaul, the trams being towed up from Victoria Street by a cable car.

In 1906 the single track between Avondale Corner and the depot was doubled. The following year two more cars arrived, being numbered 69-70, and

by 1911 two further cars, 68 and 67, brought the total fleet to sixteen. The year also saw the first Sunday cable car service being introduced; it had long been a heated election issue. In April, 1908, a fatal accident to a partially-sighted man at the top of Victoria Street resulted in a flagman being employed both summer and winter, despite the fact that cars could stop in two or three yards. The same year a boilerman died from heat stroke. By 1914 the cable cars were still losing money to the extent of about £1,000 a year. This contrasted with the profitable horse trams which could be relied upon to profit to the extent of £12,000 a year.

The Corporation formally took over the horse trams on 2nd January, 1902 with a civic turn out, led by Mayor Samuel Webb, rides being free up to noon. Mr Stephen Robinson was appointed manager of the Corporation's new transport department. The fleet of horse trams now totalled 36, these being numbered 2 to 37. No 1 had started life as a single deck winter saloon but was changed to a double-decker in 1894, though it had disappeared before the take-over. No 1 remained vacant until 1913 when a new saloon was given that number. The 36 cars were stored at Derby Castle though

A cable car on the link line with the horse trams at the foot of Victoria Street, about 1897. (F. Frith / Manx National Heritage)

when part of the area was made into new offices, and with further cars on order, the decision to build a new tram shed in Waverley Road was made. Additional stabling had become available when No 1 Strathallan Crescent was purchased in 1891, the house being used as offices. The yard and stables of the house became known as 'The Brig'. Together with the original 'Lightfoot' stables behind what became known as Tramway Terrace, stabling for 68 horses was now available.

Tram horses were limited to eight return journeys in any one day. No such limits were placed on the drivers and conductors who received 26s 6d for working a week which could be anything up to 114 hours. The men were demanding better conditions and Mr Robinson was confronted by a day-long strike in July, 1911, which saw all horse trams (now 45) and cable cars stopped as the height of the summer season approached. The Tramways Committee sanctioned new terms which were accepted, the horse tram men gaining a 72 hour six day week for 27s, with overtime payment and an extra 4s 6d for Sundays. The cable men also had a reduction in the working week to 72 hours, drivers being paid 30s and conductors 27s. There was no overtime available but extra was paid for Sunday working.

Since 1905 the Tramways Committee had considered the introduction of motor buses but it was not until 1914 that the decision was made to purchase two buses to replace the horse-buses operated under contract on the Peel Road route. In

Thursday, 2nd January, 1902, was a civic occasion when the Corporation took over the horse trams and cable cars. Free rides were available until twelve noon. On the top deck of one of the horse trams, Council members and officials can be seen with Mayor Samuel Webb in the centre. (Keig Collection)

September the two buses began their service at Peveril Square (Victoria Pier) and went via the Quay, Peel Road, Belmont Hill and returning via Circular Road, George Street and Bank Hill Corner. But in August of that year the Great War had begun and the town would suffer profoundly from its effects. Hopes were dashed of exceeding the record 1913 total of 615,726 summer visitor arrivals - a total which would never be surpassed.

This splendid photograph shows part of the fleet of horse trams hard at work on the tracks which were extended to the foot of the Victoria Pier in 1902. That year also saw the completion of the Harbour Commissioners' ornate Pier Building on the triangle of reclaimed land opposite the Peveril Hotel. (Cowin and Co.)

THE TOWN'S WATER SUPPLY

His Excellency Sir Henry Brougham Loch left the Island in March, 1882 after being Lieutenant Governor for nineteen years. Destined for higher things, he eventually became Lord Loch, Governor of New South Wales, Australia. His departure was the source of much sadness and approbation; the memorials to his public works are still a major feature of Douglas. He and the good Lady Loch did much to relieve the plight of the sick, the poor and the orphans of the town through many charitable works. He was quick to introduce compulsory vaccination following the outbreak of smallpox in 1877 and appointed the first Public Analyst to monitor the town's water supply. One of his regrets on leaving was that there were still people in Douglas living in insanitary conditions which could only be remedied by the provision of better housing. He was also pressing the Town Commissioners to close all wells still being used within the town.

The first steps to provide a supply of clean water were taken following the disastrous outbreaks of cholera in 1832-33. The following year Tynwald promulgated the Douglas Waterworks Act which authorised a company to collect water and distribute through pipes to all households in the town, at least to those which could afford it. Fresh water was also to be made available for the watering of ships in the harbour.

The Douglas Water Company built its first reservoir at Burnt Mill Hill; the mill is thought to have been one of the Onchan corn mills situated where the villa Min-y-don was later built in the 1830s. The name Burnt Mill Hill gave way to Summerhill at the end of last century, following the building of Summerhill House at the top of the rise to Onchan. This first reservoir had a capacity of 250,000 gallons but soon had to be supplemented by a similar

One of the breweries to be found in old Douglas was the Lake Brewery built originally in 1779, flanked by Bank Hill with Big Well Street to the rear. It was completely 'modernised' when it became Clinch's Brewery in 1868. For its water supply a spring beneath the premises was tapped by Tube Wells, the water being forced to a large cistern in the top of the main building by means of steam pumps. The brewery boasted of its fine ales produced, including the common 'jough' popular throughout the Island.

Steam cranes at work on the early stages of constructing the 300 feet wide embankment in West Baldwin. (Tom Cowell)

capacity reservoir built immediately above the first one on the stream running through the Bemahague estate. The remains of these can still be seen in what is now Summerhill Glen. The necessities of the town, however, soon showed that the company would have to obtain a new watershed and the next move was the erection of the Ballacain reservoir in Onchan, with a capacity of 450,000 gallons.

In the course of time the Water Company was forced to consider a reservoir of much greater magnitude and this resulted in the construction of the Clypse 24,000,000 gallon reservoir much further up the Groudle river beyond Ballacain. To this new undertaking was added a pumping station at the mouth of the Groudle river, water being pumped to a small reservoir on the adjacent hillside of Howstrake from where it flowed by gravitation into the Ballacain main.

The requirements of the town continued to grow and the company had considerable difficulty in maintaining a constant supply of water in the summer months. Besides the complaints of private consumers, considerable friction existed between the Town Commissioners and the Water Company with regard to the limitations of supplies for public purposes, such as street cleaning, watering and sewer flushing etc. The result was that the Town Commissioners took steps to acquire the undertaking. Prolonged negotiations resulted in the Douglas Water Company offering to sell its undertaking for £144,000. Acting on the advice of Mr George Henry Hill, the eminent water engineer, the Commissioners agreed with the offer and in 1890 the necessary statutory powers of borrowing were obtained and the water undertaking was transferred to Douglas Town Commissioners.

The transfer included certain arrangements for acquiring land to build another storage reservoir on the Kerrowdhoo Farm, just below the Clypse. As the demand for water continued to grow no time was wasted and the Kerrowdhoo Reservoir

was completed in January 1903, the capacity being 50,000,000 gallons. Cost amounted to £17,000. To facilitate the supply to Upper Douglas a new main was laid from Kerrowdhoo and in the same year a new main was laid from Summerhill to supply the steamers and for other non-domestic purposes.

The Borough now had at its disposal a capacity of nearly 75,000,000 gallons in normal circumstances. The Waterworks Committee, however, realised that the only wisdom with respect to the water supply of a rapidly growing visitor resort was to provide an unlimited supply of pure water. It was in October, 1897 that the Committee recommended the adoption of the West Baldwin reservoir scheme. This was agreed and Messrs G.H. Hill and Sons were engaged to prepare the necessary plans and details. Tynwald gave approval to the scheme in 1899. Orders were placed with English firms for the necessary pipes and valves etc. but it was decided that it would be cheaper for the construction work to be carried out by direct labour.

The magnitude of the reservoir scheme was formidable: a 300,000,000 gallon reservoir with a maximum depth of 70 feet and with a surface area of 60 acres. A railway was essential for carrying materials so a line of 3 ft. gauge was built from Sir George's Bridge three miles up to the dam site. Nine timber bridges were built to cross the River Glass. The line was completed by January, 1901 and the first locomotive, to be named *Injebreck,* was purchased from the Isle of Man Tramways and Electric Power Company following the completion of the electric railway line to Ramsey in 1899. The same source also provided rails and waggons. Later Injebreck was joined by three other locomotives - *West Baldwin, Ardwhallin* and *Hannah.* Under resident engineer Mr Thorpe the local labour force available had to be augmented by Irish navvies, bringing the total to 250 men.

Vast quantities of clay were hauled up from Ballacreetch to provide the waterproof core within

One of the steam locomotives with some of the trucks which brought 8,000 tons of stone for lining the outer faces of the embankment. (Tom Cowell)

September 6th, 1905. The great enterprise is complete as flags fly in readiness for the Inauguration Ceremony. A band is playing beneath the large banner emblazoned with the Borough Coat of Arms. (Tom Cowell)

the embankment which began to take shape as half a million tons of stone and soil were removed from the valley floor, once the fields of three farms which would disappear. Steam cranes helped the men in this laborious work. Apart from clay some 8,000 tons of stone was also required for facing the 300 ft long embankment; when local quarries had been exhausted the railway line was extended to a new quarry opened at Hillberry. As final 'setting stone', sandstone was brought by traction engines from Peel, and limestone from Castletown.

The vast undertaking had taken nearly five years to complete and there was much cause for celebration, as recorded in the Isle of Man Examiner of 9th September, 1905. "The Inauguration Ceremony for the Injebreck Reservoir Scheme was held last Thursday afternoon. The day had dawned windy and the marquee, necessary for refreshments, had been prostrated so men were rushed from Douglas to replace the canvas and poles. A goodly number of people journeyed from Douglas to witness the proceedings and these for the most part took advantage of the cars which the Douglas Car Association, with commendable enterprise, had provided for the conveyance of sightseers. The Lieut. Governor, Lord Raglan, and Deemster Kneen were driven to the scene by Mr J.W. Orde, Secretary of the Automobile Club of Great Britain and Ireland, and Sir William Drinkwater in a car owned and driven by his son Mr Geo. Drinkwater. Others made the excursion by bicycle and even a few pedestrians travelled to the picturesque lake which has been formed in this lovely valley. The great municipal venture had cost over £90,000 and has a capacity of 301,000,000 gallons.

"In honour of the occasion the embankment had been decorated with flags conspicuous among which was a banner gorgeously emblazoned with the fearful and wonderful device which passes muster for the arms of the Borough of Douglas. As the time of the ceremony approached the procession of the assembled dignitaries moved across the embankment, the bands of the Douglas Volunteers and the Douglas Town Band playing selections awhile. Arriving opposite the valve shaft a halt was called as Alderman Goldsmith M.H.K., Chairman of the Water Committee spoke as follows: "It is now my duty and pleasure to request the Mayor to unveil the tablet commemorating this great water undertaking." Whereupon the Mayor, Alderman Kaye J.P., carried out his duties on behalf of the Council, the engineers of the work and the official staff (applause).

"The entire gathering then descended the embankment to a platform which had been erected near the relief well and in view of the concrete channel which carries the overflow. With everyone in their places Ald. Goldsmith gave a brief history of the attempts to supply Douglas and the surrounding districts with a plentiful supply of water. "With demands increasing each year we now have a magnificent reservoir of the best workmanship and the best materials and amply adequate to supply Douglas for many years to come. It will not only serve this generation, but generations yet unborn (applause)."

The Mayor had much to say about the construction of the embankment, the difficulties of acquiring the land, setting compensation, and paid tribute to all who worked together in harmony to ensure that all work was completed on time. With the assistance of the young Mr Hill he vigorously twisted the large key which turned on the flow of water from the 18" pipe at the mouth of the tunnel. A superb volume of water rushed through the pipe, whereupon a mighty cheer was raised. The proceedings concluded with more speeches and presentations after which all those present partook of the welcome refreshments provided."

HERE THEY COME !

It is hard to imagine, but this was late-Victorian Douglas. A smoke-belching steamer arrives at Victoria Pier. The place is crowded: black-painted minstrels strum banjos and fiddles for the ha'penny or farthing that may be thrown their way; wandering 'gleemen' and costumed women sing for the crowds, vagabond urchins run hither and thither trying to peddle souvenirs...or pick the pockets of the unwary; touters tug at the sleeves of arriving holidaymakers and try to persuade them to go to a hotel not of their choosing. Porters with coloured slatted wooden wheel carts to carry luggage are all addressed the same: "Hi, Kelly!" Aren't all Manxmen named thus? think gullible tourists.

Everywhere the atmosphere is one of hustle and bustle; match sellers, women and girls with fruit and flowers for sale blocking free passage. Loiterers against the sea wall watch the world go by. Street corner gangs argue and swear. Soon there will be a purge on it all but for now tough Irish police pensioners help to control it. They're the best in the world, say the Manx authorities who have drafted eighty of them in to help keep the peace in what can be a drunken summer. In 1894 Tynwald had passed the highly controversial Boarding House (Licence) Act. Churches are strong on temperance but the pubs and music halls pump out the beer and wine. Many day-trippers return to the paddlers at night senseless on handcarts.

Along the promenades (laced with overhead telegraph wires which link the town to Cornaa where the Island's submarine cable link begins to St. Bee's Head) and in the mud-rutted streets, sprayed frequently by Corporation water carts to keep dust down in dry weather, there is music: violinists, accordionists, a man with a performing monkey on his shoulder: all licensed buskers who earn a living from the ready giving of holidaymakers. There are 67 designated stands for them, some for mornings only, others for afternoons, some for an hour only outside hotels after breakfast or lunch, many from 9am to 10pm. All are supervised by an inspector but there can still be trouble. Established entertainers claim specific sites as their own but the official rule is: first there gets its use . . . except for a bagpiper who haunts the market area. Residents are so fatigued by the wail of pipes he is banned from the stand!

On Harris Promenade there is singing and music on a bandstand from pierrots: entertainers in black polka-dotted dresses with pointed hats. Town bands vie for popularity. There is the official Douglas Town Band and a military Volunteer Band. Councillors encourage competition to get the cheapest performing price for events! On the fore-shore the Salvation Army band draws crowds. Indoors in assembly rooms and hotel concert rooms there is music too. A nuisance, say some, but the visitors love it!

Children, some barefoot, others in leather-topped and wood-soled clogs, seem to be on almost every street corner selling wares or calling the headlines of newspapers they have for sale. Some stand on their heads or turn cartwheels when tourists are driven by. They call: "Kelly - pitch a penny," and tourists respond by throwing them a coin. "Selling in the gutter" is what one newspaper describes it. Little happiness or brightness enters their lives, say the socially aware. There are 150 of them licensed by the Corporation. Trading licences are restricted to under-14s unless they are 'mentally deficient' or physically handicapped. One such character is 'Fat Jack', known so because of his pondering weight. He's inclined to lie against doorsteps and spit. Eventually, in 1910, when he's deemed old enough to know better the Corporation withdraws his licence "to l'arn him a lesson," says a Corporation official. Behave himself and he'll get his licence back, he's told...and so he does.

The young are adept creators of opportunity. When a laden coal cart passes by they nip unseen to the rear, pull out a lump of coal to loosen the load then when the cart turns a corner a few lumps inevitably fall to the road and are hastily gathered.

Everywhere (except Sundays when bye-laws prohibit it) there are bootblacks anxious to shine shoes for a penny; a big business given the muddy nature of roads and footpaths and their contamination with horse droppings. Not many of them are Manx, though; a fact that's resented locally and sometimes the cause of trouble. Many want the 70 stand licences issued by the Corporation restricted to the Manx and for all to wear a common uniform, but the Corporation thinks it impracticable. The nearest thing to a common uniform comes in 1911 with the free issue by Douglas police on behalf of a shoe blacking company of blue check overalls with bright buttons. These are given to the thirty best behaved bootblacks. There's a joke about shining shoes for Manxmen: "Lor! Three legs," says the bootblack. "I'll charge a penny-ha'penny!" So appreciated is the joke there are china souvenirs depicting it. They are destined to be sold or won at coconut shys in their thousands.

Along the sea front parasol-carrying girls link arms and promenade four and five deep in their long skirts. It's a way they have in Man, they say. Waiting for the 'male' boat is another!

On the pebbled high reaches of the shore bed linen is laid out to dry in the summer sun. It's the way many boarding houses do their laundry. Young urchins mount guard.

Lower on the sands there are wheeled bathing huts - one section for women only; another, operated by a separate licensed concessionaire for men. These are the days of separate bathing. Long gone are the days when millworkers of both sexes frolicked totally nude on the shore. Now Douglas

A view of the Harris Promenade at the turn of the century, with its band stand from where pierrots entertained the passing crowds. Note the gas lamps and the poles carrying the telegraph wires linking the town to the submarine cable brought into Cornaa. (Cowin and Co.)

bye-laws, dating back to 1870 and amended in 1891, prohibit the two sexes coming within a hundred yards of each other and everyone aged over ten must be clothed. Men must wear 'suitable drawers'; women an appropriate 'gown or dress'. Eventually the dislike by families of being divided will lead to the licensing of a mixed bathing 'reservation' well concealed from the general public at Port Jack; then later the bye-laws will be ignored totally and broken with impunity. But for now that lies in the future. Meanwhile, where there are no bathers the sands are a 'free park' for cricket, golf, tennis, running and jumping; even crab races with eager betting on which is fastest.

Further in town, down back lanes where even milking cows are known to wander, can be heard the bleating of sheep and the bellow of cattle. Twenty one butchers slaughter animals on their premises. Above the clamour can be heard the sing-song calls of fish salesmen as they wheel their carts through town: "Fresh herring - red herring!" Their customers are not only locals; visitors, too, buy from them for many are on self-catering holidays. They pay for their room but must provide food for their landlady to cook.

Come dusk, lamp lighters wander the town. They use poles to light gas lamps. (Some in lower Douglas burn sewer gas - methane drawn from the sewers rather like a safety valve to prevent it accumulating.) Gas has been supplied by the Douglas Gaslight Company since 1836, the company having being formed the previous year. It can now boast as being the oldest company incorporated by Act of Tynwald.

Everywhere there is the sedate clip-clop of horses - and their droppings. The car trade is one of the town's big industries. In little more than a generation the drivers and proprietors are to become redundant, victims of 'automobilism', but now if anyone suggested it they'd laugh. The industry is so big it is considered vital to the town. Hence the vetoeing by Councillors of a plan by a Blackpool man for Japanese-style two wheeled rickshaws! People hire gigs for country rides. There are hundreds of landaus on the seafront... and everywhere so many car men tout for trade they are branded a

On the sands - bathing huts and donkeys, while Punch and Judy shows add to the fun. (R and L Kelly Collection)

public nuisance. Waiting areas are carefully controlled by Corporation bye-laws. Less of a nuisance are the horse droppings. They provide the town with a useful profit. Nearly four thousand tons of it a year are sold as manure - much of it despatched into the countryside by rail.

Incineration is official town policy for combustible refuse - but is a private responsibility. Householders are required to consign their vegetable peelings and food scraps to their home fires leaving only ash to be collected for disposal from ashpits. Thus the naming of the collectors as 'Ashmen'. The ash is taken to sea aboard a hopper barge called 'Mona' and dumped in 50 ton loads

While the Town bye-laws concerning separate bathing for men and women were strictly enforced, convention was broken when family bathing was permitted in the sheltered creek of Port Jack. (Cowin and Co.)

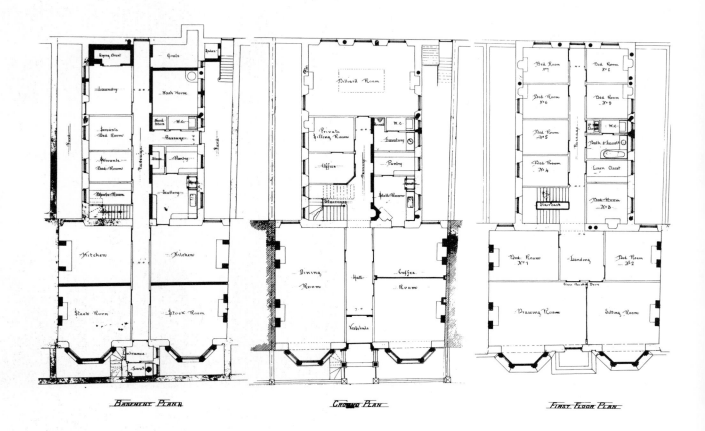

BASEMENT PLAN   GROUND PLAN   FIRST FLOOR PLAN

SECOND FLOOR PLAN   THIRD FLOOR PLAN   FOURTH FLOOR PLAN

34

supposedly three miles off Douglas Head. Harbour Commissioners doubt the exact distance covered; others fear that the incoming tides return the refuse to the beaches. But the Corporation is adamant: the barge is going the required distance and according to experienced seamen tidal curents are such that the refuse can't be brought inshore. It's cheaper, more efficient and more sanitary than tipping on land, say Councillors.... but the barge is old, the practice of towing it out to sea and leaving it there whilst tow-boats do other work is considered dangerous, and there are complaints that it smells in the harbour. It is destined not to last.

Nor is another practice: that of farmers coming with their horses and carts to gather the troublesome wrack which is piled in ridges on the beach by late season storms. Later the Corporation will have to pay for it to be removed. Now, when labour is cheap, the farmers take it freely - to recycle it as one of nature's best fertilisers. When they don't Corporation workmen merely push it back into the sea!

Thus is Douglas, canopied with smoke from thousands of coal fires; a place not so much Manx as 'cosmopolitan'. Here, more than anywhere else, there are Irish and English, Scots and Welsh, Lancashire and Yorkshiremen especially. They are the business adventurers and risk takers. Around them the capital of Man grows bringing an air of prosperity unknown to the townsfolk. They go forward into the twentieth century with confidence and security. Many visitors become family friends who return year after year for their annual respite from the industrial towns of the north of England and beyond.

ACCOMMODATION

Accommodation facilities in the hotels and boarding houses are basic: hot water brought in jugs to bedrooms every morning for washing and shaving. Later comes the daily ritual for chambermaids of 'slopping out' - emptying water basins and chamberpots into buckets. A typical boarding house would have no more than a single bathroom and two indoor toilets with round earthenware bowls in box fittings, the bowls having coloured patterns. Usually each landing would have a tap and lead-lined sink for filling ewers.

The kitchens were serviced by large earthenware sinks. Cooking was on open coal ranges with heavy iron pans and kettles, the ranges often being locally-made. Coal for heating, cooking and gas production was imported in huge quantities, making use of the improved quay facilities of Douglas harbour. Coal fires were in most rooms, including bedrooms for which an additional charge was

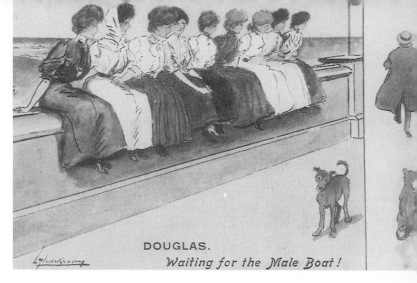

DOUGLAS.
Waiting for the Male Boat !

Two early (coloured) postcards capture the holiday spirit of Douglas in the the 1890s. (R and L Kelly Collection)

DOUGLAS.
A Scramble over the Rocks at Port Jack.

made. All lighting in the hotels and boarding houses was by gas with fittings provided in halls, landings and kitchens. Dining rooms and sitting rooms were adorned with chandeliers. Many of these fittings were provided by the local firms of Gelling's Foundry and Todhunter and Elliot.

When it came to the building of hotels and boarding houses speculators and developers responded with true Victorian entrepreneurial zeal. The lodging houses in the older parts of the town were rapidly succeeded by a new generation of hotels and boarding houses which transformed the appearance of the town by the end of the century. What was started on the Loch Promenade continued on the sloping fields behind the old shore line and cliff faces. New terraces appeared which could all boast either a 'sea view' or being 'within easy walking distance' of the sea front. Local

---

(Opposite) Plans of the Belvedere Hotel as originally built in 1878: Downstairs in the BASEMENT were the stock rooms (2), kitchens (2), scullery, pantry with store, servant's bedrooms (2), wash house, laundry, coal store and drying closet. There was also provision for a WC, an ash pit, wand (broom) room, food lift to the dining room above, a boots room under the stairs and lavatory. The GROUND FLOOR, with its vestibule and hall, contained the large dining room with coffee room opposite which could be divided into two. Beyond these were the still-room with food-lift from basement; a pantry; an office; a private sitting room and a large billiard room.
The FIRST FLOOR contained a drawing room and a sitting room overlooking the promenade; behind these were nine bedrooms, bathroom and WC, and a linen closet.
The SECOND and THIRD FLOORS were virtually identical, with 15 and 16 bedrooms respectively, a single WC and a housemaid's closet. In the Attic on the FOURTH FLOOR were a further seven bedrooms. (Frank Cowin Library)

The construction of the Sefton Hotel on the Harris Promenade was a later development, the site being originally part of the Villa Marina grounds belonging to Mr Henry Bloom Noble. It was built to the design of W.J. Rennison for Mr Quayle, a local hotelier. The centre section was completed in 1892 and its wings were completed three years later. (Frank Cowin Library)

newspapers produced supplements announcing the arrivals of families and where their holiday accommodation could be found.

It was also the time for architects and builders to display their skills. Foremost among the architects was W.J. Rennison who hailed from Stockport and set up his office in Douglas. One of his first commissions was the design of the Villiers Hotel which opened in 1877-78 with 200 bedrooms and 20 sitting rooms; by 1889 it was advertising 300 bedrooms and charging three guineas a week for full board, considerably less than an equivalent London hotel. It was Mr Rennison who went on to design most of the boarding house establishments on the Loch Promenade, thus giving this part of Douglas seafront its classic Victorian appearance. Most of these boarding houses were family run and were either single-fronted or double-fronted, the latter having 47 bedrooms. An example of the latter was the 'Belvedere' for which the original plans still exist and are shown here. It was completed as a 'Temperance Hotel' in 1878 for Mr Robert Cowell. The hotel was managed by a staff of six - a manager, cook, scullery maid, two housemaids and 'boots' with additional laundry maids

as required. The public rooms included a large billiard room, sitting room and drawing room.

Probably the most prolific developer during the late Victorian era was Alexander (Alec) Gill whose buildings are still around us and are memorials to his enterprise. He was a Town Councillor from 1904 to 1909 but began life as a tradesman building with his own hands his first home in Melbourne Street. Subsequently he was responsible for developing a substantial portion of the seafront as we know it today, many of the roads leading off it and, as a contractor, building the Palace Opera House and Coliseum, and the Gaiety Theatre. Huge quantities of slate were quarried from behind the South Quay and from the cliffs at the foot of Summer Hill. Masons were paid by result and earned three old pence for each cubic yard of quarried slate used for walls etc., their handiwork still evident in the rough stonework of the foundations. Personally, Alec Gill owned about 150 boarding houses and hotels. His practice was to give tenancies to comparatively poor but ambitious people and then stand security for them for bank loans to enable them to furnish and equip the premises.

Hotels vied with each other to provide attractive surroundings in their reception areas. One of the most splendid was Milne's 'Waverley' built before the end of last century on the Queen's Promenade. The decor was based on an armorial theme as evident in this postcard of the Oak Room. (Peter Kelly)

CUNNINGHAM'S HOLIDAY CAMP

Douglas was the pioneering base for Britain's first holiday camp - though many residents weren't happy about it at the time. Its instigator was Joseph Cunningham; a Liverpudlian baker involved in working lads' institutes. His original concept was an all-male tented village; the most popular meal: kippers and jam!

Mr Cunningham and his wife, Elizabeth, came to the Island after disagreements over organising summer camps in England. He launched his own camp site overlooking Groudle Glen at Howstrake and soon it catered for 600 men a week. It was such a success that in 1904 Mr Cunningham moved his 'International Young Men's Holiday Camp' (later known as the 'Canvas City') to five acres of land at Victoria Road, Douglas. Eventually an estimated 1,500 bell-shaped tents were pitched there, all with sprung beds, a mirror on a central pole and wooden bases which were raised every ten days for cleaning underneath. With eight men to a tent, it was claimed to be the largest holiday resort in the world, self-sufficient in almost all camping needs. It grew its own vegetables, had its own bakery and even a piggery! All campers wore badges so they could recognise each other outside of the camp and "pal-up."

Soon known simply as Cunningham's Camp, between March and September each year it brought thousands to the town, thus swelling the arrival figures. Mr Cunningham claimed they were visitors who would not otherwise have come to the Isle of Man but hotel and boarding house keepers thought otherwise. They resented the competition and there was a particular sense of unfair trading when it was claimed that despite its size the camp was valued for rating purposes at only one seventh of that of one 40 roomed boarding house. Only permanent buildings were valued. The tented land was classed as agricultural. Protests and public meetings to condemn the camp continued for years. Critics said the camp was illegal. It had not received planning approval; nor were its tents subjected to Douglas bye-laws. Legal advice was divided. Some said a tent was a building and Douglas Corporation should enforce its bye-laws in respect of the camp. Others argued that there were no bye-laws applicable to such a situation, especially when the tents were renewed every year.

So heated did the arguments become that there were incitements to violence: for people to tear down the tents. Others appealed to the Home Office for action. Others gave dire warnings of what might happen if women were ever admitted into the camps. Eventually it became clear to Tynwald that the only way to resolve the issue was to introduce legislation governing the operation of the camps and this was done in 1912. For the first time there were standards for a camp to satisfy - and women were banned from staying at them.

In response to constant criticism about such a large camp medical inspections found it to be well run and managed - but pressure was maintained even so for proper 'framed' buildings and many years later the camp eventually conformed. The Cunninghams became a highly respected family and did much to support local charities. Mr Cunningham became Island Boy Scout Commissioner; Mrs Cunningham, Commissioner of Girl Guides.

ENTERTAINING THE VISITORS

Douglas in the 1890s was over-rich in places of entertainment. Small theatres, music halls, assembly rooms and dance halls vied for business, locked in a contest of diminishing returns. They had proliferated following the pioneering success of High Bailiff Laughton in the development of a small variety theatre and dance hall at Derby Castle. At first some had made big profits; then, as others had come along, these had shrunk. The shares of the Derby Castle Company had halved in value.

In 1896 one of the first places to greet arrivals at Douglas was a new wooden Cirque built by circus entrepreneur Albert Hengler on Steam Packet land known as 'The Eiffel Tower site' because it had been the site for a proposed tower. Twenty years earlier Hengler's Circus, based at one time on the site now occupied by the The London Palladium, had set up in a special building on a site opposite St George's Church, now occupied by the Athol Garage. With the concentrated development of the town's Parade (the seafront) he decided on a permanent presence there. The wooden Cirque, later destined to be the Steam Packet's warehouse, had a seating capacity for 1,800 and was lit by its own generated electricity. The circus featured 50 performing horses, ponies and terriers but soon added a bioscope for animated pictures and an electric fountain with water chute.

Near the Cirque was the Grand Hotel and theatre complex in Victoria Street. Its theatre was run by Southport showman Alfred Hemming and featured comic operas staged by professional companies including D'Oyly Carte. There was a music hall too, a bowling alley and the Victoria sea water swimming baths heated to 70 degress Fahrenheit. These opened from 6am to 9pm on weekdays and 6am - 10am on Sundays.

Adjoining the Sefton Hotel was The Marina, otherwise known as The Pavilion; a dance hall used also for variety shows. Further along on the former Castle Mona estate was the Palace Pavilion, 200 ft long by 100 ft wide, and an adjoining Opera House, a small cosy theatre. Above it and overlooking it was the Falcon Cliff Pavilion of similar design: off the promenade but providing easy access to it was

A view of Victoria Street at the turn of the century showing the Grand and Villiers buildings. Within the Grand was the Grand Hotel and the Grand Theatre and sea water swimming baths. Later, the 'near' end of the Hotel became the popular Yates's Wine Lodge. (Cowin and Co.)

a twin track cliff railway which rose 110 feet. It lasted from 1887 to 1896. Then at the north end of the promenade was the Derby Castle.

In Regent Street there was the small 550 seat Empire Theatre; at the top of Prospect Hill, the original Gaiety Theatre (now occupied by the South Douglas Friends Association). Elsewhere hotel concert rooms were styled music halls, most notable of them The Star Music Hall on Prospect Hill. A large ground area of the Villiers Hotel on Loch Promenade was given over to a cavernous concert room. Elsewhere there were the inevitable waxworks and aquariums; at the Bowling Green Hotel, a large oval cycle track; in Buck's Road an indoor skating rink; then on the town's periphery the incredible Belle Vue (now the site of the National Sports Centre). It had beeen laid out for an international exhibition in 1892 and its facilities had remained. These included a lake on which was moored a replica of *HMS Victory*. There were side

Away from the promenades, the Bowling Green Hotel in Derby Road had plenty of entertainments, including its bowling green, skating rink and circular cycle track, the latest bicycles being available on hire. In 1894 the cycle track became the site of the Eastern District Secondary School. (R and L Kelly Collection)

shows, balloon ascents for the daring, athletic and horse race tracks (complete with grandstand), a variety theatre and usually a resident circus.

Competition was destructive. One of the directors of the Derby Castle Company, John Archibald Brown (editor/proprietor of the *Isle of Man Weekly Times* and *Daily Times*) described it as ruinous. Actually it was to prevent that competition heating up that the others had acquired the Castle Mona estate. The picturesque grounds around the Castle Mona Hotel included a waterfall cascading down a cliff face to the shore. When the owners had decided to sell because they couldn't get a reasonable return on the site's capital value Mr Brown and his colleagues had feared the emergence of a new pleasure garden. The rival Derby Castle and Marina companies had been unable to fund the estate's £80,000 purchase so Mr Brown had formed a syndicate of businessmen with an ostensibly "patriotic objective." The estate had been acquired then offered to Tynwald as an appropriate location for Government House. When this had been rejected the syndicate had offered it instead to Douglas Town Commissioners as a park and the basis of a town museum which many felt was necessary. Payment was to be deferred for ten years apart from a small down-payment.

Such a scheme would have neutralised the estate. Unfortunately for the other entertainment companies the offer had been rejected as being beyond the Commissioners and the syndicate had had to fall back on its reserve plan: better for it to develop the site than some rival concern. Thus the syndicate had carved up the estate, sold off the hotel, some land for housing (after the waterfall had been enclosed in a vertical pipe down the cliff face) then had built the Palace Pavilion and created the Olympia race course and sports centre behind it. One of the attractions of this had been the appearance of a touring American Wild West Show featuring legends of the west and real Indians re-enacting their bloody battles. Olympia had never been a financial success, however. Now, as Douglas Corporation was incorporated, it was apparent that an urgent solution had to be found to ease the competition.

Mr Brown's solution was the merger of the strongest competitors: the Palace, the Marina, the Falcon Cliff and the Derby Castle companies. This was achieved in 1898: the new Palace and Derby Castle Company emerging under Mr Brown's chairmanship. The Falcon Cliff's dance hall was closed and its land allocated for housing. Meanwhile, there were hopes that the Falcon Hotel and five acres of river land around it could be turned into a health hydro with a lake, tennis and croquet grounds. That never happened but the redevelopment of the Marina Pavilion did. No longer required as a dance hall the new owners lavished a fortune on it, employing Frank Matcham, the greatest Victorian theatre architect, to redesign the building within the existing shell. The work was supervised by Alex Gill, a director of the Palace and Derby Castle Company and the new theatre was named The Gaiety Theatre. It first opened its doors on 16th July, 1900 with a performance of 'The Telephone Girl' with Ada Blanche from the Theatre Royal, London, in the title rôle.

The elegant landmark of the Falcon Cliff Hotel was joined by a monster Dance Pavilion in 1887, although the latter was demolished in 1896 after succumbing to its competitors.

The Palace Pavilion of 1889 was the last of the huge ballrooms to appear. The roof was badly damaged by fire in 1902 but the building was soon repaired and modified by its new owners, The Palace and Derby Castle Company Ltd. (R and L Kelly Collection)

In September 1902 the Palace Pavilion roof was destroyed by fire. Thus was created the stimulus for the company to develop the site now that two competing dance halls had been removed. The outcome was one of the finest dance halls in Europe. Capable of accommodatimg many thousands of dancers, its success gave the company the impetus it needed to develop a new theatre on what had been an outdoor skating rink and tennis court in front of the ballroom. Elsewhere the Grand Theatre in Victoria Street was having a lean time. Even shows starring Harry Lauder, Houdini the famous escapologist and George Robey, had played to half empty houses. Still the Palace remained confident and proceeded with the construction of The Coliseum which was opened in July, 1913 by music hall star Vesta Tilley. It was designed in the "modern renaissance style" and seated 3,500. A special cover way led from the theatre to the ballroom enabling aftershow audiences to have a dance or two before going home. This became known as 'The Bridge of Joys' as it linked two centres of pleasure.

The Palace and Derby Castle Company tried to eliminate opposition but even as it did others arose such as the opening in 1905 of a wooden Pier Pavilion in Walpole Avenue for vaudeville performances. Fred Buxton's famous pierrot troupe who performed on the Corporation bandstand on the seafront also expanded when moves were made to get rid of the bandstand because it was causing

In 1877 the former Derby Castle residence of Major Pollock was acquired by Douglas advocate Mr N.A. Lawton who built the first Dance Hall in its grounds. In 1884 the Derby Castle Company Ltd. was formed and the company proceeded to double the size of the Dance Hall, the interior of which is shown below. It could accommodate 5,000 dancers. In 1893 this first entertainment complex of Douglas was developed by the building of a Theatre which hosted many of the top Music Hall stars of the day, including Florrie Forde.

The splendid Coliseum was opened in 1913 and had an integral passage way connecting the Theatre with the Palace Ballroom. (R and L Kelly Collection)

The interior of the Coliseum. The theatre was a popular venue for Sunday night concerts with an audience of 3,500. (R and L Kelly Collection)

congestion. People sympathetic to the pierrots intervened to help, one of them being Henry Bloom Noble who lived in the nearby Villa Marina. He had so enjoyed listening to the 'operatic pierrots' he viewed their possible departure with sadness so he took Mr Buxton to some land he owned further along the promenade and offered it to him. Thus was born on what is now the Crescent site the Pierrot Village and Tea Gardens.

Another sympathiser was the vicar of St Matthew's Church. Saying it was a "downright shame" that the pierrots should be lost he gave Mr Buxton wooden benches from the old St Matthew's Church. Using these around a small wooden platform, Mr Buxton launched his new open air venture, retaining his rights at the bandstand during the day as long as possible and staging performances at the new site only in the evenings. But soon it became a substantial full-day operation attracting daily audiences of up to 4,000. Performances ran continuously for twelve hours a day. By then a wooden covered stage and terraced seating had been established alongside the Empress Hotel, and other wooden buildings featuring alternative attractions had been erected alongside. It was here that the song 'Flanagan, take me to the Isle of Man again,' was popularised. The village prospered despite all the opposition until the outbreak of the Great War in 1914.

Another building on the site of the Pierrot Village was occupied by the Buxton Picturedrome, forerunner of the Crescent Cinema. The cinematograph was the big novelty among most places of enter-

tainment. In 1896 its future could not be guessed but public interest was keen. One of the regular attractions at the Grand Theatre were lecture nights by a professor, his geographic talks illustrated with 'animated' pictures. Later the Pierrot Village projected images of lions and tigers onto a screen for sharpshooters to aim at. Movements stopped when rifles were fired accurately.

Probably the first pure Picturedrome in Douglas was Wellington Hall, formerly the Waterloo Theatre and then a skating rink for the town's elite. In 1901 it was fitted out by the Royal Animated Picture Company and provided film shows in the afternoons and evenings. These were mainly scenic views from all over the world, including some of Douglas. It was claimed that nearly 15 miles of film were projected every day.

Later, when car racing came to the Island a newsreel company actually developed and edited their material locally for screening at the Palace within the day!

The first local live theatre victim of the cinematograph was the Empire Theatre in Regent Street, owned and run for some years by Charles Dare whose minstrels had been a success on Douglas Head. It was converted into a cinema known as the The Empire Electric Theatre.

The first purpose-built cinema, The Strand, was opened in 1913 by a company independent of the Palace and Derby Castle Company. And as this co-incided with the building of the Villa Marina Royal Hall, the Palace Company's dream of a monopoly in entertainment was thwarted.

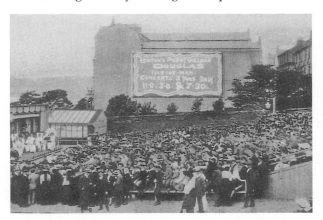

Fred Buxton's famous Pierrot Village and Tea Gardens were located on what eventually became the 'Crescent' site.

The holiday sprit is captured in another postcard from the R and L Kelly Collection.

41

No building typified the splendour of Victorian architecture more than the Palace Ballroom, set in the former gardens of Castle Mona. It had 16,000 sq.ft. of parquet flooring on which 3,000 couples danced to the best of orchestras. It could justifiably lay claim to be the largest and finest ballroom in the world. For concerts the building, with surrounding balcony, could seat an audience of 5,000.

ALL THE FUN OF DOUGLAS HEAD

Most of Douglas Head remains a part of the Nunnery Estate to this day but the principal parts of it - subject to certain omissions - were dedicated in perpetuity in 1870 to the people of Douglas for ramblage and recreation by Sir John Goldie-Taubman of the Nunnery. Effectively the Town Commissioners became the headland's guardians: their Highway, Sewering and Works Committee the specific department responsible. The omissions were an acre of land at the top of the headland where a stone tower had been erected in the 1820s as a guide to shipping. Another half acre of land known as the War Office site was purchased by the Corporation in 1910.

On the headland being dedicated to the town, paths were laid out, many of them financed by the Isle of Man Bank for Savings in Athol Street, known to many as the Penny Bank as it was primarily aimed at attracting savings from the poor.

At first people went to the headland for its scenery but soon there were other attractions. Probably the first was the development of Port Skillion Creek. The sheltered cove became a popular spot for men bathers all year round at a time when mixed bathing was banned. From here some swam to the Tower of Refuge and back. Eventually an open air pool, its contents replenished at high tide, was built by Douglas draper Robert Archer of Evans and Co., in Victoria Street. It was reputed to be the first public open-air pool in Britain. Mr Archer spent between £2,000 and £3,000 on building concrete walls to create a pool 80 ft long by 60 ft wide and varying in depth from two to eight feet. This enabled swimmers to perform 'headers' into the sea. Towels and bathing drawers were available for hire but to change behind rocks was considered so indecent that anyone who did so was forbidden from swimming in the pool. The hire fee, therefore, was in effect an admission charge.

By the mid 1890s the pool had become so popular that ferries plied between Victoria Pier and Douglas Head - and female voyeurs located themselves at vantage points. One newspaper reported the regular presence of "modest nymphs with powerful field glasses!" In 1921 the pool was bequeathed to the Corporation under Mr Archer's will and after storm damage in 1932-33 the creek was restored to its original state.

It was probably the Port Skillion pool and female interest in it that prompted Rochdale entrepreneur James Fielding to erect the Great Union Camera Obscura on the headland in 1887. The eleven lensed 'spy camera' secretly captured headland scenes and projected them onto panels in a darkened room. Destroyed by fire in late October, the circular wooden building was rebuilt in time for the following summer and became notorious for spying on courting couples. Significantly it was sited directly overlooking Port Skillion.

Without control the headland would have become saturated with funfair-style side shows and rides but the Corporation limited what was permissible, sharing what rentals were received on a 50-50 basis

The 'Rose' was one of three similar ferries which plied across the outer harbour from the steps of the Victoria Pier to the Battery Pier, shown above. Musical entertainment added to the holiday spirit of those making the short crossing to Douglas Head. (Cowin and Co.)

with the Nunnery Estate. Bye-laws controlling the headland were introduced in 1894 and a uniformed full time inspector supervised everything to "preserve order and good conduct." One of the Corporation's principles concerning what was permitted was 'taste'. Thus a proposed exhibition of a "clock-eyed woman" was refused; so too were exhibits of a new baby incubator and displays of strength by a man named Sampson. In an effort to preserve some of the peace of the area fun fair rides such as a patent switchback steeplechase, a bicycle railway and a toboggan run were refused. The other principle was that there should be no business or trade on the headland which would compete with that operated by ratepayers in the town. Thus Mr F. Woodcock, a photographer was refused permission for a photographic studio and Mr W. Cottier Cubbon of Liverpool in respect of a 50 seat cinematograph pavilion. Among those who were approved was a phrenologist, a lecturer on electricity, an exhibitor of a battery, another who used electricity to "test nerves"; a silhouette artist and incredibly a professor who operated a revolutionary new X-ray machine. What levels of radiation were permitted defy the imagination! Minstrel troupers were permitted but restricted to morning and afternoon concerts. Evening entertainment had to remain in the town. The sort of numbers they could attract was demonstrated in 1896 when an amateur singer from Eccles accompanied by a member of the Palace orchestra attracted 3,000 people for a charity performance outside the Douglas Head Hotel! What he raised went to the R.N.L.I.

Town Council controls were unable to protect the headland totally. On land not vested in the Corporation, and incorporating within it the stone tower once used as a guide for shipping, there was

The Lighthouse and Bathing Place, Douglas, I.O.Man.

Constructed as a private venture the Port Skillion open-air swimming pool was one of the first attractions of Douglas Head. (Frank Cowin Library)

The Port Skillion sea water pool was strictly for men only, and hardy ones at that! The scene made interesting viewing for the ladies from the slopes above. (R. and L. Kelly Collection)

A visit to the famous Grand Union Camera Obscura was a 'must' for all holiday makers who enjoyed the sequence of eleven headland scenes. (Frank Cowin Library)

built the Douglas Head Hotel and an exhibition of curiosities. A little later a music hall and dance pavilion was added to it. Then, nearby, dominating the skyline, there was erected in 1899 a slim 150 ft iron tower with a revolving observatory platform capable of seating 200. This was known as the Warwick Tower after the London engineer Thomas Warwick who had obtained a concession from its American designers to build a chain of them at British resorts. The first British tower had been erected at Great Yarmouth in 1897 and there were others at Scarborough and Morecambe. The first in America had been built in Atlantic City, New Jersey. For a fee of sixpence a steam-powered lift raised the platform and viewers to the summit for views of Douglas and the coastline.

Soon the tower gathered around it a 'shantytown' of wooden buildings with peep shows, fishing ponds and other amusements; a "hideous rattrap," according to one newspaper. Then at 10 pm on August 28th, 1900 these were destroyed by fire, providing a spectacle for thousands of visitors during the Oldham Wakes. Destroyed in the fire were automatic machines - 'Cosmoscopes', 'Eriscopes', 36 waxwork figures and a jewellery stall. The base of the tower was twisted by the heat but the tower itself survived. Subsequently a pleasantly-styled Pavilion was erected at the tower's base by insurers and as an added attraction the revolving tower was fitted with 'flying boats' thus converting it into a whirligig which reputedly made passengers sick! The 'boats' were suspended on long metal chains so that as the tower revolved they would fly out from the structure. However, according to its critics the venture was a 'dead loss' and when fire struck again in August, 1906 it was welcomed by many. This time the iron tower was reckoned to be beyond saving. Town Councillors had the Borough Surveyor inspect it as to its safety and report his findings to the police. In March, 1907 it was demolished. A controlled fire at its base heated the iron supports until they were bright red, then a steam traction engine used a steel rope to tug the weakened structure down. Disapproved though it might have been it did have a successor of sorts: a giant 'Joy Wheel'.

Another 'attraction' frowned upon by many yet popular was a small gypsy encampment. The Boswells and Harts claimed to be genuine Manx gypsies; three generations born on the Island. During the 1890s they set up camp every summer on land just outside Corporation control and thousands of visitors and locals alike went to the tents to have their fortunes told after the traditional crossing of palms with silver. In 1896 the authorities tried to get rid of them under a provision in a new Vagrancy Act. This stipulated that it was deception to 'pretend or profess' to tell fortunes.

To prove that only pretended fortune telling was taking place two young police officers in plain clothes were despatched to the encampment in the early summer of 1896. On paying their fortunes to be told they were warned: their sweethearts were false; they were flirting with others. Both constables had been 'done out' of fortunes by near rela-

The ill-fated 'Warwick' Tower which was a landmark on Douglas Head from 1899 to 1907. (Frank Cowin Library)

tives but prosperity would come one day for them and they would be successful in their courtships. On the basis of this two of the fortune tellers were hauled into court accused of deception. This called into question whether an offence had been committed so a compromise solution was reached. The prosecution withdrew its charges after the High Bailiff managed to extract a promise from the gypsies that they would never tell fortunes again. "The telling of the future is not for you to tell," he observed; "whether people die or marry or receive great fortunes, you have no power of knowing and it is only deception on your part to persuade people that you know these things."

The encampments still continued for some years thereafter and the chances are that a more tolerant society eventually accepted the fortune telling. Certainly, following a relaxation in earlier standards, the Corporation allowed a 'lecturer' on palmistry to have a stall on the Head. When the families had need of a new site to pitch camp, however, and sought Corporation approval to one on Council-controlled land for 1906 it was refused. Subsequently the gypsies moved to Onchan Head where they acquired land of their own.

Open-air church services for holidaymakers on Sunday afternoons were a more 'approved' feature of Douglas Head. These were started by Bishop Rowley Hill and continued by his successors; also on occasions by other religious groups such as the Town and Seamen's Mission. In the mornings a reputed 20,000 and sometimes 30,000 walked or

A view from Douglas Head towards the end of the 1890s. In the foreground, on the left, can be seen the gypsy encampment - gypsy fortune tellers being one of the popular 'attractions' at this time. (Cowin and Co.)

Probably the most popular attraction of Douglas Head was the Charles Dare Minstrel Show which gave performances in the mornings and afternoons throughout the week, except Sundays. (R and L Kelly Collection)

Steam Packet vessels rest at the Battery Pier while the crowded ferry 'Shamrock' arrives with more visitors on their way to Douglas Head. (Frank Cowin Library)

rode from town to Kirk Braddan for its famous services in a field. Afterwards, on a good, warm afternoon upwards of 10,000 were recorded at Douglas Head. Collections by means of a box or plate in a fixed position were for local charities such as Noble's Hospital, the House of Industry, the R.N.L.I. and a fund for nurses. On wet days the services were switched to Hengler's new Circus in the Parade. Later the Free Churches wanted to stage services without collections on weekdays but these were not pursued. One of the problems would have been the clash with other entertainments, particularly the minstrel shows.

Charles Dare of Greenwich came to dominate these. His Anglo-American Minstrels had appeared earlier in the Regent Hall, Douglas. But he had soon established exclusive rights to provide minstrel shows on the headland, paying Douglas Corporation what was described as "a very large rental" for use of the tiered semi-circular arrangement around a small stage. These he planked at his own expense. His minstrels offered "Fun without vulgarity" twice a day, performances starting at 11am and 3pm, and not once was there a public complaint to Councillors. For Mr Dare it was an amazing risk. He paid rent and paid his minstrels what he claimed to be "a good weekly salary." Yet he couldn't charge admission to the shows. They were conducted in the open-air and the headland was a public place open to ramblage. He had to rely, therefore, on the sale of song books for audience singalongs and the public being so delighted with the entertainment that they gave willingly when collection boxes were passed around. These made their rounds twice a performance to allow for the constant comings and goings of the audience. For some reason the Corporation refused him permission to sell programmes.

Despite that Mr Dare and the Corporation had an excellent relationship. Councillors were unable to give him a lease of the headland theatre which he sought but when other minstrel troupes made offers for the concession they were told: The Corporation felt that Mr Dare's minstrels were entitled to priority in consideration. Clearly it was a success for the open-air shows on the headland continued until the 1970s, many of the performers augmenting their incomes with hotel cabaret work at night. The remains of the open-air theatre and its stage are still visible.

So popular was Douglas Head that efforts were made to make it more accessible. In 1896 a hydraulic-powered swing bridge was erected across the mouth of the inner harbour, thereby shortening the land route to the headland for those prepared to pay a toll. It was designed to admit vehicles also but pedestrians were the biggest users. Amazingly when crowds gathered for the first official turning of the bridge it was found that the concrete circle in which part of the mechanism worked was fractionally too small. Builders had to be summoned hurriedly to chip away some concrete to let the mechanism complete its circle! (The bridge continued to be a feature of Douglas harbour until its replacement with a similar pedestrian bridge in 1979.) For those who walked across the bridge there remained still a big climb up steep steps to reach the Head Road.

Another more leisurely route to Douglas Head was across the outer harbour - from the Victoria Pier steps to the Battery Pier. By 1900 the first ferries were replaced by the larger oblong open-decked *Rose*, *Thistle* and *Shamrock*, owned first by Lawrence Boni then by Mr R. Knox, provided a service every three or four minutes. The ferries were fitted with bench seating round their railings and a small steering deck raised slightly round their central funnels. Fares were a penny each way. Music was provided by pianists and violinists playing the popular tunes of the day. On reaching the breakwater passengers followed the winding path lined by stalls selling shell fish, souvenirs or offering to weigh people on chair scales. To ease the strain of the final ascent to Douglas Head a privately owned double track 4ft gauge railway took passengers up the incline starting from near Port Skillion.

The winding pathway, flanked by the inevitable kiosks, led to Port Skillion and the incline railway which took its passengers up the final steep climb to the top of Douglas Head. (R and L Kelly Collection)

BY "THE DOUGLAS SOUTHERN" TO PORT SODERICK

In the early part of the nineteenth century the lower part of Douglas Head, overlooking the harbour and Douglas Bay, had become a favoured place for 'desirable' residences, such as Harold Towers and Fort Anne. As Douglas developed as a holiday resort the headland, by the 1880s, had also become a place of resort and entertainment for the holidaymakers. Its main drawback was its inaccessibility, the only route being by the old stone bridge at the top of the harbour. This was a challenge to speculators and ambitious schemes for constructing a high-level suspension bridge were seriously considered. The promoters of the Douglas Head Suspension Bridge Company included Major Goldie-Taubman of the Nunnery. The company was to build a tower for access to the bridge, the tower being a rectangular building with a hydraulic lift. The foundation stone was actually laid in October, 1890 but by the end of the following year the scheme collapsed through want of funds. The site was later used for Hengler's Circus and, in turn, was occupied by the Steam Packet's goods department.

Better progress was made by Douglas Head Marine Drive Ltd who saw the possibilities of a roadway along the spectacular coastal scenery formed by the contortions of the Manx slate. It would be open to pedestrians and vehicular traffic, the landowner, Major Goldie Taubman, being paid 5% of receipts. The roadway had reached as far as Wallberry, covering 1.5 miles, by 1891 and entrance was by means of an ornate gateway which still bears the

date of its construction. The Drive included an elaborate wooden bridge across Pigeon Stream. But the scheme then ground to a halt through lack of finance.

A group of Lancashire businessmen came to the rescue in 1892, and the following year saw the construction of massive bridges across the deep clefts at Wallberry and Horse Leap and a turning place for horse-drawn carriages at Little Ness. To reach here had required the engineering contractors to cut shelves into the slate cliffs. A marquee luncheon to celebrate the achievement was held at Little Ness and there was the first hint of an electric railway being constructed along the drive. By November, 1893, the drive had reached as far as Keristal. Then, once again the money ran out.

Two of the main shareholders in the Marine Drive company were partners in an Old Trafford engineering firm. They secured the concession from the Marine Drive Company to build a tramway and then sought a contractor to build the line, payment being largely in shares. Agreement was reached with the Electric and General Corporation from Westminster in 1894, the same year that the Douglas and Laxey Coast Electric Railway Company had reached Laxey. The Marine Drive company now dealt with the contracting company direct but the main concern was still the access to Douglas Head. In March, 1895, agreement was reached with Major (now Sir John) Goldie-Taubman to construct a 35-foot road from the South Quay to Douglas Head. (Matters were

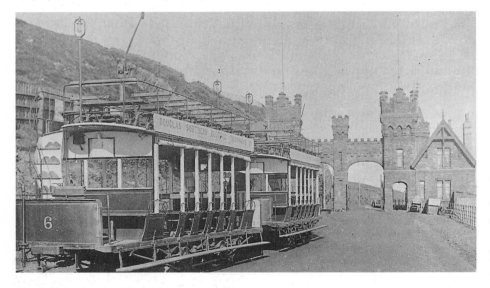

A car and trailer seen here in 1896 just inside the entrance gates to the Marine Drive. The toll gate house no longer survives but the entrance towers remain as a memorial to another great Victorian enterprise. (Warburton/Manx National Heritage)

Extraordinary feats of engineering were required to traverse the difficult cliff formations along the Marine Drive. Here, on the right, the double span bridge crosses Wallberry 267 feet above sea level and beyond is the Horse Leap bridge. (Warburton/Manx National Heritage)

also helped by the Harbour Commissioners constructing a swing bridge across the harbour). The idea of the railway starting at the foot of the new roadway, and even round the harbour to Victoria Street was abandoned. In October, 1895, a separate company, Douglas Southern Electric Railway Ltd., was formed to own and operate the new tramway when completed. Sir John Goldie-Taubman was its chairman and Dr Edward Hopkinson (of the Laxey electric railway fame) was employed as consultant engineer. The tramway company would pay 1d per passenger to the Marine Drive Company. Work was underway early in January, 1896, as the single 4' 8.5" track, with passing loops, was laid on the landward side of the already existing carriage drive, this being widened where necessary. Pigeon Stream was crossed by a three-span lattice-girder bridge but the most spectacular engineering feats were the bridges crossing Wallberry and Horse Leap. The 256 foot long Wallberry bridge was in two sections, slightly angled on a central pillar which supported the track 267 feet above sea level. The main depot, with car shed and workshop, was built on the seaward shelf at Little Ness - 1 .75 miles from the Douglas Head terminus which was sited overlooking the harbour and 400 yards before the Toll Gates. The depot was built of wood and corrugated iron. Of similar construction was the power house built on another shelf at Pigeon Stream, whose water supplied the two coal-fired boilers for the two engines and generators.

The 2 .75 mile track as far as Keristal was completed by July, another marvellous tribute to the engineers and workmen of those days, where the absence of modern mechanical aids was compensated by Victorian vigour. Official inspection required many safety features to be incorporated and when these were provided the first public service ran on 7th August, 1896, beating the Douglas Cable Tramway by a few days. When the season finished at the end of September 53,536 passengers had been carried. Twelve cars (six motorised and six trailers) were available and once in its stride the tramway was carrying an average of over 200,000 passengers a year.

The tramway undoubtedly affected the receipts of the Marine Drive Company which went into receivership and was unable to complete the Drive as far as Port Soderick. But the tramway company pressed on and its track was extended in 1897 to complete the three miles to a point 180 feet above its goal - the beach and facilities at Port Soderick. A pathway with 90 steps led to the beach

but a double cliff lift, once used below the Falcon Cliff Hotel, was installed in 1897 and privately operated. It consisted of two 4 ft. gauge trams driven by an oil-powered engine. By 1900 Douglas Head also had its double track funicular extending from a point near the steps leading to Port Skillion upwards for 450 feet to the terminal building which also contained the engine house, oil being the fuel used. The lift brought passengers to within easy reach of the tramway terminus.

PORT SODERICK

Port Soderick was famed principally for its caves and oyster beds but there was also a glen on its landward side which could be explored. Inventive Victorians marketed it as an old smugglers' cove. The oyster beds were equally as imaginative - they weren't naturally Manx. They were artificially 'seeded' every spring!

The attractions of Port Soderick were largely the result of the enterprise of Mr M. Forrester and family who built the promenade in 1897. A date stone is inscribed 'Built by M and T Forrester, 1897'. The Forrester family had previously been tenants of Laxey Glen Gardens and were proprietors of the Victoria Cafe on the Victoria Pier. For many years thereafter the Forresters were a well known local hotel family. One of the features at Port Soderick was a Camera Obscura and at either side of the cove marine parades led round the headlands to caves which could be explored. At first admission to the parades was two old pence but later it was made free to enable Port Soderick to be advertised as the only free glen on the Island. One parade led through an area grandly called the Cathedral Gates.

An inevitable pub and various stalls catered for tourist demands. Local oysters were much in evidence and fresh farm produce was such a feature of the restaurant that milking cows were kept in the glen and every day were brought down to the beach to be milked as visitors sat on benches to watch!

Port Soderick became a 'must' for all visitors and Port Soderick station handled many thousands who travelled by the steam railway from Douglas. The Douglas Southern electric tramway also did good trade while enterprising Douglas boatmen made Port Soderick a sea trip as well - one which Government officials admitted later helped to distort season arrival figures. Everyone who returned from Port Soderick was recorded at Douglas as a sea arrival!

Port Soderick in the early 1900s. The cliff lift on the right linked with the Marine Drive tramway, while on the skyline can be seen a rival train of the I.O.M. Railway. Port Soderick station was one of the busiest on the Port Erin line.

TOWN PERSONALITIES

THE FIRST MAYORS

The first Mayor of Douglas was Alderman Thomas Keig JP, FRPS, a cabinet maker and amateur astronomer who helped pioneer photography on the Island. The photographic business which he established when his amateur interest turned commercial is still in family hands, some 136 years later. Alderman Keig became the town's first Mayor in 1896...but not for long. The ardent 67-year-old local preacher, five times Chairman of the Town Commissioners and regarded as 'father' of the incorporation scheme, had been ill for some weeks prior to his appointment, but managed to recover sufficiently to attend the Council meeting which elected him. Thereafter his health deteriorated. A specialist was brought from England to operate on him but his condition worsened. In such esteem was he held that hourly bulletins were issued outside his home on Prospect Hill and when he died the Town Clerk, Thomas Nesbitt, was at his bedside. A depressive gloom spread throughout the town.

For his funeral the Corporation closed its departments and suspended all 200 outdoor labour so they could attend. They wore black crepe rosettes and marched two by two from the Town Hall to Prospect Hill where a crowd of several thousand had gathered for the start of the funeral procession. There were 40 vehicles in the procession to Loch Parade Church, the Council staff marching in columns of four. All houses on the promenade had their blinds drawn and hotel doors were closed.

Alderman Keig had joined Douglas Commissioners in 1874. Reputedly present at all subsequent demolitions of old buildings and the erection of new ones, he recorded them photographically as well as taking an interest as a member of the local authority. Once when the Commissioners got rid of an engineer because of cost they turned to Mr Keig for advice as "an amateur engineer" and he was credited with saving the town a lot of money.

Alderman Keig was not the Corporation's first choice as Mayor. That was Samuel Harris, one of the founders of the Isle of Man Bank in 1865, a member of the Manx Bar for 63 years and High Bailiff of Douglas for 41. He had been the first Chairman of the Douglas Town Commissioners and responsible for building the first promenade. Though not a member of the Corporation any longer it was felt he should be honoured for what he had achieved. Councillors and Aldermen agreed unanimously to offer him the post but he declined it, saying he did not think he could give it the time it needed. Mr Harris died in 1905.

Within the Corporation Alderman Keig's natural successor was another Douglas businessman, Alderman Samuel Webb. But there were many who believed the Mayor should be above local politics and this time by a 14-8 vote they got their way. Their choice was wealthy South Douglas MHK Major Robert Swan Stephen of Spring Valley mansion. He remained in office for the remainder of that municipal year and for a full year following, then stood down following the death of his wife.

Never again did the Corporation bring in an outsider as Mayor, and Alderman Webb was elected to succeed the Major. Samuel Webb originated from Warrington and set up his first shop in Duke Street. This shop was demolished when Victoria Street was being built whereupon Mr Webb moved to Strand Street and occupied the site where today's Marks and Spencer stands. Known as Webb's Lounge and Grand Bazaar it was referred to also as the Louvre Promenade because of its arcade qualities and high arched roof windows. Few

Advocate Samuel Harris guided Douglas into town status and became the first Chairman of the Town Commisioners in 1860. He became the High Bailiff of Douglas in 1864, a position he held until his death in 1905. Although no longer a Councillor he was invited to become the town's first Mayor in recognition of his services. Because of his other commitments he turned the offer down. He was also a founder director of the Isle of Man Banking Company and was its Chairman from 1872 to 1894.

Thomas Keig had the honour of being the first Mayor of Douglas though only for a brief period because of illness. He first become involved in town affairs in 1874 and was Chairman of the Town Commissioners on five occasions, playing a leading part in the town's incorporation of 1896. He was a man of many talents and founded a photographic business which today is one of the town's oldest commercial concerns. He was also a Primitive Methodist local preacher and his engineering skills were applied to the construction of Loch Parade Methodist Chapel.

stores outside London could rival it and the huge emporium became one of the most successful businesses on the Island. One feature was a Grand Orchestrion (an automated orchestra) which entertained visitors with Manx national music. Another was a free reading gallery with newspapers and periodicals, and desks with writing material for visitors.

Alderman Webb became a Town Commissioner in 1881, was elected an Alderman in 1896 and was serving one of his three years as Mayor at the time of the Dumbell's Bank crash. Although one of the principal sufferers as a bank depositor it was recorded: "His large heartedness never allowed himself to shut his pocket." When he died in 1903, aged 72, all Douglas shops closed for two hours so their staff could attend the funeral which was "an extraordinary affair" according to one report. Two bands joined the procession of many hundreds which followed the cortege from Strand Street to St. George's. It was Alderman Webb who presented Douglas Corporation with its Mayoral mace as a memento of his mayorality.

TOWN CHARACTERS

There are many Douglas personalities remembered more for what they did than their names: like the 'Flitter man' who chipped the limpet shellfish known as flitters off the rocks on Douglas beach, cooked them then sold them in town on lengths of wire.

In a time when there were no licensed 'turf accountants' or betting shops, there were the illegal bookies' runners who toured the pubs. Some said they were known as runners because they ran from the police! There were the rag and bone men who wandered the town with their carts and helped people rid themselves of their old clothing, bottles and jars which were capable of being recycled. Then there was a man who bought rabbit pelts from those who went rabitting in the country. He sent them to England for glove making.

The 'Onion Men' came every summer with a small boatload of onions on lengths of string. Wearing berets they wandered the town with a wooden pole across their shoulders and strung onions dangling down either side. People bought the onions by the length of string and hung them in their kitchens.

One Italian who was much liked was Caramouche Valerio. He used to carry a small hurdy-gurdy suspended round his neck and a monkey on his shoulder. When he stopped to play the organ it was supported by a stick. Sometimes he also provided fortunes through caged budgies. These were trained to pick up fortune cards in their cage.

A Douglas pioneer in his trade was sugar boiler John Kelly of 69 Strand Street. It was he who invented the traditional seaside rock, devising a production system whereby the Three Legs symbol and the words 'Isle of Man' could run through a stick of rock. Soon he was supplying Blackpool and other seaside places with rock bearing appropriate wording until local sugar boilers could produce their own. Mr Kelly died in 1938, aged 88, and his pioneering exploits were recorded in the *Daily Mail*.

Other obscure people who have earned a place in the town's history include grocer's assistant David Corlett and draper's assistant, Stephen Clague. The personal price they paid for what they achieved was such severe victimisation that they were compelled to work off the Island. At the turn of the century there were no controls on shop hours. So keen was competition among shopkeepers that before they would close at nights they would send out spies to see whether rivals were putting up their shutters. As a result, even in winter, shops stayed open until 10pm.

Employees were expected to work 60 hours a week

Samuel Webb arrived from Warrington and set up his first shop in Duke Street, but moved into Strand Street when Victoria Street was being planned. On today's site of Marks and Spencer, he built Webb's Lounge and Grand Bazaar - an emporium which had few rivals anywhere. In 1881 he became a Town Commissioner and then a Councillor in 1896. As an Alderman he was Mayor of Douglas on three occasions between 1898 and 1902.

and could be expected to do more even on a Sunday without notice or overtime. Eventually Corlett and Clague with the assistance of others inspired fellow workers to walk out at 8pm no matter what their employers said. The outcome, in the days before organised union labour, was an agreement on a maximum 56 hour week (7am to 6pm with an hour for dinner) for five days and 7am to 1pm on Saturday. A spin-off for Douglas Corporation was prompter evening meetings. Although timed for 8 pm many didn't start until an hour later because members couldn't leave their work. Now they were more punctual and there was less debating into the early hours of the morning!

Other achievers included William Clucas Joughin, a story writer for children's comics, particularly the *Boys' Own Paper*. One day he wrote some verse about 'Moaning Minnie', the Douglas foghorn provided by the Northern Lights Board when steamer masters said they were finding it difficult to make port in foggy conditions. Its noise had plagued the town. Now, through his light hearted approach he achieved what others had failed in doing. He got the foghorn moved round the headland to minimise the disturbance to the town. Mr Joughin emigrated to Calgary, Canada, in 1911.

Dawsey Kewley captured the public imagination when a short-sighted doctor walked off the end of the pier. Dawsey jumped in and supported the doctor in the water for 20 minutes before help arrived. Subsequently he saved 22 more from drowning and as a member of the Douglas lifeboat crew righted the boat and got it to the harbour when it was overturned and most of the crew were drowned.

Postcard salesman Henry Hough, a printer who came to the Island in 1906, failed in his ambitions to seek election to the Town Council but earned a place in history nevertheless for his humour and willingness to censor it. Church protests that obscenity had crept into comic postcards and that there was a street of ill-repute in Douglas led him to persuading fellow retailers to introduce a voluntary form of censorship - the first and only one of its kind in the British Isles. In 1912 a committee of retailers led by himself started to vet all cards offered by publishers and gave the police copies of rejected ones so they could prosecute anyone who sold these cards. Eventually the task of censorship was taken over by a Government committee but that wasn't until 1933.

Mr Hough died in 1926 aged 60 but his sense of humour survives in his pretended ownership of a rare breed of Manx dog. So famous did 'Prince Toby Orry' become that Mr Hough produced postcards of him and an English manufacturer produced souvenir china figures of the dog. Visitors were invited to call at Mr Hough's International Card Depot in Strand Street to see a three-legged dog, the last of a breed which had inspired the Manx Three Legs symbol. The truth was that the dog had lost a leg in a cable car accident!

THE MUSIC WORLD

Within the town's world of music and entertainment several names dominated. There was the innovative Harry Wood, band leader and director of the Derby Castle and later the Palace and Derby Castle Company. His school of music produced many instrumentalists; his concerts entertained thousands - and it was his inspiration that prompted the fledgling Douglas Choral Union, formed in 1896, to embark on the staging of comic operas, until then the province of professional companies brought to Douglas at great expense. Harry's younger brother Haydn eventually established an international reputation as a violinist and composer. The First World War song 'Roses of Picardy' was his. But he never forgot Douglas and returned many times to perform here, sometimes bringing famous stars with him. He also composed a wide selection of Manx music.

Another member of the Wood family was Miss M.L. Wood, brought to Douglas by her London parents in 1857 when eighteen. Within a year she was composing music and ten years later became a music teacher. When she died in Albert Terrace, Douglas, in 1925 she had achieved such a reputation that her friends and former pupils had a memorial tablet erected in the hall of Douglas Library. It remains there to this day proclaiming her as 'The Mother of Music in the Island'. A living memorial to Miss Wood is the Manx Music Festival

The Music Hall star Florrie Forde appeared for many years at the Derby Castle and became known as 'the darling of Douglas.' She was famous for her voice which could fill any theatre without amplification and for her rapid costume changes, her costumes being made locally at Miss Curphey's. (R and L Kelly Collection)

which she founded in 1892. Thousands of boys and girls have sung one of Miss Wood's compositions. It's "Honour the Old School Colours" - the school song of the Eastern Secondary School, forerunner of the Douglas High Schools.

London music publisher Bert Feldman made his mark after visiting the town in 1910. To promote the sale of sheet music and songbooks he opened a couple of 'music shops' which were, in fact, large singing halls where people were encouraged to sing the popular songs of the day before buying the sheet music. The last Feldman's Hall, as it became known, lasted until the early 1950s in Strand Street.

One of the Music Hall's biggest stars, Florrie Forde, was the darling of Douglas, returning season after season. It is her the Island has to thank for changing the Music Hall classic 'Kelly from the Emerald Isle' to 'Kelly from the Isle of Man'.

Lawrence Boni was one of the large pool of amateur musicians in Douglas who tried to make a living from his talents. He first sprang to the attention of Douglas Corporation in 1896 when he applied for a licence to operate a barrel organ. It was refused; so too was an application for a musical trio to tour the town led by Mr Boni, one of them a pianist, one a harpist and a third, a mandolinist. Undeterred, Mr Boni soon became known for bigger things - like running all the seasonal kiosks on Douglas seafront; seven shops in Strand Street with his wife; the Steam Ferries across Douglas harbour; then running the biggest hackney carriage business in town. But disaster overtook his enterprises with the coming of World War 1 in 1914.

John James Kelly in 1888 discovered how to place the Three Legs and lettering inside a stick of rock and soon his invention was being copied in many other seaside resorts. When he died in 1938, at the age of 88, he was given a special mention in the 'Daily Mail' as 'the man who brightened seaside holidays.'

HENRY BLOOM NOBLE, BENEFACTOR

One name dominated the life of Douglas at the turn of the century. Synonymous with the health and well-being of the town, Henry Bloom Noble was a childless self-made man who amassed a fortune in land and share speculation. Following the death of his wife Rebecca in 1888 he had become a semi-recluse in his walled Villa Marina mansion house on Douglas seafront. When he died in 1903 he became the town's greatest benefactor. Even today the Trustees of his estate still function.

In 1835 Henry Noble arrived from Whitehaven with his widowed mother whose maiden name Bloom he added to his own in later years. Arriving as a young man of 19 with 'the single pair of breeches and its patches' he was determined to make his way in life and support his mother. He was fortunate in being taken on by the highly respected firm of Alexander Spittall of Douglas and Whitehaven, wine and spirits merchants. By the age of 24 he was running the firm on behalf of the young widowed Mrs Jane Spittall. The following year he applied his experience to setting up as a merchant on his own in premises at Fleetwood Corner, midway along the North Quay. In 1852 he purchased land from Mr Samuel Harris in Upper Church Street and built new premises which were eventually leased to Messrs Bucknall. At the same time he became involved in the building trade setting up his timber and slate yard in the area which became Hill Street. He was therefore in an excellent position to benefit from the late Victorian boom in building and the visitor industry.

Very soon the ambitious Henry Noble owned a fleet of schooners which traded with English and Continental ports. They were also used to export ore from the Great Laxey Mine in which he acquired a large holding. He was also prepared to lend money but was noted for the stringent conditions he imposed; failure to repay meant a visit from the Coroner. He was also a major shareholder in the Douglas Gas Light Company and was a director of The Isle of Man Steam Packet Company until he parted company with his fellow directors upon their refusal to adopt his scheme for the introduction of the new propeller-driven steamers in place of the paddleboats.

Henry Noble possibly showed his greatest business acumen when he gained a controlling interest in the Douglas Water Works Company, realising that one day The Town Commissioners would have to gain possession of the company. His asking price was £144,000 but his insistence of payment in cash was the source of furious indignation within The Town Commissioners, and within the town in general. It appeared he had little confidence in the Dumbell Banking Company who were the Commissioners' bankers and whose manager, Alexander Bruce, was the Commissioners' Treasurer. In the end Henry Noble got his way and in 1890 Alexander Bruce handed over the requisite sum in Bank of England notes. This was deposited with the Isle of Man Banking Company of which Henry Noble was a founder director and which had been bankers to the Water Company.

When Villa Marina, the property of Samuel Harris, came on the market following the untimely death of Governor Pigott at the end of 1862, Henry Noble purchased the prestigious residence where he lived with his newly-wedded wife and elderly mother. The house and its spacious grounds were bought for

A Marshall Wane study showing Henry Bloom Noble with a group of orphans in the orphanage founded by his wife Rebecca. (Manx National Heritage)

£7,000 which some said was foolishly high; it would become the last green belt on the seafront and as such became extremely valuable though he refused to sell. He later purchased the land and a large property to the south west for £5,400; he then sold off plots on which was built the Pavilion Theatre and the Sefton Hotel, making £10,000 profit in the process.

Henry Noble's wife was Rebecca whose elderly parents Samuel Thompson, a retired sea captain, and Margaret Heywod Thompson lived in Clifton House, 14 Mona Terrace. She was a formidable lady and supportive in all her husband's enterprises. When she inherited Clifton House she made available the land above and adjoining Crellin's Hill to the Douglas Hospital Committee who had for some time been searching for a site on which to replace the old hospital of 1850 in Fort Street which, with its 14 beds, was now totally inadequate. Rebecca laid the foundation stone on 26th July, 1886 of what was to be called Noble's Isle of Man Hospital and Dispensary in recognition of the munificence of the Nobles who endowed the hospital to the extent of £20,000 to build and equip one of the finest hospitals anywhere. When completed two years later it had two main wards of 18 beds with consulting rooms, an operating theatre, kitchen, stores and accommodation for doctors and nurses. Henry Bloom Noble became one of the town's leading philanthropists. Providing Christmas dinners for residents at the House of Industry was just one of his many charitable commitments. His wife was responsible for founding an orphanage for destitute children.

HENRY BLOOM NOBLE TRUSTEES

Following his death in 1903, in his 87th year, Henry Bloom Noble was buried in Braddan (new) Cemetery, his grave being marked by a modest monument. He bequeathed his entire fortune for the betterment of the community, his entire estate to be administered by reliable Trustees he appointed whose "discretion was to be uncontrolled". There was a host of beneficiaries; then the Trustees applied themselves to many major projects. Extensions to the hospital were being considered but when they were told a new hospital on a greenfield site would be preferable the Trustees financed the building of a 57 bedroom hospital in Westmoreland Road. They equipped it with the latest devices including its own generating plant and X-ray machine and endowed it with £20,000. The new Noble's Hospital opened in 1912, the old hospital becoming the home of the Manx Museum in 1922. (Prior to this the Trustees provided Ramsey with its Cottage Hospital, opened in 1907).

Westmoreland Road was created through the acquisition of land for another venture - the building in 1905 of Noble's Hall at the junction of Princes Street and Tynwald Street. For 21 years the Douglas Soup Kitchen had been run for schoolchildren. Now a purpose-built hall with dining provision for 500 children was provided. Elsewhere, fields at Glencrutchery Road were acquired and given to the town as playing fields, to be known as Noble's Park. Part of the land was used for the building of a new church, St. Ninian's, £10,000 being left for this purpose in the will.

Another £10,000 was advanced to enable Douglas Corporation to acquire the run-down privately-owned swimming baths in Victoria Street and their re-development as Noble's Baths. Such a scheme had long been the dream of Councillors. In 1902 the baths had been criticised as being insanitary. One newspaper correspondent had observed: "Abandon soap all ye who enter here." So enthusiastic were Councillors now, they overspent on the venture by £7,000, naively thinking that what they were creating would last for 200 years. The Trustees funded the difference with a low interest loan. Two seawater swimming pools were provided, one for men amd one for women, each 75 feet by 30 feet and illuminated by four 800 candle power intensifying lights. The proud boast was that the water, drawn by pipe from the sea at high tide, was crystal clear whereas in many other resorts bathers had to be content with water "like coffee." Admission was free for children. Russian Baths were also later provided.

To make all that and many other endowments possible, including scholarships to King William's College and Liverpool University, the Trustees had to disillusion some Councillors. It had been the dream of many that the eight acre Villa Marina estate would be bequeathed to the town as a public park. Instead, the Trustees offered it for sale to the Corporation. The price of £60,000 in low interest Corporation bonds was condemned by some as excessive but in reality was considerably less than valuations had the land been sold for development. In return for buying the site Councillors were offered a grant of £20,000 towards demolishing the mansion and laying out the grounds as parkland and the building on part of the site of what is now the Villa Marina Royal Hall, then known as the Kursaal. There was just one provision. The Corporation should remove the large public shelter on the Harris Promenade opposite the Sefton Hotel which formed part of the Noble estate. Its removal promised to enhance the seaviews of the hotel and increase its value.

In 1909, though some thought the venture would be "a white elephant", Councillors agreed. Pessimists tried to stop it, even appealing to London for the Royal Assent to be withheld from the Villa Marina Act, 1910, which had been necessary to enable the purchase to be made but they failed despite it being raised in the House of Commons. The Villa Marina Park was opened to the public in 1911 with music provided by local pierrot leader Fred Buxton. In the first week alone 7,000 people paid a penny each to visit it.

Delays occurred before the building of the Royal Hall. So conscious were Councillors that they wanted something special that they held a competition for designs and inspected buildings in other resorts. Eventually the Noble Trustees advanced £25,000 to pay for what was planned and in July, 1913, equipped with its own electric lighting system, it was opened amid great celebrations. Mayors and Town Clerks from many British tourists resorts and over 60 journalists were among the invited guests. Lt. Governor Lord Raglan and his wife broke their summer holiday in London to attend - and for them the occasion was more memorable than for most. The noise of the excited crowd made their horse rear and plunge so badly they had to switch carriages!

54

SOME NOTABLE TOWN EVENTS

One of the most significant moments in Manx transport history occurred on Douglas quayside one June day in 1899. That was when the first 'horseless carriage' arrived at Douglas. According to Manx law, which had never anticipated such a vehicle, it was classed as a steam roller and as such someone was required to walk in front of it carrying a red flag. Steam rollers were limited to four miles an hour but this Coventry-built 5.5 horse power wagonette of the Daimler-Panhard type was much faster and capable of over 12 m.p.h. The solution of the Manx Cycle and Hiring Company, which had brought the vehicle to the Island to test it on Manx hills, was to give the red flag to a young boy cyclist, and he pedalled furiously ahead of the automobile as it chugged up Prospect Hill to the company's premises at the junction of Prospect Hill and Athol Street. Later in the countryside such formalities were ignored. The vehicle's throttle was opened wide and it sped round the Island startling horses and dogs. Even people scrambled over hedges!

Thus had arrived the automobile age. Few thought of it at the time as anything but a noisy curiosity. But within five years, though there were still but a handful of cars on the Island, Douglas was destined to make a major contribution to the future of the British motor industry. In 1904 Britain needed somewhere to stage speed trials for cars so that a national team could be chosen to represent Britain in the International Gordon Bennett race. Mainland authorities refused to close public roads so the fledgling R.A.C. turned to the Isle of Man. The prospect of a 'Motor Week' and the tourists it would attract resulted in Tynwald passing the Road Closure Act of 1904, enabling roads to be closed for the trials themselves, but not for practising. At a meeting in Douglas Town Hall meanwhile, local businessmen pledged half the cost of staging the trials and promised to give their staff an extra half-day off work so they could help marshal the event!

Thus motorsport came to the Island. Next year, inspired by the Hon. Charles Rolls of Rolls Royce fame, the **first car T.T.** was launched; the start at Woodlands. It was the first race of its kind in the world and brought a new, exciting atmosphere to Douglas.

With it there was also a new awareness among horsemen that their days were numbered. Dismissively they condemned the smelly machines which threw up clouds of dust behind them, startled horses and generally disturbed the peace. Automobilists were condemned as 'speed cranks'. But by 1907, as leading Manx people acquired automobiles the town's (horse) car trade became worried about the potential challenge.

At first they persuaded Councillors not to license automobiles for hackney carriages. Their speed and liability for serious accidents would deter visitors from healthy riding in carriages, they claimed. This would inflict a cruel and calamitous injury to a six days a week industry (never on a Sunday!) which was of the greatest importance to the town. What they bought themselves, however, was but a temporary respite. The motor age had arrived and couldn't be stopped.

One of the more memorable events of 1902 was the unexpected visit of **King Edward VII** and **Queen Alexandra.** Reputedly the king had visited the town *in cognito* a number of times but this would be his first official visit and coming only a short time after his coronation and a subsequent illness it was a complete surprise. The royal couple were on a cruise aboard their yacht *Victoria and Albert* accompanied by a cruiser and two torpedo boat destroyers when one Sunday in late August they decided to visit the Island.

Early that summer Douglas had celebrated the coronation with a procession, bonfires on the headlands and candle-lit illuminations along the seafront featuring fairy lights and Chinese lanterns in hotel windows. The burning in the bay of an old hulk laden with tar barrels had been planned too - but someone had forgotten to get her out of harbour before low tide!

Now as an unsuspecting 10,000 people took part in an open-air church service on Douglas Head the royal flotilla came to town. By late afternoon it could be seen approaching. By 5.30pm it passed the breakwater and the royal standard could be seen on the yacht. The word flashed round town: "The king's here!" A small cannon at the Fort Anne Hotel, traditionally fired to welcome the arrival of steamers, gave a welcoming salute and within half an hour, as the flotilla anchored in the bay, there were thousands on the seafront. Every harbour boat was chartered and circled the yacht with passengers cheering the royal couple who could be seen on deck.

Speaker of the House of Keys and local historian, A.W.Moore, who raced to the harbour after seeing the flotilla arrive, chartered one of the small boats and was permitted to board the royal yacht to deliver an official Manx welcome. Later, following Mr Moore's departure, the flotilla up-anchored and sailed to Ramsey where conditions were considered better for a royal landing the next day.

On 25th August King Edward and Queen Alexandra landed on the Queen's Pier and embarked on a tour of the Island by carriage, greeting amazed passers-by with waves of the hand. Wherever they went crowds

The scene on the quayside prior to the 1904 Gordon Bennett Trials - the first race of its kind which brought a new, exciting atmosphere to Douglas and which, ninety years later, remains as strong as ever. (R and L Kelly Collection)

gathered quickly - but even bigger crowds awaited them as the news got around that the royal couple would arrive in Douglas by early evening.

First they went to Cronkbourne, the home of the Speaker, for tea then were driven to Douglas. Thousands had gathered outside the Legislative Buildings in the expectation that the royal couple would be shown round the parliamentary chambers but they didn't stop. Instead they went down Prospect Hill and Victoria Street pressed in on all sides by a cheering crowd that followed. It was an unprecedented sight: a sovereign among his people, a few police running alongside the royal carriage but their presence unnecessary because of the people's respect for the king and queen. Along the promenade it was the same; the destination of the royal couple, the electric railway terminus at Derby Castle. There an official welcoming party awaited them including Mayor Webb and Town Councillors, with the double-deck horse cars providing a convenient grandstand for onlookers. The royal couple then made a swift return in a saloon tram to Ramsey.

It was a memorable occasion made all the more so because of its total surprise and the fact that His Majesty had chosen the Island to be the first place outside the U.K. to visit since his coronation. For Mayor Webb it was doubly memorable for shortly afterwards he learned that in gratitude for the welcome he had received at Douglas the king had conferred on him a coronation medal. This was delivered to him at his home whilst confined to bed with a painful nerve condition.

One of the most emotional issues to confront Councillors was what became known as **'The Preaching Nuisance'** in 1905. That summer a number of evangelists descended on the town and to gather a crowd relied on preaching on the promenade. To prevent seafront congestion one of the town's bye-laws prohibited public gatherings within 200 yards of the sea wall but the preachers refused to move onto the sands. Being so removed from the crowds would lose their impact, they said.

Such open defiance of the law couldn't be ignored and eventually four of them were arrested. Their subsequent prosecution before High Bailiff Harris was an emotional one, the Court House packed with sympathisers. When they were fined a shilling each (5p) and told they would be imprisoned for four days if they didn't pay, women shrieked hysterically and the preachers prayed in the dock. One woman actually stepped forward and kissed one of the defendants as they were led from the courtroom. Given time to think about their situation the determined preachers promptly returned to the promenade and preached again in defiance of the bye-law.

Again they were arrested and prosecuted; then the Rev. Somerset McTaggart was charged a third time, swearing he would go to prison for 21 days rather than pay a further fine of 21 shillings. Douglas Town Missioner William Kelly, a local preacher for 27 years, was equally determined to accept imprisonment: in his case for 14 days, but eventually the secretary of the Mission prevailed on him not to do so. Passions subsided - and as the summer ended so too did the 'Preaching Nuisance'.

In 1907 the **First Division of the Channel Fleet** which included six 16,000 ton battleships and two cruisers visited Douglas. On their anchoring in the bay a steam tug took the Mayor, Councillor Joseph Sharp, out to welcome the Admiral and he was greeted aboard the flagship by a guard of honour. The steamers *Mona* and *Tynwald* took sightseers round the bay and Douglas boatmen reaped a rich harvest by taking people to inspect the warships. Those which flew yellow flags accepted up to 500 visitors a day during the afternoons.

During the visit a regatta was held in the bay; warship crews known as 'blue jackets' were given shore leave; then between 10pm and 11pm the battleships gave a memorable searchlight display.

Probably the greatest celebrations in Douglas were staged in mid-summer 1911. They not only marked the **Coronation of King George V** but also the completion of 50 years of municipal government in the town. Linking the two, Councillors partnered Tynwald and others to stage a **Coronation and Jubilee Carnival** marketed as a major tourist attraction. Even horse racing on Douglas beach was permitted! Historic milestones were achieved with the following:

* *The switching of the now famous TT races from the short St. John's circuit to the new Snaefell mountain course with a start in Quarterbridge Road, Douglas.*
* *The staging of the first electric illuminations in any British seaside resort.*
* *The first visit of flying machines to the Island and the staging of a unique race between one of them and the Steam Packet's turbine steamer Ben my Chree.*
* *The presentation to Douglas by the Noble Trustees of the new Noble Playing Fields, now Noble's Park,*
* *The opening to the public for the first time of the Villa*

August, 1902 brought an unexpected Royal Visit and the townsfolk turned out in their thousands to give King Edward VII and Queen Alexandra an enthusiastic welcome. Here the royal procession passes between the Public Shelter on the Harris Promenade and the Gaiety Theatre. (Manx National Heritage)

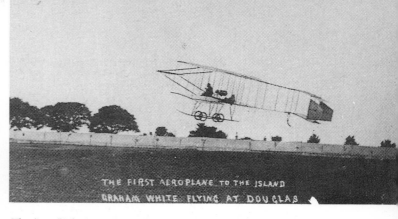

THE FIRST AEROPLANE TO THE ISLAND
GRAHAM WHITE FLYING AT DOUGLAS

Claude Graham-White and the Farman biplane - stars of the great Douglas Carnival of 1911. (Keig Collection)

The first flight into Manx skies took place on 4th July, 1911 from the Noble's Park Playing Fields. Spectators were charged admission - hence the screens round the 'aerodrome'. (Keig Collection)

Marina grounds. Sunday band concerts were introduced there that year - although not originally provided for in contracts given to the bandsmen. The Corporation had suddenly become less 'Sabbatarian', according to one observer.

To arrange everything a special committee was estalished containing within it sub-committees for particular events. These included a world-class marathon race with international athletes; a battle of flowers and confetti carnival; various sports and even motorcycle speed trials for TT riders over a flying kilometre between Little Switzerland and Broadway on Douglas promenade. This was marketed as a 'mini-TT' and unofficially riders were permitted to practice on the seafront for an hour every morning as long as it was before 7am.

The celebrations were between 28th June and Saturday, 8th July. To promote them the organising committee had 250,000 eight-page leaflets distributed throughout Britain and 2,500 pictorial posters. In England there were rumours that Douglas boarding houses were doubling their tariffs but this was heatedly denied.

June 28th was declared a public holiday on the Island and although the Coronation had occurred the previous week this was specifically given over to celebrate it. At twelve noon 21 maroons were fired over Douglas as a royal salute and this was the signal for five thousand flag and banner carrying schoolchildren to parade from their respective schools to the pier. There they were joined with others in the singing of the National Anthem then paraded along the promenade, finally lining up on either side to watch a civic procession from the Town Hall, led by the Mayor, Alderman William Joughin and featuring massed bands to the Villa Marina grounds. Finally everyone gathered there for singing and speeches.

Later that day the Noble Playing Fields were officially declared open. Then that night an estimated 20,000 people, residents and visitors, gathered on Douglas promenade for the start of the illuminations, designed by Mr Edmonson, manager of the Manx Electric Railway, and funded by donations from local businesses. Originally the committee had planned to buy the necessary equipment then sell it afterwards but after establishing the high capital cost had decided to hire equipment from an English contractor.

At 10.15pm an aerial bomb signalled the big moment. Scores of rockets flashed across the night sky; three more bombs exploded then the official switch-on drew gasps of amazement. At a time when electricity was still a novelty no one had seen anything like it. Everyone was rapturous in their admiration. Fairy lights had been distributed free for window displays in seafront hotels and boarding houses. Added to them now were thousands of light bulbs festooned from one end of the promenade to the other as well as some 300 chinese lanterns suspended from poles, whilst searchlights on Douglas and Onchan headlands probed the sky.

Every night thereafter for the duration of the Carnival period the illuminations astonished everyone. More than anything else this captured the public imagination; so much so that when the celebrations were over the contractor gave the town an extra night of lights free of charge. The Council members were also impressed and they placed a contract with the Electric Street Lighting Apparatus Company of London for permanent decorative street lighting, with the Manx Electric Railway Company supplying the current until 1923. Thus Douglas was able to boast of being the first seaside resort to have such illuminations.

In 1911 the T.T. Motorcycle Races moved from the St. John's Course to the more challenging Snaefell Mountain Circuit. Here a rider leaves Bray Hill, little more than a country lane, as he approaches the start and finish which for that year was on Quarterbridge Road. (Motor Cycle)

THE VILLA MARINA KURSAAL

1912. Work begins on laying the foundations for the Kursaal in the Villa Marina Gardens. (R and L Kelly Collection)

1913. The stage in the Villa Marina Kursaal as it was for the opening ceremony in July. (R and L Kelly Collection)

1914. Holidaymakers crowd into the Villa Marina Gardens during what could have been another record season but for the outbreak of war. The Gardens would be almost deserted for the next four years. (Frank Cowin Library)

For the aviation displays and race two aircraft - a 'bird-like' Bleriot parasol monoplane to be flown by George Barnes, and a 30 ft wingspan Farman biplane, piloted by Claude Grahame-White - were brought to Douglas in crates and assembled at the new Noble's Playing Fields. A temporary hangar was erected for the planes making the playing fields the Island's first aerodrome. The runway was a cricket pitch. Unfortunately spectators who paid a shilling admission were destined to be so disillusioned on occasions by the lack of activity that there were near riots when they demanded their money back. Language was 'painful but free'. One of the problems was the weather; another the late arrival of Mr Grahame-White, and the inability of Mr Barnes to take off as a result of a cracked propeller.

Eventually, Grahame-White decided to risk it and took off in his Farman - held together with piano wire and powered by a 1,000rpm Gnome engine. Megaphones announced the start of the race and the *Ben my Chree* set off across the bay. The Farman appeared 'doing an incredible 60 mph' and circled the ship two or three times before returning to its aerodrome. The pilot had decided that wind conditions were too risky to go further; in doing so many people in other parts of the Island were disappointed as the plane was supposed to make landings at Lewaigue, Ballagyr near Peel and Four Roads Farm at Port St. Mary. The Ben steamed on and made the round-the-Island trip in a record three hours, and as she approached Douglas Grahame-White took off again and 'escorted' the ship into the bay treating everyone to a display of 'twisting and manoeuvres exciting in character'.

That night Claude Grahame-White appeared at the Fancy Dress Carnival in the Palace Ballroom where he received thunderous applause from those who had witnessed his daring exploits. The aviator was flying again the next day and began taking fare-paying passengers bold enough to sit behind the life-jacketed Grahame-White. The wife of a King William's College master was the first passenger and she described her flight as 'a delightful experience'. As they circled the town, down below they could see men working on the new St. Ninian's church. However, Council officials and even the Lt. Governor Lord Raglan declined the chance of free flights. Said Lord Raglan: "If anything happened to me the loss would be too great for the Island to bear." Despite all, the first aircraft to be seen in Manx skies was a memorable spectacle.

An unusual attraction in Douglas in 1911 was the mooring in the inner harbour of what was claimed to be the last Australian **convict ship**. The *Success*, built in Burma in 1790, used in Australia as a convict hulk, sunk then raised from Sydney harbour and restored, had been converted into a travelling museum marketed as 'a lesson in prison reform'. Sightseers were able to tour

72 original cells and see models of 120 convicts and wardens; also some of the various tortures used to discipline the convicts including branding and the cat o' nine tails. Guides told stories too of a murder plot against the captain of the *Success* and the depredations of the Kelly gang.

Later that year the *Success* became Manx-owned. Among the investors were Charles Fox of the Palace and Derby Csatle Company, and John Philip Smith, owner of the Metropole Hotel. Famous Manx novelist Hall Caine was also reputedly involved. The *Success* was towed by paddle-steamer from Douglas harbour and fitted out in Liverpool for a 96 day trans-Atlantic crossing in 1912 to Boston, U.S.A. Thereafter she toured the States and was Manx-owned until 1922. In 1946 she was destroyed by fire.

The success of the 1911 celebrations prompted Douglas to repeat some of the features in a **1914 Carnival Week** staged between 29th June and 6th July. The promise of frequent parades, confetti and flower battles, fireworks and aviation displays was credited with attracting 15,000 visitors, all greeted on their arrival at Douglas by a decorated arch across the promenade near the pier declaring 'Welcome to our visitors'.

The big attraction arranged by the Douglas Carnival Committee was the appearance of two *Daily Mail* flyers and their machines. Mr Salmet, a Frenchman flew a Bleriot two-seater monoplane which was assembled at Noble's Playing Fields. The second was an Avro 504 fitted with floats and was flown by Mr Raynham and positioned in a hangar on the grass area of Queen's Promenade from where it could be hauled down to the water's edge. The Bleriot was the first to appear and flew at low level over the beach and then climbed to give aerial displays. When the tide was out the plane would land on the sand and pick up passengers who had filled in a coupon in the *Daily Mail* and were lucky enough to be chosen. Actually one of the first passengers was Miss Mildred Buxton, daughter of the famous owner of the Pierrot Pavilion.

Mr Raynham also joined in these activities and on his first take-off from the water climbed to 3,000 feet over Douglas Head before giving a splendid display. Spotting an incoming steamer the Avro went out to give it a greeting by hopping over the ship from side to side, much to the delight of the passengers who cheered loudly while loud blasts could be heard from the ship's horn. After landing on one occasion the Avro was caught by a wave which buckled the tubular frame to which the floats were attached. Replacement struts later arrived by steamer; in the meantime wheels were fitted and the shore used as a runway. The 1914 Carnival Week had been another great success. But within a month of the departure of the aviators Europe was plunged into war.

The Avro 504 floatplane was one of the big attractions during the 1914 Carnival Week. (Keig Collection)

EFFECTS OF THE FIRST WORLD WAR

The outbreak of the Great War in August, 1914 came to be seen as the onset of one of the most catastrophic times in the history of the town. However, at first the full realisation of its possible impact was not appreciated. All over Britain people believed that it would be "all over by Christmas" and young men were anxious to get into the war before it ended. Here the same belief persisted. Indeed, one of the most interesting news items of that time was that a Douglas Town Councillor, a Mr Knox, had introduced into the town the first motor taxi-cabs, "three speedy cars with self-contained means of propulsion".

Still, although the likely impact of the war failed to trouble people's minds at this early stage, other matters had to be dealt with. With headlines such as "Armageddon in Progress" in the local press, the Orchestra then playing in the Villa Marina was obliged to change its name from that of the 'Imperial Vienna Orchestra' to one with a less Teutonic flavour. Similarly, it was thought right and proper to drop the word 'Kursaal' from the Villa Marina entertainment complex.

By the autumn, however, it was becoming clear that the war was going to have direct and very immediate consquences on the Island in general and on Douglas in particular. Although the war had not started until well past midway in a season confidently expected to break all records, the reported drop of a quarter of a million visitors rapidly produced sober reflections in people. By the end of the year it was already being described as a disastrous season and the Boarding House Keepers Association was reporting that many of its members were finding it hard to pay their rents.

Of more immediate concern perhaps was the creation of a detention camp on the site of Cunningham's Holiday Camp. The camp, like the rest of the town, had been enjoying a bumper season with the Bolton and Nelson Wakes coinciding at the beginning of August. The declaration of war saw a mass exodus of over 2,000 campers as they rushed home to volunteer for military service. Many of the 200 camp staff also left. Within a month the camp had been commandeered and turned into an internment camp for enemy aliens and by the end of September the first prisoners had arrived. The barbed wire, the sentries armed with 'ball ammunition', the perimeter lights reflected in the night sky and visible as far away as Castletown were soon features of the town. The Camp, oddly enough, was split into three; the Privilege Camp where the wealthy could buy better rations and even employ a prisoner servant, the Ordinary Camp and the Jewish Camp. Such divisions however did little to allay the worries of the townsfolk. The sanitary arrangements seem to have been a source of constant concern while public anxieties were far from being allayed by the report in mid November of the riot in the Camp which left five prisoners dead and 14 injured.

Other forms of enemy activity also caused worry. The bombardment of the East Coast English seaside towns by units of the German Navy compelled the Council to extinguish the gas lamps along the promenade, notwithstanding the fact, as was pointed out, that the detention camp was brilliantly lit!

The turn of the year, the realisation that the war would not reach a rapid and satisfactory conclusion, forced everyone to a more realistic appraisal of the situation. The Douglas Gas Light Company had already reduced its prices, the directors of the Peveril Hotel had foregone their remuneration, the Council's road widening scheme at the bottom of Lazy Hill had been abandoned, but the really important development had been the requisitioning of the larger and faster vessels of the Steam Packet Company by the U.K. Government. By late spring it was obvious that 'disaster' as applied to the forthcoming season was, if anything, too conservative a term. Not only were the better boats no longer available but the U-boat menace in the Irish Sea was also a significant deterrent. In the Council it was pointed out that in Douglas, with a population of 21,000, there were those who had been forced to abandon their boarding houses; for example, half of the prestigious houses of Loch Promenade were vacant. In the *Isle of Man Examiner* of May, 1915 it was reported that of the thousands of boarding and lodging houses many were on the verge of bankruptcy and starvation. The Boarding House and Lodging House Keepers Women's League went to see the Governor, Lord Raglan. His solution was that they should go in for shirt making; to which one of the ladies replied furiously that "shirt making wouldn't keep them in salt."

By mid summer the full extent of the catastrophe was clearly evident to all. Douglas was described as "a dull and unsocial place under a blacker cloud than any other resort in the British Isles...and the great bay of light is a semi-circle of darkness...the beach is given up to the gulls and the seats are deserted." The great majority of the young men of the town had obeyed the call of 'King and Country'. Hundreds of horses which once crowded the promenades and streets had been commandeered by the Army, never to return. The horse trams kept sufficient horses to maintain the normal winter service throughout the year.

Distress Committees were set up; a National Relief Committee chaired by the Governor established; and a series of public meetings, with the Mayor presiding,

After the outbreak of war Cunningham's soon changed from a thriving Holiday Camp to an Alien's Camp. Here some of the 2,600 internees are mustered for roll call.

There was no dancing at Derby Castle during the war years. Instead, the spacious ballroom became a factory where local women were employed as machinists producing garments and ballonets, the latter being used in the construction of airships. (Frank Cowin Library)

were held in the Villa Marina during the summer and autumn. So stormy were the meetings that the Mayor was unable to make himself heard. There were several solutions proposed, many to do with financial relief. The Public Meetings produced proposals for the total non-payment of rates; for the authorities to collect only one third of them; an agreement for landlords to reduce rents by two thirds; that the Manx Government could issue personal loans and last, but by no means least, that the Imperial Government should provide substantial relief as part of its constitutional obligations. Other schemes caught the imagination too. Novelist Hall Caine suggested that 20,000 well-to-do aliens should be imported to fill the Douglas boarding houses; others put forward the view that the houses could well be used by convalescing wounded; others still that they were ideal to be used by soldiers training for Kitchener's New Army.

One man who took pity on his many boarding house tenants was Mr Alex Gill. He reduced rents to one third then said that if they still could not pay they would not be disturbed. Other landlords, alarmed at the precedents he set, said he was mad. Eventually his mortgage charges exceeded his rent income and he had to sell properties to meet the charges but he persisted, confident in making money again after the war. He told critics: "We may lose all we have but it is not so bad as losing one's son."

But the cargo boats were still full of furniture being sold at knock-down prices by desperate boarding house keepers, and when the Imperial Government finally produced a grant of a paltry £25,000 for the whole Island, and the Manx Government dodged the responsibility of increasing its own financial resources by introducing Income Tax, there were many at those public meetings who saw, and strongly advocated, annexation by the U.K. as the only sensible solution to widespread social distress in the town. Foremost among the many voices demanding action by Lord Raglan, and even his resignation, was that of Samuel Norris. He took up the cause of the Douglas landladies and in many a rousing speech advocated that rates should only be paid in part and that auctions should be boycotted. He caused many a problem for the authorities, so much so that he was found guilty of contempt and imprisoned in Victoria Road gaol by Lord Raglan. Only after Mr Norris's apology for 'unwittingly causing contempt' was he released though he was to continue his campaign for constitutional reform and action from the seemingly silent and impotent Tynwald Court which was firmly in the control of the Governor. Only after the war, when he was elected one of the Douglas M.H.K.s, would he see some result for his efforts.

Another gentleman who took action, though non political, was the Rev. Copeland Smith, minister of Victoria Street Methodist Church. At his instigation, and with the help of businessmen connected with his church, a company called the Manx Industries Association was formed in July, 1915. Knitting machines were obtained and eventually 200 women from destitute backgrounds in the town were employed who, by the end of the war, had produced millions of socks and garments mostly for the armed forces. Elsewhere there were more jobs for women when the spacious Palace and Derby Castle Ballrooms became factories for the production of silk envelopes used in the construction of airships.

The coming of 1916, however, saw little improvement. The question of the rates still dominated the agenda with more and more finding it impossible to meet the demands. Arguments were advanced that Tynwald should use the Accumulated Fund to offer relief, but with little success. The progress of the war too did little to relieve the misery. The introduction of conscription in the Island in early spring and the appalling stalemate on the Western Front made it clear that an early end to the war was unlikely. In Douglas the 'War Rights Union' attacked the impassivity of the Manx Government and demanded Home Office intervention and so on. Public meetings at the Villa Marina attended by upwards of a thousand were notable by the absence of the Douglas M.H.K.s from the platform.

Soon this feeling within the town was reflected in general Manx affairs and although during the year the rates and rents issue remained dominant, Tynwald Day, 1916, saw scenes never before witnessed on the Island. Slogans like 'We want a new Governor', 'Taxation of Wealth', 'Use the revenue from the Camps to relieve War Distress', and the public meetings on site at which they were shouted made for a very exciting National Day. The original War Rights Union had, it would appear, been superseded or perhaps taken over by the 'Fight for Freedom' movement which with its frequent public meetings, some on Douglas foreshore, some in Wellington Hall, was forming the vanguard of complaint.

All, however, was not doom and gloom. Despite the fact that the Imperial Government had left the Steam Packet Company with only three of their smaller vessels there were signs that in 1916 there might be a little revival in the number of visitors arriving in Douglas. This proved in fact to be true and the arrivals increased from 33,000 to 52,000, giving a faint hope of optimism. The reason would appear to have been that the worry about U-boats operating in the Irish Sea seems to have receded. But a more sober appraisal was that if the war continued into 1917 then the unmitigated disaster would continue.

The distant war was brought a little closer when the Island's first air raid warning sounded shortly after midnight on 29th September, 1916. Suddenly maids hid under tables; women fainted and some had hysterics. The alarm was raised by the firing of three maroons. At first people assumed that German submarines known to be close to the Island had opened fire on the Palace factory. But the truth was that a Zeppelin was headed for the town. About six were raiding the north west of England but strong winds had blown them off course; one of them out to sea in the direction of Douglas. Five minutes after midnight the Field Marshall commanding the Home Forces sent an urgent telegram to the town: "Take air raid precautions," and minutes later uniformed members of the Manx Volunteers, from their headquarters at the Drill Hall in Peel Road, toured Douglas ordering the extinguishing of lights. Then the waiting began, the town defenceless against air attack. The only weapons available were single barrelled rifles which fired standard ammunition. After three hours the 'All Clear' was given; the Zeppelin hadn't reached the Island.

The New Year of 1917 saw not only the continued distress in the town but also the realisation that the war had not only precipitated cataclysmic changes in the Insular economy but also in general social attitudes. It was repeatedly asserted that not only would men demand a living wage but that "women having shown their competence in the management of machines will insist on maintaining their economic independence." Heady and revolutionary notions indeed!

But Easter 1917 saw the fewest visitors yet and in Douglas the common saying was that "even eels get used to being skinned." Meetings on Douglas foreshore continued and the constant complaint was the reluctance of the Manx Government to do anything to relieve the extreme distress of the citizens of Douglas. This was despite the fact that in both 1916 and 1917 Budget surpluses had been declared, largely because of the enemy alien camps in Douglas and at Knockaloe and their consumption of dutiable goods. The prosperity produced by the camps was not, it was claimed, directed to the relief of the distress of the boarding house keepers and the small businesses of Douglas. As usual there was little response. Instead the Government continued to issue circulars advising how food shortages could be overcome with suggested amounts of bread, sugar and meat for each person. Food was distributed on this basis, but rationing was never introduced. When there was a potato shortage then turnips should be used as a substitute, and fishing parties in the pleasure boats should be undertaken to relieve the shortage of meat.

Matters came to a head when in the summer of 1918 it was announced that the subsidy to maintain the price of a large loaf of bread was to be withdrawn, with the prospect of the nine pence loaf rising to a shilling. The U.K. Government had sanctioned the subsidy of £20,000 a year from public funds provided that Income Tax was introduced. But even Lord Raglan could not persuade the House of Keys to pass the enabling Bill. As a result the United Kingdom withdrew the sanction for the bread subsidy; locally a movement was formed to abandon Home Rule and accept Annexation instead. Huge protest meetings were held in Douglas and throughout the Island resulting in a general strike which became known as the "Bread Strike". Few places dared to open for business and Lord Raglan ordered the public houses to be closed that day, the 4th July. The Tynwald ceremony the following day was postponed for fear of riots. Instead the Governor capitulated and the bread subsidy was brought back. The Home Office threatened to impose its own income tax but both Houses of Tynwald prevented that by passing their own Bill without delay, a permanent result of the war situation.

Samuel Norris, who gave a lead to the Douglas landladies in their pleas for retribution during the war years. After the war he became a Douglas M.H.K. and applied his outstanding political skills to achieving constitutional reforms. (Manx National Heritage)

By the end of August there was light at the end of the tunnel as better news was received from France. The month had also seen a great increase in the number of visitors so much so that Steam Packet boats could not cope. The piers saw thousands queuing all night for a passage home. But, as 1918 wore on it gradually became apparent that the war was approaching a satisfactory conclusion; the appearance of American sailors in Douglas was proof of that. Naturally, the townsfolk, and indeed the population of the whole Island, began to direct their thoughts to the post-war period. An immediate problem, of course, was the service to be provided by the Steam Packet Company, a matter serious enough to warrant the sending of a Keys' deputation to London urging the return of the *King Orry, Peel Castle* and *Mona's Queen* to support the smaller *Tynwald, Douglas* and *Fenella*. Despite some rumblings about the future of the Steam Packet Company itself, those six vessels were made ready to provide a fully established programme of sailings for the first post-war season. The Steam Packet had lost three ships including the *Ben my Chree*, pride of the fleet; but the nightmare of the Great War was over.

ROLL OF HONOUR

As the four long and grim years of war came to an end, so did the almost weekly announcements in the local press giving the latest names of those who had been killed in action, missing presumed killed or had died of wounds or accidents. Many a Douglas family would never be the same again; hardly a street escaped without losing a father or son. Of the total town population of 21,000 about one out of seven, mostly volunteers, saw service in France or one of the theatres of war. Many returned wounded but a total of 515 would not return. Their names are recorded on a Roll of Honour which the Council placed in the entrance to the Public Library, pending the erection of the Douglas War Memorial on the seafront.

PART TWO 1919-1945
TOWN HALL AFFAIRS

The immediate concern of the first years after the war was 'to restore dear old Douglas.' But such a restoration was not to be without its traumas. Not only were there immediate conflicts over the running of the Steam Packet Company but the provision of adequate lighting, possibly electric, and an augmented water supply produced their own heated arguments. Yet such was the general determination that soon things were under way again. The return of the aviators for pleasure flying was an indication of this, while Douglas Head opened up its stalls for character readings, lucky dips and the ever popular 'galvanic batteries.' Professor Holland paid a rent of 12/6 a week for his Punch and Judy site at Broadway; the peafowls in the Villa Marina Gardens had to be shut up at night because of the trouble they were creating; and the Tramways Committee had 122 tram horses working for them.

The visitors were back and, if anything, after the horrors of the war determined to enjoy themselves more than ever. Flora Woodman, 'The new Nightingale of the Concert Hall' was to be heard at the Villa, itself described, because of the dancing and whist as 'an immorally conducted institution.' To make matters worse 'promiscuous bathing' was going on outside and motor cars were being 'furiously' driven at 36 mph on the Promenade.

However, although much of the attention was directed towards the restoration of the town as a premier holiday resort, other equally, perhaps more important matters needed attention. The provision of housing for the 'artisan' population of the town was one such matter. By 1921 the rents of the artisan dwellings in James Street and King Street had had to be raised by 40%; those in Lord Street by 50%. The developments in the early 1920s on the Hills Estate to provide 'just the sort of houses that workmen need' were welcomed by those who were aware of the chronic housing shortage. In the same year the need to provide a decent thoroughfare from the piers to the railway station saw a scheme to widen Big Well Street from Hanover Street to the corner of Athol Street which necessitated the purchase and then clearance of the old properties along the route, to be replaced later by the Corporation tenements. The construction of these new estates produced one unexpected problem as the builders were getting their sand, tons of it, from the foreshore in contravention of the bye-laws! By 1926 there were 300 applicants for only 60 houses. The Pulrose Estate, bought it was claimed as a disposal area for the town's rubbish, was seen as the site of further houses but the recommendation that a Golf Course be laid out was accepted in 1926. Similarly, the Olympia Estate was bought in 1928 for housing development.

There is little doubt that the problems of poverty, of unemployment, of inadequate housing and sanitation were almost overpowering issues of the time. Mass meetings of the unemployed were held at the Market Place, newspaper articles and other meetings encouraged emigration to Australia; and the comment in 1926 that not all the people from the Fairy Ground and Big Well Street could move to the new houses at Pulrose because 'many could not afford the rent of a whole house' are sufficient indication of the seriousness of the situation. But the Corporation still had to find time and interest to ensure the success of the Public Library. It was only allowed a one penny rate and it ended the year with £38 in hand.

Facing the future: Councillors and Town Hall officials of 1919. Front row, left to right - William Knox; James Craine; John T. Faragher; the Mayor John Kelly; William Quirk; R. Corlett; David Gray. Second row - A.B. Cuthbertson (Deputy Town Clerk); Thomas G. Kelly; Sydney T. Shippam; T. Kermeen (Mace Bearer); Alex Robertson (Town Clerk); George Gilmore; John J. Quine; Edward Corrin; H.A. Bridge (Borough Surveyor). Back row - Thomas H. Cowin; David Collister; Robert C. Cain; Noah Moore (Villa Marina Manager) (Warburton Studio Photograph)

DOUGLAS WAR MEMORIAL

Shortly after the conclusion of the war, the Douglas Town Council appointed a committee to prepare a memorial for all those from Douglas who had fallen in the conflict. A design by Mr Ewart Crellin, ARIBA, a Douglas architect, which took the form of a 40 foot granite column topped by a 10 foot statue of an infantry soldier, was unanimously accepted at a public meeting. It was estimated the cost of the memorial would be £3,400 and this was raised by public subscription. Various sites were considered including Greensill's Corner, Villa Marina front, the old Bandstand on the Harris Promenade, and Queen's Promenade. Harris Promenade was chosen though difficulties with the bandstand and the nearby roadway resulted in the memorial being sited on the embayment opposite. Mr T.S. Quayle, a stonecutter of Douglas, obtained the contract for its construction and the statue of the soldier, weighing three tons, was sculptured by Mr H. Hemms of Exeter.

The Town Clerk, Alexander Robertson, had the difficult task of listing all the names of Douglas men to appear on the Roll of Honour. He was assisted by a Committee of Ladies and the total number of names came to 700, including those who had enlisted with overseas forces such as Canada, Australia and New Zealand.

The unveiling ceremony and service of dedication of the memorial took place on the afternoon of Thursday, 29th May, 1924. A huge crowd attended and the singing was led by the Manx Ladies Choir and 3,000 school children conducted by Mr Noah Moore. They were accompanied by the Douglas Town Band conducted by Mr Fletcher Kinrade. The Earl of Derby had graciously accepted the invitation to unveil the memorial which was then dedicated by the Lord Bishop. The Mayor, Alderman A.B. Crookall, MHK, JP, accepted the custody of the memorial on behalf of the Borough.

Earlier in the day, Lord Derby had been made the first Freeman of the Borough, he being considered worthy of the honour not only because he was head of the famous Stanley family, who, for nearly four centuries were Kings and Lords of Mann, but also for his outstanding contribution to the war effort. Among his many roles he was the leader of the Recruiting Campaign, Secretary of War in charge of military operations and Ambassador in Paris.

(Above) The ten foot sculpture, weighing three tons, which surmounts the war memorial.
(Below) The Earl of Derby KG, PC, GCVO, CB, who unveiled the war memorial and was the first to be granted the Freedom of the Borough.

A photograph showing part of the huge crowd which gathered on the Harris Promenade for the Unveiling of the Memorial on Thursday, 29th May, 1924. (Warburton Studio)

That significant social problems then were created by the development of the town is clear; the pattern of employment alone saw to that. Nevertheless it was the thrust provided by the position of the town in the centre of the visiting industry that equally provided its prosperity. The new 15 inch water main laid in 1926 from West Baldwin was essential to meet the increased demand from the boarding houses. Plans were produced in 1925 for the improvements to the harbour facilities that are uncannily similar to those effected over half a century later, while in the same year thought was being given to widening the Loch Promenade.

Of all the schemes, however, the one which did come to fruition in this period perhaps the most felicitous was the construction of the War Memorial in 1924. It was paid for by public subscription but not without controversy. Some thought the site unsuitable for a holiday resort. The thousands who in 1924 saw it dedicated by Lord Derby would find little to favour in that opinion, and the hundreds of thousands who have seen it since have not failed to be moved by the stark dignity of the battle-worn infantryman.

TOWN HALL ALTERATIONS

In 1928 the Town Hall underwent major internal alterations to provide additional and improved accommodation for the staff. This was rendered necessary by the increased work entailed by the growth of the Borough and the numerous additional branches of activities and duties associated with the work of the Corporation. In applying for Tynwald's approval to borrow the cost of £3,000, it was pointed out that the total capital debt of the Borough was £895,794 in 1926 of which £31,532 had been redeemed by March, 1927. The total revenue from rates and trading revenues was £116,475 in 1926 with an additional £31,364 from the Water Undertaking. The Borough rate for 1927 had been set at 10s 8d in the £, this being made up as follows: Borough and Library 5s 3d; Asylum etc. 6.5d; Education 1s 11.5d; Domestic water 2s 0d. The population of the town within the confines of its boundary had risen from a total of 19,223 in 1900 to 20,192 in 1926.

The Corporation now had 280 artisans' dwellings in the form of houses or tenements; motor bus services were being introduced and increasing responsibilities incurred as a result of Tynwald enactments through the Local Government Board. These included such matters as the Shop Hours Act, National Health Insurance, Rent Restrictions, Meat Inspection, Common Lodging Houses together with Poor Law Guardian and Education elections. In addition, the trading undertakings meant increased administration through the tramways, markets, Villa Marina, Pulrose Estate, Playing Fields, Public Baths and the Water and Electricity undertakings.

The alterations carried out to the Town Hall saw the removal of the stone entrance and pediment in John Street to a new opening in Ridgeway Street giving access to a large entrance hall and the staircase leading to the Council Chamber, Mayor's Parlour and Committee Rooms. The walls of the old corridor from John Street were removed as were other division walls to create

BY=LAWS RELATING TO THE FORESHORE

RUBBISH NOT TO BE PLACED ON SHORE.

No person shall deposit, place, or leave, or cause to be deposited, placed, or left, any night soil, offal, putrid meat or fish, or entrails of fish, carrion, dead animals, blood, dung, manure, oyster shells, bones, glass, china or earthenware, dust, ashes, refuse of vegetables or fruit, soaper's waste, gas tar or tar water, stones, lime, mortar, soil, clay, sand, or rubbish of any description, or any other offensive matter or thing, upon any part of the shore, or upon the slips or approaches thereto.

SAND OR GRAVEL NOT TO BE CARTED OFF SHORE.

No person shall cart or carry off or from, or cause or procure to be carted or carried off or from the shore, any sand, gravel, or stones.

PENALTY.

Every person offending against or acting in contravention of any of the foregoing Bye-Laws, shall forfeit and pay for such offence a sum not exceeding Five Pounds.

No person shall in or upon any part of the unenclosed foreshore or sea beach of the district, and belonging to the Commissioners, or in or upon any boat or bathing machine standing, lying, or being on the said beach, beg or solicit alms, or expose any painted, printed, or written matter or thing soliciting alms, or referring to any infirmity of mind or body, sell or offer for sale with importunity so as to cause annoyance any wares, exhibit any puppet show, posture making or other like performance, wilfully and indecently expose his person, conduct himself or herself in an indecent manner, sing any profane or obscene song or ballad, or use any profane or obscene language, and no person shall, without the consent of the Commissioners, in or upon any part of the said unenclosed foreshore, belonging to them place any vehicle, barrow, structure, stall, photographic apparatus, stand, show, or tent, carry on or exercise any trade, handicraft or calling, exhibit any advertising board or placard, let to hire any seat, form, stand, or platform, or play any musical instrument: Provided always that nothing herein contained shall prevent fishermen or boatmen or bathing machine owners from exercising their respective callings.

No person shall within a distance of twenty yards from the promenades or public roadway preach or hold or conduct any religious service, recite, or read aloud any passage or extract from a book or pamphlet, or deliver any public speech, lecture, sermon, or address of any kind or description, on the unenclosed foreshore belonging to the Commissioners.

No person shall, between the hours of eight o'clock in the morning and ten o'clock in the evening, beat or shake any carpet, drugget, mat, rug, or fabric, upon any part of the unenclosed foreshore, or sea-beach of the district, and belonging to the Commissioners, within a distance of fifty yards from the promenade or public roadway.

Every person who shall offend against or act in contravention of any of the foregoing by-laws in which no pecuniary penalty is mentioned shall, at the instance of the Commissioners, be liable for every such offence to a penalty not exceeding two pounds ; and, in the case of a continuing offence, to a further penalty not exceeding one pound for each day after written notice of the offence from the Commissioners.

PUBLIC NOTICE is hereby called to the foregoing By-Laws. By order of the Committee, May 9th, 1924. **ALEXANDER ROBERTSON, Town Clerk.**

Victoria Press, Douglas.

A view of the Town Hall before the main entrance in John Street was moved into Ridgeway Street in 1928. On the left can be seen the entrance to the Town Library. The occasion is thought to be the granting of the Freedom of the Borough to Alderman J.T. Faragher in April, 1926.

three new offices for the Town Clerk and his clerical staff. Steel girders were installed to support the Council Chamber above. A corridor leading to the library was removed and a series of glass partitioned offices belonging to the Accountancy Department was formed, all with access to a Public Counter in the new hall. This was for the purpose of rate and wage payments, issuing of licences etc.

Originally, a Tower, with staircase, at the rear of the building had been incorporated as a Public Entrance to the Council Chamber. As this staircase was no longer needed the Tower was reconstructed to contain another office on the ground floor with a store room above. The original Borough Surveyor's offices on the ground floor were given over to the Water Department, Sanitary Inspector and the Car and Market Inspectors. The remaining space was used as the Firemen's Assembly Room with access from the Fire Station. A new staircase was built leading to the first floor where the Borough Surveyor and his staff were accommodated with separate offices for his Deputy, drawing staff and Building Inspector. The staircase leading to the Caretaker's quarters on the next floor was restructured leading to a new landing.

Throughout the later years of the 1920s plans made earlier came steadily nearer execution. By 1928 the Promenade and Victoria Pier widening scheme was given the go ahead. The first demolition of the old

The Council Chamber in the early 1930s.

66

properties to make way for the New Street scheme began. Along the sweep of the Bay plans were advanced to improve the Villa Marina by demolishing the old wall along Colonel's Walk and replacing it with a colonnade, balcony and shopping arcade. Within the harbour, a scheme to replace the old Red Pier with a new one was started in 1930. At the same time it was planned to widen the Peel Road and to rebuild the old stone bridge at the top of the harbour.

There can be no doubt that by 1930 Douglas was a booming town with developments going on apace. During the August Bank Holiday of that year 40,000 visitors arrived in Douglas. As Sir Hall Caine, the famous Manx novelist said, "There is not a town in Europe so absolutely given over to enjoyment as Douglas in the month of August." But the old problems continued to persist - lack of housing, high rents and serious winter unemployment. When in the General Election of 1929 of the five Douglas members, three represented the Manx Labour Party the concern was clear.

On a different note, as the workmen cheated the tides on Douglas foreshore under lights at night, the wrath of those whose sleep was disturbed knew no bounds. Equally, the noise of the dredgers on the new pier evoked a similar complaint. Shopkeepers complained about the new shops planned for the Villa Marina Colonnade and seemingly everyone argued about the responsibility for the maintenance of King Edward Road at the north end of the Promenade. The Corporation bowling greens apparently remained deserted, however, because prices were too high. Along the Promenade police raided the 'shebeens' - unlicensed boarding houses which were known to be selling alcoholic liquor. At Port Skillion the crowds were so great that a young lady, fully clothed, was 'squeezed' into the water. Fortunately, it was only six feet deep and her fiance pulled her out.

The early 1930s produced grave concern about the effects of what was to become known as 'The Great Depression.' The concern was, on the one hand, about its effects upon what appeared to be almost the endemic problem of unemployment in both the entire Island and in Douglas especially. On the other hand, of course, the principal worry was the likely consequence of massive unemployment in the major industrial centres of the North of England in a reduction in the number of summer visitors. However, despite such anxieties, despite an increase in the Borough component of the Douglas rate of over 25% (from 6/8 to 8/6) the various schemes of improvements in the town were advanced. They were, in fact, advanced to some purpose. The recognition that the old town of Douglas, or the parts left, really had to go produced far-reaching and indeed far-sighted housing schemes. Shaw's Brow and Barrack Street, Chester Street and Wellington Square, the old Fairy Ground with its 120 properties, involving a total of 160 families and 600 people, all were earmarked for clearance and rebuilding by the early 1930s. Had these schemes been completely accomplished, the centre of Douglas may still have been inhabited by people rather than by cars. There were further demands for an improved water supply to the town while the expansion of the Corporation bus services necessitated the town being given the authority to

The Rt. Honourable Sir John Gilmour M.P., Secretary of State for Home Affairs, address-es the Council during his offi-cial visit to open the Marine Gardens on Loch Promenade, 23rd June, 1934. In the chair is the Mayor, Alderman James H. Skillicorn while seated below the dais is Borough Surveyor H.A Bridge and, wearing glass-es, Mr Leonard Costain who was appointed Borough Treasurer in 1932.

Lady Butler, wife of His Excellency Sir Montagu Butler, turns on the water for the foun-tains watched by the Mayor. In grey top hat is Sir John Gilmour M.P. In front of him is Councillor W.C. 'Gussie' Craine, Chairman of the Works Committee, and, with his file of papers, Mr Percy Shimmin, Town Clerk since 1931.

The Water Committee's Filter House off Glencrutchery Road was completed in 1934 to the design of the Water Engineer, Mr T.C. Greenfield B.Sc. Its object was to treat all water arriving from the reservoirs and to improve the quality of the town's water supply by purification. The treated water was stored in enclosed service reservoirs at Glencrutchery and Ballaquayle before supplying the town, a system which has remained basically unchanged.

impose its own regulations regarding bus sizes and so on. Perhaps surprising to modern attitudes the possibility of siting a police station in Pulrose was thought to be 'an insult to the inhabitants'! Also at this time there were strident demands for an open-air swimming pool somewhere along the foreshore or possibly in the Villa Marina grounds.

By the mid Thirties, indeed as early as 1934, a major issue was dominating the considerations of the Town Councillors. The steady growth of Douglas, despite The Depression, demanded more land for housing, for roads, for sewers, for schools and so on. The obvious solution was to take land from the neighbouring parishes of Onchan and Braddan. And as, so it was argued, quite

clearly Onchan village had become nothing more than a dormitory suburb of Douglas it was only logical that it too should be absorbed into the town. The resulting uproar can well be imagined. 'Will Douglas drag an unwilling bride to the altar?' and 'We strenuously oppose the proposals in toto' were two of the more restrained headlines appearing in the local press. A difference of 4/6 in the rates was a major factor. The row sparked and fizzed for many many months before being considered and reported on by a Committee of Tynwald. By early 1936 Douglas had lost the battle to incorporate the Onchan Village District into the town, being left far the greater part with what they considered the less useful and less valuable areas originally considered. Indeed,

A view of Douglas harbour in 1935 in which the cranes working on the new King Edward VIII Pier can be seen. The pier was officially opened the following year and is one of the few public works named after that monarch.

In 1936 the town's Fire Brigade received two new fire engines from Merryweathers of London. One, MAN 875, was equipped with a motor-driven turntable fire escape (with 100 foot extension) and fitted with a turbine pump. The second fire engine, MAN 876 also shown here, had its own pump and also a trailer pump. Its other equipment included a first-aid reel and 45 ft extension ladder. In uniform is the brigade's first full-time Chief Officer, Stephen (Bert) Caugherty whose father, also Stephen, had been Superintendent.

to add insult to injury the Onchan Commissioners then succeeded in getting hold of 'the sausage', the area immediately north of the Glencrutchery road, long coveted by Douglas. Further salt was rubbed into the wound when the Onchan Village Commissioners petitioned for the return of the £500 from the Douglas Corporation that Onchan reckoned the boundary battle had cost!

Despite their major problems, however, other matters great and small occupied the minds of Douglas citizens. By 1935 the new road from the Railway Station to Victoria Pier was at last absolutely completed, fifty years after it had been first mooted. In 1936 the brand new King Edward Pier was opened, ahead of schedule. By the following year the far-sighted scheme to widen Peel Road from its junction with Circular Road to the Quarterbridge was completed and the scheme to widen the Queen's Promenade at Derby Castle had been embarked upon. All these developments changed the face of Douglas to an extent that was to prove of inestimable value later in the century when all forms of road traffic increased at a rate and to a volume scarcely credible even to those directly involved.

More matters that occupied attention was the discovery that the Fire Brigade ladders were 20 feet too short for the taller boarding houses; that Corporation houses were distributed in what some believed an unfair manner; that the Corporation cafe in the Villa Marina was competing directly with rate-paying private cafe owners. Troubles perhaps, but on the other hand, the Augusts of those years could see something like 70,000 people arrive and depart in a 24-hour period. The Depression over, arrivals climbed and 1937 saw 578,498 visitors arrive during the season, with equally good summers to follow.

In May of 1937 the town celebrated the Coronation of King George V1 and Queen Elizabeth. A magnificent procession stretching from Peveril Square to the Villa Marina was made up of the school children of the town taking part in historical pageants. Having reached the Villa the younger children were given the treat of a cup of tea and a bus ride, infinitely more attractive than having to listen to the speeches from the assembled dignitaries.

That year saw attempts to provide a new Fire Station. The old horse-drawn steam fire engine had given way to new motor driven fire engines and the original Fire Station within the Town Hall was too small to accommodate all the new appliances. A tentative proposal to build

a new establishment at the top of Woodbourne Road near the Douglas High School for Boys was quickly squashed. Also considered was the building of a new Town Hall and Fire Station on the cleared area on the old Fairy Ground between the North Quay and the new Lord Street. Such a scheme, however, was put on hold and the area used as the town's first car park. (It seems almost beyond belief now, but in 1938 it was recognised that Douglas found itself with car parking problems!) Meanwhile, extra garaging for the fire engines was found across Lord Street where they remained until 1977. More positive was the opening in 1937 of the new school at Pulrose with spacious windows. It was dubbed the 'sunshine school' and was grandly described as the 'finest in the civilised world.'

As the end of the decade approached there were still many problems to contend with. There was still a need for more housing with the remaining slum areas awaiting demolition. More attempts to take land from Onchan failed. One answer was found in the building of the flats in Lord Street. Shopkeepers bemoaned the loss of their customers to estates on the outskirts of the town while it was hinted that St. Barnabas Church might have to close because most of its congregation had been transferred to Pulrose! Then there was the constant spectre of unemployment with 400 or more men and youths of the town huddled on street corners in the winter months, presenting a dismal appearance relieved only when some found employment in the winter works schemes.

By the early months of 1939 it was becomimg clear that despite the determination to push on with the town's summer season as usual the international situation was deteriorating rapidly. The name of Adolf Hitler became familiar to all and everyone was aware that Nazi Germany was giving backing to their entries in the T.T. Races in a determined effort to win the Junior, Lightweight and Senior classes. In the event they only won the Senior race. But later that summer the Manx Territorials were called up and on 1st September the *Isle of Man Examiner* carried under the headline 'Late News' the fateful sentence 'Germany attacks Poland.' Two days later the Island along with the United Kingdom was at war. A very successful season was drawing to a close and there was no mass exodus as had occurred in August, 1918. But with the effects of the First World War still remembered there was considerable dismay as to what was going to happen this time.

FIRST FREEMEN OF THE BOROUGH

One of the characteristics of a well-founded and successful borough throughout the ages has been the creation of its own Freemen. Douglas was no exception and but for the onset of the First World War it is arguable that the honour may have been conferred earlier than it was. However, in 1924 the first Freeman of Douglas was created and it was decided in March of that year that the Earl of Derby should be the first the receive the accolade.

On Wednesday, 23rd April, 1924 the Earl, who had travelled to the Island from Liverpool on the Steam Packet vessel *Viking*, put exclusively at his disposal and taking only 3 hours 20 minutes, proceeded to the Town Hall where the Mayor, Alderman A.B. Crookall and the Councillors bestowed the signal honour upon him. He received also a Certificate engrossed on vellum by Archibald Knox and a silver casket bearing the Borough and Derby Arms. He was described rightly by the Mayor as an outstanding figure for his country and his Empire, which the Mayor added was "the noblest and greatest Empire the world had ever seen."Derby had been chosen of course as the first Freeman because of the long connection of that family with the Island.

When Sir John Stanley was granted the Island in 1405 few could have anticipated it remaining a family possession for the next three and a half centuries. The family, despite the vicissitudes of the Civil War, prospered and although a branch was finally to sell the Island to England in 1765 the connection remained strong. (The Eagle and Child, representing the Derby family, are incorporated in the Borough Arms). The 17th Earl had enjoyed a long and distinguished public and diplomatic career. As a Member of Parliament for some fourteen years he had demonstrated his sincere and genuine character. As Secretary to Field Marshall Roberts he had been mentioned in despatches in the South African campaigns while in the Great War he had been Director of Recruiting and later Secretary of State for War. Later still he received the appointment as the British Ambassador in Paris.

ALDERMAN J.T. FARAGHER J.P.

It is hard to conceive a greater contrast with the Earl of Derby than the gentleman who was made the second Freeman of Douglas in 1926. John T. Faragher may honestly be described as a self-made man and one whose strength and integrity of character were put to the service of the town throughout a long and distinguished public career. Born in Foxdale in 1847 he started his working life in the mines before seeking advancement in Douglas in 1885, where he established an agricultural and auctioneering business. The business prospered and by 1890 he had been elected as a representative in No.1 Ward. His ability and probity were soon evident and he became Mayor first in 1905 and later from 1916 to 1918. He chaired every committee and in 1926 became a Justice of the Peace. The respect he gained from his strict impartiality and enthusiasm was no doubt enhanced by his reputation as a local preacher. He had been on The Plan since 1866 and his patriarchal figure was known throughout the Island. He was prominent also in the Oddfellows and Rechabites where his personal qualities were equally valued. He remained in public office virtually until the end of his life, and when he died on 5th October, 1931, Douglas lost one of its great figures, a man who had seen and indeed helped create the rise of Douglas to one of the great holiday towns in the north of Great Britain.

SIR HALL CAINE K.B.E.

There have been few Manxmen whose name is so instantly familiar to Manx people of all ages as Hall Caine, and on 23rd July, 1929, the Mayor of Douglas, Alderman William Quirk, conferred the Freedom of the town on this distinguished literary and political figure.

Born in 1853 Hall Caine trained as an architect, became for a short time a schoolmaster in Maughold, spent another six years as a leader writer on the Liverpool Mercury and finally journeyed to London where he established an enduring friendship with the poet Rosetti. The literary career, for which he earned a world-wide reputation with his novels translated into many languages, began in 1882 with his first published work while of his 14 novels, seven were set in the Isle of Man. His political activities brought him equal fame. He spent eight years as a Member of the House of Keys and his work for the British Government during the Great War earned him his K.B.E. in 1918 and his elevation to a Companion of Honour in 1922. One of his least publicised actions was his production of a semi-official document in 1916 setting out the need for a 'Union of Nations' after the war, perhaps the seed from which the League of Nations grew. The esteem in which he was held may best be judged by the personal tributes from such as Ramsay Macdonald, Stanley Baldwin, Lord Leverbrook, George Bernard Shaw and Viscount Cecil on this special day in Douglas.

On that Tuesday the Council Chamber was packed, the adjoining rooms and staircases crowded as was the street outside; indeed loudspeakers had to be set up to broadcast the proceedings to the people. After the Mayor had delivered his speech Hall Caine embarked on his reply. For 40 minutes he presented 'a truly monumental ovation' employing in its delivery 'infinite shades of tone and accent.' Indeed, this was a remarkable effort for a gentleman of his advanced years. The silver casket with which he was presented was illustrated not only with views of Douglas Head and Douglas Town Hall but also of Greeba Castle, his home for many years. He was able to enjoy his place as a Freeman of the town for only two more years. He died in 1931 but his reputation shines as bright as ever it was.

ALEXANDER ROBERTSON O.B.E.

The fourth Freeman of the Borough to a certain extent enjoyed a career that paralleled Alderman Faragher's in that both men had been heavily and directly involved in the almost meteoric development of Douglas from the 1890s onwards. Alexander Robertson, however, was a

Alderman John T. Faragher J.P. receiving the silver casket from the Mayor, Alderman A.B. Crookall, during the ceremony in the Council Chamber on 26th April, 1926.

paid official of the town and to that extent the honour was an unusual one. As was said at the time: "There must be few cases in the British Isles where a town clerk has been so honoured, but then there are very few town clerks of the worth, the value and the all-round general excellence and capability of Mr Robertson."

Alexander Robertson had been born in Douglas in 1864 and was brought up in the town. After a brief flirtation with banking he took up the position in 1890 of Deputy Town Clerk to the then Board of Commissioners, succeeding as Town Clerk in 1898. For the next 30 years or more he was at the centre of all the major developments of the town. The reconstruction of the old town and the new Council houses, the provision of an adequate water supply, of electricity, the Noble's Baths and Recreation Ground acquisitions, the Villa Marina and so on, all benefitted from his complete grasp of the subject matter and his courtesy and incomparable tact. His shrewdness in financial affairs was demonstrated when he withdrew £20,000 of ratepayers money from Dumbell's Bank just days before it crashed, thus helping to avoid the dire consequences suffered by others.

A staunch Methodist, Mr Roberston was active in the affairs of the Church, and whatever spare time was left was devoted to in almost every case responsible positions in the many voluntary organisations such as the National Relief Committee and the Crookall Maternity Committee existing at that time. He was also the founder member of the Isle of Man Municipal Association and its secretary for twelve years.

At three o'clock on Wednesday 29th October, 1930, Mr Robertson became a Freeman of the town that he had served so ably and with such distinction throughout virtually all his working life. During that time he had been awarded the O.B.E. and it is said that staff working in the Town Hall looked upon him more as a father than a master. Happily he was able to enjoy a long retirement during which he became a director and Chairman of The Isle of Man Steam Packet Company Ltd. Mr Robertson died in 1951.

ALDERMAN R. CORLETT J.P.

At a formal ceremony on 20th July, 1932 Alderman Robert Corlett J.P. became the fifth Freeman of the Borough. Like the other three Manx Freemen of the town

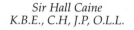

Sir Hall Caine
K.B.E., C.H, J.P, O.L.L.

Mr Alexander Robertson
O.B.E.

Robert Corlett had had a long and distinguished period of public office spanning those years that had witnessed the remarkable development of Douglas. Born in Lezayre, Robert Corlett arrived in Douglas in 1878 as a qualified joiner and millwright. Once established in the town he soon became concerned in local politics and in 1894 became a Town Commissioner. Upon the incorporation of the Borough he was returned unopposed to the new Town Council in 1896 and so continued his 38 years of service.

By 1907 Robert Corlett had become an Alderman; from 1912 to 1914 he held the position of Mayor and in 1919 became a J.P. He held at one time or another the Chairmanship of every Committee. He was actively and directly involved in all the advances in the town - the widening and improvements of the promenades both at the south and north ends, the water supply, the provision of an adequate sewer network, the trams and so on.

Throughout all those years Robert Corlett was characterised by his straightforwardness and his concern for the citizens of the town. When in 1932 he received the traditional silver casket containing the vellum scroll his description as a man of 'distinction, dignity, and ability' had been well-earned and was throughly merited.

The Mayor, Councillor Wm. James Corkill J.P., presenting the Freedom of the Borough to Alderman R. Corlett J.P. on 20th July, 1932.

TOWN DEVELOPMENTS 1919-1939

The Town Council welcomed the Armistice with two main objectives in their minds - houses fit for heroes, and a new street linking the passenger landing piers with Peel Road and the west of the Island. Inevitably, things took a long time returning to normal after the Great War and it was not until 1922 that Tynwald gave the nod to the Council to proceed in their avowed objectives by passing the Douglas Town Improvement and Artisan Dwelling Act. This Act empowered the Council to carry out street improvements and to purchase and demolish properties so as to enable a new street to be formed, initially from the top of Bank Hill to Ridgeway Street. Further properties could then be acquired so as to continue the street as far as Parade Street.

At that time the traveller wishing to proceed along the line of the present day Lord Street from Peel Road would first pass down Big Well Street as far as Quine's Corner. The latter had a distinct double dog-leg and it joined Big Well Street several yards further east than at present. Then came a short stretch of Barrack Street from which Hanover Street branched off, and this extended as far as Church Street, which runs up behind the Town Hall. A much shorter Lord Street came next crossing the comparatively new Ridgeway Street and terminating at Duke Street. At this point, the road straight ahead was a cul-de-sac called Duke's Lane so it would have been necessary to turn down Duke Street (or what is now Market Hill) and proceed along New Bond Street, or along the Quay, and into Parade Street, a somewhat tortuous journey.

The sting in the tail so far as the Act was concerned was the clause which decreed: "No occupier shall be required to vacate premises in the New Street area until accommodation in artisans dwellings be offered." It was here that the Council encountered their first difficulties. They experienced a shortage of building materials and also of suitable tradesmen, and this prevented them from getting their building programme under way. Consequently, they could not proceed with the demolitions necessary for the New Street scheme.

Their first building plot was Hills House which stood immediately to the west of the modern Post Office Headquarters building in Circular Road. For more than a century it had been the Douglas base of the powerful Moore family of merchants, but in recent years it had become derelict and was gifted by the Henry Bloom Noble Trustees to the Council as a likely site for municipal housing. The Trustees also included some empty plots in Peveril Street, Orry Street and Allan Street. At the same time the Council acquired a large part of the Hills Estate stretching from Westmoreland Road to Peel Road, and adjoining the new hospital. The Council had succeeded in erecting several houses on the rear of the Hills plot in Princes Street as early as 1922, but two years elapsed before the old house could be razed and the Circular Road/Westmoreland Road houses put up.

By then the supplies position had improved somewhat and work was proceeding quite satisfactorily on what was to become Hillside Avenue. Deciding not to build on the Peel Road frontage, the Council sold off the plots between Belmont Terrace and Belmont Hill to private enterprise at a handsome profit.

With 300 families on the housing list and a similar

Another look at the problems facing the Council in the years after the First World War - the removal of the warren of streets and squalid habitations of old Douglas. (Keig Collection)

number waiting to be included, the Council were aware that they were only scratching the surface of the housing problem. To add insult to injury, Tynwald was expressing concern at the delay in advancing the New Street scheme. How could the Council speed up the building process? The answer came in an approach by the Universal Housing Company who claimed they could erect whole estates of houses within one month from cutting the first sod to putting in the tenants. The Town fathers were invited to view examples of these wonderful houses at Rickmansworth and they returned to the Island very impressed. One of the favourable features they noted was that the houses were erected using sheet asbestos on both inside and out.

The Council already owned the Pulrose farmland, having purchased it in 1915, ostensibly for use as a dump for the town's rubbish. They then decided to utilise the land by erecting 100 of the Universal Housing type of dwelling. The Universal Housing Company were awarded the contract in September, 1926 and by the following July former occupants of the New Street area were being moved into their new homes. A further 50 houses were commissioned and residents and Councillors alike were praising the ideal site with its healthy elevation and fine views. Meanwhile the Electricity Committee of the Council were searching for a site for its Power Station!

The Council were still looking at other likely sites for housing and took an option on almost forty acres of Ballakermeen. This was bordered by Noble's Hospital, Eastfield, Ballabrooie and Peel Road, and was at what was felt to be a reasonable price of £10,000. After a long battle and acceptance by the Keys, their plan was thrown out by the Legislative Council. This was only the first of several schemes rejected by the 'Upper House', but what particularly incensed the Town Councillors was the anti-votes coming from the two Deemsters and the Attorney General, all unelected officials.

The Council had more success in the acquisition of the Olympia site at the top of what had been the Castle Mona Glen. By 1930 they had erected 66 houses in Victoria Crescent, Marathon Road and Falcon Cliff Terrace.

With their housing stock now approaching 500 units, the Council were able to make some progress in the New Street area, having cleared sufficient of the old properties to open up from Peel Road to Ridgeway Street. Tynwald was anxious to provide work for the unemployed and was only too willing to grant the Council compulsory purchasing powers so they could speed up the clearance and so remove the vermin infested hovels that mainly occupied the area between the Market, the Quayside and Parade Street. But before they could embark on these final clearances, the Council still needed to enhance their housing stock by a considerable amount. They commissioned a further 100 houses at Pulrose and asked their technical staff to draw up plans for tenement style housing. These were to be built in the by now devastated area of Big Well Street and lower Barrack Street, and were intended for tenants on lower incomes.

The draft plan for the flats was approved by the Council in March, 1929 and the units were ready for occupation by May, 1932. They comprised the 78 flats in four blocks on the north side of Big Well Street with two blocks opposite Quine's Corner, and two large lodging houses on the corner of Queen's Street. These latter two properties were eventually converted into flats following difficulties experienced in attracting suitable managing tenants. It was at this point that the Council made a formal decision to delete Big Well Street as a name now that it had been absorbed into Lord Street. An amendment to similarly 'lose' Quine's Corner was heavily defeated.

THE COFFEE PALACE

Although coffee houses were recorded in Douglas almost a century earlier, it was only the Coffee Palace, first noted in 1883, that attracted the attention of early photographers. This sole bastion of temperance stood, in football terminology, on the right wing in a forward line of inns and taverns placed on the quayside to entice the seafarer, perhaps ashore for the first time in weeks. It is unlikely that many of the itinerant travellers partook themselves of that beverage in the premises of the Douglas Coffee Palace Company. More likely it served as a meeting house and, possibly, a restaurant. In any case, the temperance connotation did not prevent it being demolished with most of its neighbours during the clearances of the New Street scheme.

It is often a matter for speculation as to how many licensed premises were swept away in the 1930's clearances, and no doubt there are elderly gentlemen

still around who may well have been patrons of some of them and who could clarify the matter. There may be more but the fourteen inns and taverns that can be identified are as follows: the Ellan Vannin Arms and Manchester Hotel in Fairy Ground; the Market, King Orry and the Step-down Inn in New Bond Street; the Laxey Inn in Chapel Row; the Manchester and Liverpool Arms, Masonic Hotel, Oddfellows Arms and Hare and Hounds - all on the North Quay; the Crown Inn on the corner of Muckles Gate and Duke's Lane; the Ramsey Inn in Almshouse Lane; and the Sheffield and Criterion Hotels on Parade Streeet. The latter had earlier been the home of Nessie Heywood, famous for having travelled to London in 1792 to plead the cause of her younger brother Peter who was standing trial for his part in the Bounty mutiny.

This particular area of slum clearance was levelled and provided Douglas with its first car park which remained as such until the 1960s.

With 250 houses now occupied at Pulrose, the Council cast their net further afield and purchased three fields abutting the Castletown Road and adjoining Pulrose. Before developing this land, however, it was decided to erect a further 150 houses in what was to become upper Pulrose. It has to be borne in mind that despite all efforts by the Council to extend the town boundaries, the predominance of the Country members in the Legislature was preventing this, and so Pulrose was still technically in the parish of Braddan. Consequently, the Braddan Commissioners felt they had a contribution to make to the Council's plan for upper Pulrose as they considered the new houses would be too near the tip and that there was a strong possibility of infectious diseases affecting the residents. In order to progress the scheme, the Council brought in experts from England to reassure the critics that this would not be the case.

By October, 1934 the first houses in upper Pulrose were occupied and the demolition of the New Street area was almost complete. It was reported that workmen demolishing one of the last houses in the area, known as 'Old Sweetman's House', encountered millions of bugs and numerous 'long-tailed fellas'. It appeared to be the last retreat of all the vermin in the district, and so the workmen proceeded to set the house ablaze and continued their work untroubled the following morning.

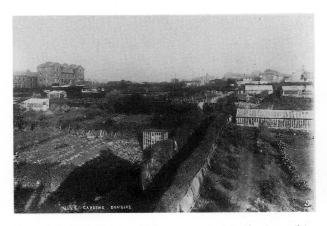

Part of the Hills Estate which was acquired by the Council in 1922, enabling them to build the first post war housing for displaced families. In the background can be seen Noble's Hospital, opened in 1913. (Keig Collection)

The derelict Hills House which was demolished in 1924 making way for Corporation housing at the Circular Road/Westmoreland Road junction - next to the Post Office Headquarters of today. (Keig Collection)

STREETS OF OLD DOUGLAS
- making way for the new Lord Street

Part of Big Well Street which took its name from the well, situated in the right foreground and which supplied this part of the town.

(Top) Another view of Big Well Street, this time after the demolitions and looking towards the buildings of the Railway Station and Peel Road. (Above) In 1888 the Douglas Schools Committee built Hanover Street School, a fine red brick building which stood out in contrast to the old stone buildings of the area.

Hanover Street with the school to the left and the 'Old Brig' and other buildings on the site of what is now the Salvation Army Citadel

Looking west along Hanover Street to Barrack Street

ALL ILLUSTRATIONS ARE FROM THE KEIG COLLECTION

Quine's Corner as it was in 1930, looking towards Big Well Street.

Then came one of the more controversial proposals by the Council. They announced that they wanted to erect 168 houses on the Ballacurry and Hague estates in Onchan. This was vetoed by the Government Property Trustees as being too close to Government House but the Council persisted with a revised plan to utilise Ballacurry only. The residents of Onchan village were aghast at the thought of having common council housing on their doorstep but their fears were unfounded, the scheme being rejected by the Legislative Council after a narrow acceptance by the House of Keys.

The ambitious proposals by the Council with regard to boundary extensions that would have taken in large parts of both Braddan and Onchan parishes, as well as Onchan village, had been watered down considerably by the time Tynwald came to vote on the matter. All the town eventually gained was the area around Pulrose.

A change of Governor saw a change of attitude towards housing in the proximity of Government House, and the Council were surprised by Government's offer of land in front of Bemahague. This was on the south side of Blackberry Lane which was costed at £6,320. In addition they were being asked for a contribution of £3,200 to release the restrictions on the fields they already leased on the north side of Blackberry Lane. In view of their previous difficulties and the inevitable opposition from Onchan Commissioners and residents, the Council were reluctant to spend any money on the site until it was clear they could proceed. In the end the Council were unable to come to a satisfactory agreement with Government regarding housing subsidies and so the scheme was abandoned before the battle with Onchan commenced.

The last couple of years of the decade saw the war clouds gather again over Europe, so the Council shelved any further housing plans for the foreseeable future. Nevertheless, they could look back with the satisfaction that they had increased council housing more than eightfold, from 94 to over 800 during the previous two decades. While the town's population remained static at 20,000 during this period, it could now be claimed that the vast majority of the poorer classes were living in modern hygienic conditions.

In 1937 two other significant developments took place within the town. There had been many calls to

The old Stone Bridge which had stood at the top of the harbour since 1778. This photograph shows work commencing on its replacement which was opened in 1937

build a new bridge at the top of the harbour in place of the old 'Stone Bridge' which had survived since 1778. Having a carriage-way of only 15 feet it was woefully inadequate to cope with the growing amount of motor traffic wishing to cross from the Old Castletown Road and the South Quay on the one hand, and the North Quay and Bank Hill on the other. But it was not until 1937 that the old bridge was demolished and the new one of concrete construction was formally opened. Such were its proportions that it even provided space for car parking, a convenient facility for the new garage of E.B. Christian Ltd. That year, and with traffic also in mind and as a continuation of the new Lord Street, Peel Road was widened from the end of Circular Road to Quarterbridge. With commendable foresight the road was brought up to modern standards and has stood the test of time.

The twenty years after the First World War also saw a proliferation of private housing which reached a peak in the second half of the 1930s. It was during this latter period that many new streets and roads of mainly semi-detached dwellings appeared, as exemplified by Westbourne and St. Catherine's Drives on Ballakermeen; Western Avenue and Westminster Drive on the old Ballabrooie quarterland; Thornton Avenue, parts of Alexander Drive, Somerset Road and St Ninian's Road, and the villas on Lazy Hill. But by far the most ambitious and largest development took place on the slopes overlooking

A view along Peel Road from Allan Bank in Circular Road, home of Keig's the photographers. Work is in progress on the new road completed in 1937. The 'Brown Bobby' is still standing which was a pub named after a racehorse. In the distance can be seen the Pulrose Power Station and cooling towers. (Keig Collection)

Another view of the old Peel Road with the entrance to Burleigh Manor on the right. On the left is one of the old gas street lamps and one of the new standards for electric lighting. (R and L Kelly Collection)

STREETS OF OLD DOUGLAS
- demolished relics of a past age

The famous Coffee Palace was a lone bastion of temperance in this part of old Douglas which had a preponderance of pubs and hotels. The Coffee House and the warren of streets behind this part of the North Quay disappeared in the great clearance of the 1930s. In the distance can be seen the Royal Hotel which survived until recent times and was used by the Steam Packet Company as its freight office. During 1957-59 this part of the quayside was re-constructed but it is still known as the Coffee Palace Berth

(Left) View along the Fairy Ground past the Clarendon and Douglas Hotels to the Fish Market made of cast iron. (Centre) Drury Lane seen from the Fairy Ground and with Bond Street going out of picture to the left. (Right) Looking east along New Bond Street with Almshouse Lane branching off to the left at Mrs Rowland's shop.

(Left) View from Chapel Row along Chapel Lane to Duke Lane. The door surround in the right foreground has been preserved at the Finch Road entrance to the Manx Museum. (Centre) Looking west along Seneschal Lane with the projecting porch of Smagg's House. (Right) St. Barnabas Square, looking towards the old Records office which was used by the Town Commissioners as their Town Hall. It survived as the Customs House, known as Seneschal House, until recent times.

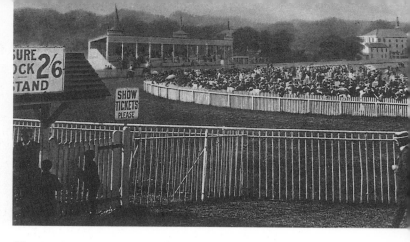

The Corporation's first double-decker bus on duty at the Belle Vue sportsground in the early Twenties. Race fans are queuing up for the return to Victoria Pier. (J.H. Corris)

The popular racecourse at Belle Vue which was opened in 1912. It was forced to close in 1931 following Tynwald's ban on betting. (Keig Collection)

Port-e-Chee, the development which was known as 'The Garden City.' Bray Hill, once a country lane on the outskirts of the town, was now very much a part of Douglas and what few plots remained were left vacant until after the end of the Second World War.

BELLE VUE

Although it was outside the town until the boundary extension of 1937, Belle Vue, as it is still affectionately known to the older generation, has provided the venue for a wide variety of sporting events for over a hundred years. Being at the confluence of the Dhoo and Glass rivers, it was virtually an upper extension of the Nunnery Lake and was subject to regular flooding. The developing visiting industry, and particularly the success of the Sports arena at Falcon Cliff in the 1880s, convinced a consortium of local businessmen of the viability of a second cycling and athletic track in the town area. At that time the River Glass, and consequently the parish boundary, ran directly across the land and so it was necessary to divert the river around the perimeter before the track could be laid.

The first sports meeting in 1889 was only moderately successful owing to the dearth of local competitors, and this situation continued although a New Zealand runner is reputed to have established a world best for the quarter mile hurdles in 1891. The following year the promoters temporarily closed the sports field to make way for the Great Exhibition. This was the greatest show the Island had put on to attract visitors and was a spectacular event that included a circus, a picture gallery, a wild west show, demonstrations of the latest scientific marvels, a switch-back railway, a boating lake and a model of the *Victory*.

That same year a third sports stadium was opened at Olympia on Victoria Road. There was certainly insufficient support for three venues and Olympia closed after its second season and Belle Vue ceased promoting after 1896. Falcon Cliff resumed its monopoly until the turn of the century when it too closed leaving Belle Vue to have a fresh lease of life. Sports meetings continued to be held for several years but without enthusiasm.

It was in 1912 that Belle Vue entered its second phase - as a racecourse. This was due to the efforts of Harry Fisher of Manchester who formed a company in the January and put on his first race meeting in July of that year. The old racecourse at the Strang was still in use but the facilities at Belle Vue were much superior. These included a grandstand accommodating a thousand spectators, refreshment rooms, proper changing rooms for the jockeys, and spacious stables for the horses. All these attracted the punters and successful racing was enjoyed. The Great War halted the activities but they soon resumed after the cessation of hostilities. While the authorities frowned upon the course-side betting, they realised that horse racing was a great attraction for the visitors.

Although a Betting and Gaming Act existed, it included an exemption clause for Belle Vue, and this happy situation lasted until 1927 when there were plans for a greyhound track at Onchan Head. This was the catalyst that House of Keys member, J.D. Qualtrough (a future Speaker) needed and he introduced a Bill in the legislature to ban all betting. He succeeded in killing off the greyhound track and eventually forced through his Bill which consequently sounded the death-knell for Belle Vue. The Bill was passed at the end of 1928 with a three year exemption for the racecourse. All attempts to have this exemption extended failed and Belle Vue became obsolete after the 1931 season. There was much public disquiet at the intransigence of the politicians and this one piece of legislation led to the formation of the Manx Reform Association whose members felt that the Keys and Legislative Council were out of touch with reality, and with the wishes of the people.

When the racecourse came on the market it was snapped up by the Town Council who saw the opportunity of creating a much-needed sports ground of which the town could be proud. This was in 1935 and early the following year, when King George V died, it was decided to name the Park in his memory. The King had visited the Island in 1920.

To prepare the ground, the Council brought thousands of tons of slag from Foxdale mines with a special railway branch line onto the site. By this means the whole area was raised six feet before turfing and seeding the surface began. This was under the general guidance of the Town's Gardening Superintendent, Mr Eric Coward and woe-betide anyone who did not treat the park with the respect he required. Mr Coward was also responsible for the creation of the Corporation's Ballaughton Nursery containing 12.5 acres which was purchased in 1938/39.

It was not possible to complete the King George V Park until after the Second World War when it became a fine sports ground. On one occasion it hosted a series of cycle races in which the famous world champion Reg Harris was the star performer; on another occasion, race walk specialist Paul Nihill set up an unofficial world record of 69 minutes for the ten-mile event. The Bowl, which became the Manx Wembley, was built at a later stage.

The above aerial view is one of a series taken from an aircraft of the Royal Air Force about the time of the end of the Second World War in 1945. This one is particularly valuable as it shows, in the centre, the car park formed after the demolition of the old streets around the Fairy Ground area. The car park contains a fire tower used by the wartime Auxiliary Fire Service; also in view is one of the static water tanks which were placed in various parts of the town for emergencies. (One still remains close to the Manx Radio station on Douglas Head.) Close by the car park is the Lord Street bus station used by the red buses of Isle of Man Road Services.

In the foreground is the old Sea Terminal Building in front of the Peveril Hotel. Behind Walpole Avenue can be seen the chimney of Noble's Baths and then the steeple of St. Barnabas Church. The swing bridge leads across to the South Quay behind which are the quarries from which much of the building stone of the town was obtained. In the distance rises the smoke haze from the Douglas Gasworks. (R and L Kelly Collection)

An aerial view of upper parts of Douglas showing the completed Ballakermeen High Schools and the first developments on the Ballabrooie estate which had taken place by 1939. The first houses on Devonshire Road and Crescent had also been completed. (R and L Kelly Collection)

THE VILLA MARINA : PRIDE OF DOUGLAS

Saturday, 19th July, 1913, was indeed a red letter day both for the Corporation and the townsfolk of Douglas. It was the day that the Villa Marina Kursall was officially declared open by His Excellency The Lieutenant Governor, Lord Raglan, and Lady Raglan. Great care had been taken in the arrangements which commenced with a Civic Procession leaving the Town Hall at 2.30 p.m. As the carriages made their way down Victoria Street onto the Loch Promenade and thence to the new Villa Marina entrance in Broadway, over 400 invited guests took their places in the grand circle balcony while members of the public took their seats in the main part of the Hall, doors being closed at 3.00 p.m. The curtains remained closed as the Mayor, Councillors, the Governor's party and the Douglas Town Band and artistes arrived on the stage. Then Lady Raglan appeared with a silver bell, presented to her by the Corporation, and 'rung up the curtain'. Miss Katie Cowin, the youthful daughter of the Deputy-Mayor (Councillor R. D. Cowin) came forward and presented 'in pretty fashion' a fine bouquet to Lady Raglan. The Douglas Town Band struck up with the National Anthem, the singing being led by the artistes engaged for the Kursaal's opening concert. Then came the speeches, with the Mayor of Douglas, Alderman R. Corlett J.P., being the first to be given a warm reception:

"Your Excellency, ladies and gentlemen - This is an important day in the municipal history of Douglas. We are met here to ask Lord and Lady Raglan to declare this magnificent hall open. This event has been looked forward to by the inhabitants of Douglas for more than a generation. The undertaking is a great one and only such as the municipality of a progressive town would undertake. . . .

"The town has developed rapidly since gaining town recognition with all the utilities in place for a modern resort, and with private enterprise playing its part in providing both accommodation and amusement for our visitors. Many people had hopes that the late Mr Noble would leave Villa Marina to the town, but that was not to be as, on his death in 1903, it was disclosed that he had left his large estate to Trustees to be used for charitable purposes. The Finance and General Purposes Committee appointed a subcommittee of five to negotiate with the Trustees with a view to acquiring the residence of Mr Noble and its grounds. The Trustees intimated that they were open to suggestions as to the acquisition of the property and to the purpose of the same. Provisional agreement in detail was reached by the Council in February, 1910 and the necessary Act of Tynwald was promulgated in September of that year . . .

"The Trustees offered prizes for a competition for the design of the building and laying out of the grounds. The competition was advertised and Professor Adshead of Liverpool University Department of Civic Design was appointed assessor by the Royal Institute of British Architecture. In January, 1911, it was announced that the winning design was that of Percy Robinson F.R.I.B.A. and W. Allan Jones, architects, of Leeds. The contract for the construction of the building was awarded to Mr Paul Rhodes after his tender of £15,985 was accepted. Work began in December, 1911 and has been completed without accident of any kind (applause) . . .

"In terms of agreement with the Trustees, £21,750 was provided to carry out the whole of the work, including the furnishing and equipment and the provision of an organ. The committee, under Alderman Craine, and their architects visited various resorts including Harrogate and Bournemouth before giving final recommendations as to the decoration and furnishing. In order that the Council could carry out most of these recommendations the Trustees generously agreed to a further grant of £3,500 (applause). It was also decided to install electric light and this work has been carried out at a cost of over £3,000 . . .

"In conjunction with the Villa Marina scheme, several other valuable improvements have been carried out. Notably, the removal of the Shelter, and the improvement of the junction of the Harris and Loch Promenades. The Council will in the near future be called upon to decide on

The Mayoral procession from the Town Hall to the Kursaal was witnessed by thousands of holiday makers from the North of England and Scotland. (Manx National Heritage)

The Lieutenant Governor's carriage arrives at the Broadway entrance. Lord and Lady Raglan are on the left and they are accompanied by the Earl and Countess of Bessborough. (Manx National Heritage)

the widening of the Harris Promenade and the further improvement of the Colonel's Road. Another street improvement is the widening of Broadway, a work which for many years has been desirable - 750 square yards have been taken from Villa Marina and used for this purpose. The Villa Marina scheme so far is complete in itself, but there are yet developments and extensions with splendid possibilities for increasing the attractiveness of Douglas as a high-class resort. The adjoining property between Villa Marina and the Gaiety Theatre belongs to the Corporation, and has yet to be dealt with, and in this connection we believe we have the sympathy and interest of Your Exellency and the Trustees, and we sincerely trust that this property will be used in such a practical manner as to prove of great public advantage to the people of this Island and our visitors. I have the greatest pleasure in asking Your Excellencies to declare this building open (loud applause)."

Lady Raglan, with silver bell in hand, then came forward and made a short but charming speech in which she congratulated everyone involved in the great undertaking of providing such a 'beautiful and delightful Kursaal which must have a refining and elevating influence on all who visit it.' She hoped that the sound of her bell would fill the atmosphere with joy, and peace, and harmony. Lady Raglan then declared the Villa Marina Kursaal open. In reply to a vote of thanks, Lord Raglan added his own congratulations and alluded to Villa Marina Gardens and Kursaal as providing for a class of holiday-maker of which Douglas had hitherto been neglectful. Large numbers of our visitors care little or nothing for dancing and variety turns, nor do exhibitions of cinemaphotography appeal to them with any amount of force. Nevertheless they appreciate entertainment more staid and more elevating of character and is just

the sort of entertainment which it is intended to provide in connection with the beautiful gardens and hall now owned by the Corporation.

After the speeches, the curtain was lowered and the platform party took up their places in the grand circle in preparation for a short concert 'of admirable quality' presented by visiting artistes. At the conclusion of the concert Lady Raglan unveiled on the main foyer staircase a tablet commemorative of the building of the Kursaal with the following inscription:
"Villa Marina Estate was purchased by the Corporation of Douglas for the sum of £60,000 and the building was erected and furnished at a cost of £25,000 out of funds provided by the Trustees of the late Henry Bloom Noble and opened by His Excellency the Lieutenant Governor, Lord Raglan, and Lady Raglan, on the 19th July, 1913."

The party then moved to the front of the grounds where Lady Raglan was requested to turn on the water in connection with the marble fountain erected on the south promenade of the Kursaal, to commemorate the visit of King Edward V11 and Queen Alexandra to Douglas in 1902. Cheers greeted the consequent playing of the jets in the bright sunshine.

The previous evening, Friday, the Mayor entertained a host of journalists who had travelled to the Island that day as guests for the opening ceremony. The journalists represented nearly eighty national and regional newspapers and journals including 'The Times', 'Daily Telegraph', 'Daily Mail', 'Daily Express' and 'Observer'. An excellent meal was partaken in the Kursaal cafe, the catering being in charge of the manageress who was assisted by Mr J. Ritchie, Isle of Man Steam Packet Company, and Mr Wilson, proprietor of the famous restaurant in Victoria Street. The convivial

evening, attended by Lord Raglan, was brought to an end by an hilarious 'symposium' given by the Douglas Head Concert Party. If publicity was the object of the exercise, no one could have been disappointed with the many glowing and detailed newspaper reports about Douglas being 'the great Island playground of the North' and about the Kursaal which 'gives an atmosphere of charming continentality to the picture of the bay, with its fringe of fashionable boarding houses'.

THE KURSAAL BUILDING

The following is taken from the official description of the Kursaal:

'The Gardens of 8 acres form a welcome relief amid the buildings of the sea front, and with their background of trees possess a natural charm. About half the site is now laid out as a lawn in the centre of which a bandstand had been erected. This is not of a usual pattern but is a small open-air theatre designed in the Chinese style, enclosed at the back with wooden trellis work and flower baskets giving it a garden-like appearance. Deck lounge chairs and tables are provided so that visitors may partake of afternoon tea while listening to the music and performers. A raised promenade terrace runs parallel with the sea frontage and below this terrace the street pavement is covered over forming a verandah for shelter.

'At the north end of the grounds has been erected the Kursaal which, together with the grounds, is to the design of the architects Percy Robinson and Allan Jones of Leeds. The style of the building is an adaption of the classic style and is a departure from the hybrid and restless character of many sea-side buildings of similar class; viewed from the grounds the building is reminiscent of some of the old stuccoed Italian private palaces.

'The general internal arrangement of the building consists of a large concert hall, designed for orchestral concerts but adaptable for other forms of entertainment. The concert hall is octagonal in shape, 100 feet in diameter, and has a total height of 66 feet to the ceiling of the lantern. The hall is a light and airy apartment surrounded on all sides by a raised promenade corridor, 300 feet long, with a series of arched openings permitting a good view of the stage. A similar promenade extends all round at the gallery level with openings on to a series of open-air roof gardens.

'On three sides of the octagonal concert hall and promenade are placed a fine series of rooms measuring from end to end 350 feet and 22 feet wide. These comprise foyers, lounges, rooms for refreshment, reading, writing, conversation etc. Current periodicals, writing materials and other conveniences are available for the use of visitors. These rooms are also available for local functions during the winter. The refreshment rooms are panelled in American oak, eight feet high, with the furniture in cane. Oak furniture is provided in the other rooms with a suitable number of settees and arm chairs. Two of the foyers, including the east foyer with the two main staircases, have marble mosaic floors in green and white. Over the whole of these surrounding rooms are a series of open-air promenades and roof gardens with two summer house pavilions in which refreshments can be served.

'In addition to the foregoing accommodation and the usual cloakrooms, artistes' rooms. manager's room etc. there are also provided large public conveniences, entered from the street, with a ladies' parcels office at

The lower part of Broadway was widened at the same time as this entrance to the Villa Marina Gardens was built in 1913. (Keig Collection)

the busy corner of Broadway. Broadway has also been widened and the old stone wall supplanted by iron railings which permits a peep into part of the grounds of Villa Marina.

'A power house has been erected wherein electricity is generated for lighting the grounds and building. The electric fittings for the building generally are of the semi-direct form of lighting, avoiding the unpleasant glare of the naked lights.

'As regards the general construction of the building it is of a substantial and permanent character with Ferro-concrete being largely employed. It is said that the main roof of 100 feet span, which is constructed in Ferro-concrete in the Kohn system, is the largest roof of its kind in England without lateral support, being executed by the general contractor, Mr Paul Rhodes of Leeds, without accident of any kind. The walls are constructed in the local manner of rubble walling with cement and pebble-dash facing. The building is heated throughout on the low pressure system of hot water. It is anticipated that the hall will hold 3,000 comfortably in plush seating.'

The Manx Language Society objected strongly to the use of Kursaal in the Villa Marina's name. It thought it inappropriate and not Manx in character. They submitted a Memorial to the Corporation which suggested alternative Manx names but these were turned down. Suggested titles included: *Halley ny Bingys as Garey ny Ferrishyn* - 'Hall of Music and Garden of the

The shelter along Colonel's Walk which survived from 1913 to 1930 (Keig Collection)

A view of the Colonnade and Sunken Gardens which were completed in 1931. (Reg Quayle Collection)

THE GARDENS, VILLA MARINA, DOUGLAS, I. O. M.

As part of the 1930/31 scheme a Colonnade was added to the south side of the Royal Hall. (Reg Quayle Collection)

A prize winning photograph showing visitors relaxing in the south Colonnade which provided an extension to the Cafe. In the background can be seen the Pavilion where revue parties performed. (Douglas Corporation Guide)

Fairies'; *Plaase ny Maynrys* - 'Palace of Happiness'; *Garey ny Feay* - 'Garden of Rest' and *Oayll Ferrishyn* - 'Haunt of Merrymaking'.

The great enterprise was one of the largest and most onerous ever embarked upon by the Corporation. Herr Simon Wurm's Viennese Orchestra was the big resident attraction for 1914. Attired in picturesque uniforms the musicians were famous for the popular Hungarian waltz melodies which were in keeping with the continental atmosphere of the Kursaal. However, the coming of the Great War foreshortened that season and, being of alien origin, Herr Simon Wurm and his musicians were arrested and interned at Knockaloe Camp. Also, as a result of its Austro-German connotations, the name Kursaal was dropped and subsequently replaced by the title 'Royal Hall' following the visit of King George V and Queen Mary in 1923. During the war years the hall was used for a very different purpose to what had been intended. Here were held meetings where the destitute boarding-house keepers aired their grievances in an attempt to assuage their plight.

It was not until 1920, with the summer season returning to pre-war proportions, that the Villa Marina complex was to prove the great asset to the Corporation that had been envisaged. In 1919 Mr Noah Moore L.R.A.M. was appointed its General Manager. A leading figure in Manx music circles, he was renowned as a conductor of choirs with a long series of successes gained both in the Manx Music Festival and 'away' Festivals, such as Blackpool and London. His appointment meant that he had to leave his profession as a schoolmaster, but his many talents were applied to making the Villa Marina a centre of excellence in the world of entertainment where he became a well-known figure to professional artistes. His daughter Nora, after four years training at the Royal College of Music, became a successful concert soprano and made regular appearances at the Villa Marina. The Sunday Night Celebrity Concerts brought the finest talents of the music world to the Island: Peter Dawson, Paul Robeson ('Old Man River'), Sir John McCormack, Heddle Nash, Kreisler and Bratza (the world's finest violinists) and Flora Woodman of 'Hiawatha' fame.

In 1925 a Garden Pavilion was built to provide alternative entertainment with Concert Parties being engaged each season. Under Mr Moore's guidance the Villa Marina became a profitable undertaking, but it

To make way for the Arcade these buildings next to the Gaiety Theatre, including a guest house and the photographic studios of Mr Warburton and Miss Kirton, were demolished in 1930. (Keig Collection)

was not until 1929 that the Council felt able to proceed with the remainder of the developments originally intended. The Public Amusements Committee, with Ramsey G. Johnson as Chairman, employed architect F. Prentice Mawson of the Lancaster firm of Thomas H. Mawson and Sons, eminent landscape architects, to submit designs for the project which would involve the following: a Verandah and Colonnade with shops along the Colonel's Walk; an Arcade shelter, with shops and public conveniences, extending from Colonel's Walk to the road in the rear; a Colonnade and Verandah extending along the south wall of the Royal Hall providing a sheltered extension to the Cafe overlooking the Gardens. Construction of the Arcade would mean purchasing the properties adjoining the Gaiety Theatre, including the photographic studios of Mr Warburton and Miss Kirton. The scheme was approved by the Council and application made to Tynwald to sanction the borrowing of £42,322 - though this had to be amended at a later date when it was realised that architectural fees of over £10,000 had not been included!

The Villa Marina Amendment Bill was duly passed by Tynwald at the end of 1929, but not without a certain amount of criticism. Was the Corporation deviating from the original intention of having the Gardens freely available to the public at all times. Was the provision of shops bringing the Corporation into unfair competition with the shopkeepers of the town? Did visitors come to Douglas to spend their time sitting under shelters? Was the Corporation increasing its

The Villa Marina Arcade as completed in 1931. Seating was provided at a later date. (Reg Quayle Collection)

The steps leading to the upper part of the Arcade. Hand rails and seating were a later addition. (Reg Quayle Collection)

indebtedness at a time when it should be concentrating on new streets in the town? On the other hand it was not denied that the people of Douglas were desirous of the Villa Marina extensions. Nor could the Corporation be blamed for making the most valuable property on the Island into a profit-making asset. The Bill was duly passed and work began in earnest on what was regarded as a winter work scheme over the next two years.

The Colonnade took preference and the four shops were in occupation for the 1930 season bringing in an income of £1,175. The tenants had all applied for a renewal of their tenancies while applications had been received for the nine proposed shops in the Arcade. By June, 1931, the Arcade was nearing completion with all the heavier reinforced concrete work in position. The nine shops were already in occupation and the extensive lavatories taking shape with many of the fittings in place. In fact, the entire scheme of the Villa Marina extensions were completed in time for the season with the Colonnade being regarded as one of the most beautiful and useful improvements made in Douglas for many years. The Arcade soon proved its worth with its attractive shopping facilities and provision of welcome shelter for the visitors.

Shelter was also at the heart of the next scheme embarked upon by the Corporation which would give the main entrance to the Royal Hall an entirely new look. The original raised entrance to the foyer, accessed by double steps from ground level, was replaced by a new entrance and foyer at ground level. The steps and original facade were demolished and the new frontage built of brick with cement rendering. A canopy was incorporated to provide shelter over the new entrance. From the foyer, incorporating new pay desks, twin enclosed stairways led up to the original foyer. The plain frontage was designed in the Art Deco style of the 'twenties and 'thirties, being in sharp contrast to the original classic design. The front was embellished by the use of neon strip lighting in green and red, while the glass 'boxes' on either side were illuminated from within. The new front to the Villa Marina was completed in time for the 1939 season.

While the Sunday Celebrity Concert was the highlight of the week, dancing took place in the Royal Hall on other nights with the best of orchestras providing the music. Orchestras were made up of the finest of musicians playing an abundance of strings. A high standard of decorum was required from the dancers who moved round the ballrooms always in an anti-clockwise direction. While the great Harry Wood's orchestra entertained at the Palace, competition was now provided at the Villa Marina by orchestras such as that of Percy Kahn. Jewish by birth, he was also a brilliant pianist and accompanist. He regularly featured in the Sunday Night Concerts and accompanied his wife, Olive Kavan, a famous singer. 1929 saw the arrival of Jack Howard's Band with clarinets and saxophones, to cater for a new generation of dancers brought up in an atmosphere of ragtime, jazz and syncopation. Before coming to the Villa the band was appearing at the Royal Opera House, Covent Garden. The bandleader struck up a romance with one of the local beauties. He would leave the stage, usually for a romantic waltz, and dancers were intrigued by the relationship; but strong opposition from her parents put an end to the romance! Jack Howard was followed by Al Davidson whose band was also in the modern idiom. He had first appeared with a small show band in the Onchan Head Pavilion but secured the appointment at the Villa Marina with a full-sized band. He was a brilliant musician with a degree from Cambridge, where he had been a don for some time, and wrote many of his own arrangements.

Whilst visitors flocked to the great centres of entertainment, the locals also had a feast of shows and dancing to enjoy. What was so great about the Villa Marina, and the Palace, was that they were able to purchase season tickets for as little as £1 each. These entitled the holders to attend all afternoon and evening performances, excepting Sunday evening concerts. A very large percentage of the young people of Douglas had season tickets for either the Villa or Palace. Many of the older generation also bought them so they were able to go to the Villa Pavilion revues or the Palace Coliseum shows and afterwards watch or join in the dancing in the respective ballrooms. Again, they could enjoy the Garden concerts in the afternoons. The Derby Castle also had good shows and bands but was rather frowned upon because of the several bars around the ballroom. Neither the Villa nor the Palace was licensed, so they were favoured as suitable and pleasant places for teenagers to spend their evenings.

A 1938 view of the Villa Marina and the Harris Promenade. (Douglas Corporation Guide)

DOUGLAS TRANSPORT

While the promenades were served by the horse trams, and the upper parts of the town by the cable cars, one part of the town which was not so well served was the North Quay, Peel Road, Belmont Terrace and Circular Road area. While the idea of introducing the new motor buses had long been mooted, the Tramways Committee shelved matters by using, on a contract basis, private carriage companies to provide horse buses during the summer months. Although never a financial success the horse buses served the area from 1907 to 1913 after which the committee once more considered the introduction of motor buses. Not until May, 1914 was the decision made to purchase two buses - a Tilling Stevens and a Straker Squire. The decision does not seem to have met with the approval of the Tramways Manager, Mr Stephen Robinson who presented the committee with a copy of the 'Report with respect to accidents to the Motor Buses.' Of like mind was the Cable Tramway Engineer who was suspended from his duties and subsequently resigned his position before the arrival of the two brand new buses in October, 1914. They were numbered 1-2 (MN 589-590) and were introduced for all-year service on the Peel Road routes. However, it was now wartime and one was used to augment the horse trams which were short of horses, most of which had gone to France. There was also plenty of work in transporting workmen to Knockaloe where a huge camp for enemy aliens was being built.

By the end of the war these two buses, which had been heavily utilised, were in need of replacement and in 1920 the Committee bought four new Tilling-Stevens petrol-engined 28-seaters and numbered 3-6 (MN 1328 - 1331). They were supplemented by two more in 1922 - 7 and 8 (MN1879-1880), the first being a saloon type and the second with a double-deck open-top 49 seat body. By 1925 six further buses of the saloon type had been acquired, bringing the total fleet to twelve; but by the end of 1929 this total had been increased to 31! At the same time the older Tilling Stevens with solid tyres were also being gradually replaced by the newer models with saloon bodies by Northern Counties and fitted with pneumatic tyres.

END OF THE CABLE CARS

In 1926 buses were allowed to operate on the promenades, thus competing with the horse trams. At the end of the following year the horse trams ceased for the winter and became a seasonal service only as from 1928. The cable cars had already been reduced to seasonal use from 1921 following heavy winter losses the previous year; the introduction of buses hastened their demise. They had never been financially viable and the Tramways Committee were faced with mounting costs not only for repairs and renewals but also for coal. The system was also becoming decidedly noisy as the track, cable and pulleys wore out. Further noise in the enclosed saloon cars, called 'Devils' by the locals, was caused by the rattling of the windows. Only by shortening the summer period of running did the cars survive until a halt was finally called in 1929 when the cable cars were in service for a very brief season lasting from 23rd July to 13th August. Nearly 79,000 passengers had been carried but receipts were well short of the expenses incurred. Soon afterwards the *Isle of Man Weekly Times'* reported: "What a strange quiet place Douglas was on

(Above) Corporation bus No 2 was a 25-seater Straker Squire which was acquired in 1914 along with a Tilling Stevens. It continued in occasional service until 1936. (Below) Bus No 7 was one of two Tilling Stevens which arrived in 1922. This type, and its future developments, was adopted as the standard single-decker by the Transport Committee.

(Above) A final view of a cable car passing Prospect Terrace where the road was later widened. The last cable cars ran in August, 1929 after serving Upper Douglas for over 30 years. (Below) More and more Tilling Stevens single deckers came into service, now equipped with pneumatic tyres. Shown here, at the Borough Cemetery entrance, is No 39, a 34-seater which served from 1930 until 1944. (Alan Kelly Collection)

Three double-decker horse trams, crowded with happy holiday-makers, at Victoria Pier in 1930.

One of the popular open toastracks, with awning, in 1932. Profits from the horse trams were used to subsidise the introduction of the motor buses.

Tuesday, the clanking noise had gone - the cable trams had stopped. Monday was their last day - perhaps for ever."

Thus, without ceremony, the cable cars, which had been part of the life of the town for 33 years, came to an end. The cable was soon removed from its slot but filling the conduit and lifting the track was a considerable job which took three years to complete. Some of the track was used for a new lay-out for the horse tram terminus at Victoria Pier. The winding engines were broken up for scrap and the 16 cars were all sold to Charles McArten of Spring Valley with the object of converting them into holiday bungalows. The York Road Depot became a ready made garage and workshop for the growing fleet of motor buses.

Meanwhile the horse trams, with a fresh stock of horses, had got back into their stride and were as popular as ever and could be relied upon to make a useful surplus for the Transport Department as it built up its fleet of buses. Replacing the track, which was showing signs of wear, was a major expense, and brought into question the tramway's future. While work on widening the Loch and Harris Promenades began in 1928 it was not until 1934 that work on realigning the track from Greensill's Corner to the War Memorial was completed. Then, with the future of the horse trams seemingly assured, the renewing of track was completed as far as Summer Hill in 1935, winter closures being a help. Early in 1935 new offices were built on to the Derby Castle depot using up two of the original depot roads.

The pre-war fleet of cars remained the same until 1935 when three new cars were purchased at a cost of £505 each. They were numbered 48-50 and were covered 'toastracks' but equipped with sliding screens for bad weather. By now all cars had been fitted with ratchet brakes together with battery-operated electric side lights for night operation. The number of tram horses then stood at 135.

Passenger figures, as with summer arrivals, fluctuated according to economic conditions prevailing in Britain. Whilst the 1913 record of over 615,000 was never surpassed, an average of over half a million visitors annually could be relied upon during the inter war period, with 550,000 not uncommon. This was achieved, for example, in 1934, when the horse trams carried nearly two and a half million passengers - an astonishing figure compared with the town's population of just 20,000! The following years from 1935 to 1939 were also 'bumper' years with the horse trams carrying a record 2,750,000 passengers in 1938. That year the Douglas Transport operations with the horse trams and buses made a gross profit of nearly £10,000 to the relief of the rates.

NEW TRAMWAYS MANAGER

On 9th May, 1932, Mr Stephen Robinson retired as the Borough's Tramways Manager. He was succeeded by Mr C.F. Wolsey, A.M.Inst.T who had gained experience with tramways in Stockport and Lowestoft before successfully applying for the Douglas appointment. His chief engineer at that time was Mr T.A. Clague A.M.I.A.E, A.M.Inst.T. One of Mr Wolsey's first concerns was to ensure the future of the horse trams and it was his scheme of modernisation that was implemented by the Tramways Committee.

Turning his attention to the fleet of buses he recommended the purchase of AEC Regent double-deck buses as the first step in replacing the Tilling Stevens single-deckers, though examples of these would survive for many years. The new AEC, with a 6.1 six-cylinder petrol engine, incorporated many sophisticated developments, including a vacuum-hydraulic brake system. The 52-seat bodies were built by Northern Counties. The first two of these double-deckers arrived in 1933 and were numbered 41-2 (MN 8690-91) to be followed in 1934 by three more numbered 43-5 (MN9517-9) with another in 1935, No 46 (MAN 122). By now the Corporation buses were being popularly called the 'Yellow Buses' because of the colour scheme adopted, yellow, apparently, representing the summer hours of sunshine which could only be bettered by the Cornish Riviera.

Also during 1935 two Vulcans were purchased. These were buses of a different kind with small wheels and low chassis similar to the Vulcan which was already in use in Douglas, having first appeared in 1926 as No 17 but re-numbered 3 in 1935. The new Vulcans had unique bodies specially designed by Mr Wosley and followed similar lines to his covered 'toastrack' horse trams 48-50 already mentioned. The Vulcan buses were equipped with glazed folding screens on each side and could be opened or closed according to the weather. When the screens were closed each end of the cross bench seats could be folded up to provide an internal gangway. The new models were numbered 1-2 (MAN 123-4) and had a Bedford engine, gearbox and radiator. Capable of carrying 27 passengers, they were ideal for coping with the extra summer traffic.

The need for more conventional single-deck buses was met by the introduction of the Leyland Cub type, two of which were purchased in 1936 and numbered 9-10 (BMN 255-6) They could carry 20 passengers and came to be nick-named 'Wolsey's Midgets'! By 1939 four further Cubs had joined the fleet, these being Nos 11-12 (BMN 868-9), 8 (CMN 709) and 14 (DMN 585). Also, during those three years more AEC Regents had arrived and were numbered 47-8 (BMN 866-7), 49 (CMN 701) and 50 (DMN 585). Route numbers were introduced in 1939 but it took many years before all buses were equipped with blinds. That year the bus fleet, still with a few Tilling Stevens, included 10 AEC Regent double-deckers and 6 Leyland Cubs. No doubt there would have been many more but for the coming of war in 1939.

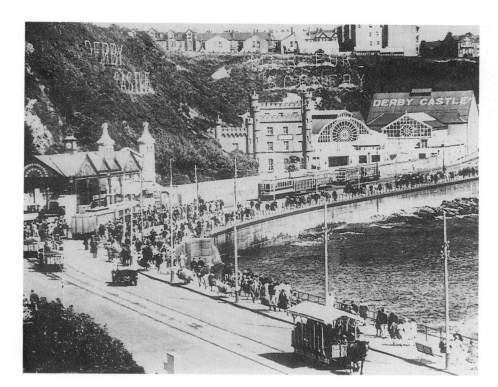

A view of the Derby Castle Terminus on a hectic day in the early 1930s. This photograph shows the original promenade before work on widening it began in 1938, work which was not completed until 1948. (Keig Collection)

This photograph appeared in a brochure published by the Transport Committee to commemorate the remarkable achievement of August Bank Holiday Week of 1934 when a total of 417,777 passengers were carried by the horse trams and buses. Posing in front of one of the new double-decker buses are, left to right: H.Price, senior ticket inspector; T Clague, chief engineer; N. Kelly, senior clerk; Cyril Wolsey, general manager; Douglas Kerruish, veterinary surgeon and Thomas Quine, chief inspector and later superintendent. (A.Q. Russell)

Transport Department officials and staff with a line-up of the five AEC Regent double-deckers which were in service for 1934. They were joined by a further five by 1939.

THE MUNICIPAL GOLF COURSE

Despite the many other enterprises undertaken by the Corporation it was felt that a first-class golf course should be one of the attractions of a holiday town like Douglas. In 1910 the Corporation, with a view to future expansion, had purchased an area of 256 acres of pasture land known as Pulrose Farm on the south-western outskirts of the town. Of this area a total of 130 acres was set aside for the construction of a golf course which would stretch from the lowest to the highest part of the estate. The Council appointed a Golf Committee and they called in the services of Dr A. Mackenzie, a leading Golf Architect, whose company, the British Golf Course Company Ltd., supervised the construction work. Much of the labour was provided by Corporation staff with Tramway horses being employed during the winter of 1926/27.

The 1st, 2nd and 18th fairways were laid on reclaimed land as a result of skilful drainage of a marshy area. From this wooded valley the course gently rises 250 feet to the open uplands with its vista of the town. The length of the course when completed was 5,587 yards and had cost a total of £5,000. One description recorded: 'Its most striking features are the four really excellent one-shot holes, and the number of tee-shots at the longer holes, which provide a good carry for the ambitious golfer to go for, without infliction of unnecessary punishment on the less powerful player by what are sometimes known as unfair cross hazards.'

A temporary pavilion was in place for the opening while awaiting the building of a Club House. Many will remember the first Professional appointed by the Corporation for the opening of the course. He was Mr J.H. Devereau who had been the Professional at the Enniscorthy Golf Club in the Irish Free State. The terms of his appointment stipulated that Mr Devereau

be paid a salary of 30 shillings a week with the right of the sale of golf clubs, balls and accessories, and fees for lessons and practice. He was also required to assist in the management, maintenance and upkeep of the Course during the winter months when he was paid 45 shillings a week. He was also granted one of the new houses being constructed on the Pulrose Estate.

On 28th August the Golf Links was officially declared open by the Mayor Alderman A.B. Crookall M.H.K., J.P. and he and Councillor 'Gussie' Craine were the first to tee-off for the first game. Alderman Crookall had been the principal instigator of the links, one of his objectives being to preserve some of the Pulrose estate from housing developments. His enthusiasm was believed to be all the more remarkable because he owned the Castletown Golf Links . . . and the Municipal links was charging less than any other course.

Golfers now had access to three courses within the Douglas area. Howstrake Golf Course on its present site has a history going back to 1894. At the opposite end of the bay a new golf course was opened in 1906 on Douglas Head and was known as the Fort Anne Golf Links. It was operated by Morris and Thomas Forrester who purchased the former private residence of Fort Anne in 1901 and developed it into one of the foremost hotels. The Golf Links was laid out under the supervision of John Norris of Hoylake and was considered by eminent golfers to be the finest on the Island. Situated across the Head Road from the Fort Anne Hotel it extended along the Marine Drive and covered an area of about 2 square miles. It survived the Second World War but went out of use in the early 1950s. The enterprising Forresters had developed Port Soderick and also ran the Falcon Hotel. Mr Morris Forrester was a Town Councillor from 1922 until his death in 1926.

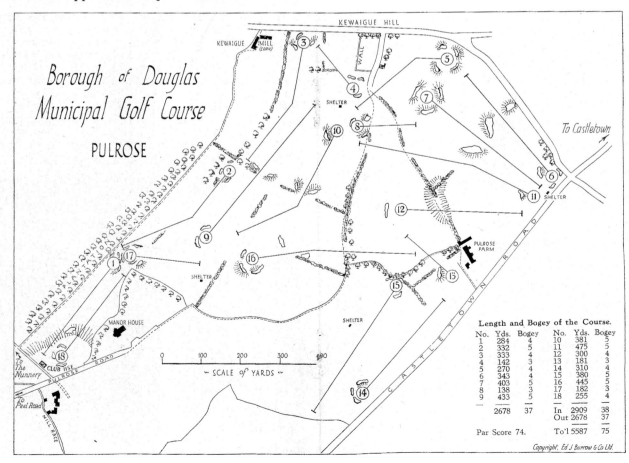

Length and Bogey of the Course.

No.	Yds.	Bogey	No.	Yds.	Bogey
1	284	4	10	381	5
2	332	5	11	475	5
3	333	4	12	300	4
4	142	3	13	181	3
5	270	4	14	310	4
6	343	4	15	380	5
7	403	5	16	445	5
8	138	3	17	182	3
9	433	5	18	255	4
	2678	37	In	2909	38
			Out	2678	37
Par Score 74.			To'l	5587	75

THE ELECTRICITY UNDERTAKING

In the early years of the nineteenth century the only means of illumination for moving about the narrow and dingy streets of Douglas at night was by oil lantern or candle. But in 1822, Mr Gelling of the Foundry demonstrated an alternative. He lit his iron-mongery shop on Market Hill by gaslight and it was an immediate source of wonder with crowds flocking to Market Hill to see not only his shop lit up, but also the street outside. The gaslight had a "brilliant and pleasing effect" as one newspaper reported. Soon a few others followed and some shops in the fashionable Duke Street were similarly lit. The enterprising Mr Gelling had set up a gas plant in his Foundry on the South Quay when this new form of lighting was still in its infancy and still unknown in most towns in the British Isles. The demand for this new form of illumination grew steadily, so much so that Mr Gelling was encouraged to enlist support for the formation of a commercial undertaking to supply gas. Thus in 1835 the Douglas Gas Light Company was established by Act of Tynwald.

As a result of Mr Gelling's enterprise the first gas mains were laid on the South Quay and went across the stone bridge at the top of the harbour, up Bank Hill and along Athol Street to St. George's Church, the first church to be so lit. From there the new lighting spread gradually to other parts of the town to meet the demands of shops, offices and households. As Douglas expanded and the building boom in hotels and boarding houses got under way hundreds of tons of iron and lead piping were laid so that all the new premises could be supplied.

The Harbour Commissioners were the first to use gas as a form of street lighting and lamps appeared along both the South and North Quays. This official recognition was followed by the Town Commissioners embarking on a programme of street lighting 'on the rates' which would reach all parts of the town by the end of the century. Quarterly prices were agreed with the Gas Company according to the hours required on a seasonal basis, no lighting being required during the month of June. The lamplighters with their ladders became familiar figures going about the streets and returning to extinguish the lamps 'no sooner than 11 p.m.' However, adhering strictly to the specified hours was made difficult by the fact that the lamps took an hour for the men to light and a similar time to extinguish.

On 14th February, 1897 Town Clerk Mr Nesbitt wrote to the Isle of Man Tramways and Electric Power Company to ascertain the cost of illuminating the promenades by electricity during the forthcoming season. The company had installed generators at their Derby Castle depot for such a purpose and already had various customers in the Onchan area. The brand new Douglas Bay Hotel was the first hotel to use this revolutionary form of lighting in 1894, closely followed by the newly completed Derby Castle Theatre.

Chairman of the Tramways Company, which by now also controlled the horse trams, was Mr Alexander Bruce who was also the Borough Treasurer. He responded to Mr Nesbitt's request with a challenging offer. His company would light not only the promenades but also Victoria Street and parts of the Upper Douglas route, free of charge, in return for the right to sell current in Douglas to private consumers. The company would also undertake to electrify the bay tramline by overhead wiring at a cost of £20,000. It was the latter that was the subject of much debate within the Council. A Special Committee was set up and Mr Nesbitt prepared a lengthy report on the subject.

With the support of Mr Bruce the Committee of eight, together with the Town Clerk and Borough Surveyor Taylor, embarked on a continental tour which included London, Paris and Berlin to study municipal electric tramways. They returned full of enthusiasm for electric traction using the overhead system and their recommendation was duly presented to the Council. However, strong protests were being voiced concerning the effects it would have on the bay tramline. Memorials were received from hoteliers along the promenades together with strong objections from car proprietors and drivers who feared for the loss of business. The Council deferred making a decision until after the November elections only to be informed by the Tramways Company that its offer had been withdrawn. Thus the idea of electrifying the bay tramway was dropped, and the people of Douglas were denied the opportunity of being supplied by this new form of light and power. It would be Douglas by gaslight for many years to come although the situation encouraged private companies to generate electricity but on a very small scale.

Following the Corporation's take-over of the tramways in 1902 the question of electrification and the introduction of a public electricity supply arose once again. The cable cars continued to lose money and electrification

Another of John Miller Nicholson's fine street studies from the mid 1890s. On the right can be seen the gas lamp over the entrance to Well Road Methodist Chapel while, in the distance, one of the gas standards on the Loch Promenade can be seen. (Manx National Heritage)

Interior view of the North Quay Power Station opened in 1923 and which remained in constant use until after the Second World War. It was during the latter years that one of the flywheels of the diesel engines disintegrated and flew out of the building causing damage to surrounding buildings, a large piece crashing through the roof of Brown's Isle of Man Times office in Athol Street.

Mr Bertram Kelly (centre), the Borough's first Chief Electrical Engineer, making a retirement presentation in the Ridgeway Street showrooms and offices of the Electricity Department.

could well be cheaper than the cost of the large amounts of coal being consumed. From 1907 onwards expert reports were called for almost annually right up to 1919. But usually they were 'noted' and no action taken. There were those who considered the service of the Douglas Gas Company was perfectly satisfactory, so why undertake unnecessary expense? There were even those who suggested that the Gas Company should be taken over. On the other hand the 'modernists' believed that a premier resort such as Douglas should be in the forefront of using modern inventions and enabling the hotels and boarding houses to keep apace with those in rival resorts. The debate went on. Nevertheless, whereas Douglas had been one of the first to have a public gas supply available, it would be one of the last towns in the British Isles to have its own public electricity supply.

In 1920 Tynwald was presented with The Douglas Corporation Light and Power Bill and the subsequent Act was promulgated on 5th July, 1922. The Electricity Committee staged an Electricity Exhibition in the Villa Marina at the end of October, the object being to demonstrate the advantages of electricity as a source of light and power. Also that year the town's first Electrical Engineer had been appointed - Mr Bertram G. Kelly A.M.I.E.E. A Manxman, Mr Kelly had studied at the Royal Technical College, Glasgow and, after gaining experience with various electrical companies, he was appointed in 1907 as chief assistant engineer to Mr Edmonson, Manager of the Manx Electric Railway.

The site chosen for the Power Station was on the North Quay, between Ridgeway and Queen Streets. On 20th December the foundation stone was laid by the Mayor, Councillor Arthur B. Crookall M.H.K., J.P. The limestone building, designed by Mr E.J. Teare, was of modest dimensions, the builders being Creer Brothers of Kensington Avenue. The eminent electrical engineering firm of Handcock and Dykes of London was appointed as the main contractor. At the beginning of 1923 work began on digging the trenches in which the supply cables from the Power Station would be laid along the main streets. Provision was also made for extending the supply into other streets where a sufficient number of households applied.

Mr Kelly made regular progress reports to the Electricity Committee, whose Chairman was Alderman Robert Corlett, regarding the building, installations and the arrival of equipment including meters and street lamp standards. Customers had been promised that current would be available by Whitweek, the traditional start of the season. At the beginning of May, Mr Kelly reported a delay in the delivery of meters, parts of the switchboard and cable. The Committee wrote to the contractors pressing for immediate delivery. More perturbing was a letter received from Mr Dykes informing the Committee that he had found it necessary to lay an additional main in Strand Street, the one along the seaward side of the street not being sufficient for both sides. This would mean the other pavement would have to have the flags removed and another trench dug causing inconvenience to tradesmen. The additional cable was despatched in haste from Liverpool and Mr Dykes, himself, arrived to ensure that all was in order for Whitweek.

Direct Current was supplied at 220 volts for lighting, cooking, heating and small motors as in vacuum cleaners; and 440 volts for large motors. Tariffs for lighting, heating and power was charged at 10d. a unit from dusk until midnight and at 2.5 d. for the rest of the day. Larger establishments were accepted into a flat rate tariff of 7d. per unit for lighting and 2d. for heating and approved power.

Almost immediately, Messrs Handcock and Dykes were advising that the generating plant was incapable of meeting the growing applications for current. While being granted a monopoly status it was the statutory duty of the Corporation to meet all demands within a certain area in two years. A sub-committee led by Alderman Corlett embarked on a tour of inspection in London, Blackpool and Morecambe and elsewhere to judge the merits of rival systems of installation. The result was an order being placed for two 6-cylinder Rushton diesel engines while the two existing engines were replaced by two more powerful 4-cylinder engines. The new engines were installed in 1924 and the capacity of the station was trebled to 1,200 kilowatts. There was also an increase in the amount of vibration caused by the engines which led to many complaints from nearby properties; their complaints were answered by a reduction in their rates. In 1928 the area of supply was extended in all directions to two miles outside the Borough boundary. The first Show Rooms in Ridgeway Street were opened in October, 1929 for sale, demonstration, hire purchase and hire of cookers and water heaters and other electrical appliances. The administrative offices of the undertaking were also housed in the same building which was later purchased by the Corporation.

Work in progress during the 1935-36 extension and structural alterations to the Pulrose Power Station.

The turbine room of the Power Station showing the 1936 turbo-alternator in the foreground.

Pulrose Power Station after the 1935-36 extensions had been completed.

Alderman Corlett and the Electricity Committee were almost in constant session monitoring the situation as the demand continued unbounded. The little building on the North Quay was obviously unsuitable for further expansion so the search began for a new site to build a much bigger station. This resulted in the choice of a swampy area at Pulrose, though tests showed that the ground would be suitable for the purpose. Borrowing powers were authorised by Tynwald and work began in October, 1928, Handcock and Dykes again being the consulting engineers and Mr Teare the architect.

Some 200 piles were sunk 20 feet into the ground to secure the concrete foundations of the steel-framed building finished in brick, and resulting in a building of handsome appearance. The initial equipment consisted of two watertube boilers each capable of evaporating 15,000 pounds of water per hour. They were fed by mechanical stokers supplied by means of an elevator and conveyor. The single turbine provided power to drive the 1,000 kw. Mather and Platt alternator generating 3,300 volts at 50 cycles per second. Output of the High Tension feeders and Low Tension circuits were controlled from the Switchboard Gallery. A tall wooden structure, some 75 feet high, acted as the cooling tower for carrying and circulating water in the event of the river being too low to provide a continuous supply. The Power Station was designed to allow for future expansion, and a further boiler and 1350 kw turbo-alternator were installed in 1933, together with a second cooling tower.

Alternating Current was generated as opposed to DC from the North Quay. Alternating Current had by now been standardised throughout Great Britain, being more suitable for distribution and rectifying. Rectifier sub-stations were positioned at Pulrose, Tromode Road and Summerhill, Onchan. (A supply of current for Onchan Village was commenced at the beginning of 1930). The cost of the new Pulrose Power Station and sub-stations amounted to £60,000 though this figure also included the cost of a small extension to North Quay to accommodate two motor alternating sets for converting current generated at Pulrose for distribution within the town.

The Douglas Gaslight Company responded to its new competitior by appointing Mr Alec Bissett first Manager and later a Director of the Company. He was a most enthusiastic and colourful Scot who soon entered into the life of the town and in 1928 he organised the first of the Highland Games during the annual 'Scotch Week'. The event proved to be one of the greatest tourist attractions ever staged bringing many thousands of visitors to the beautiful setting in the Nunnery Grounds. Apart from being a highly successful businessman he was also devoted to Gaelic history and culture, and was closely involved with the Manx culture movement.

As soon as the increased capacity of Pulrose Power Station was completed in 1933, the newly constituted Isle of Man Electricity Board began taking a supply of bulk current as the Board embarked on an Island-wide programme of providing the towns and villages with electricity, though it would be many years before rural areas and farms were connected. Pulrose was in an ideal central position and thus began a long and co-operative period between Tynwald and Douglas Corporation which would last until 1950 when the Electricity Board was in a position to generate its own requirements. However, the constant rise in demand from Pulrose meant that the Electricity Committee had to embark on yet another scheme to increase output,

The two original cooling towers were joined by a third and larger one in 1936.

involving the enlargement of the Pulrose Power Station.

Work began in Ocotober, 1935 with English contractors again being employed. More cement piles were sunk into the soft ground to provide the foundations of the extension to the original building. The extension housed a 3,750 kw turbo alternator driven by a steam turbine with its own boiler, the combined weight of the new generating set being 350 tons. The two original cooling towers were joined by a third and bigger tower capable of dealing with a quarter of a million gallons of water an hour. Space was left inside the extension for an additional turbo-alternator to be installed in 1937 which then brought the total capacity of Pulrose Station to 10,500 kw, sufficient to meet all needs for many years to come. The number of consumers in the town and surrounding area stood at 4,904 in March, 1936. The number of public street lamps was 626 while 187 were still lit by gas.

The total cost of the 1936 extension amounted to £45,000 and the electricity undertaking from the commencement was self-supporting without aid or Government grant of any kind. The new extension was officially declared open on 29th October by His Excellency The Lieutenant Governor Sir Montagu Butler. During the ceremony Alderman Robert Corlett was the subject of much praise for his interest and pertinacity in guiding the Electricity Committee through its difficult years. In fact the Alderman had been honoured in 1932 with the Freedom of the Borough in recognition of his services.

(Left) Alderman Robert Corlett, Chairman of the Electricity Committee from its inception. He had been Mayor of Douglas 1912-1914 and was made a Freeman of the Borough in 1932. He was first elected to the Council in 1904 and remained in office until his death in 1940. (Right) Mr Bertram Kelly A.M.I.E.E., the Borough's first Electrical Engineer and Manager from 1922 to 1947.

LOCH PROMENADE WIDENING

January, 1929, saw the commencement of an ambitious scheme, which would last six years, to widen the Loch Promenade. It was undertaken by the Corporation, with Government providing half the funds as a means of relieving the unemployment situation during the winter months. Planning was in the hands of Borough Surveyor H.A. Bridge M.Inst., C.E. and his staff, including the Deputy Surveyor, J.C. Bregazzi. They had the challenging task of building a sea wall which would add 100 feet to the 80 feet of the original Promenade of 1875. Behind the new sea wall would be added an extra six acres of reclaimed land. The first phase was spread over three years with the Harbour Commissioners being responsible for an area reaching from the Victoria Pier to the town boundary at the Peveril steps from where the Corporation took over as far as a point opposite Regent Street.

For the municipal section of 1,000 feet, a concrete foundation of shingle and Portland 'Blue Circle' and Ferrocrete cement was laid, being 14 feet wide and reaching 6 feet below the beach surface. On top of this foundation the sea wall, backed by mass concrete, was made up of precast shingle and cement blocks with a facing of granite chippings, each block weighing two tons. The dimensions of the sea wall are 11 feet wide at the base tapering over a height of 20 feet to a width of 4 feet at the top. The wall was then surmounted by bull-nose blocks each weighing four tons. All the concrete blocks were cast on the old Promenade and for this work large quantities of shingle were obtained mainly from the White Strand near Peel and from Castletown Bay. The in-fill behind the sea wall was made up of huge quantities of Manx slate and grit quarried from the two municipal quarries on Douglas Head, the quarries being known as 'The Happy Quirk' and the 'Howe'.

While much of the work was by pick and shovel, special items of equipment were brought in. These included two travelling steam cranes and portable hand cranes; concrete mixers of various kinds; electric pumps and flood lights. As work could only be carried out for two hours before and after low tide it was necessary to work every tide and so two shifts of 4.5 hours were worked each working day. Progress was often held up when on-shore winds affected the height of the tide. The site had to be pumped continually in sections made up of steel piling during working periods. While one section would be used as a sump for the pumped water another would be filled with concrete and a third would be excavated. The two ton face blocks were craned into place and bolted in position to secure them while the concrete backing was setting. When one section was complete the bolt holes were then grouted up to bind the whole face together.

During each winter, from November to April, an average of 160 men were employed who were mostly unskilled. About 80 men were on shift work, and they were employed in two gangs with one doing foundation work while the other worked on the sea wall itself. The shift men worked every tide using powerful flood lights when necessary. In the quarries about 20 men did the drilling and blasting while 30 were employed in carting and haulage. Many of the lorries were privately owned and converted from the charabancs used in the summer.

Work on the second phase started in 1931 and 1,824 feet of sea wall was completed by 1933. Progress was quicker as the men became more skilled and construction was aided by the fact that for the final 400 feet, up to the War Memorial, the sea wall was set on rock rather than shingle. The entire scheme had required 51,600 tons of concrete for the foundations and the making of 3,406 facing blocks. For filling-in a total of over 200,000 tons of rubble slate was required. Other materials used included 4,000 tons of shingle. 11,000 tons of granite chippings and 6,000 tons of cement.

At the beginning of November, 1933, the whole of the surface of the old Promenade was removed for a new foundation of Portland cement reinforced with steel fabric. The tram lines were also relaid using old track as sleepers to which the new rails were bolted. The final road surface was made of two inches of asphalt. The new road was 65 feet wide with pavements of 10 and 5 feet on either side. This left 50 feet for the gardens and 50 feet for the footway on the seaward side which was surfaced by coloured asphalt. To complete the scheme the public lighting was modernised using ornamental steel standards with artistic double brackets. The standards were placed on either side of the

A view of the Loch Promenade in 1928 before the widening scheme began at the beginning of the following year.

Another view of the Loch Promenade showing the old wooden posts used to support the public lighting.

new promenade and carried two parallel lines of decorative lighting consisting of 12,000 15-watt coloured lamps.

THE MARINE GARDENS

At the same time the Marine Gardens were taking shape, these being planned and supervised on behalf of Messrs Dickson's Nurseries of Chester by Mr John Denman of the British International Horticultural Association. The six gardens, five of which are separated by public shelters, were sunk below the footway to give protection to a total of 32,000 trees, shrubs, plants and bulbs set in 3,000 tons of soil. The garden walls were made of 2,000 tons of local stone.

From the south end to Regent Street the first section was designed as a shrub and flower garden, using many exotic varieties. The paths, outlined in turf, were made of Macclesfield sandstone flags of various shades. At the south end was erected an artistic sundial with eight faces, it being the original dial which stood in the gardens of the Duke of Orleans at Twickenham, London. The second section, from Regent Street to Howard Street, is the rock garden using 500 tons of stone from the Douglas Head quarry. At either end ornamental lily ponds were built and on either side of the winding pathway of crazy paving a profusion of shrubs and plants was placed between the rocks.

The third section, from Howard Street to Granville Street, was designed as a rose garden made up of 36 beds. The beauty of the garden was heightened by a central electrically illuminated fountain, with changing water shapes to which a variety of colours were added at night time. The fountain is placed in the middle of a lake from which the water is drawn.

Next, from Granville Street to Senna Slip, came the children's yachting pool. The pool itself was a generous 200 feet by 25 feet - big enough for children of all ages to spend endless hours sailing their yachts and motor boats. It was the haunt for countless young visitors and town children, many of whom would discover, by accident, the depth of the pool to be 15 inches - enough to give a good soaking! Children today will find that the pool has been filled in and replaced with a children's playground.

The final two sections from Senna Slip to the Gaiety Theatre, and without a dividing shelter, were made up of a bamboo and flower garden and, finally, another flower garden ending with a wall fountain which fed into an ornamental pool. Each of the gardens and shelters was provided with teak seating which was also positioned along the footway, these being placed on concrete supports set in the walls.

The entire six-year scheme, which has largely remained unaltered, cost a total of £173,000. On 23rd June, 1934, the new Loch Promenade and Marine Gardens were formally declared open by the Secretary of State for the Home Department, the Right Honourable Sir John Gilmour M.P.

One of the steam cranes used to lift the two ton sea wall blocks which were precast on the old promenade.

Some of the 3,406 faced concrete blocks awaiting delivery to the sea wall.

The sea wall takes shape backed by mass concrete and the rubble in-fill.

While the new roadway receives its topping of asphalt, the final touches are being put to the sunken Marine Gardens.

The rose garden which was divided by the fountain producing patterns made all the more spectacular at night when a variety of colours illuminate the sparkling waters.

The popular children's yachting pool was a great attraction. Note the new steel ornamental lighting standards which also date from 1934.

A general view of the completed Loch Promenade widening scheme which ended at the site of the Douglas War Memorial.

SHOPPING IN THE TOWN

The development of Douglas during the nineteenth century was accompanied by the town becoming the major shopping centre of the Island. Leading from the North Quay, with its market, a profusion of shops could be found in Duke Street, Strand Street and Castle Street. The creation of Victoria Street, intersecting Duke Street, led to a new generation of shops and stores leading to Prospect Hill and Bucks Road. All tastes and pockets were catered for and the arrival of the summer influx of visitors meant a considerable increase in business. Many shops, the great majority being family concerns, became household names, flourishing for varying periods only to be replaced by new names as businesses came and went.

An observer in the early 1930s noted that many alterations were taking place with the drab fronts and small windows of Victorian times giving way to lighter and more open aspects with attractive displays. One who was singled out for praise was Percy Dawson who ran the Magnet gents' outfitters on the North Quay. He had taken over the vacant premises of 12, Castle Street which combined a shop and boarding house. (This was quite normal with the shopkeepers living over their shop premises, thus requiring two entrances). The shop was gutted and then rebuilt incorporating the side entrance to the house above which became Mr Dawson's dwelling house. Tiling was used beneath the mahogany window and the entrance to the recessed door was similarly tiled, 'artistically arranged in a futuristic style'. Concealed electric lighting was used to display the ladies' blouses and lingerie in the shop front. At the same time, in 1931, Duke Street had a new bazaar built to 'striking modern architectural design' for Messrs R.H.O. Hills. The front comprised three show cases with two doorways between them leading to the sales department occupying the entire ground floor. The first floor was used as a storeroom with goods arriving in the yard behind being carried on an overhead rail. On the third floor was a canteen and kitchen for the eighty girls employed.

Percy Dawson was just one of many well-established names in the 'thirties. R.C. Cain's occupied about five shops in Duke Streeet with departments dealing with ladies' and gents' clothing, gloves, stockings, handbags, umbrellas, and curtains, besides all the haberdashery. Across the lane at the back was the furniture and carpet department; all goods were noted for being moderately priced and of good quality. As with most of the larger establishments a system of overhead wires connected with the pay office. Bills and cash were

A view of Webb's Public Lounge which was part of the Grand Bazaar opened at 18 and 20 Strand Street in the late 1880s

Marks and Spencer Ltd. arrived in Douglas in 1904 and opened their Penny Bazaar in Duke Street, near Lord Street. It remained there until 1924.

In 1918 Marks and Spencer opened a second shop, this being in Strand Street next to Maley's the Chemist, which can be seen here with gas lamps for illumination.

The front of Webb's Bazaar with the adjoining millinery shop which displayed the latest French styles brought in by Madame Janvier, the French wife of Harry Webb.

placed in a shuttle-like container which was propelled along the wires to the central pay desk. The receipt and change would then be returned to the counter concerned. The system fascinated many a bored schoolboy. The staff seemed to stay for most of their working life and got to know their customers by name, making R.C. Cain's something of an institution. Nearby, a welcome break could be had in Cannell's cafe which must be the longest established cafe in 'the street'. Another institution was Sayle's in Victoria Street which specialised in soft furnishings and materials for dressmaking and curtains. Buttons of all shapes and sizes were stocked and could be purchased singly for matching up. A winding staircase led upstairs where ladies' clothing of all kinds was displayed. T. H. Cowin's shop on the corner of Duke Street and Wellington Street was older than either Cain's or Sayle's and was popularly known as 'Tossie's', the Manx pet name for Thomas. The large showroom displayed an enormous number of hats while dresses were also on display and could be made to order. Fashion shows were a regular feature and the arrival of the spring stock of millinery brought in the crowds.

When it came to fashions the ladies had plenty of alternatives including, at this time, such shops as Emmet's Ladies Shop in Duke Street, Vogue in Victoria Street, Madame Moore's (for millinery) in Strand Street, Madame Janvier's (for French styles) - a shop run by the wife of Harry Webb (son of Sam) whose famous Lounge was next door. Miss Curphey, a court dressmaker, moved from Ramsey and set up her high-class 'Manxonia' in 47/49 Victoria Street. Then there was Lyons (from Blackpool) which first set up a branch in Castle Street before moving to Strand Street. The shop in Castle Street was retained by the company and became Sally Mae's which sold inexpensive garments. Lyons completely refurbished their Strand Street shop in a modern style. The downstairs had walls of walnut veneer and mirrors, with chairs of chromium and leather; a smart page-boy was stationed at the entrance. An equally attractive upstairs was where the high fashions of the day were on display and dresses of the highest fashion were available or made to order. The shop was also noted for its window display which was illuminated until late each evening to attract those returning home from the cinemas.

Men were catered for by such shops as Arthur Clague's and Fred Bridson's - both outfitters in Strand Street. One of the best tailors to be found in the town was Fletcher's in Nelson Street. There was also Percy Dawson's on the North Quay and Christian and Maddrell in Ridgeway Street. Other well-established businesses included Devereau's and Higgins' which offered the best in fish and poultry in their shops in Castle Street; Blakemore's in Victoria Street was the only shop to supply the musical wants of the town; Maley's, which ran two chemist shops in the town - in Strand Street and at Greensill's Corner; Holmes and Davidson's in Strand Street - the opticians also noted for their excellence in silverwear and fancy goods; the Art Store offered high class glass and chinaware as did Dibb's in Duke Street; in Strand Street could also be found Bateson's, famous for its sausages and pies, and Gray's the pork butcher; Quirk's and Elder's supplied bread and confectionery. Hardware could be found in the ironmongery shops of Gelling's Foundry in Victoria Street, Todhunter and Elliot's in Duke Street and Cannell and Harvey's in Thomas Street, opposite the entrance to Victoria Street Church.

During the 'twenties and 'thirties many of the English 'chain' or 'multiple' stores established branches in Douglas. Woolworth's first set up its 'threepenny and sixpenny' store in Strand Street in 1924, next to Crellin's kipper shop. About the same time Boots the Chemist arrived, taking over the shop on the corner of Duke Street and Victoria Street. Soon neighbouring shops were added with passageways linking them together. Apart from their range of pharmaceuticals, cosmetics, stationery and fancy goods, Boots was also popular for its lending library which became a rival to the town library. For groceries Strand Street offered three well-stocked stores in close proximity - Lipton's, Home and Colonial and the Maypole - all competing as regards variety and price. Service was personal, but slow, as butter, cheese, sugar, currants etc. were weighed out. On the other hand, orders could be left to be delivered by van.

Webb's Bazaar was taken over by M and S in 1928 when the adjoining millinery shop became known as Reid's. By 1931 the latter shop and the one to the left had been bought to make way for expansion.

MARKS AND SPENCER'S

One shop which has witnessed more changes than most is Marks and Spencer's, which can claim to be one of the longest established businesses in 'The Street.' In fact, its local history dates back to 1904. Twenty years before that a young Michael Marks had arrived in Leeds after escaping the harsh Czarist rule in Russian Poland. The Jewish emigré arrived in London at first but he made his way to Leeds where a certain Mr Isaac Dewhurst of the English Sewing Cotton Company was always ready to help emigrants by way of giving them £5 cash. But young Michael asked for cotton goods instead. This was arranged through Mr Dewhurst's bookkeeper and Michael set up his first stall in Leeds market. The bookkeeper was named Tom Spencer, a bluff Yorkshireman some 12 years older than Michael Marks who was then 31. By 1894 Michael had spread his stalls in market places and halls into other towns and invited Mr Spencer to join him as an equal partner in his enterprise. This was agreed in 1903 and Marks and Spencer Ltd. was formed, with headquarters in Manchester. By 1903 they had established 40 outlets - all run under the name of Penny Bazaars. They then turned their attention to Douglas and in 1904 acquired the property of 12, Duke Street. This was made ready

and the Penny Bazaar was opened in January, 1905, with many of their goods geared to the holidaymakers.

In 1918 Marks and Spencer's opened a second shop, this time in Strand Street next to the well-established Maley's the Chemist, dating from 1895. It had a roll up and down shutter across the frontage though this was later altered to having windows and a door as a protection against inclement weather. Prices were kept low though the concept of the Penny Bazaar was abandoned. One could walk around the shop and gaze. In the Twenties, Marks and Spencer revolutionised female underwear and brought to the less well-off attractive garments, which could be easily washed and at prices they could afford. This was achieved by introducing new materials known as artificial silk or rayon (not to be confused with nylon). Underslips and panties, lavishly trimmed with lace, could be bought for an amazing 4/11 (25p) though colours were limited to beige and black.

The Duke Street shop was closed in 1924 but a major step forward was taken in 1928 when part of the famous Webb's Emporium was purchased opposite the Strand Street shop. By 1931 the remaining part of the Emporium, which had become known as Reid's, and a further property were acquired, making way for future developments. The Examiner of 5th June, 1931,

The ground floor of the former Webb's Bazaar as set out by Marks and Spencer's. In the background is the stairs leading to the upper floor.

A view of the upper floor specialising in fancy goods. Note the arched roof of the former Bazaar which disappeared in 1936 when the combined premises were completely rebuilt.

Marks and Spencer's 'New Super Store' takes shape in the spring of 1936, covering 14 to 22 Strand Street.

reported: "Outstanding among the alterations which have been taking place in Strand Street is the conversion of the premises previously owned by Harry Webb into an extremely handsome cash store by Marks and Spencer Ltd. The imposing triple windows, floodlighted at night, is the latest thing in exterior work. Wide spaces and passages among the counters is one of the features of the main sales department on the ground floor. There is a second sales department on the first floor to which access is gained by two sets of stairs at the far end and one on the left hand side. On this floor are also the offices and canteen kitchen. In the cellar beneath are innumerable wooden shelves for receiving the stock. An interesting and commendable feature is the fact that practically all the stock is British made. Practically all the clothing, especially the cotton goods, comes from Lancashire, and the leather goods chiefly from Birmingham and London. All the sales staff are local girls and the manager, Mr Williams, is both surprised and gratified at their capabilities."

The completed store as opened in May, 1936. On the right can be seen a glimpse of the popular Felices cafe also seen on the previous photograph showing Reid's

The London construction firm of Bovis was called again to undertake a complete rebuild of the premises in 1936. This was completed in just five months and in readiness for the summer season. The front of the building took on a new appearance and the building has remained largely unaltered for the past sixty years, modifications being made only to the street display windows and entrances. The new building was given three floors with the upper floor providing offices, medical attention for staff, a canteen and store space. An innovation in 1939 was the opening of a cafe on the first floor which proved most popular with shoppers during the war years and into the 1950s.

In 1939 space was made available on the first floor for a cafeteria which remained open during the Second World War and into the 1950s. (Photographs are courtesy of Marks and Spencer Ltd.)

RUNNING A BOARDING HOUSE

The boarding house keepers were the backbone of the visiting industry. It was they who provided accommodation, at reasonable rates, for the mill and factory workers who were intent on enjoying their brief respite from their daily labours. Most of the houses were run by the lady of the house as a means of supplementing the wages of her husband, many of whom would also be employed in seasonal jobs connected with the industry. As distinct from the larger publicly licensed establishments and high-class hotels, the boarding houses offered more 'homely' accommodation. Following the highly controversial Boarding House (Licence) Act of 1894 it was possible for private hotels and boarding houses to apply for licences to supply 'intoxicating liquor' to their guests. While many of the larger houses, with 30 or 40 bedrooms, were granted this facility, licences were, in fact, hard to obtain and for the next fifty years or so strong opposition to new licences was mounted by the Temperance organisations. The great majority of the smaller houses with as few as 3 or 4 bedrooms never became licensed.

At the cessation of hostilities in November, 1918, many boarding house keepers were in an impecunious state. Mountainous debts, accumulated during the war, would have to be paid. These, for many, included rent and rates, for which payment was waived until the war was over. But the boom summers of the early 'twenties alleviated the position and enabled the boarding house and hotel keepers to regain financial stability. All businesses prospered. Money was plentiful and, as the visitors were having their first holiday for four years, they were not loath to spend it.

Contrary to general belief, boarding house proprietors rarely made a fortune. Mrs Kelly, Clague, Cowin, Christian. Kewley, Quilliam etc. worked extremely hard, night and day, in the summer when their premises would be overflowing with visitors; but it would be a long winter which followed. Unless they had another source of income, debts would gradually mount up, and these would have to be settled in the summer. There were exceptions among the larger houses and private hotel owners. Those with sound business acumen, which catered particularly well and endeavoured to provide their guests with every possible comfort, could profit enormously. The ranks of the boarding house keepers were joined by those from 'across' who realised their ambition to settle on the Island. In one instance seven members of a Lancashire family each took on a boarding house or private hotel. They were able to order goods in bulk and each of their enterprises flourished successfully.

As soon as January arrived, preparations began for the ensuing season which traditionally began during Whit Week. The proprietor, aided by members of the family, would commence the decorating of bedrooms where necessary. All bedrooms would be thoroughly cleaned and any repairs to furniture attended to. Public rooms, such as the lounge and dining room, would also be cleaned and orders made for replacement carpets and chairs etc. The household linen would be checked, repaired and replaced where necessary. This linen checking and mending was often made into a social occasion - usually in the evenings. The lady of the house, with two or three helpers, would gather in the private sitting room. A sewing machine was much in evidence, and a roaring fire made the room very comfortable. The evening usually ended with a light supper.

Kitchens would have a complete spring-clean with cupboards made ready for the provisions which would be delivered before the season. An order would be given to a grocer, usually a wholesaler, for all goods which could be stored and which would be necessary in the catering. As these goods would be used they would be replaced, so that there were always full cupboards and pantries. There were no freezers as yet. The aim was to have all preparations for summer concluded by Easter, when some houses had early visitors - football teams and supporters, for example. Others liked to have a free week so that they could attend the Guild (the Manx Music Festival) all day and every evening. The Guild took place in the Palace ballroom the week after Easter.

As soon as the bright windy days arrived, blankets would be washed - a few at a time. This washing took place in large tin baths and a barrel-shaped container called a 'dolly tub'. After washing, the blankets would be put through a large wooden mangle, then taken down to the foreshore and laid out on the stones to dry. As time went on, this custom ceased and people sent their blankets to the laundry.

Advertisements would be placed in the guide produced by the Board of Advertising and in English, Scottish and Irish newspapers. The resulting bookings, with compulsory deposits, would be eagerly awaited. The deposits received were often used to pay for the stock when it arrived. This would ensure a good discount. Many visitors came back to the same house year after year and were important in building up a good connection. This was especially true of the Lancashire mill workers who returned annually *en masse* during the towns' Wakes Weeks.

Accommodation improved tremendously in the 'twenties and 'thirties. The bedroom floor coverings, which had been linoleum with rugs, were now replaced with carpets. Although the public rooms had been carpeted, fitted carpets were not in use. The reason for this was that broadloom carpeting had not yet been manufactured. A fitted carpet could be obtained by having narrow strips, the width of a stair carpet, joined together. They were joined by sewing and, although looking good when new, wore badly along these seams in a very short time. An ordinary carpet had no joins and was finished with a fancy border. So, now the bedrooms had patterned carpets, usually with a surround of linoleum or stained and varnished floorboards.

Gone were the days when the guests washed with cold water provided in large jugs accompanied by a bowl in which to wash. Small jugs of hot water were now being delivered by the chambermaid to enable the men to shave. Boarding houses of any size now had wash-basins with hot and cold water installed in their bedrooms. As many boarding houses were rented, the cost of installing these wash-basins was shared between landlord and tenant. Hot water could now be supplied from a boiler in the kitchen or outhouse. This was a terrific boon both to guests and management. There were as yet no en-suite bathrooms. The general rule was one w.c. per floor and one bathroom per house. A chambermaid had to be informed when a guest wished to have a bath, when a small charge would be made. With the availability of electricity the custom of candles in bedrooms died out. Candles had been a necessity as, although the houses had been fitted with gas, for some strange reason it very rarely reached the bedrooms. When electricity was installed every room was lighted, including basements and attics. A few of the taller houses on the Promenade and in the Drives installed lifts so upper rooms were now as important as those lower.

Some houses had a dining room but no lounge. This sometimes caused difficulties if the weather was wet or stormy, when the guests would not want to go out. The dining room would need to be cleaned and the tables set for the next meal. There might be what was euphemistically called a 'smoke room' which must have retained its title from an earlier age. As more liquor licences were obtained these rooms became 'lounge bars'.

101

Meals were prepared in the kitchen, very often situated in the basement. They were transferred to the dining room by means of a lift constructed with two or three shelves, sometimes called a 'dumb waiter'. It was pulled up to the dining room by ropes and, when it arrived, the waitresses would then lift the meals off and serve them to the visitors. The dirty crockery, dishes and silver would duly be returned to the kitchen by the same means. In a large house there might be found at the back of the dining room a small utility room which was known as the 'still room'. In this room were housed cutlery, tea and coffee pots, tea and coffee cups and saucers, sugar basins, cream jugs, cruets, sauce bottles, small jugs for mint sauce and all glassware, cake dishes etc. Tea and coffee were made here, a large urn supplying the hot water.

By the 1930s most of the guests stayed on a 'Full Board' basis which meant providing breakfast, mid-day dinner, high tea and light refreshments in the evening. The high tea meant that mountains of bread had to be cut and buttered sometime in the afternoon. Hand machines were used to cut the bread but it took a long time to butter. There were also the 'Non-Boarders' to contend with. These were guests who bought their own food which they handed in for cooking. This food would comprise meat, fish, bacon etc. and whatever else they required, other than vegetables, soups or puddings - these could be purchased from the day's menu as required. What was brought in had to be labelled and kept separate for the non-boarders for their breakfasts, dinner and tea. Many stories are told of guests looking for their own names written on the boiled eggs! Thus the larger establishments would have to cater for seventy or eighty boarders and, at the same time, for twenty or thirty non-boarders who would have their meals cooked separately. However, a feature of this period was the gradual disappearance of the non-boarders which greatly simplified the catering arrangements.

While Full Board was still available, Dinner, Bed and Breakfast became the norm with visitors having lunch out in Douglas or wherever they were visiting during the day. Thus life was made a little easier for the boarding house keepers. One hazard which persisted was the abundance of flies in the hot weather. Few had refrigerators so the only protection for food was the use of 'meat safes' which were cupboards with fine metal netting kept in as cool a position as possible, usually the back yard. Cooking was done mostly by gas, usually on more than one huge gas stove with a hotplate nearby to keep the innumerable pans hot. Frozen foods were not yet in use and items like vegetables, for instance, would be either fresh, tinned or dried.

All guests were expected to adhere strictly to meal times and to be in at night by a given time, usually midnight for 'Lights out. If there was a late function of any kind which would be finishing after this time guests could make alternative arrangements. Visitors were accepted on a week-to-week basis. The Steam Packet Company had so many ships then that they arrived at many different times, as well as the regular services. This meant some very early rising for the staff.

The changeover of the weekly guests was extraordinarily hectic, and any friends or relations were called on to lend assistance. Saturday was changeover day when the entire house emptied. The hall would be chock-full of departing guests' luggage early in the morning. The first quota of new guests could not have possession of their rooms until ten o'clock so, from about 5.30 am they would sit on the Promenade surrounded by their luggage. If the weather was wet they would make for their boarding house and room would have to be found for their luggage. A complicated business indeed! There were two sittings for breakfast and as the departing guests left all available staff and helpers commenced

cleaning their vacated bedrooms. The bed clothes and towels had to be collected and made into bundles with appropriate lists enclosed, ready for the laundry to collect. Saturday night saw everything in order once again and some very tired people went to bed thankful another Saturday was over.

Where it was necessary to engage extra staff problems could arise. It was ideal to have the same girls returning each year but this was not always possible because of the seasonal nature of the employment. The alternative was to advertise for waitresses, chambermaids, cooks and kitchen staff in local and mainland newspapers or via the Labour Exchange. Many came from Liverpool or Ireland and it was something of a gamble as to their capabilities. The first essential, however, was honesty - especially in the case of chambermaids. They would be entering and working in bedrooms where guests were notoriously careless in leaving jewellery and money lying about. As to the efficiency or otherwise of staff, there was little that could be done once the season got under way. In order to have a full complement of staff for the season it was necessary to take them on early in May ready for the busy T.T. Race period. After this there was a lull until the second week in July which was Scotch Week. From then on it was the peak period until the Amateur T.T. Races, later called the Manx Grand Prix, early in September. When there was a lull the girls engaged for the season would have free time to go about town when they would meet others and discuss the wages and tips they were receiving. Some had little loyalty to their employers and would leave if they thought they could better themselves. So having kept the girls during the quieter times, the employers could find themselves short of staff just as the busy time arrived when replacements were hard to find.

Another hazard was when the employer had been so misguided as to engage two or three girls who were friends. If there was any trouble with one, then sacking was out of the question as they were all liable to walk out. Sometimes staff who had been engaged never even reached their appointed destination. Some of the larger hotels had their own conveyances to meet their guests. But the drivers could be sent on an entirely different mission. They would be sent to look for likely staff, get into conversation with them and persuade them to come to his hotel to work - with better wages, of course, being offered. These were just some of the things which could happen on occasions to add to the problems of the busy boarding house keepers.

In the 1920s Douglas had the reputation of being 'dear but delightful' with the emphasis being on the 'dear'. This was the result of those involved in the industry trying to recoup their wartime losses during the post-war boom. This image resulted in something of a phobia and everything was done to dispel the notion of Douglas being an expensive place for a holiday. By the early 1930s there was little to complain about. Prices varied according to the style and luxury desired, but it was possible to obtain Full Board at private hotels on the Promenade for 7s 6d, 8s and 8s 6d (42.5p) a day. Not far from the seafront there were scores of houses which provided tea or dinner, bed and breakfast at 5 shillings (25p) a day. These tariffs meant that Douglas was no longer considered 'dear'. In fact, tariffs were now less than many an English resort, thus giving an additional incentive in choosing Douglas for a holiday, especially for families and young people.

The adverts shown on these pages appeared in the 1939 Official Guide to Douglas which was issued under the Authority of the Douglas Town Council and published by The Douglas Boarding and Apartment Association.

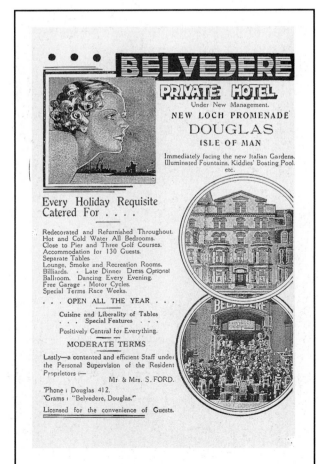
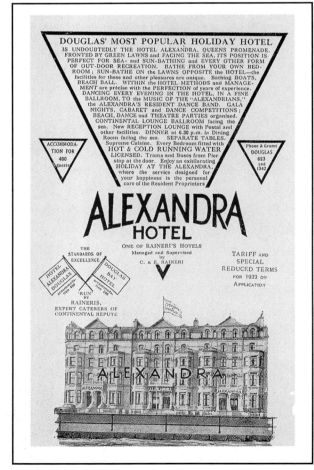
104

"HAPPY DAYS ARE HERE AGAIN!"

The beginning of 1919 saw Mr Joseph Cunningham and his wife Elizabeth being inundated with requests for the Camp Herald and booking forms, these requests coming mainly from those who had survived the trenches in France and were keen to taste again the delights of a holiday at Cunningham's Young Men's Holiday Camp. They were joined by many newcomers, of all classes, now able to afford a holiday. Although it was not until March that the last internees departed, preparations were made to receive the first campers in May. Thus began another prosperous period which would last for the next twenty years.

While the spirit of the campers remained unchanged, times were changing. Gone were the stiff three-piece suits and in came the loose fitting trousers, jackets and open-necked shirts. The management reacted to all the latest trends providing cinema shows while the ballroom echoed to popular dance bands playing the latest hit tunes. Alternative music was provided by a grand orchestreon, or automated orchestra. But it was the band that was the great favourite and inevitably it started up with 'Happy Days Are Here Again.' Eventually the BBC broadcast dance music from here on a regular basis. Teetotalism was strictly enforced and whereas the camp was for men only, women became part of the social life and joined in the morning and evening dances. To make access from the promenade easier an electric escalator was installed in 1923. The lift took the form of a line of collapsible single chairs which operated virtually non-stop. Campers rode free.

Much prominence was given to sports of all kinds. A Camp P.E. instructor coached in boxing and swimming lessons were given in the indoor pool. Keep fit classes, for those who wished, started the day at 7.30 am. Organisers arranged tennis tournaments and the Little Switzerland sports field was used for cricket matches and athletics. Indoor games included billiards and badminton. Campers had a private grandstand at Governor's Bridge from which to view the TT and Manx Grand Prix Races. Competitors were provided with facilities to garage their machines.

Catering for such large numbers was a gigantic task, with four meals being provided daily - breakfast, dinner, tea and supper. An army of waiters was required in the vast dining hall and the campers could eat as much as they liked. The Cunninghams had taken over 850 acres of farmland and created Ellerslie Farm in 1915. Some of the wartime internees helped in its construction and the latest methods in farming were employed. The farm supplied milk, vegetables and potatoes. The kitchens were equipped with the latest gadgetry. The butcher's department dealt with hundreds of carcases a week. The bakery turned out thousands of loaves and bread rolls and 700 hams were cooked weekly. Custard was made in 100 gallon pans. Much of the cooking was done in vast pressure cookers. When Mr Billy Butlin came to find out how to run a holiday camp he was not permitted to inspect the kitchens and the catering organisation!

The maximum number of campers which could be accommodated rose to 4,000. The tents were gradually replaced by wooden bungalows and dormitories, while chalet tents were also introduced. The latter were more spacious than the old bell tents although anyone who wished to camp out in the old style could still do so. By the coming of the Second World War, Cunningham's Holiday Camp had accommodated over a million men. There was little need to advertise!

THE CAMP HERALD
SEASON 1920

· THE CUNNINGHAM
YOUNG MENS HOLIDAY CAMP
"SWITZERLAND" QUEENS PROMENADE
DOUGLAS I.O.M.
ESTABLISHED 1887

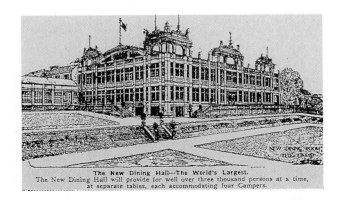

The New Dining Hall—The World's Largest.
The New Dining Hall will provide for well over three thousand persons at a time,
at separate tables, each accommodating four Campers.

ENTERTAINING THE VISITORS

In the latter years of the Great War Fred Buxton returned to Douglas. After touring with pantos and other shows in England, and opening several cinemas there, he took over the running of the Villa Marina in 1917 and 1918 and secured an important cinematograph first for the Villa. Hall Caine's book 'The Deemster' had been made into a movie film and Mr Buxton offered the production company £200 for the world premiere rights - and got them! This was about twenty times the normal price for a film. Mr Buxton bought the run-down Grand Theatre in Victoria Street, reseated it, installed electric lighting and re-opened it with a professional company staging the comic opera 'The Belle of New York.' Unfortunately his health failed and although he hoped his teenage son, Douglas, would take over from him this was too soon. Mr Buxton sold out to the Palace and Derby Castle Company. Subsequently Mr Buxton died aged 52 of cerebral degeneration. A specialist brought to Douglas couldn't save him; then, on seeing the afternoon steamer crossing the bay, lamented that he would be stuck on the Island for another day when there were so many patients in London who needed his attention. When the Steam Packet was told of this, the steamer was recalled to harbour!

For Douglas Corporation the Villa Marina prospered, sometimes in unexpected ways. Twice in the 1920s roller skating crazes supplanted dancing. Towards the end of the decade a new maple floor was laid over the dance floor for skating and sessions were held in the mornings, afternoons and at night. Demand for skates far exceeded supply! A special floor was laid in the Reading Room for learners. Its popularity attracted families and to the disapproval of some, children were encouraged to dance. Critics alleged that children of up to seven could be found dancing at 11 pm ! Official Corporation policy, however, was that children were to be removed from the dance floor by 9 pm. Subsequently the managership of the Villa Marina, conducted by Mr Noah Moore, was described as "probably the most unenviable and thankless public position in all Manxland." There were so many

On board one of the steam ferries that carried holiday-makers to and from Douglas Head. Johnny Ventro with his violin and accompanied by a pianist, entertained with the latest popular songs. Seated left, with pipe, is well-known local journalist Arthur Moore.

critics! Two other issues which raised tempers were Mr Moore's opposition to free passes for Councillors and a wish by him to open the Villa one night a week free of charge for the poor of the town. But it was in August, 1934 that the Villa's Royal Hall had an all-time record box office for a Sunday Night Concert. Over 3,000, many standing, attended a concert given by internationally acclaimed negro singer Paul Robeson. Huge crowds had to be turned away.

Provision of a Garden Pavilion at the back of the gardens, first capable of seating 600, then later up to 1,300, enabled concert parties to entertain. Meanwhile, the erection in 1931 of a Collonade, Verandah and shopping arcade adjoining the Gaiety Theatre enhanced the Villa's frontage. A popular feature of the Colonnade was a restaurant

In the 1920's the highly popular concert parties on Douglas Head were provided with a stage and changing rooms. Deck chairs were provided for patrons on the tiered terraces. (Mannin Collections)

with views of the promenade on one side and the Villa grounds on the other. Later, in the early Thirties when Port Skillion swimming pool was lost in a storm and Town Councillors considered the provision of a replacement open-air pool, complete with water chutes, the Villa grounds were suggested but nothing came of it. The grounds were too popular on sunny afternoons for band concerts and bathing beauty competitions. Thereafter the gardens were opened free in the winter as a public park.

Hopes to stop the decline of Douglas Head failed to materialise too. Though many of its attractions still had years of life left in them, and the letting of deck chairs for hire had been introduced there by the Corporation at the same time as on the beach (1928), the headland's hey-day had passed with Port Skillion. In 1930 mains electricity was provided to the headland for the first time in the hope of stimulating activity there, particularly evening performances by concert parties - an idea originally frowned upon. But there was no stopping the decline and Douglas Head never re-established itself as an attraction for the hundreds of thousands of pre-war visitors. Briefly in 1937 new plans were prepared by the Borough Surveyor for a new and bigger open-air swimming pool at Port Skillion. Other sites in the town could not be used without spoiling the amenities of the area, said Councillors. However, the plan was never implemented.

Nevertheless, the steam ferries operating across the harbour were able to maintain their busy schedules, augmented by about a dozen rowing-boat operators licensed to row people across the harbour. Their rewards were only small, however, because of constantly increasing licence fees. Many said they were worse off than men on poor relief. They had to row 2,000 people across the harbour to pay for their licences. One of the main attractions still was the Douglas Southern Railway to Port Soderick. The track, bridges and electric trams were made ready for the 1919 season and the following season was exceptionally good. However, the pre-war average of over 190,000 passengers per season would never be exceeded. During the 1920s the tramway was combined with the surviving Douglas Head Marine Drive Company. To encourage an increase in traffic a combined ticket was introduced giving travel to Port Soderick via the harbour ferry, incline railway, Marine Drive tramway and Port Soderick cliff lift for 1s 6d return. In 1933 the steam-powered generators at Pigeon Stream were sold off and power taken from the Douglas public supply. While safety was never neglected, only prudent management enabled the tramway to survive until 1939, passenger figures having fallen to well below the 100,000 seasonal mark.

Port Soderick, under the Forresters, continued to enjoy wide popularity and was well supplied with patrons who travelled in great numbers to the Steam Railway station at the top of the glen. Trains to this point would often consist of 12 or more coaches requiring three locomotives on the gradient from Douglas.

Back in Douglas there were plenty of fresh devel-

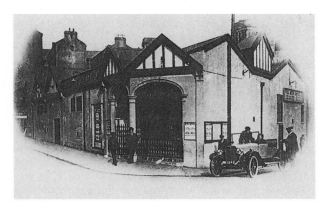

The Pier Pavilion in Walpole Avenue, dating from the end of the nineteenth century, was demolished to make way for a new cinema.

Men of local builders Creer Brothers at work on the timber scaffolding as the new cinema takes shape.

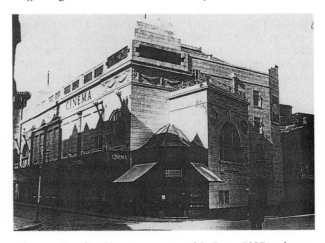

The new Royalty Cinema was opened in June, 1927 and was regarded as a British pioneer in its design. (Photographs by kind permission of Stephen Pitts)

opments in the entertainment world. In Strand Street the Picture House was opened in July, 1921, and a new dance hall, the Palais de Danse, was built in time for the 1927 season by the owners of the Strand Cinema and Picture House. (Eventually these were all taken over by the Palace and Derby Castle Company). Later the Palais became a popular venue for boxing and wrestling matches, and even for indoor roller skating, requiring a special floor. But by far the most dominant feature in entertainment during the inter-war years was the expansion of the cinemas - the 'flicks' to many because of the flickering nature of early films. The introduction of 'talkies' in 1927 marked the closure within two years of the Empire Electric Theatre. Presumably it was too small for the necessary investment. But other cinemas prospered, which was bad news for the amateur musicians who had provided musical accompaniment for the silent movies. At one time the Picture House alone had employed a pianist, violinist and 'cellist. The 'talkie revolution' made them redundant.

Two live theatres were lost permanently to cinemas: the Pier Pavilion in Walpole Avenue which was redeveloped as the Royalty Cinema in 1927 and regarded as a British pioneer in its design; then the Grand Theatre in Victoria Street. First it became the Grand Cinema; then in 1935 after a major internal rebuilding which retained nine dressing rooms in case a theatrical use would be required, was renamed the Regal Cinema. Even the Gaiety Theatre was almost lost. Occasionally in the peak period of the silent movies it was used as a Picturedrome during the winter, music being provided by Harry Wood's Bijou Orchestra.

Cinemas came to dominate the entertainment scene, some changing their main features three times a week - one film Monday to Wednesday, another Thursday to Saturday and then a different programme for a Sunday. Programmes ran continuously from about 2.30 pm and in the mornings too on wet days. In the summer major films were sent to Douglas for a trial run before general release. The town's great picture palaces during the Thirties were the Royalty, the Regal, the Picture House and Strand in Strand Street, and the Crescent on the promenade. The Royalty and Crescent were mainly seasonal; the others all year round. One novel feature of the Strand, which was enlarged in 1930, was that its roof could be slid back during intervals to vent cigarette smoke. In 1935 it also pioneered the introduction of a lift to the Circle so the elderly and infirm didn't have to use the stairs.

The 2,000 seat Crescent 'Super Cinema', built in 1930 on the site of the earlier all-wooden 'Picturedrome' (part of the Pierrot Village), was the biggest and also the most decorated. Its interior was like that of a Tudor castle with imitation tapestry walls. Its stage, which could be used for theatrical requirements and did so occasionally, was styled like a portcullis. There were proposals to build a new theatre, shopping arcade and winter garden alongside the Crescent on the site of the Pierrot Pavilion but the onset of the Great Depression in the Thirties put paid to that. The Pavilion remained and did so until the 1960s.

One of the features of the Regal was the rainbow effects which changed with the mood of music at intervals around the stage area whilst from the pit a fabulous illuminated Compton organ played by Dr George Tootell would rise up for musical interludes. This was the first entirely electronic organ produced by Crompton. Previous models had relied on wind. On Sunday nights the cinema would be packed for half hour pre-film sing-alongs to the accompaniment of the organ. Words were projected by slide onto the screen. A similar but

The wooden building of the Picture House, part of the Peirrot Village, was removed and the site prepared for the Crescent Cinema. Creer Brothers were the main contractors.

Men at work on the balustrade surrounding the front section of the cinema. Plans to build an identical theatre on the left of the site, with a shopping arcade and winter garden between, were not completed.

The finished Crescent 'Super' Cinema was opened in 1930. With 2,000 seats it was the largest cinema in the town. Its ornate interior was designed in Tudor castle style with imitation tapestry walls. (Photographs by kind permission of Stephen Pitts)

smaller organ was used in the Picture House. The proud claim of Douglas in the mid-1930s was:

* Ten thousand people could dance every night
* Eight thousand could be accommodated nightly in its cinemas
* Five thousand could be seated in its theatres and concert halls

Variety shows were said to be so up-to-date that many leading London music publishers tried out future hit songs here first. At least one of the performing companies at the Palace in 1928 would have a dubious reception today because of its name; an insight into how things change. Its name? The 'Gay Dog's Company'! In June, 1931 the Company made history by having its show transmitted 'live' by BBC radio. The performance was sent to an English-based transmitter by submarine cable.

The historic show business event of 1935, though few could have realised it then, was the arrival in Douglas immediately after the T.T. Races of a production crew from Associated Talking Pictures Ltd. of Ealing. Their mission was the production of the T.T. comedy classic 'No Limit', written by author of 'Love on the Dole', Walter Greenwood under the title of 'Take me to the Isle of Man'. Their budget: £50,000. Co-starring with Florence Desmond, who had Manx relatives, was George Formby Jnr - so named because his father had been in show business too and had appeared at the Palace Opera House at Douglas. Most of the picture was filmed on the Island - even the scene where George 'Shuttleworth' falls over the side of a Manx ferry, supposedly at the Liverpool Landing Stage. That was at Douglas harbour.

The entire cast and most of the crew stayed at the Majestic Hotel. The stunt men used for the various crashes were soon out of action and could be seen with bandages and sticks hobbling round the hotel. They were not used to riding motorcycles and it was at that point that the Peveril Motor Cycle Club were called upon to help. Five or six of its members took part and they had an interesting and lucrative

week. It was one of the members, Cyril Standen, who did the crash into the Ballacraine Hotel and the leap at Sulby. Other locals helped with props. The donkey which George tries to ride to the Grandstand from Douglas Head was known throughout Douglas as the one which hauled Harry Winter's fruit and veg cart around town.

For the ukulele-playing George this was his first big movie. It was a tremendous success, made a mint of money, and led to many movies thereafter. It also earned George a place in T.T. history. The Palace Company acquired a print of the film and its screening every T.T. period became an annual tradition until the 1980s by which time the print was in poor condition. 'No Limit' survives through occasional showings on TV and its release on video: hence the Island's continued warm affection for George and the erection of a bronze statue of him in Strand Street near its junction with Regent Street.

A journalist from the rival resort of Blackpool captured the holiday spirit of Douglas in an article which appeared in the Blackpool Gazette' in 1931:

"I hesitate to have to confess it, but compared with the liveliness on the Douglas Promenade on a sunny afternoon even a Blackpool August Bank Holiday crowd seems the height of respectability . . .
"Shops in Douglas keep open as long as they please: the hotels are open all day and until 11 at night. Holidaymakers appreciate these extended facilities. Only on Sundays are there irritating restrictions. It is a short season in the Isle of Man and a long winter, and as the Island is almost entirely dependent on the visiting industry it doesn't mind staying up late to entertain its visitors . . .
"Prices everywhere are reasonable and you can ride the full distance of the promenade for twopence, compared with threepence last year. Whether you are on the horse trams or the modern motor buses makes no difference. Most visitors prefer the former and when, if ever, Douglas dispenses with its horse-drawn 'toast-racks,' it will lose a big attraction . . .
"Cheap travel on the steam railway means that no fares

The original poster advertising the 1935 film 'No Limit' which starred George Formby and Florence Desmond. George is seen here on his Shuttleworth 'Snap' which brought him TT glory. Members of the local Peveril Motor Cycle Club assisted in the riding sequences in the film.

Enjoying the sunshine and relaxing on the 'two miles' of sandy beach. (From the 1938 Douglas Guide)

Dancing in the Palace Ballroom, one of Europe's largest. Both dress and dancing were strictly formal. (Keig)

are more than three shillings return. There is also available two-day tickets for a similar amount giving unlimited travel while for an extra half a crown you can have the freedom of the buses for the same period. The Manx Electric Railway offers five shilling 'rover' tickets for two days of travel on its 50 miles (i.e. both sides of the track!) of panoramic beauty, including a trip on the Snaefell Summit Railway . . .

"The dearest motor-coach trip is the full-day tour round the Island. There are stays of half-an-hour at Rushen Abbey, Port Erin and Ramsey; and one of an hour-and-a-half for lunch at Peel. You see every part of the Island from the Calf of Man to the Point of Ayre. And all for five shillings which compares with half a guinea some

years ago. The coach drivers make sure you are back in Douglas by 6 o'clock for your evening meal.

"The evening admissions to the Palace and Derby Castle remain at 1s 6d but this includes both dancing and revue. Theatre prices range from 6d to 4s 6d. And the programmes - the handiest programmes I have ever seen - are 'price one penny.' Cinema admission charges range from 6d to 2s, and all the plays or pictures have yet to be seen in Blackpool!

"If Manxland can keep its present moderate tariff, can maintain its holiday spirit, then its steamship service, already the largest, finest and fastest of its kind in the world, will have to be increased to deal with the million

SOME NOTABLE EVENTS

When peace returned, so did the 'flying machines' which had made such a lasting impression during the Carnival of 1914. In the spring of 1919 the A.V. Roe Company approached Douglas Corporation for a concession to use part of the beach and grass area on Queen's Promenade for use as an aerodrome. From here the public would be given the opportunity of participating in 'pleasure flying' which became a craze in the post-war years. Permission granted, A.V. Roe despatched from Manchester two of their 504K aircraft, wartime machines which had been converted to carry two passengers. In charge of the operation was Lt. Moxon who announced his arrival over Douglas Bay by giving a display of aerobatics to demonstrate the safety of flying. His first passengers were the Mayor, 70 year old Alderman John Kelly, and the Town Clerk. There was more pleasure flying the following year with many enjoying a 'flip' round the bay. But there were objections, and a memorial signed by twenty persons was presented to the Corporation claiming an infringement of rights. They were objecting to the loss of the grass area in front of their hotels for the benefit of their guests and for the purpose of drying bed linen. In court the appeal was upheld and the aerodrome facilities were withdrawn. That same summer of 1920 saw the beginning of a daily service between Windermere and Douglas flown by Captain Pixton using an Avro seaplane. Its purpose was to deliver copies of the *Daily Mail* ahead of its rivals which were brought aboard the afternoon steamer. But poor weather and the economics of the venture ended in the service being scrapped after a fortnight.

The first year after the war was a time for victory celebrations. There was a Manx National Thanksgiving Fete and a one-day Carnival in Douglas in aid of war funds. Boy Scouts led a torchlight procession through town but a planned spectacular of 800 star shells fired from Douglas and Onchan Head failed to materialise. Only a few shells arrived. A Manx National Reception for soldiers and sailors was staged at the Nunnery in September, 1919 and attended by 10,000. Overhead Lt. Moxon gave a spectacular display but he was unable to land his aircraft at the Nunnery because of the weather conditions. More memorable was the overflying of Douglas on a test flight to Ireland of the world's largest airship, the R34.

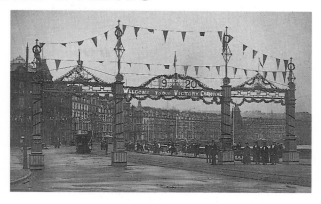

The archway built on the Loch Promenade as part of the Victory Carnival held in 1920. (R and L Kelly Collection)

The end of the war in which most of the Steam Packet fleet had been lost raised the question: what future was there for the Company? Some shareholders wanted to sell what ships remained, realise the British Governments's compensation for what had been lost and then wind up the Company. In a two day meeting of shareholders the matter was hotly debated; opinion was divided - then a non-Manx shareholder threw his vote in favour of the 'carry-ons' and so one part of the traditional features of Douglas harbour was assured.

Socially these were times of change. Those who had fought a bitter war were unprepared to settle for how things had been before, especially restrictive practices. Increased militancy led to concessions. It was established, for example, that one Douglas bye-law which prohibited the use of car stands on Sundays was illegal, and had been for 30 years! One of the most important concessions saw the introduction of old age pensions. The first were paid in March 1920, many of the first recipients of ten shillings (50p) being in Douglas. When it came to wages, however, reformers were less successful. Demands that Manx building trade workers should be paid the same as in England - two shillings (10p) an hour - were rejected and led to one of the most protracted strikes in Manx industrial history. It lasted several months.

In July of that year, during the strike, King George V and Queen Mary arrived in Douglas with an escort of

The Queen's Promenade was used as an aerodrome by Avro aircraft in 1919. When the tide was out pleasure flying 'flips' were made round the bay. (R and L Kelly Collection)

30 ships of the Royal Navy. They included five 'super Dreadnoughts' and an early aircraft carrier described as 'resembling a travelling warehouse.' A heavy sea, however, prevented the royals landing at Douglas as planned and to the bitter disappointment of crowds who had braved bitterly cold weather at the pier they had to switch to Ramsey. One of the highlights of the two-day visit was the gathering of 5,000 school children all dressed in white in the Villa Marina grounds to welcome Their Majesties. There the children sang the two National Anthems before Douglas Corporation greeted the royals in the Villa's Royal Hall where they were presented with an Address designed by Archibald Knox.

Barely had the royal visitors departed than Douglas lost the Palace Ballroom, known as the 'White Palace' to many, to fire. Rebuilt after the fire of 1902 it was the finest in Europe with a splendid parquet floor. By the time the Douglas Fire Brigade arrived with its manual appliances and steam engine the fire had taken a strong hold with flames leaping 150 feet through the collapsed roof into the early morning sky. By demolishing the connecting corridor the firemen were able to save the Coliseum. Building workers on strike thought the disaster played into their hands. To get the Palace rebuilt in time for the following season the Palace and Derby Castle Company agreed to pay workers the required two shillings an hour. But it was a hollow victory, though the King sent a telegram of congratulations on the speedy re-building of the Palace. Once the Palace had been re-erected pay scales offered by employers reverted to lower levels. It was only at the outbreak of the Second World War in 1939, when English contractors were required to build military facilities here, that it was accepted that to overcome a shortage of local labour United Kingdom rates of pay would have to be introduced.

In June, 1923 the Royal Navy provided another spectacular at Douglas. This time ten ships of the Fifth Destroyer Flotilla of the Atlantic Fleet came into the bay. Sports were organised for the crews ashore. Later they were admitted free to some places of entertainment in Douglas and for half-price at the cinemas. That night thousands lined the promenade for a send-off preceded at 11.30pm by a half-an-hour searchlight display by the destroyers.

In February, 1923 the combination of a south-east gale and one of the year's highest tides (20 feet 9 inches) caused flooding in lower Douglas. Water in the inner harbour overflowed at The Tongue and swept through the shopping area with such force that promenade seats were broken from their mountings and carried away. Strand Street and Castle Street were flooded to a depth of between six inches and a foot.

The following year Britain's National Strike in the late spring threatened a greater disruption to the town. Most Manx workers were excused by their unions from striking because it was accepted that their actions couldn't affect the issue in the United Kingdom. However, faced with the prospect of a protracted dispute and shortages of fuels, Tynwald requisitioned the latest cargoes of coals and rationed them, prohibiting places of religion and entertainment from receiving any. The big fear was that the strike would destroy the summer season. Steamers couldn't operate without coal it was pointed out. To enable businessmen to hear the latest news a radio with loud speakers was established at Government Office in Douglas. Eventually the strike ended in May giving the June Effort and Season Extension Committee time to market the Island. Services of Thanksgiving were held in most churches.

A view of Strand Street in February, 1923 when one of the highest tides on record caused widespread flooding in the lower parts of the town. (R and L Kelly Collection)

As its contribution to the continuing success of the TT Races, the Corporation built a permanent steel Grandstand at a cost of £2,000. Built in 1926 it lasted for sixty years. (Keig Collection)

One of the big 'events' of the week was the Sunday morning open-air service held at Kirk Braddan. Loud-speakers broadcast the service to the thousands who attended either walking or travelling by special trains, buses or coaches.

That year, 1926, was also the year that Douglas Corporation saved the T.T. Races. The previous year the Auto-Cycle Union had warned that it might not be able to continue running the races unless some financial help was forthcoming. Town Councillors had formed a committee to see what could be done and had identified the annual erection and dismantling of a wooden grandstand towards the bottom of Glencrutchery Road as a substantial burden for the A.C.U. The latter agreed that if it was relieved of the grandstand this would go a long way to resolving its financial difficulties, certainly sufficient for it to guarantee that the T.T. would continue for at least three more years. So in return for a share of the grandstand receipts and the adjoining enclosure the Corporation spent £2,000 on building a permanent steel grandstand on land acquired for the purpose opposite the Borough Cemetery - slightly forward of the present one but otherwise on the existing site. It was a rush job. When riders arrived for practising in 1926 the structure was still being completed. Nevertheless, it was destined to last for sixty years.

An ambitious event staged in June, 1929 with the backing of the June Effort and Season Extension Committee was the renactment at Douglas Harbour of a famous World War 1 naval raid on Zeebrugge. Some of those invited to participate had actually taken part in the raid. The idea occurred to its promoters when similarities were noted between Douglas Harbour and Zeebrugge. Motor yachts were disguised as naval vessels and submarines, and large quantities of fireworks including rockets replicated the actual gunfire and smokescreens. Approximately 20,000 seats were provided for spectators on the Battery and Victoria Piers. The weather was good but the evening event was disappointing. The general verdict was that the spectators were just as confused about what was happening as were the Germans in the original raid!

The 1930s, marked by the Great Depression and mass unemployment, started dramatically. The worst floods in living memory hit the whole Island in September, 1930. At Douglas a new bridge serving the electricity power station and the Pulrose Council estate was swept away.

For three years in the 1930s Douglas became Britain's Monte Carlo. 'Round the Houses' car races had been introduced in the principality of Monaco so successfully that the R.A.C., after many promptings from the Isle of Man and offers of financial assistance from Douglas Corporation and local businesses, decided to copy the idea in Douglas. The result in July 1933 was the staging of two races - the Mannin Beg (Little Man) and Mannin Mooar (Big Man) races over 50 laps of a 4.6 mile circuit. Described by some English newspapers as the most dangerous race in the world (a race of 500 corners per lap, it was estimated) the course started in front of the Villa Marina (with pits on the seaward side of the road) went south to Church Road and Finch Road; from there to the top of Woodbourne Road and Governor's Bridge, into Onchan then down Summer Hill to the promenade. For safety reasons some tramlines and telephone poles had to be removed temporarily. Douglas Corporation embarked also on a two-year phased programme of lifting the now redundant cable car lines in upper Douglas.

Race enthusiasts thought the event to be a success despite reports of women shrieking with fright and fainting when seeing cars approach them at over

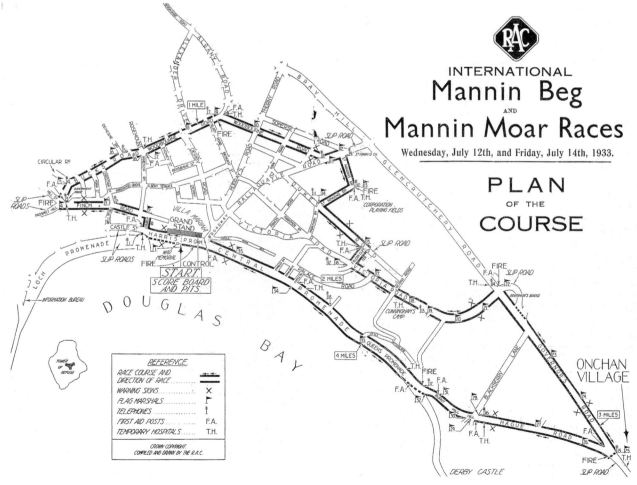

113

Crowds of spectators watch as cars in the 1933 Mannin Beg race pass through Church Road on their way to Finch Road and the upper parts of the town. (Manx National Heritage)

Scene of the start of the Mannin Beg 1934 race opposite the Crescent Cinema, in front of which a large grandstand had been positioned. (Keig Collection)

100 mph whilst they spectated from gardens! There were crashes which, but for luck, could have been serious. One involved a car, out of control with no brakes, heading for a barrier behind which were hundreds of spectators. As they scrambled for safety the driver averted disaster by deliberately turning his car into a dining saloon.

Danger, however, wasn't what attracted criticism. What did was disruption of the town at the height of the season. Access to the beaches was denied to people from Upper Douglas during practices and racing; meanwhile tourists were trapped in their hotels if they did not get away early enough. To ease that problem the races were brought forward in 1934 to the end of May and early June when there were fewer non-race tourists, and the course was reduced to 3.7 miles by avoiding the heart of the town. This was done by starting cars opposite the Crescent Cinema. The course turned up Broadway, went to Ballaquayle Road, York Road and the base of Bray Hill, up the hill to Glencrutchery Road, on to Onchan then down Summerhill to the promenade.

In 1935, presumably to increase spectator interest on the promenade by increasing the action there, the start returned to the Villa Marina. Cars went south to the Sefton Hotel, did a U-turn, then returned to ascend

Broadway. The rest of the course was unchanged; the disruption to seafront traffic no less. Only a small entry was received, however, and few were able to last the distance. Competitor and spectator interest was so small that afterwards it was decided that the cost and inconvenience of staging such a race again wasn't worth it. However, a course on the outskirts of the town was introduced the following year, starting at the grandstand and then via Parkfield corner, Cronk ny Mona and Onchan. Winner of the 1936 RAC International Light Car Race was Dick Seaman driving a Delage and the following year the honours went to Prince Birabongse of Siam in his famous ERA 'Romulus.'

In May, 1937 the Coronation of King George VI and Queen Elizabeth was marked by great celebrations in Douglas. School children gave displays of fitness and physical training in the Villa Marina grounds and at night there was one of the longest and grandest carnival parades ever. A float entered by Douglas Corporation attracted a lot of praise. It was a detailed replica of Westminster Abbey. One of the Corporation double-decker buses retained its bunting and flags from a slightly earlier celebration. It had just become the first double-decker to serve the new estate of Pulrose.

The start and finish for the 1935 races returned to the Villa Marina. Here is Mannin Beg winner P.G.Fairfield in his supercharged 1909cc six-cylinder E.R.A. after completing the 600 mile 'round the houses' race at 67.29 mph. Freddie Dixon in a non-supercharged Riley was second. (R and L Kelly Collection)

SOME TOWN PERSONALITIES

In 1919 according to a future Deemster and Town Councillor, Ramsey Johnson, the most powerful man on the Isle of Man was a Douglas printer - a linotype operator with the Isle of Man Times. Alfred Teare had been one of the pioneers with printer and publisher Sam Norris in the Island's socialist movement, a campaigner for working men's rights, foremost in the formation of the local Workers Union and launching the Labour Party. The previous year Mr Teare had led workers in a campaign for the Island to follow the U.K. on bread subsidies. Inspired by his Treasury bosses in London, Governor Raglan had said the Island couldn't afford it. Then introduce income tax, said the campaigners, and an all-out strike had so paralysed the Island there were suggestions that the U.K. should send a warship to Douglas to collect stranded holidaymakers. Scenes included a thousand demonstrators outside Government Office. By the second day, acting on instructions from London, Lord Raglan capitulated and a mass meeting of over 2,000 at the Jubilee Clock was told the news.

Subsequent attempts to force Mr Teare off the Island failed. John Brown, owner/editor of the *Isle of Man Times* was threatened with the loss of advertising and printing contracts if he did not dismiss Mr Teare but he refused to be coerced. Later in 1919 Mr Teare was elected to the House of Keys for South Douglas and started a 43-year record of service in Government which saw many changes now taken for granted. He also became Secretary of the Workers Union and, in 1933, a member of the Town Council. He remained a member until 1965 by which time he had been made an Alderman and had been honoured by being awarded the M.B.E. Deemster Johnson described him as "human and lovable . . . trusted by everyone."

The future Deemster became a Town Councillor himself in 1921, his principal claim to fame being his youth. He was 15 years younger than any other Councillor. Elected after a campaign for covered accommodation at the Victoria Pier and the abolition of singing rooms in Douglas, Mr Johnson achieved some control of the latter when elected later as an M.H.K. His verdict on ten years as a Councillor? "There were some very inferior members who took delight in hindering the transaction of public business."

Another distinguished Labour campaigner was Walter 'Gussie' Craine, first Labour Councillor in 1926, and first Labour Mayor in 1937. He remained a Councillor until 1959 during which time he was also an M.H.K. for South Douglas. Earlier Mr Craine had been the first Labour candidate for the Keys in 1908. Two businessmen each bet him a new hat that he wouldn't get a hundred votes. In fact he got 282 - not enough to be elected but enough to win him two hats!

One of the new-rich created by the Great War was Arthur Binns Crookall, Blackpool-born but raised in Douglas. Whilst a painter and decorator, and summer caterer he became a Councillor in 1911. He then made his fortune when Knockaloe became an internee camp during the war. He obtained the concession to feed 20,000 plus internees. His post-war pre-eminence in the Corporation as an Alderman was recognised as Mayor for a remarkable five successive years, between 1922 and 1927.

Political reformer Alderman Alfred J. Teare M.L.C., M.B.E., J.P. He served in the Legislature from 1919 for a period of 43 years, representing South Douglas as a Member of the House of Keys. He was also a member of the Town Council on which he served from 1923 to 1965.

Alderman Crookall instigated the widening of the Loch Promenade and inspired the formation of the North American Manx Association after a U.S.A. tour in which he addressed Manx Societies. But he is remembered most for philanthropic acts like dressing as Father Christmas for many years and distributing personally-financed Christmas presents to a thousand poor children of the town. One year the girls' presents were known as 'The Crookall Dolls.' He bought them, local women dressed them and they were displayed in the Town Hall before their new owners were invited to the Villa Marina by postcard. For another year Alderman Crookall persuaded the Town Clerk, Borough Treasurer and Noah Moore, manager of the Villa Marina, to dress as Santa and they toured Douglas separately distributing presents.

Alderman Crookall's interest in children led him to realising there was a need for a Maternity Home and deciding to establish one at his own expense in memory of his late wife, Jane Crookall. In 1927 he bought and equipped premises in Demesne Road and it was run by Trustees and an honorary surgeon, Dr Dorothy Pantin. The name survives to this day though the Home has changed premises twice and is now run by the Health Services as part of Noble's Hospital. Alderman Crookall resigned from the Corporation in 1932 on becoming Chairman of Tynwald's Electricity Board, the formation of which he had originally opposed. Three years later he died aged 62. His last gift to the town was a bequest of

£10,000, with which the proceeds of the sale of the first Maternity Home and donations from his children, was enough to finance a new and larger Jane Crookall Maternity Home, opened in 1939 and vacated only in recent years.

Douglas newspapers have produced many personalities: one of the most accomplished of them William Cubbon. At first joint proprietor and editor of the *Manx Sun* then editor and manager of the *Isle of Man Examiner*, his academic interest in Manx history led him in 1912 to becoming Borough Librarian; ten years later, Librarian to the Manx Museum; then in 1932, Director of the Museum, a post he held until 1947. His massive two volume 'Bibliography of the Literature of the Isle of Man' published in 1933 remains the most important guide ever produced to early published material about the Island. In recognition of his achievements Mr Cubbon was given an honorary degree of Master of Arts at Liverpool University in 1940 and the Order of St. Olaf of Norway.

Another newspaper man who made an impact on the Island was T.R. Radcliffe, director and editor in chief of the *Examiner* for 33 years until his death in 1956. As a Lancashire orphan he had 'gone to the mill' at the age of ten but later had become the business manager of the *Oldham Chronicle*. On coming to Douglas he bought a debt-burdened *Examiner* - "a brand plucked from the burning," it was said later - and transformed it. In 1934 he gave the Island its first illustrated newspaper, front page news instead of small adverts and splash treatment of news. Almost overnight circulation doubled and thus began the *Examiner's* dominance of the local media.

The name of 'Tossie' Clucas survives in the Tromode-based laundry which he established. As a boy 'Tossie' used to carry laundry parcels for his mother to Cowen's laundry in Union Mills. Later, after seeing how things were done, he launched his own laundry in a house in Circular Road. Six years later business had grown enough for him to transfer it to A.W. Moore's former sail cloth factory at Tromode. Eventually it expanded into the production of 'Manx Cat' branded brushes for export, the acquisition of the dye-works and laundry in Union Mills and all property in Tromode village. An M.H.K. between 1933 and 1946, 'Tossie' Clucas was co-opted onto Douglas Corporation during the Second World War when elections were temporarily suspended. He sold his business in the late 1940s and died aged 70 in 1950.

A father and son dynasty in the Corporation-controlled fire brigade was a remarkable achievement. In December 1935 Stephen Caugherty retired as Superintendent of the brigade after 40 years service. He had been Captain since 1922 and Superintendent since 1929. His successor as from January, 1936 was his son Stephen (Bert) Caugherty, a member of the brigade for ten years and, at the time, secretary and first engine driver.

Another outstanding Corporation personality was Eric Coward. He came to Douglas as its first Gardens Superintendent in 1935, two years after the Corporation had leased Summer Hill Glen from the Government Property Trustees for 99 years. It had been created in 1932-33 by 187 young men aged 18 to 22 on a 'Work for the Workless' scheme. Mr Coward

Mr Arthur B. Crookall M.L.C., J.P. He was a member of the Town Council from 1911 to 1932 during which time he was made an Alderman and was the Mayor of Douglas for a remarkable five successive years from 1922 to 1927. He was famous for acting as Father Christmas to the children of Douglas, as seen in the above cartoon by well-known local artist Dusty Miller.

supervised its further development as a winter work scheme. The sunken gardens on Loch Promenade had just been completed. However, a disaster was to follow when it was discovered the salt-water spray washing over the gardens in winter killed off the thousands of plants put there in 1934. One of Mr Coward's first acts was to institute annual planting.

It was Mr Coward who pioneered the opening of the Corporation's nurseries in Brunswick Road; then in 1938-39 the acquisition of 22.5 acres of nursery land at Ballaughton. He replanted the enclosed gardens at Hutchinson Square, Woodbourne Square and Derby Square when they were vested in the Corporation in 1938 and 1945. Mr Coward also undertook major improvements at Noble's Park (now known simply as 'The Rec'). This included the regular cutting of the grass - which was condemned by some as a waste of money! Mr Coward retired in September, 1973 with one dream unrealised. That was the conversion of Port-e-Chee meadows into a park with lake and walks.

One man remembered for the pleasure he brought was 'The Hurdy Gurdy Man,' believed to have been a Mr Collister of St. George's Street. What he operated around town, however, wasn't a hurdy gurdy (a boxed string instrument), nor a traditional barrel organ (a piped instrument which had air admitted to its pipes via a revolving disk fitted with pins). On board his pony-drawn cart was a piano-organ, rather like a pianola. This was operated by a hand wheel on one side. Mr Collister led the pony and an assistant used to stand at the back of the cart to steady the instrument. The strains of the 'Hurdy Gurdy' added to the gaiety of the promenade in pre-war days and again after the war. But they came to an end in the late 1940s and in 1950, on the opening of the Home of Rest for Old Horses - then only a field and stable at Whitebridge, Onchan - the 'Hurdy Gurdy' pony, Jessie, became one of its first recruits; a retirement that lasted just one year.

Places of popular resort well into the first half of the century were the town's herb beer shops. Two of the principal ones were in Walpole Avenue and ideally situated for patrons of the vaudeville theatre who would rush out on Sundays when no pubs were allowed to open and order a 'half and half.' That was one part herb beer, the other sarsaparilla. Some drinks were slightly alcoholic but they were not required to be licensed. Their products were based on old herbal remedies and were considered medicinal. This was particularly so in respect of the dark, cavernous and smoky premises operated by the Blackburn family. Fresh herbs gathered from secret locations in the countryside were hung from the ceiling. One of the popular concoctions was for 'cleaning the blood.' The Moore family ran the other shop and it continued under different ownership until the late Fifties. Although window displays offered herbal cures it survived latterly mainly through providing refreshments for the young like hot Vimto and sarsaparilla. Later it was converted into a newspaper shop.

In Nelson Street the one-armed Bill Corrin earned a reputation for bottled herb beer, sarsaparilla and ginger ale brewed in front of the fire in his tobacconist and sweet shop. When a boy Mr Corrin lost his right arm in a horse tram accident. One knocked

Well-known character around the streets of Douglas was Billy Corrin who is seen here outside his shop on the corner of Nelson and Wellington Street. (Mrs Janie Moore)

him down; another coming in the opposite direction ran over him. In recognition of that invalidity and probably a sense of responsibility because it was a tram that had injured him, the Corporation granted Mr Corrin for the rest of his life a special licence to push a hand-cart round town (one shaft on his shoulder) selling home-made ice cream. It was the only one of its kind permitted. Ice and coarse salt provided the insulation. A special gadget was devised on his wooden cart which enabled him to fill a wafer with one hand. A swivel on it ejected the wafer when completed. Many people used to watch in admiration at his dexterity. Then he was so accomplished with one hand that he could even play a concertina! One half was held between his knees! At a time when people did not have refrigerators at home Bill Corrin provided an important service. His route through town was well known. He had no need to shout his arrival or ring a bell. People anticipated his arrival and emerged with basins for so many scoops of ice cream. Mr Corrin died in 1953. In his later years when he was less mobile the Corporation permitted him to stand with his cart on the promenade by the paddling pool opposite the Falcon Hotel.

Summer Hill Glen was developed and opened to the public after being leased from the Government Property Trustees in 1933.

117

DOUGLAS DURING THE SECOND WORLD WAR
(1939-1945)

Douglas had enjoyed the long, hot summer of 1939 with the beaches packed in the daytime and the dance halls, theatres and cinemas crowded in the evenings. An atmosphere of merriment was prevalent as though those on holiday were determined to enjoy themselves despite the deterioration in the international situation. Prime Minister Neville Chamberlain's 'Peace in our Time' was now being seen as diplomatic optimism while behind the scenes preparations were being hurriedly put in place should the worst happen. At the end of August territorials of the Manx Regiment embarked on the *Fenella* for Liverpool. On 2nd September the *Mona's Queen* blew a long and sad farewell as she left Douglas to join nine other of her sister ships commandeered as part of the emergency plans by the War Office. The Manx Grand Prix races had been abandoned. Then, on the morning of Sunday, 3rd September came the Prime Minister's announcement on the wireless that 'Britain was at war with Germany.' People heard the news at home, in churches and chapels, or in hotels and boarding houses. That night the town was ablaze with light for the last time as the blackout restrictions were introduced. The promenade illuminations were switched off and the 652 electric street lamps and 178 gas lamps would not be used again until after the war.

Drapers' shops were well stocked with heavy cotton blackout curtain material and there was great activity as people hurriedly endeavoured to sew their curtains. Shutters, unused for many years, were found to be an excellent way of blacking out light from rooms. Shopkeepers had to cover the backs of their windows and ensure no light came onto the street when the entrance doors were opened. The transformation was completed in a remarkably short time and the total darkness was a weird experience to which was added a certain amount of excitement. There was much singing and laughter as people bumped into each other, especially those still on holiday. During the week there was a rush to buy electric torches which had to be dimmed to emit only a narrow shaft of light. As the dark winter nights approached the blackout restrictions were rigorously enforced by Wardens empowered to report offenders. The Wardens were men of the Loyal Manx Association who worked with the police throughout the war. A £5 fine and names reported in the newspapers were an extra deterrent.

Following in the steps of the U.K. Government, Tynwald, beginning in 1937, devoted considerable time to enacting a series of Orders covering Air Raid Precautions, Civil Defence and National Service. The Spanish Civil War had demonstrated the horrors of bombardment from the air, and while few believed the Island would suffer such an attack, the matter was taken seriously. Chief Constable J.W. Young was appointed Chief Air Raids Precautions Controller for the Isle of Man. In March, 1938, the Mayor, Councillor W.C. Craine, appealed through the newspapers for citizens of the town (men, over 30, and women) to come forward for training as A.R.P. personnel. Heavily involved were the police, the St. John Ambulance Brigade and the I.O.M. Red Cross Society. First Aid Posts were set up and equipped with stretchers and medical equipment; vans were made ready to act as ambulances and the Masonic Temple prepared as an emergency hospital.

The onset of war gave greater urgency to all the preparations though it would be well into 1940 before all the items of equipment required were in position. Early in 1940 the Chief Constable expressed his concern about the lack of air raid shelters in the town, especially in the busy shopping area of Strand Street. The Council responded by erecting three shelters in the Loch Promenade sunken gardens - opposite Regent Street, Howard Street and Granville Street. Built to the design of the Borough Engineer they were made of concrete with roofs reinforced by railway lines. Additionally a shelter was constructed under the Villa Marina Colonnade at the main exit from the Gardens. Each of the shelters could accommodate 200 people. The Town Hall cellar was also designated an official Public Shelter as were the York Road bus depot, the Villa Marina toilets and certain cellars under hotels and shops. Further shelters were provided beside Noble's Hall and on Shaw's Brow. Schools were to make their own arrangements and where satisfactory shelter was not available children were to be sent home or to the house of a nearby relative or friend. Expenses were borne by Government who also issued to households literature dealing with air raids and civil defence.

The War Emergency Committee set up by the Government in August, 1939, became the War Committee of Tynwald the following year, under the Island's wartime Governor Vice Admiral The Earl Granville, whose wife Lady Margaret Rose Bowes-Lyon, was the younger sister of Queen Elizabeth, now the Queen Mother. The Committee had executive powers and amongst their many concerns was the state of

With the 41st and 42nd Batteries already in England, volunteers were hastily recruited for the 129th Battery, thus completing the formation of the Manx Regiment (Royal Artillery). Here members of the new battery are seen marching to Howstrake Holiday Camp for final mustering before leaving the Island in October, 1939. Many of this ill-fated Battery were taken prisoner in Crete during May, 1942.

fire brigades throughout the Island. Their deliberations resulted in the Local Government (Fires) Act which became law in February, 1940. Seven Fire Authority Areas were created, Douglas being designated No 1 area which included Onchan, Braddan and Santon. The same year an Auxiliary Fire Service was formed to support the fire brigades. Volunteers were called for and 140 men underwent training by the Brigade staff, the Barrack Street Mission Hall being used for this purpose. Equipment was very limited to begin with and was dispersed among the twelve Fire Posts set up within the area. It would not be until May, 1942, that the necessary additional trailer pumps and vehicles arrived. Fire watching was put on a compulsory basis throughout the town and the post on top of the Douglas High School at St. Ninian's was linked by telephone to the Fire Headquarters in the Town Hall. The Lord Street Car Park was the site for practical training where a tower was built. Here also was one of the static water tanks placed in various parts of the town. The tanks were an emergency supply for the trailer pumps.

In November, 1940, gas masks were issued from Victoria Street Methodist Church schoolroom. Whilst the carrying of the gas masks was not taken very seriously, all children were required to take them to school in a cardboard box slung over a shoulder, a habit which would last for the next two years. As part of the precautions Decontamination Centres were set up, one of them being Noble's Baths, the method being to hose down casualties with water.

In January 1941 the Borough set up its own War Emergency Committee to supervise all A.R.P. work in its area with the Town Clerk appointed as Controller. The Town Hall became its headquarters and Wellington Hall was used for stores. From here 225 stirrup pumps were distributed to street parties trained in their use. Also buckets and 162 tons of sand were distributed throughout the town. The wailing sirens gave notice of frequent practices to ensure that the civil defence arrangements worked smoothly. However, these practices were abandoned when the Chief Constable discovered that there were many who were taking little notice of them! In future the sirens would only sound when danger threatened.

The Luftwaffe, after failing to destroy the R.A.F. fighter squadrons during the summer of 1940, turned to the safety of the night skies and during the winters of 1940 and 1941 no city was safe from the effects of the Blitz. Liverpool, Belfast and Glasgow were frequently attacked which brought the war a little closer to the Isle of Man. Fighters based at R.A.F. Jurby were part of the defence of the North West and were frequently called upon. The sirens would sound and the civil defence and rescue services would take up their positions. Daylight alerts were usually of short duration as an enemy aircraft passed high overhead while reporting on shipping in the Irish Sea. On moonlight nights the drone of bombers could be heard as they passed overhead on their way to Belfast. On the nights of 20th and 21st December, 1940 there were two alerts each lasting five hours when Liverpool and Manchester were being heavily attacked. It was a sobering experience to stand on the promenade and feel the vibration underfoot from the heavy bombardment taking place, and to see the fiery glow reflected in the distant sky. The docks had been heavily attacked and later that week the *Victoria* was mined as it left Liverpool. Those on board survived as did the ship but it was enough to make the Steam Packet Company move their mainland port to Fleetwood for the remainder of the war. A single sailing a day meant that newspapers and mail only arrived on the Island every other day.

The first enemy bomb to fall on the Isle of Man was on the night of 18th September, 1940, when high explosive bombs caused four large craters in the Dalby area though without damage or injury. Such cases were the result of a Heinkel or Dornier either being lost or being chased by one of the R.A.F. night fighters. On the nights of 7th, 15th and 16th April, 1941, enemy bombers were again over the Island. On the first occasion the sky was illuminated by flares and an incendiary bomb landed near Port Soderick. On the 15th an h.e. bomb caused damage to the Cronk Ruagh Sanatorium near Ramsey and the following night a bomb fell near the radar station at Scarlett in the south of the Island. The following month considerable alarm was caused when two bombs fell on the outskirts of Douglas on the night of 8/9th May. The sirens had given warning and aircraft could be heard overhead. It was then that the first of two jettisoned bombs exploded in a field at Ballaoates Farm and the small bungalow on Ballaoates corner had its roof blown off and windows smashed. Within seconds the other bomb exploded in a field above

A wartime Civic Sunday. The mace-bearer leads Mayor Councillor John C. Faragher J.P. and fellow Councillors to Rosemount Methodist Church on 17th November, 1940. On the Mayor's right is ex-Mayor Councillor Walter C. Craine J.P., M.H.K. followed by future Mayor Councillor Stephen Quirk.

Willaston Corner. Houses were shaken along Ballanard Road and windows smashed as far away as Park Avenue and Norwood Drive. The air raid sirens sounded a total of 43 alerts, 32 of them in 1942, but fortunately there were no casualties.

Through the National Service Act conscription was introduced when war was announced, men in the 20 to 22 year age group being first to be called up followed by a succession of year groups as the months went by. In 1939 the Town Hall employed over 450, mostly men, in the various departments including the Borough Engineer and Surveyor's office and the Treasury, Electricity, Water and Transport Departments. As a local authority, the Corporation was entitled to retain certain staff in what were called 'reserved occupations.' However, it was decided that the Borough could operate on a greatly reduced staff relying on those who were over 40 and those who failed the medical test. Thus all the functions of the Town Hall continued as normal though strict economies were introduced and it was even possible to reduce the Borough Rate, thus helping to compensate for a general rise in the cost of living. As the men of the town received their call-up papers the women also responded, some joining the 10th (Isle of Man) Company of the Auxiliary Territorial Service - the A.T.S. Others enlisted in the Women's Royal Naval Service (W.R.N.S.) and the Women's Auxiliary Air Force (W.A.A.F.).

THE HOME GUARD

As the Germans circumvented the 'impregnable' Maginot Line by way of the Low Countries and drove into France in May, 1940 a call was made to all able-bodied men at home to join the Local Defence Volunteers. Those with First World War experience came forward to help organise the volunteers who, after a day's work, turned up for training, equipping themselves as best as they could with shotguns, .22 rifles and even broom handles! To some, L.D.V. meant 'Look, Duck and Vanish'! But as the German invasion fleet massed in the French ports after the Dunkirk evac-

uation and the Battle of Britain was raging, Winston Churchill gave his famous rallying speeches to prepare for the worst. On 28th July it was announced that the L.D.V. was to be renamed the 'Home Guard' and brought to a higher degree of preparedness. The Isle of Man would form two battalions, the 1st Battalion based in Douglas and responsible for the eastern sector of the Island. Deemster Sydney J. Kneale was made Lt. Colonel of the 1st Battalion with Mr R.T. Wetherill as Adjutant. Mr G. W. Howie of the Knockaloe Experimental Farm was placed in charge of the 2nd Battalion responsible for the rest of the Island. Men came forward in their hundreds, men who were too old for the Armed Forces or who had failed their medicals on call up. But most of the men were in reserved occupations and had been prevented from enlisting because of their value to the war effort at home, such as men involved in food production, transport and the medical services. Many were skilled tradesmen who were detained by the War Office to maintain the many commandeered properties within the town. The 1st Battalion, with its Headquarters at the Tromode Drill Hall, was divided into companies with 'B' Company containing the men from Onchan. 'D' Company consisted of men employed by the railway and bus companies. Ballakermeen High Schools were used as a centre for signals and communication training while the Old Drill Hall of 1896, next to the Brown Bobby on Peel Road and in use as the Wool Centre, was used for simulated gas practice.

Training was on a regular basis with these part-time soldiers expected to emulate the regular army. Chief Petty Officers from H.M.S. St. George, the Royal Navy training ship housed at Cunningham's Camp, gave basic training in drill, bayonet practice, and lectures on map reading, moving under cover and the use of camouflage. The first 'official' rifles came from the Douglas Police Station where they had been stored since the First World War! Then a supply of Ross rifles from Canada was received which had been stored in grease and took many hours to clean. These were eventually replaced by the modern Lee Enfields and practice firing took place at Ballnahow, Santon. American Browning

Douglas men who were commissioned into the 1st Battalion (Manx) Home Guard following its formation in July, 1940. Many are wearing ribbons of First World War medals. Those that can be identified are as follows: Back row, left to right - G.H. Corlett, jeweller; - ; - ; G.E. Moore, advocate and wearing R.A.F. uniform; Mr Leeming, Corlett, Sons and Cowley; Percy Shimmin, Town Clerk; - ; Leonard Holroyd, Isle of Man Bank; Ramsey B. Moore, H.M. Attorney General.
Front row, - ; Alfred Corlett, Norwich Union Insurance; Harold Cain, future M.H.K.; James M. Cain, Ocean Insurance, appointed Major in command of 'A' Company; James Caine, draper; Stanley Keig, photographer; T.C. Greenfield, Water Engineer; B.J. Pendlebury, Douglas High School for Boys and Louis Meyer, Meyer Box Company.

machine guns were also received and fired on the butts at Langness. Special pens were built on Douglas Head and used for practice throwing of grenades.

To make training realistic Home Guard units observed the manoeuvres of the infantry Officer Cadet Training Unit based at the Villiers Hotel. Some of the men from 'B' Company attended a night exercise when a simulated river crossing was being made on the Kionslieu Dam, below the Eairy Dam. Live ammunition was being used - machine guns opened up, tracer bullets criss-crossed the dam and the night sky was lit up by flares. Then something went badly wrong as one of the dinghies making the crossing was blown sky-high as a result of one of the parachute flares landing on the dinghy and detonating the live ammunition on board. It was an horrific experience with six cadets losing their lives. The 'B' Company men were rushed back by lorry to the Drill Hall and were sworn to secrecy by an officer from the O.C.T.U.

These were the dark days of the war and while there were many stories worthy of television's 'Dad's Army' the matters in hand were taken most seriously. Regular training brought proficiency so the men were able to undertake a variety of duties with confidence. They had to be prepared for a coastal landing or one by enemy parachutists; then there was the possibility of saboteurs, spies, escaped prisoners and internees. The most important duty was the guarding of strategic points and installations. The men were required to undertake guard duties one night in six at various points covering Douglas and the Eastern sector. Coastguard points were set up stretching from Banks Howe in Onchan to the Marine Drive, Port Soderick and Port Grenaugh. Inland was covered by a series of observation points and road blocks made of sandbags were positioned on all the main roads on the approaches to Douglas. Guard was also mounted at vital points such as the Onchan reservoirs and the G.P.O. telephone station above Creg ny Baa. In town the Telephone Exchange in Dalton Street, the Power Stations and the petrol installations around the harbour were considerred to be particularly vital.

SHORTAGES

As everything became geared to the war effort, and with heavy shipping losses in the Atlantic, shortages became inevitable and the drive for salvage began. The Town Hall, through the Borough Engineer and

Surveyor, organised collections within Douglas. Paper was first called for with children in the elementary and secondary schools being called upon to play their part. The dust-bin wagons were part of the operation and, amongst other things, collected bones which were taken to Litt's in East Baldwin to be turned into bone-grease and glycerine. Scrap metal was also vital and the town was scoured for iron (including inessential garden gates and railings), lead, zinc, copper, brass, tin and aluminium - the latter to help in aircraft production. Hundreds of tons were dumped in the Lord Street Car Park ready for shipment. Records indicate that a total of nearly a thousand tons of paper was collected, together with 54 tons of bones, 74 tons of tin, 10 tons of rubber and 12 tons of textiles. Petrol was severely rationed for private cars, many of which were laid up 'for the duration.' St John's Woollen Mills produced khaki and grey wool for the ladies of the town who spent endless hours knitting such garments as scarves, balaclava helmets and gloves. These were collected by the Red Cross and made up into 'comfort' parcels with chocolate and cigarettes for the troops.

Everyone was affected by food shortages and in November, 1940, rationing was introduced. It was organised by the Government Food Control Office with local authorities issuing the ration books. These permitted the holder to receive a weekly supply of 2 ounces of butter, margarine, lard, bacon and tea, and 4 ounces of sugar. Butter was served from a barrel and sugar weighed into heavy blue paper bags. Chocolate and sweets were also rationed so children had a difficult choice to make. A bar of Cadbury's blended chocolate and a piece of liquorice or cough stick was a typical weekly ration. Other items of food were put on points which could be used for jam, syrup, biscuits, and dried fruit. Tinned foods, once frowned upon, were now considered a Godsend. Imported fruits such as oranges and bananas disappeared completely. Housewifes took great care in planning their weekly visit to the grocer's but shopping was on a much more personal level and grocers got to know the needs of each family, pointing out what items they had available. Ration books were marked and points cut out. As part of the wartime community spirit there was a great deal of swopping with one family's surplus being exchanged to help another's shortage. The system worked well. Meat was also rationed with weekly allowances of fresh meat being reduced from 2 shillings to 10 (old) pence per person. Here again, the family butcher was very

Douglas men of 'B' Company photographed at Tromode Drill Hall. Seated centre, with gaiters, is Company Commander Major Dawson Quilliam. (via Barry Quilliam)

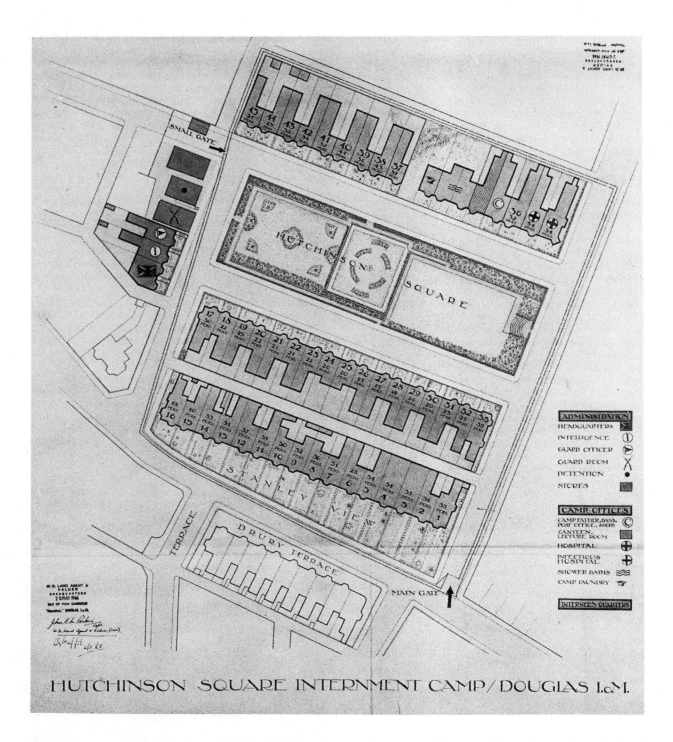

HUTCHINSON SQUARE INTERNMENT CAMP / DOUGLAS I.oM.

helpful ensuring fair shares of the unrationed offal and sausages. Local rabbit became a welcome addition at many a table. Fish was plentiful and 'spuds and herring' came back into their own. Eggs were also fairly plentiful.

Households were encouraged to 'Dig for Victory' to help overcome a general shortage of vegetables. Thus gardens were turned over and great pride was taken in providing for family wants. Ballaughton Nurseries were used for vegetables and the Corporation provided 53 allotments on the Ballakermeen Estate and a further 18 at Pulrose. These were rented out for 10 shillings a year. Mr G.W. Howie, the Island's Agricultural Organiser, was making great efforts to bring every available acre of land under cultivation for increasing corn, potato and green crops. When he turned his attention to Pulrose Golf Links the suggestion was that it be

given over to sheep grazing and a quarter of the area put under the plough and returned to productive cropping. When the Board of Agriculture persisted in their demands the Corporation took the matter to Appeal. In the end the Governor ordered that seven acres of the better land near Kewaigue be ploughed over. This happened in the spring of 1942. Cocksfoot grass seed for hay crops was normally supplied from Norway but now that that country was in Nazi hands an appeal was made, through the schools, for children to collect seed from cocksfoot grass growing on waste ground and by the roadsides. The appeal was supported by the Corporation cropping all its own land when the seed had set. Children also picked huge quantities of blackberries on half-day holidays during the autumn term. The blackberries were used at the Rushen Abbey jam factory to eke out supplies.

VISITORS OF A DIFFERENT KIND

For the summer of 1940 the Corporation engaged Phil Richardson and his band for a seventh time at the Villa Marina in the hope that there would be some sort of summer season. But there was only a trickle of visitors, a trickle which would continue throughout the war for those intent on a brief respite from the bombed cities and long hours in the munition factories. There were also about 800 children sent as evacuees. It could well be that the boarding house keepers would be in the same predicament they endured in the First World War. But the situation in the spring of 1940 ensured otherwise. As the threat of invasion grew following the evacuation from Dunkirk, there was frenzied activity to round up and detain all those of German origin who were thought to be a risk to national security. The net was thrown far and wide in a controversial exercise which saw pro-Fascists mixed with those who had been welcomed in their escape from Nazi Germany. June, 1940, saw the lists grow longer as Italy joined Germany as the common enemy. While Canada and Australia accepted a limited number, the British Home Office searched elsewhere. The Isle of Man, detached from the British mainland, was an ideal place and the Defence Regulations (I.O.M.) Act was quickly put in place.

The middle of May saw blocks of boarding houses being ringed with barbed wire fencing to form internment camps in Douglas, Onchan, Ramsey and Peel. The Steam Packet ships *Snaefell, Rushen Castle* and *Victoria* worked overtime to bring in the internees by the hundred and by the thousand. To the landladies it was a guarantee that their rents and rates would be paid, and that there would be compensation for damage. But it was a traumatic experience to be given just seven days notice to vacate the boarding houses, find alternative accommodation and sort out a small allowance of furniture, bedding and personal possessions. Everything else, the hundred and one items required to run a boarding house, had to be left behind. These were listed by a Government valuer and a small quarterly payment made as rental for their 'use by His Majesty's Government'. Carpets and all floor coverings were removed for storage at Derby Castle. Smaller houses behind the seafront, which normally took visitors, were used as billets for the soldiers sent to guard the camps.

The first Douglas camp to receive an intake of internees was Central Camp in mid-June. The camp was made up of 34 houses on and behind Central Promenade and by the end of the month contained 2,000 men. Next to open was the Palace Camp made up of 28 of the larger boarding houses, and which by the end of the month was filled to capacity with over 2,900 men. Overlooking the camp was the Falcon Cliff Hotel which was turned into a hospital for all internees. July saw the first Italian internees arrive, these being housed in the Metropole and Hutchinson Square Camps. Other camps made ready later in the year were the Granville, Regent, Sefton and Falcon Camps, the latter being above the Palace Camp. Only two of these smaller camps were actually used - Granville until October, 1941 and Sefton until March, 1941. During 1940 the male internees held in all camps on the Island reached a maximum of just over 10,000, to which must be added 4,000 women who were accommodated in Port Erin.

As the threat of invasion subsided, the Home Office instituted a more thorough screening of those interned. Those deemed to be true enemy aliens - the 'A' catagory - would remain until the end of the war, but many in categories B and C were 'repatriated' and even played their part in the war effort. The process was slow and the cause of considerable unrest in the camps. To outsiders looking in the internees were a source of curiosity but behind the wire Camp Commanders allowed appointed leaders considerable freedom to organise the daily routine and occupational activities. The internees were well fed with meat provided on five days a week and fish on two. Derby Castle became the centre for romantic reunions between men and their interned wives from Port Erin.

As numbers dropped, reorganisation took place which saw all detained Italians housed in Metropole and Palace Camps. The latter saw clashes between Fascists and anti-Fascists while December saw different nationalities arrive as the war spread. There were over 500 of these including Japanese, Hungarians, Romanians and a large number of Finns who were mainly merchant seamen. Throughout 1942 the numbers dwindled as a result of releases and transfers and by November the Palace Camp was finally closed. Metropole also saw numbers drop following the collapse of Fascism in Italy, but it would not be until October, 1944 that the last of the Italians left, being transferred to Ramsey. Throughout 1943 and 1944 many of the internees opted to undertake work on the farms as a relief from the camp boredom. At first they were accompanied by guards but later they were collected from the camp and established friendly relationships with the farmers' families.

Hutchinson Camp was in many ways an ideal camp made up of a quadrangle around the central gardens and away from the public gaze. Its population was made up of Germans and Jews many of whom were highly intellectual and well educated. They were the ones who felt the restrictions most irksome. Not for

A group of internees inside the Hutchinson Camp. (Manx National Heritage)

A guard on duty at the Palace Internment Camp. (Manx National Heritage)

Giovanni (John) Moneta's wartime oil-painting of Douglas as seen from his room at the Metropole Internment Camp. On the right can also be seen part of the Palace Camp

them sitting around sunning themselves when possible and playing cards. There were scientists, medical consultants, writers, artists and musicians. They organised themselves and gave lectures, art and sculpture exhibitions, and concerts. Perhaps most famous among their number were the famous piano duettists Rawicz and Landauer. Here also was developed a wide variety of crafts from tailoring and carpentry to watch mending. They were encouraged to make articles for sale in a shop specially provided in the Villa Marina Arcade. Here could be found many beautiful things such as handbags, model boats and jewellery. These craftsmen could work wonders with the leg of a chair or a piece of floorboard or curtain material. Under guard, the internees were taken for walks along the promenades and attended special matinees at a cinema or a play at the Gaiety Theatre. By March, 1944 only 228 inmates were left in Hutchinson, mostly of the 'A' category. These were transferred to Peel and Hutchinson Camp was closed. As the internment camps were emptied most of them were transferred from the jurisdiction of the Home Office to the War Office and put to alternative use.

In 1940 the War Office commandeered the Villiers Hotel as the base for 166 Officer Cadet Training Unit. Additional accommodation was found in the adjoining hotels, Walpole Avenue and in Peel Road. Full board and lodging were provided though this was later changed with the arrival of A.T.S. cooks which supplied more realistic Army rations. The Falcon Hotel was taken over as the Officers' Mess. Lord Street Car Park was used for the parking of military vehicles including Bren gun carriers. Each intake of cadets underwent a rigorous 17-week course of infantry training where physical fitness and qualities of leadership were developed. The culmination of each course was a Battle Week spent in remote parts of the Island, the highlight of which was a 'river crossing' of Kionslieu Dam. Real ammunition was used with flares and charges to represent enemy shells. A stiff examination decided which cadets would be commissioned and the passing-out parades and presentation of a belt of honour became a popular spectacle in the town. There were inevitably casualties during the training and the Hotel Majestic in Onchan was commandeered and converted into a fully-equipped Medical Hospital for the Royal Army Medical Corps. (One of the surgeons was Major

Bob Lamming who remained after the war to work at Noble's Hospital). Altogether a total of 4,000 cadets were awarded commissions and went on to play a distinguished part in many regiments of the Army. Over a thousand further officers were trained for the Royal Navy, Royal Marines and the R.A.F. Regiment.

The R.A.F. Regiment was formed in 1942 for the specific purpose of defending airfields. Its Headquarters was the Empress Hotel which had already been taken over in March, 1940 as Headquarters of No 1 Ground Defence Gunnery School based at Ronaldsway. In March, 1943 the Gunnery School was absorbed into the R.A.F. Regiment, thus leaving Ronaldsway available for the Admiralty to develop the aerodrome into a major training establishment for the Fleet Air Arm, known as *H.M.S. Urley.* The vacant Central Internment Camp was now filled with intakes of Air Force personnel for their training period. The Corporation made available part of the Villa Marina grounds, close to the Broadway entrance. Here was built a large black concrete dome which housed a Bofors anti-aircraft gun which could be trained at 'targets' projected on to the roof of the dome. Also at the end of 1942, the Palace Camp became the signals school for the Royal Corps of Signals.

The Granville Camp (stretching from Granville Street to Regent Street) was taken over by the Royal Navy to provide accommodation for ratings who would undergo tuition at No 1 Radar Training School which was ideally positioned on Douglas Head. The 'hush-hush' training base had been built and equipped at an estimated cost of £3 million and the whole area bristled with masts and radar scanners. The Douglas Head Hotel was divided into classrooms each equipped with radar sets, as was Collinson's Cafe and even the ticket office at the top of the incline railway. A new three-storeyed concrete block containing 18 classrooms was also constructed, the building now being the home of Manx Radio. The station was commissioned in July, 1941 as *H.M.S. Valkyrie* and continued its work until the end of the war during which time some 30,000 radar operators were trained for service in the Royal Navy from battleships to submarines. Occasionally the Steam Packet's *Manxman* took part in the training but more noticeable was the Chesapeake aircraft based at R.A.F. Andreas. With almost monotonous regularity it howled across the bay as it dived on Douglas Head to provide a 'target' for the trainee radar operators.

H.M.S. ST GEORGE

During the summer of 1939 Cunningham's Holiday Camp had enjoyed another busy season and no doubt would have closed as the last campers left in September. But it was to remain open for the entire war period as plans were announced of making the Camp a training school for young sailors of the Royal Navy. By the end of August the first of the town's wartime residents had arrived - the advance guard of officers to plan the lay-out and training of the school. Dressed in their smart uniforms the officers caused quite a stir and the local girls regarded them with considerable interest.

The Admiralty had decided that, in the event of war, their Boys Training Establishments should be moved to a safer location and away from air attack. Thus the seaman boys training ships such as *H.M.S. Ganges, St. Vincent* and *Exmouth* were all brought together in Douglas in what became known as *H.M.S. St. George*. Nautical terminology was applied so the boys lived 'aboard ship' and when they visited Douglas they 'went ashore'. The Camp was divided into two sections - an upper part and a lower part separated by the tunnel going under Victoria Road. To get from one part to the other meant passing through the palm court with marble pool and fountains. This became known as the 'quarterdeck' which had to be crossed at the double by the boys, while officers had to salute as they walked through.

The first arrivals in September had the usual Camp waitress service for a short while until the kitchens were taken over for the usual navy type messing. Boys slept in the chalets - usually four to a cabin. These were found to be decidedly cold in winter until heat was installed. So many boys arrived at first that some had to be accommodated at Howstrake Holiday Camp. All the boys had entered as 'Continuous Seaman Boys' having chosen the Navy as a career and signing on for 12 years. The first six weeks were spent in teaching basic seamanship - knots, splices, boat pulling and sailing etc. After this initial period the boys were divided into ordinary seaman and communication branches. The latter had Boy Telegraphists, known as 'sparkers' and Boy Signallers, known as 'bunting tossers'. The practical side of all instruction was taken by regular naval officers and the theoretical side by schoolmasters.

Ballakermeen High School had been completed in 1938 and was to be part of the Island's innovative 'multi-lateral' system of education where all children of secondary school age were to be educated together. It was due to open in September, 1939, but its classrooms were taken over and its first pupils were the boys of *H.M.S. St. George*. The boys were mustered in the Post Office building in Linden Grove and marched to Ballakermeen. The well-trodden route was via Duke's Road, St. Ninian's Road, Somerset Road, Selbourne Drive and Westminster Drive - a distance of nearly two miles which had to be walked in all sorts of weather. During the summer months the classes were held on mornings and afternoons; in winter this was changed to mornings and nights to allow the afternoons for sports activities.

Tha academic ability of the boys aged 15-16 varied, some having already passed their School Certificate (G.C.E.). Lessons were given in such subjects as Mathematics; Magnetism, Electricity and Navigation; Further Electricity; Naval History and English. The Communication course lasted a year before the pupils sat the examinations. Those who were keen were able to see action before they were 18 years old. They were usually drafted to the larger ships - battleships, cruisers and aircraft carriers. Unfortunately many lost their lives in the early years of the war on such ships as *H.M.S. Repulse, Prince of Wales* and *Hood*.

The boys lived under strict discipline according to the Boy Seaman's Book of Rules. All orders had to be obeyed immediately and without question. Failure meant severe punishment. All had to be clean, tidy and properly dressed at all times. Smoking was forbidden as was alcohol; pubs in the town were out of bounds. A maximum of half a crown (12.5p) pocket money was allowed when going ashore. Bad language, quarrelling or fighting were strictly forbidden, as was entering a tattoo parlour ashore. Captain Bell was noted as a stickler for discipline. He had commanded *H.M.S Exeter* which, together with the cruisers *Ajax* and *Achilles* had successfully chased the German pocket battleship *Graf Spee* into Montevideo where it destroyed itself in 1940. Less severe was Captain Poland who had spent most of his time on destroyers and was a popular Captain at St. George. Gradually, the discipline was relaxed to that of a well-behaved senior school.

The boys pay was about five shillings (25p) a week and they were allowed three free afternoons a fortnight when they could spend one of their shillings. This usually went on a herbal beer (2d), a visit to a cinema (4d) leaving sixpence for a feed of egg and chips at the Salvation Army canteen. Sunday afternoon 'leave' was looked forward to as there was a tea dance in Derby Castle and they could walk their girlfriends through Groudle Glen. Such liaisons had interesting sequels. As the boys were being returned from Ballakermeen on dark nights (with lights to the front and rear, and a drummer keeping all in step) there could be seen the

A rather poor wartime photograph showing the entrance gate to H.M.S. Valkyrie. Across the roadway can be seen one of the air raid shelters built in the sunken gardens along the landward wall. (Manx National Heritage)

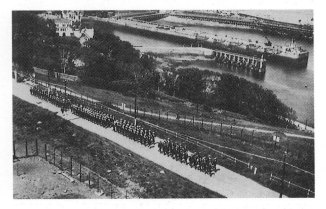

Naval ratings of H.M.S. Valkyrie on their way to the Radar School on Douglas Head. Here were trained the radar operators found in all ships of the Royal Navy. (Manx National Heritage)

The Douglas Head Hotel, with its ancient watch tower, is seen here bristling with radar masts. (Manx National Heritage)

One of the many Nissen huts found on Douglas Head as part of the Radar School. A concrete block of classrooms was also built which today houses Manx Radio. (Manx National Heritage)

flicker of a cigarette, the sound of drinking from bottles and the smell of chips. It was, of course, the girlfriends responding to the requests of their 'jacks'!

Inside the camp the boys had a cinema show every Sunday night and there were concerts given by outsiders. But the end of each term saw a special concert given by the talented boys and staff, not forgetting the W.R.N.S. Full use was made of the Camp's sports facilities with regular soccer and cricket matches between the boys and staff; one of the great events was the annual sports with boys and all staff participating. There was great rivalry between the teams (divisions). Use was also made of the small swimming pool. There were practices for special parades for such occasions as St. George's Day and Nelson's Day, and especially Tynwald Day at St. John's.

After over six years H.M.S. St. George was finally disbanded at the end of 1945. It had trained over 8,677 seaman boys in the classrooms of Ballakermeen who went on to play their part in the great wartime fleet of the Royal Navy. Some of the commissioned staff remained on the Island which had become home to them. One such was Sub Lieutenant Jack Gair who became a master at Ballakermeen and headmaster of various local primary schools. But the town's long association with *H.M.S. St. George* will long be remembered with affection.

Hotels and boarding houses just about the whole length of the promenades were put to some sort of wartime use. Sundays and off-duty evenings saw the town thronged with men and women in all sorts of uniform, with a preponderance of Navy blue including French and Dutch. Saturday nights saw trainloads arriving from Jurby, Andreas and Castletown. They were made most welcome and there was plenty of entertainments arranged. The 'chippies' did good trade though fat shortages meant on occasions 'no frying

H.M.S. St. George was based at Cunningham's Holiday Camp throughout the war. In true Navy fashion the 'ship' had to have a quarterdeck. The palm court with marble fountains at the Victoria Road entrance was adopted for this purpose. Officers passing through had to acknowledge the quarterdeck by saluting.

Seaman Boys of H.M.S. St. George passing the saluting dais in the grounds of Cunningham's Camp whose facilities were used throughout the war. (Manx National Heritage)

A high ranking W.A.A.F. officer addresses guests at a passing out parade in the Glencrutchery field. Listening intently is Alderman Francis Gale, Mayor of Douglas from 1941 to 1943. (Manx National Heritage)

tonight'. The pubs and hotels supplied the local brews but whisky was not always available, most of it being exported to America to help pay for the war effort. While there seemed to be plenty of tobacco, cigarettes were in short supply. Regular local customers had to rely on 'under the counter' supplies. The ladies of the town 'manned' the canteens of the Y.M.C.A. above Burton's in Victoria Street and the Salvation Army in Strand Street. To many the Walpole run by Mr and Mrs Cave and their two daughters in Walpole Avenue was 'home for home' to many a serviceman. The large boarding house provided overnight accommodation for those from the out-of-town stations or those leaving on the morning boat. There were several cinemas open - the Royalty, Regal, Picture House and Strand. Visiting concert parties appeared from time to time while other concert parties were organised by service personnel and local residents. During his stay at *H.M.S. Valkyrie* Sub Lieutenant Jon Pertwee, who had survived the sinking of *H.M.S. Hood*, joined forces with the Manx Amateur Dramatic Society from which emerged the Service Players. Performances at the Gaiety Theatre were played to packed houses. Navy concerts were occasionally presented in the Palace and the Villa Marina was opened for special occasions. It would be packed for dancing on New Year's Eve. But by far the most popular venue for dancing was the Palais de Danse in Strand Street. This was an elegant and beautifully furnished dance hall and had been, since its inception, a meeting place for local young people, and some not so young. It was not licensed for liquor but had a cafe; it was a most respectable and delightful place. It remained open throughout the war years and was well patronised by members of the forces each night of the week. Saturdays saw it packed with locals and service men and women. As well as this, special dances were organised; these were late dances, finishing at one or two am. They were wonderful glittering occasions, in contrast with the wartime drabness and shortages.

As the war progressed in the Allies' favour the Home Guard was disbanded following a Stand Down Parade in the Villa Marina on 3rd December, 1944. Over a thousand men from the 1st and 2nd Battalions (Manx) Home Guard from all over the Island assembled in the Lord Street Car Park. Led by the Band of the Royal Naval School of Music based at the Howstrake Holiday Camp, Onchan, the men in company formation marched along the Loch Promenade where His Excellency the Earl Granville took the salute, from the War Memorial in his uniform of a Vice Admiral. The Guard of Honour was made up of men from all over the Island in charge of Major Dawson Quilliam, officer commanding 'B' Company, 1st Battalion. Major Quilliam had served with the Coldstream Guards in the First World War. Assembled in the Villa Marina, a short service was led by Archdeacon C.V. Stockwood. The singing of 'Guide me, O Thou great Jehovah' was most moving, with the second verse sung unaccompanied. Earl Granville expressed the appreciation of all for the many hours the men had given to training and carrying out their duties. He was also full of praise for the high standards that had been achieved since the L.D.V had been formed over four years ago. Then armed with little more than 'patriotic spirit' the Home Guard had become a well-trained, well-armed and efficient military force. He thanked especially those from *H.M.S. St. George* and the O.C.T.U. for their valuable assistance in training.

A grim reminder of the battles being fought out on the Continent was brought home with the arrival of the first prisoners of war towards the end of 1944. The War Office had already made plans and three empty internment camps - Hutchinson, Metropole and Onchan - were made ready for these new arrivals. The War Office had its own methods and provided all the basic furniture. This meant that the boarding houses concerned had to be emptied so there was a mammoth removal job as the Derby Castle and Theatre were filled with thousands of chairs, tables, beds and wardrobes. Parkfield, opposite St. Ninian's Church, had earlier been made secure for the accommodation of high ranking Wehmarcht officers.

The piers were closed as each batch of prisoners arrived, bringing with them their guards, mostly men of the Pioneer Corps who would be billeted in the town. The prisoners, with no belongings of their own apart from their bedraggled Wehmarcht and Luftwaffe uniforms, were marched along the promenade to the camps. Their numbers increased rapidly until a total of nearly 2,500 was reached. Realising the inevitable conclusion of the war, many of the prisoners were happy to replace the Italian internees on the farms, desperate for labour. They were allowed out in groups of 12 with a guard, this time armed with a Sten gun. On the farms they were under the control of a German sergeant. The squads brought their own food - often raw herring - and the farmer and his staff were forbidden to fraternise as with the Italians, or offer them food or cigarettes.

VICTORY CELEBRATIONS

Prime Minister Winston Churchill's 'Victory in Europe' broadcast was heard by all on the afternoon of Tuesday, 8th May; even the Manx Music Festival in the Villa Marina stopped so everyone could listen. No sooner had the broadcast ended than the air raid sirens sounded the last 'All Clear.' For nearly five minutes they echoed throughout the town and were joined by the ringing of church bells and the sirens and hooters of naval ships in the harbour. This brought out thousands of Navy ratings and their Army and Air Force comrades who crowded into Strand Street with much shouting, singing and dancing. The locals also joined in the merriment and the infectious festive mood. The Town Hall was gaily decorated with flags and bunting, as were Victoria Street, Strand Street, the Promenade and Corporation buses.

Chester Street, one of the poorest quarters in the town, rose to the occasion with the mothers combining to organise a street party and give the children a real 'victory' treat. They had baked cakes and made jellies and the youngsters, most of them with fathers still serving, had a fine party outside under the flags and with the tables decorated with the victory colours of red, white and blue. The kerbstones were painted in similar colours. At night time there were bonfires along the foreshore but the biggest was in front of Noble's Hall. Shopkeepers produced boxes of fireworks and rockets which had been hidden away since 1939. The boisterous evening was also a way of celebrating the lifting of the irksome blackout restrictions.

The VE celebrations culminated on the following Sunday afternoon with a great parade in which 2,000 took part. Headed by a band of 70 from the Royal Naval School of Music the parade left the Pier Arcade Buildings and then through Walpole Avenue onto the promenade. Joining at the end was the parade of civilian services who had assembled in the Lord Street Car Park. Taking the salute was His Excellency opposite the War Memorial, the guard of honour being provided by *H.M.S. St. George* with the bugle band also in attendance. The parade consisted of men from *H.M.S. Valkyrie, St. George* and *Urley* followed by the Wrens,

Army units from the O.C.T.U and Signals Corps, P.O.W. camp guards, A.T.S., R.A.F. Jurby and Andreas, R.A.F. Regiment, Home Guard, Army Cadet Force, Air Training Corps, and all the various civil defence services. The parade assembled in the Villa Marina Gardens to be joined by Members of the Legislature and Town Councillors. There was a short service of thanksgiving during which the Lord Bishop gave an address.

It was then back to normal as everyone turned their attention to the expected long campaign against Japan in the Far East. It was also time to remember those who would not be coming back - those who had been killed in action, were missing presumed killed or had died during the six years. Of the Island's population of 50,829, some 490 had lost their lives; of these 237 were from Douglas and their names would be inscribed around the plinth of the War Memorial. These were made up of 109 from the Army; 49 from the Royal Air Force; 68 from the Royal Navy and Merchant Navy; 6 serving with Overseas Forces and 5 from the Women's services. Throughout the war local newspapers recorded, usually with a photograph, the names of casualties, and those who had been taken prisoner. The majority of 129 Battery of the Manx Regiment had spent nearly four years in captivity following the German onslaught on Crete in May, 1942. The last of them returned to the Island shortly after VE Day. It would be much later in the year before over 40 prisoners held by the Japanese could return.

Adding to the excitement of that summer of 1945 was the visit of His Majesty King George VI and Queen Elizabeth - the first royal visit they had been able to undertake outside Great Britain since the war began. It was a three-day visit starting on Wednesday, 4th July at Victoria Pier where they were greeted by His Excellency and Countess Granville, the latter embracing her sister, the Queen. The first stop of the royal party was the Villa Marina where 4,000 school children were assembled under Mr T.C. Corris, Headmaster of Murray's Road School. There was massed singing of the National Anthems, with music provided by the

Following VE Day a Victory Parade was held on Sunday, 13th May with over 2,000 taking part. The Guard of Honour was provided by a contingent from H.M.S. St. George seen here being inspected by the Island's wartime Governor, His Excellency Vice Admiral The Earl Granville K.C.V.O., C.B., D.S.O. (Manx National Heritage)

R.N.S.M. There was also much cheering and waving of flags as the Mayor, Councillor Stephen Quirk, and members of Douglas Corporation were presented to Their Majesties. The rest of the day was spent on a tour around the Island, stopping at the towns and villages. Thursday was Tynwald Day where record crowds assembled to witness the historic occasion which saw the first King and Queen of England to take their places on Tynwald Hill. In the afternoon Their Majesties inspected a full turn-out of *H.M.S. St. George* on the field above the Camp, adjoining Glencrutchery Road. The following day visits were made to *H.M.S. Valkyrie* where the ships company of 1,800 officers and men were paraded. A vist to the installations on Douglas Head was followed by a parade of the O.C.T.U., witnessed by a crowd of 5,000. The morning was rounded off by a visit to the machine shops of the Dowty engineering works at Castle Hill, where 250 employees were engaged in making hydraulic undercarriages for aircraft. Then it was over the mountain to R.A.F Jurby where a thousand airmen and airwomen from Jurby and Andreas had assembled. A Dakota aircraft left at 3 pm to return Their Majesties to London after a hectic three days.

At midnight on Tuesday, 14th August, Britain's new Prime Minister, Clement Attlee, announced that Japan had finally surrendered. This brought huge crowds on to the promenades as the navy ships fired their guns and lit up the sky with searchlights, rockets and Verey cartridges. Wednesday was a general holiday as people celebrated VJ Day. The example of Chester Street was followed in many parts of the town with streets gaily decorated for neighbourhood parties. At night many of the pubs had to close when supplies ran out, but the

Villa Marina and Palais de Danse were packed with happy dancers. Billy Ternent and his dance orchestra had been engaged for the summer and at midnight the band appeared on the roof of the Colonnade. The band, lit up by the naval searchlights, played the latest tunes and soon the roadway and promenade opposite was packed with dancing couples. There was a repeat the following night as dancers enjoyed the perfect summer weather.

On Sunday a Victory Parade was held with over 2,000 men and women taking part, representing all the military stations on the Island and the local civil defence organisations. The proceedings were similar to the VE Parade with the O.C.T.U. providing the Guard of Honour this time, and music was by the Douglas Brass Band School of Music conducted by Mr Sam Brough. In many ways it was also a Farewell Parade. Shortly, Earl Granville would be leaving the Island to take up his appointment as Governor of Northern Ireland. And as autumn approached the training establishments and camps were closed, one by one. The barbed wire fences, which had stood since 1940, were removed, as were the air raid shelters. The boarding house keepers had the daunting task of returning to their long-vacated homes to inspect the damage and start scrubbing floors etc. Compensation was available and local tradesmen had a boom time in effecting repairs, decorating, upholstering, and french polishing. Gradually the Derby Castle was cleared as a furniture store but despite careful records there was considerable confusion with most houses ending up with a mixture of items from other houses. But the war was over; it was now time to get back to normal and make ready for the 1946 season.

An aerial view of the Villa Marina and Gardens taken during the summer of 1945. Near the Broadway entrance can be seen the black dome used for training members of the R.A.F. Regiment. The marquees in the Villa grounds are thought to be in connection with the Royal Visit in July. (R and L Kelly Collection)

PART THREE : 1945 to 1946
TOWN HALL AFFAIRS

With the ending of the war in 1945 the Island as a whole, and Douglas in particular, found itself in a position very similar to that of 1918. It seemed imperative that 'normal' activities should resume as soon as possible and that, of course, meant the immediate revival of the visiting industry. On the national stage that necessitated the release of the Steam Packet boats by the Admiralty and many and strident were the demands for that. In Douglas there were other equally pressing concerns and perhaps the most important was the release of the promenade houses and those further in the town that had been commandeered for internment and military purposes. Even when released there was a scarcity of materials needed to return the boarding houses back to their pre-war standards.

Nevertheless, the people of the town set to with a will and despite worries about food supplies the holiday atmosphere began to re-appear and by 1947 it could fairly be said that Douglas had re-established itself as a major holiday resort. The Douglas ballrooms were back in full swing; Harry Corris was packing them in at the Gaiety Theatre; the T.T. Races and Bicycle T.T. had been re-started and the promenades were crowded with summer visitors. The summers of 1947, '48 and '49 each recorded over 600,000 summer arrivals, far surpassing pre-war levels. Not all were content with their lot. There were numerous complaints, some no doubt occasioned by the dilapidated state of the houses, but one that has echoed down the years was the cry: "It costs too much to get here to start with!"

As the immediate post-war years progressed new problems emerged. For a while it seemed that the horse trams would be scrapped. A resounding No! from the boarding-house keepers put paid to that; and in 1947 the trams made a profit! There were complaints too about the promenade becoming nothing more than a glorified car park. But there were the old well-known problems too. Many of the improvement schemes abandoned because of the war were taken up once more. The Derby Castle promenade widening scheme was completed; Broadway, Glen Falcon and Derby Roads were widened - all projects revealing a far-sighted appreciation of future needs! Housing, that ever-running wound of the inter-war years, still demanded action. By 1947 Douglas had 110 houses planned or under construction at Spring Valley; there were 750 on the waiting list! The old Fairy Ground cleared away many years earlier remained as a car park and many were the voices raised for houses in that area. Indeed, failing that, a tidal basin was suggested for the site as a way of increasing the size of the harbour. And failing that again, a decent bus station either there or on what later became the site of the Sea Terminal.

But just as housing was a perennial problem so too was unemployment. And as servicemen were demobbed so work seemed to become scarcer. There were plenty of grateful people at the Douglas Soup Dispensary for their bowls of soup and their pieces of bread. Yet things did begin to improve, albeit slowly. A further 550 houses were planned at Willaston, later increased to 730. National Conferences such as the N.U.T., Rotary, British Legion and the like had the effect of extending the season and relieving the

unemployment problem. However, by the very nature of the Island's economy the Winter Works Schemes had to remain a feature of the Manx landscape. Still by 1949, although Douglas Corporation remained at loggerheads with the Electricity Board over the supply of electricity, it nevertheless felt able to install 'decorative lighting' along Douglas Promenade.

At the start of the new decade one of the major concerns was the extension of the town's boundaries to include the new estates on the outskirts - Garden City, Spring Valley and Willaston. Not only did this mean taking a considerable acreage from the parishes of Onchan and Braddan, but also an improvement in the sewage disposal structure. The undertaking, the Douglas Trunk Boundary Sewer Extension, was of great importance and its construction was to occupy most of the decade. Indeed it represented the underpinning, as it were, of ambitious plans for future extensions of the boundary. Equally, the acquisition of the peripheral estates necessitated alterations to the Ward boundaries; Spring Valley went to Hills, Garden City went to Murrays and Willaston to Athol Ward. There were other important schemes, too. King George V Park was to be laid out properly as a Sports Centre and various road-widening projects in the town planned. Other landmarks appeared at this time. Noble's Hospital gained its substantial extension whilst over the road the Nurses' Home took shape. Others disappeared. The fire at Woolworth's in 1951 altered the appearance of Strand Street for ever. Yet others were planned. A proposed new swimming pool at Port Skillion produced several 'artists' impressions, whilst demands for a new Police Headquarters recognised the new population patterns of the town.

The season of course retained its pre-eminence. Visitors still flocked here and at peak times appeals were made to private houses to offer beds. The holiday shows and the dancing halls throbbed with activity but the hire of rowing boats at 2 shillings a person was considered exorbitant. Those seeking a quiet drink complained: "There are pianos and singers in all the pubs!" The Festival of Britain produced a headline in the Isle of Man Examiner that today would raise a few eye-brows - 'Douglas to go Gay in Festival Week.' And a fierce argument ensued before the Corporation tennis courts and bowling greens were allowed to open on Sundays.

But the old problems remained. Despite the efforts of the Council there persisted major housing problems in the town. It was said that 'cattle living at Knockaloe are living in better conditions' and there were repeated calls for the demolition of old properties in old Douglas. Indeed there was a call for the demolition of the eye-sore on Douglas Head - a building later to become the home of Manx Radio. Nor did the scourge of winter unemployment disappear. These years once more saw young people leaving the Island in hundreds every autumn, never to return. The 1961 Census showed the Island's population had fallen to 48,133 of whom 18,800 lived in Douglas.

Ideas abounded regarding maintaining Douglas as a major holiday resort; a modern swimming pool; an 'inflammatory plan' in 1955 proposed the building of a casino and a swimming pool and/or a conference hall at the Villa Marina; a national sweep on the T.T.; the re-introduction of horse racing and the re-opening and improvement of the Marine Drive. A couple of years later the Marine Drive was given the go-ahead and to complete the scheme the Town Council purchased Port Soderick to save it, it was claimed, from dereliction. The other side of the coin was the elimination of old properties in the town. The Barrack Street/Hanover Place was put on the schedule to be cleared in the immediate future; the harbour near the swing bridge widened to provide extra berths; and the area by the Central Hotel at the bottom of Broadway became the subject of speculation.

The growing importance of the town was recognised at this time by an increase in its representation in the House of Keys to seven members; a battle won despite stern opposition. A complication, or so some felt, was the introduction of adult suffrage in local elections, a step which increased the number of Douglas voters from 9,400 to 16,300, which necessitated another revision of the Ward boundaries. Perhaps a reflection of the new town of Douglas was the appeal for suggestions for a new name for the House of Industry, a title considered perhaps inappropriate for the second half of the twentieth century. Perhaps also as a comment on the increasing importance of the national Government was the comment by the Borough Treasurer in 1958 that: "We have a very fine water undertaking which the Government has been told should be taken from us."

As a new decade began in 1961 it was becoming more and more clear that the days when Douglas could rely, almost without effort, upon a constant stream of visitors in the summer months were over. The steady decline in numbers, in ten years more than 20%, was beginning to cause concern. The provision of a modern swimming pool was once more on the agenda with Councillors voting in favour of one in the Villa grounds, but only with Government support. This was not forthcoming, at least for the Villa site. Plans were put forward for a new Bus Station - and Air Terminal - at the Lord Street car park, and plans for a new Sea Terminal were put in place. The cry was to provide new and improved facilities as a means of stemming the fall in holiday traffic. Despite vehement opposition, a form of registration of hotels and boarding houses was introduced aimed at improving

standards of accommodation. But despite the worries Douglas was still a scene of bustle and activity during the 'sixties. Floodlit tattoos at the Bowl attracted thousands as did the Dance Festivals at the Palace. The Casino was seen as another major attraction while the Corporation embarked on an ambitious scheme to build an Aquadrome and an innovative indoor leisure complex on the acquired Derby Castle site. Douglas was on the map as regards conferences with thousands of delegates boosting arrival figures. In 1969 no fewer than 12 separate Conferences were held bringing 13,000 delegates. The horse trams and the deck chairs still made a profit for the town.

Needless to say, many of the old concerns remained. As houses were cleared in the centre of the town and people re-located on the outskirts more disputes occurred with Onchan and Braddan. The question of Douglas expanding its boundaries came to the fore again when Tynwald received, in 1964, the Report of the Local Government (Administration) Commission. It favoured an amalgamation of Douglas and Onchan pointing out that many people in Onchan found employment in the shops and offices of Douglas and enjoyed the amenities of the town. Onchan would have nothing to do with it. The Council's Boundary Extension Committee proposed that talks should be held with Onchan Commissioners for the mutual benefit of town and village. The idea was not accepted by the full Council as they realised there was little point in pursuing the matter. Refuse disposal was another problem and as tonnage increased the inevitable rows over new sites grew in volume. Cars increased in number and the parking problems with them. Then the Council found itself fighting off what they considered the piracy of the national Government as the proposals to merge the I.O.M. Electricity Board with the Corporation Electricity Department became more strongly advanced.

The start of the 1970s witnessed the continuation of the main themes of the town since the war. Old landmarks continued to disappear such as Victory House on Prospect Hill and the old Imperial Hotel on the harbour side as the Steam Packet Company moved into new headquarters. But at the other end of the town a new shape was appearing, that of the Summerland indoor leisure complex. Opened in 1971, it was the Corporation's culmination of many years of

This photograph shows 14 Councillors who were Mayors of Douglas between 1965 and 1986. They are, back row, left to right: Mrs Mary Halsall, (Mrs Margaret Birch, Mayoress), H. Cunningham, Miss May Teare, F.J. Waterson, C.E. Burke, Mrs Audrey Ainsworth, (Mrs Emmie Corkham, Mayoress) and Ald. W.A. Moore. Front row: A. Duggan, I.A. Faragher, Ald. C. Simpson, Ald. E. Ackary, Ald. F.E. Griffin, D.T. Cannon and W.Ward.

To provide greater protection for Douglas harbour work started in 1981 on constructing a new breakwater. Two years later the last of the stabits are being placed in position.

Mayor Daniel Cannon joins children from Murray's Road School in greeting Princess Alexandra on the occasion of the official opening of the new Princess Alexandra Pier on 14th July, 1983.

thought and hard work to keep the town in the forefront as a holiday resort. Summerland was a new concept in the world of entertainment and it was seen as a solution to halt any further decline in the vital visiting industry. Such hopes were dashed two years later with the catastrophic fire and the tragic loss of 50 lives. The reputation of the town as a safe family resort was badly besmirched.

Summerland had stretched the resources of the town to the limit; there was little to spend on maintaining the Villa Marina though 1973 saw the completion of a Conference Hall adjoining the main building. Conferences were still big business. Elsewhere, there were other developments. The Loch Promenade Methodist Church went to be replaced by the striking and equally impressive Promenade Church. The Corporation embarked on the clearance of old properties in the Chester Street and Well Road Hill with the Government taking over the re-development of the area. The site for a new Police Headquarters on Glencrutchery Road was finally settled. On the other hand Fort Anne had become derelict and would not survive the decade.

Perhaps the most significant feature of these years, and one that was not fully comprehended, was the extent to which the policy pursued by the Manx Government, that of turning the Island into an off-shore financial centre, was to have on the town. One by one banks and other financial institutions moved in to begin a change in the general appearance of the town as fundamental as that of almost a hundred years earlier. And the new Government Central Offices unveiled to the public in the middle of the decade were a sign of confidence and optimism in the future. While this was going on more practical matters continued to occupy the minds of Councillors. Not least was what now seemed to be the inevitable loss of its cherished electricity undertaking. Despite reservations about the general economy of the Island there was a cautious optimism. It was pointed out at the time "the old scars are healing." The new Summerland was open as was the Chester Street Car Park - and with its construction virtually the last remnants of Victorian Douglas swept away. Noble's Baths had been sold and refurbished as a leisure centre; the old Holiday Camp site on Victoria Road was to be a new holiday complex. A traffic island of stunning proportions was to be built opposite the Sefton Hotel to facilitate the flow of traffic along the promenade. Strand Street was to be given a new look by being 'pedestrianised.' Hopes were high and

arrival figures received a welcome boost as a result of the many celebrations of Millennium Year.

Millennium Year, 1979, saw what was described as a 'tourist bonanza' that brightened up the Island as a whole and Douglas in particular, especially as it was bidding to retain its title in the 'Britain in Bloom' competition. Nevertheless, the face of the town continued to change, and for reasons other than tourism. Office blocks in Athol Street competed with new banks, and flats on the Douglas Head Road provided new landmarks - a process exemplified by the Lord Street/Station Hill developments, completed in 1989, and by the replacement of the grand old Victoria Street Methodist Church by yet another office and banking headquarters. Fayle's Yard in Back Strand Street saw a large Government office being built while, as the decade progressed the first proposal for an indoor shopping centre across the road was heard. In these years the Island was changed from a 'low' to a 'high' profile off-shore financial centre and the inevitable change in the character of Douglas, already referred to, speeded up to a degree that many of its citizens found hard to understand or perhaps approve. Yet these same people were only too well aware that the original foundations of the town's prosperity, the holiday industry, was what seemed to be in terminal decline and a new purpose had to be found.

What is perhaps surprising is that although the change was happening, and happening more and more quickly, many of the old problems continued to manifest themselves. The provision of Corporation housing, so urgent a problem much earlier in the century, continued to exercise the minds of Councillors. New estates had to be built and land had to be found. The battles with Onchan and Braddan parishes smouldering for decades once more burst into flames as the town tried, this time with some success, to find this extra land. The old estates too again made news, not only because some of the properties were left empty, but because the Pulrose and Hillside estates needed and received extensive refurbishment. The problems of the Council's policy towards Douglas promenade, where it refused to countenance the development of self-catering accommodation, caused great concern amongst those in the tourist business, while the increasing Douglas rate of 136 pence compared with some country areas of 15 pence in the pound caused concern amongst all citizens of the town. New developments in sea transport and the introduction of Ro-Ro demanded that the old breakwater be reinforced and extended. Douglas soon rang to the thump of underwater blasting as the work went ahead in the bay. The gradual introduction of late-night shopping and the licensing of street musicians might have reflected the changing social pattern but questions over the future of the Villa Marina proved that under the surface much remained the same.

The great office building boom was not only to change the physical appearance of the town but its social character as well. The clearance of the old Victorian town earlier in the century had shifted the centre of gravity as far as the population was concerned. These new developments continued the process of moving more residents out of the town and during the day at least replacing them with cars, more and more cars. Douglas, in fact, was exercising such a dominance that the other towns were almost in the situation of becoming its dormitory suburbs. Solutions, of course, had to be found. Centre parking on Douglas Promenade, having been found to be dangerous, was eventually replaced by diagonal parking on the seaward side and at peak times on the walkway itself. Pay-and-display, disc parking and a park-and-ride scheme were introduced as traffic congestion reached levels unthinkable a few years earlier.

The practical problems, and their attempted solutions, were to a certain extent reflected in a more critical appraisal of the actual government of the town. A system instituted a century earlier was not, it was argued, likely to be able to cope with the new problems of what was becoming a new town. On the other hand a system that had coped, and pretty successfully at that, with the tremendous problems of the first three-quarters of the century had, its supporters claimed, a great deal to recommend it.

However, the Government had for some time been considering the structure of local government on the Island and obviously Douglas Corporation would be bound to figure largely in its thoughts. Ministerial pronouncements about putting Douglas in order did little to oil the wheels of debate but by the end of the decade the Aldermanic Bench had gone and the number of Councillors reduced to 18.

The new streamlined Council had problems enough facing it - some from the new character of the town, others, as their predecessors had found, from the need to replace or revamp parts of their Victorian heritage. What about the Villa? Should it be re-developed at a cost of £13 million, become an Aqua-leisure Centre or be demolished? Douglas needed more houses. Could it expand further into Braddan? Was the Council to accept that the town centre was to become, as it was said, 'a desert in the evening' or should it continue to keep people there, and to review critically and continuously the Douglas Town Plan? Even in 1995 letters from concerned Douglas citizens to the Press bemoaned the absence of residential development in the town. Still, the old Market Hall was still there, even if the traders were worried about the rents; the Railway Station had been spruced up, and Her Majesty The Queen had opened the new Museum extension. The radical plans for DOUGLAS 2000, the new Marks and Spencers, the impressive new Courthouse and General Registry on Prospect Hill, the coming to fruition of the Villiers site were to a certain extent complemented by the meticulous restoration of the Gaiety Theatre entrance canopy to its Victorian splendour.

Further details regarding developments within the town since 1945 and the workings of the Town Hall today are given in later sections.

Council members and officials 1978/9. Standing, left to right: Rev G. Graham (Chaplain); A Duggan; D. Cannon; D. Martin; M. Shimmin; R. Birch; M. Halsall (Mayor); M. Teare; W. Ward; B. Gelling; A. Ainsworth; A Duggan Snr; W. Kennaugh (Messenger). Seated: H. Cunningham; W. Shimmin; Ald W.B. Kaneen; W. Mylrea (Town Clerk); Ald C. Simpson; Ald F.E. Griffin; Ald E. Ackary. Standing centre: K. Bean (Health Inspector); G. Fenton (Electrical Engineer and Manager). Seated front: D.E Lawson (Administrative assistant); E.T. Atherton (Borough Surveyor); R. Asbridge (Borough Treasurer); G. Connolly (Entertainments Manager); K. Radcliffe (Assistant Town Clerk).

HONOURS FOR THE ALDERMEN

ALDERMAN J.H. SKILLICORN

A newspaper headline on 14th April, 1950 stated in bold print: 'Baker's Apprentice to Freeman.' The reference was to James Henry Skillicorn who, the day before, had been made a Freeman of Douglas. The casket, with scenes of the Villa Marina and Baldwin Reservoir, and the scroll were presented to him by Mayor Councillor T. Radcliffe in the Council Chamber in front of some 150 townsfolk. Glen Maye born, Alderman Skillicorn had reached the age of 40 before he began his municipal career, spending some 28 years as a Councillor, and becoming Mayor in 1933. Like so many of his generation he had been actively concerned in the transformation of Douglas into a modern holiday resort and port. He had been a main advocate of the slum clearances and of the provision of a proper water supply. He was also a sterling supporter of the widening of Loch Promenade and the general improvement of that area, the first for the visitors to see. Other affairs of the town were also given his aid. A staunch Methodist he accepted an important place in that Church's affairs, and he found also time to give stalwart help to the Douglas Brass Band. None doubted Alderman Skillicorn merited the honour bestowed upon him.

ALDERMAN J.C. FARGHER
ALDERMAN A.J. TEARE, M.B.E., J.P.

In 1964 the Douglas Town Council blazed a new trail in the creation of Freemen of the Borough. They created two at once and on Thursday, 10th September two of the giants of the town's political scene had the signal honour conferred upon them. Both men were influential in the development of Douglas from the First World War through to the aftermath of the Second, a period in which far-reaching changes had been made. In A.J. Teare's case a wider political scene had commanded some of his attention (as an M.H.K. he was a member of the War Cabinet) but both had throughout their careers fought long and hard for fairness and justice for the less well off. John Fargher had been elected to the Town Council in 1928 and was worthily regarded as the Father of the Council. Alfred Teare had come on in 1933 and over the years had chaired all the Council Committees. On their caskets and scrolls pictures of the Villa Marina and the Willaston Estate confirmed their interests and triumphs as the leaders of the progressive groups of their day. It was fitting that the impressive Civic Dinner at which they were honoured was held at the Villa.

ALDERMAN T.A. CORKISH
ALDERMAN W.B. KANEEN
ALDERMAN T,D. LEWIS
ALDERMAN R.F. QUAYLE

At an impressive ceremony held at the Villa Marina on Thursday, 22nd May, 1975 the Douglas Town Council conferred the Freedom of the Borough on not one but four of its members. At this unique occasion the four Aldermen became the only living Freemen when the Mayor, Councillor W.P. Shimmin bestowed the honour upon them with the Certificate of Admission after they had signed the Roll of Honour. These men had been giants of the municipal scene for many years. All had served on the Council for long periods, 35 years in the case of Fletcher Quayle. Each had occupied the Mayoral office throughout a period of great change, a time in the growth of Douglas that demanded high ideals, sacrifices and tough bargaining. The Aldermen had earned their high honours.

ALDERMAN W.A. MOORE

On 28th April, 1985, the Lord Bishop led the prayers at a Ceremony at the Villa Marina at which one of the most respected members of the Manx

Alderman R Fletcher Quayle

Alderman W.B. Kaneen

Alderman T.D. Lewis

political scene received the Freedom of the Borough. Alec Moore had had a distinguished career beginning in 1954 when he was elected to the Council following a bye-election. He was one of the first residents of Willaston and he played a leading part in creating a community spirit within the new estate. Working with people, and his contacts through being a postman, aroused his interest in politics and he entered the Council at the first attempt. He worked tirelessly to promote Douglas as a holiday resort and it was he who first suggested that Douglas should have a casino. His idea met with strong opposition from many quarters but his persistence resulted in Tynwald eventually giving its approval. In 1965 he became Mayor of the Town, but in 1971 he resigned his seat in the Council after being elected to the House of Keys. He went on to hold important positions and was Chairman of the Water Board at the time of the construction of the Sulby Reservoir. He ended his political career as a Member of the Legislative Council, thus completing a unique career in local and national politics. A member of the Labour Party he was very much a man of the people and his innate integrity and sense of fairness was recognised by all who came in contact with him. As the Mayor, Councillor Alfred Duggan, said at the Villa Marina as he conferred the honour upon the Alderman: "This is the latest milestone in a career of many milestones." Alderman Moore now lives in retirement at Ballanard Court.

Alderman W.A. Moore,

ALDERMAN C. SIMPSON
ALDERMAN F.E. GRIFFIN

In 1986 the Douglas Town Council once again decided to confer the Freedom of the Borough on more than one individual. The Aldermen Cyril Simpson and Fred Griffin had been Councillors since the start of the 1960s. Both had been Mayor, Alderman Griffin twice. In their political careers both had served on all the Council Committees; Alderman Simpson had chaired both the Transport and Electricity Committees; Alderman Griffin the Transport Committee for no fewer than five terms

and the Estates Committee, which was probably the topic in which he was most passionately involved. At an impressive ceremony held at the Villa Marina on 29th April both men received their Certificates of Admission, which included a superb water-colour of the Town Hall by John Nicholson, and signed the Roll of Honour.

Alderman T.A. Corkish

Alderman C. Simpson

Alderman F.E. Griffin

POST-WAR ENTERTAINMENTS

The immediate post-war years witnessed a tourist boom for Douglas; packed hotels and guest houses, crowded dance halls, theatres and cinemas. Europe was closed. People flocked to the traditional holiday resorts not ruined by warfare. The Manx Grand Prix of September, 1946 saw the return of racing on the TT Course. The Senior Prize Presentation witnessed one of the largest crowds ever in the Palace Ballroom when the doors had to be closed after 11,000 people had been admitted. Seasonal arrivals peaked at over 624,000 in 1948, a figure only surpassed by the record year of 1913. Air arrivals made Ronaldsway Airport one of the busiest in the British Isles.

New fortunes were made. One man actually formed the basis of one by using his demob pay to launch a mobile potato peeling service for hotels and guest houses. But for speculators who thought it would always be that way there were losses too. When the Cunningham Camp was sold to a new company - Douglas Holiday Camp Ltd - and this was floated on the London Stock Exchange it created some of the wildest scenes witnessed there for years. Five shilling (25p) shares rocketed as people scrambled to buy them. Their value more than quadrupled fed by false rumours that Billy Butlin was to acquire the Camp for his national network of holiday camps. Speculators lost heavily when reality set in.

The Camp, now open to families, never regained its greatness. Like the town's tourist industry it declined as foreign resorts, through package holidays, attracted the Island's traditional holidaymaker. Parts decayed; its great ballroom was gutted by fire in the summer of 1972, and was never replaced. Under new ownership the site was developed as a business park, housing estate and the Island's first supermarket. The last of the Holiday Camp buildings were demolished in March, 1983.

Whilst the post-war boom lasted there was an atmosphere of gaiety; a sense of thankfulness to have survived the war. Late at night (sometime between 11pm and midnight as most landladies locked their doors against stop-outs) holidaymakers would link arms and parade up town five, six and even seven abreast singing loudly. In many boarding houses they would gather round pianos and sing until the early hours. Most places were still unlicensed but that didn't stop the drinking. Fictitious arrangements were made between guests and landladies to the effect that liquor stocks were the guests' private property being dispensed to them as required. It would be many years before the strict licensing laws were relaxed and Sunday opening was permitted.

Eventually Douglas Corporation accepted that people wanted the fun to carry on until a late hour. The result was floodlit dancing on the promenade. When the dance halls closed on Friday nights the top bands at the Villa Marina - Joe Loss and the all-girl Ivy Benson band in particular - adjourned to the war memorial site and there thousands watched jitterbugging and jiving until midnight and beyond: a memorable send-off for those who were to leave next day. Joe Loss began his long 'reign' in 1947 and the Villa Marina was packed nightly with dancers, while the balcony was crowded with those content to listen to the music and the latest songs sung by the vocalists

From 1947 to 1957 Joe Loss and his Orchestra was the great attraction at the Villa Marina with thousands dancing nightly to the latest hit tunes.

including Elizabeth Batey, Howard Jones, Rose Brennan and Tony Ventro. There is no doubt that the profitable partnership between the Corporation and Joe Loss and his orchestra brought great fame to the Villa Marina, regular broadcasts being made on BBC Radio. Joe and his wife lived at Summerhill, Douglas during each season and his two children attended the Collegiate School. The orchestra's final season was 1957 after which another big band, that of Kenny Mackintosh appeared; but there were many who were saddened at the loss of the 'magic' of Joe Loss. Twenty years later he made a nostalgic one-night return; the Villa was packed.

The Villa Marina was not licensed in those days but Miss Doris Maddrell and her cafe staff ensured there was plenty of light refreshments for the thirsty dancers, dispensing huge quantities of orange drinks and ice cream. For the Sunday night concerts, Entertainments Manager Mr Sydney Perry engaged top artistes in the world of show business. Two new names which appeared, with the support of Joe Loss, were the youthful Eamon Andrews and Max Bygraves. The Palace Coliseum also engaged leading entertainers for their seasonal shows, the most successful being comic Norman Evans, fresh from his triumph in America. His 'Over the Garden Wall' caricature of an old woman gossip was among the most memorable of his sketches.

At the Palace Ballroom, after several seasons with other bands, most notably Cyril Stapleton, demobbed RAF men who had played together during the war as the Dance Orchestra of the Royal Air Force and then later as The Squadronaires appeared from 1952 to 1964 under the direction of Ronnie Aldrich as a co-operative band. Ronnie's widow Mary, who acted as band secretary, recalled later that it was a daunting

The neon lighting gave an attractive gaiety to the front of the Villa Marina. Inside the dance floor was filled with happy dancers; Sunday night concerts were always a sell-out. (Reg Quayle Collection)

proposition trying to compete with the reputation of Joe Loss. "He was like King of the Island," she said. "Queues for the Villa Marina stretched way up Broadway."

Yet compete the Squadronaires did and crowds poured into the Palace too, especially after the Palace company was persuaded by Ronnie in 1953 to drape curtains over all the windows and on either side of the stage to get rid of irritating double and treble echoes in the vast ballroom. Ballroom dancing in the town reached its peak in the Fifties. But soon the quick steps, waltzes and fox trots were destined to be replaced in general popularity by rock 'n roll and the twist, and the traditional dance halls would succumb to electronic discotheques. In 1964, experiencing already the decline in demand for big bands, the Squadronaires disbanded and Ronnie Aldrich - since 1959 a permanent resident on the Island, first at Baldwin and then Port St. Mary - embarked on a successful international career as composer, arranger and pianist.

The popularity of rock 'n roll could not have been more marked than when upwards of 12,000 fans - an all-time record - crowded into the Palace Ballroom to listen to and scream at the rock group, The Rolling Stones. There was no room for dancing!

The first dance hall victim to changes on the Isle of Man was the Palais de Danse; turned first into a temporary store for Woolworth's during the store's reconstruction late in 1951 after a fire totally gutted the store during building work on it, and briefly threatened much of middle Strand Street. The Palais later became a market hall, then a clothing hall. In March, 1961 the ballroom was put up for sale by the Palace and Derby Castle Company directors. At a well attended sale the fine ballroom was acquired by the Maypole Dairy Company for £44,000. The Maypole had been in Strand Street, at the corner of Howard Street, since before the First World War which it now vacated after fifty years to move into its new premises. In the early 1980s the Palais was taken over by Barry Noble and opened as the sophisticated Sun Valley Amusement Arcade. But it was short-lived and today the building takes its place in Strand Street as another shopping unit.

Throughout the Fifties and beyond there was a growing awareness in Douglas that the swimming facilities of Noble's Baths, though planned in Edwardian days to last for a hundred years or more, were inadequate for modern needs. The issue of the baths was symptomatic of a feeling that there was a need to upgrade facilities to match those of tourist

The Villa Marina Gardens were another great summer attraction with Ivy Benson and her all-girl band providing the entertainment. Thursday afternoons had the added attraction of Bathing Beauty Competitions, with heats being held each week and the winners taking part in the 'Miss Isle of Man' contest at the end of the season.

resorts elsewhere but these were financially difficult years. Douglas Corporation felt it couldn't build a new indoor heated pool alone and Tynwald was difficult over providing assistance. Eventually it was forthcoming but not until after many years of negotiation and rejection. When Councillors proposed building a championship pool in the Villa grounds in the late 'fifties assistance was rejected. In 1959 the Crescent site was considered as an alternative but this too was rejected.

Thirty years on, after a swimming pool had been built at Derby Castle site, history turned full circle. Yet again it was proposed that a pool, this time called the Aqua Centre, should be built in the Villa grounds. At one point it looked as if it would go ahead in partnership with Tynwald then opposition groups, worried about the loss of the last green belt in lower Douglas, forced a re-think. The establishment of the National Sports Centre in King George V Park prompted also the idea that the Aqua Centre should be established there along with other sports facilities.

For the cinemas, television was the big challenge; weak at first but eventually overpowering. The east coast of the Isle of Man, and Douglas in particular came within range of BBC television for the first time in October 1951 when the Holme Moss transmitter became operational. Signals were inclined to fade and become lost in electronic 'snow' and whenever a car drove past a house where a television set was in use white lines appeared on screens accompanied by appropriate sound effects. This led to mounting pressure for all motor vehicles to be fitted with suppressors. In the early days of radio (even in the 1940s) a feature of the Douglas skyline had been aerial wires strung from house to house and across streets. The wireless, as it was known, had become the biggest source of home entertainment. Occasionally there were live broadcasts from the Island, especially at TT time. One of radio's highlights on 11th May, 1947 was coverage of a service in St. Thomas' Church to mark the 1,500th anniversary of the foundation of the Manx Church. Now the metal H's of TV, some fitted with amplifiers to boost the signal, replaced the wires.

Private landlords, worried about the damage collapsing TV aerials might cause to chimney stacks, demanded that tenants should increase their home insurance substantially. Douglas Corporation and other local authorities, meanwhile, banned their erection in their estates. It was rumoured that the official attitude was that if tenants could afford TV they should not be in local authority houses. This caused many confrontations within the Town Council especially when a builder's labourer erected an aerial on a twenty foot pole in his garden and was given notice to quit if he didn't take it down. Eventually, when aerials proved to be safer than they had first appeared they were accepted.

At first cinemas still attracted big queues in the summer, sometimes four or five deep; for the Picture House, half along Strand Street; for the Strand, onto the promenade; for the Royalty, the length of Walpole Avenue; for the Regal, well up Victoria Street; for the Crescent, a long chain that could wrap itself round the large car park in front and then extend to the rear of the cinema. These were the cinema's golden days. But they weren't to last. Soon the tiny nine and twelve inch TV screens would get bigger and reception would improve. In 1953 Douglas TV dealer Harold Colebourn, frustrated at the Island being regarded as an unimportant 'fringe' area for TV coverage and therefore low on the list of priorities for its own transmitter, erected an illegal booster station at Carnane so that coverage of the Coronation of Queen Elizabeth could be received in better quality. There were rows about it but it precipitated action. Four years later, after much argument over the legality of what Mr Colebourn had done, the BBC erected an official booster station. This was switched on as from mid-December 1957. The transmitter lasted until 1966 when it was demolished and replaced by a new one. These were the moves that brought TV to the masses. Thereafter, entertainment in Douglas and the Isle of Man would never be the same.

In 1955 Douglas entered a national TV knock-out talent competition on BBC known as 'Top Town.' Douglas was pitted against Bradford. The Manx opening number was "Has Anybody Here Seen Kelly?" and the final included a Manx cat. Bradford won but everyone agreed that the local team had performed well. Two years later, in August 1957, the first 'live' Manx programme, 'Holiday Town', was broadcast from the Palace Ballroom to an estimated six million viewers. The broadcaster on behalf of the new ITV channel was the programmer ABC. The BBC had tried three times to get a good signal from the Island and had failed. Now ABC did it by using three transmission routes simultaneously. This meant that if the signal faded on one route the national transmission could be switched to another. Included in the show were heats of television bathing beauty, fashion and Adonis competitions, but the highlights for local people were a Joe Loss swing version of "Has Anybody Here Seen Kelly?" and the Lon Dhoo Choir singing "Ellan Vannin." Not to be outdone, the BBC brought its Saturday night 'pop' music show "Six Five Special" to the Island soon afterwards and broadcast it from the Villa Marina.

Briefly thereafter some wondered whether television theatres were the answer to mass entertainment: people being entertained by TV in a big screen environment, but this was a non-starter. The cinema's response to home entertainment was more colour films, bigger screens such as Cinemascope and improved sound systems. The Picture House was the first cinema to be converted to Cinemascope, the screen automatically changing shape and size according to the film being screened. Its first Cinemascope presentation was the Biblical epic 'The Robe.' Eventually all cinemas were converted but none had screens as wide as the Picture House. It was able to use virtually the full width of its stage wall whereas other cinemas, still equipped with theatre stages, had recessed screens. This was poor for audiences sitting in side seats. At the Strand this was so bad that gold curtains which folded and rose vertically instead of parting had to be introduced. Later, to cater for minority tastes, some cinemas (particularly the Picture House and Strand) introduced late night screenings of specialist films. These started around 11 pm. Even so, attendances fell as the impact of multi-channel colour television was felt and, worse still, the town's traditional holidaymaker switched to sunnier climes, particularly Spain.

Soon it was apparent to the Palace and Derby Castle Co., that a major contraction was necessary. Douglas had one cinema seat for every 75 visitors compared with a ratio of one to 1,538 in the much larger resort of Blackpool. One by one the great picture palaces disappeared. The lower part of the Royalty was briefly adapted for slot-car racing, with Karma the Lightning Hypnotist, assisted by Elizabeth, performing in the upper part; but by 1970 the cinema had become a DIY store. The Regal, after opening for summers only, was demolished in the mid-1980s to make way for a banking hall and offices. The seasonal Crescent, never redecorated in its entire history, experienced a short career as a summer theatre but the Palace Company planned to convert it

Ronnie Aldrich and the Squadronaires were the 'big band' to which thousands danced nightly in the Palace Ballroom.

into a multi-purpose centre: a new 550 seat cinema in the balcony and a large entertainments centre with gaming room, lounges, restaurant and dance floor beneath it. All this relied on the Crescent being licensed as a gaming centre and when this never materialised, the cinema was sold in 1975, gutted and converted into another type of multi-purpose centre: a fun fair on the ground floor and waxworks above. In the late 1970s when skateboarding was popular it had a rink to cater for the needs of skaters, operating briefly under the name of 'Skateboard City.' Today, the cinema building is part of the Crescent Leisure Centre.

The Strand was split between a ground floor amusement arcade and a smaller cinema upstairs until 1988 when it was finally closed and is now lying derelict awaiting some future development. Also in 1988 the Picture House was closed and for a brief spell Douglas had no cinema, not until one was opened in the Corporation-owned Summerland later that year. In 1989 new smaller cinemas were developed in the old Palace Opera House and Gaming Room - Cinemas 1 and 2. The Picture House was gutted in 1994 and the site used for new shopping units.

For the magnificent Gaiety Theatre the 1940s and 1950s was the time of great danger. Increasingly it had been used as a cinema, maintaining its theatre status only in the winter when it was rented to amateur theatrical and drama societies. For a few years in the Fifties a professional Repertory Company used it also, using Manx people as extras, but it didn't last. Slowly the theatre's structure went into decline. The roof leaked and there were actually seats where the audience could get wet whilst being entertained! In 1957 Douglas Corporation tried to persuade the Palace and Derby Castle Company to lease the theatre to the Corporation so that it could ensure the

Ronnie Aldrich and the Squadronaires during their first season, 1953, at the Palace. Problems with the acoustics of the huge ballroom were overcome by the use of heavy velvet curtains over the openings and window spaces.

One of the highlights at the Palace was the annual Dance Festival Week which attracted dancers from all parts of the British Isles. This photograph is dated 1966. Note the ornate ceiling has been covered as a further measure to improve the acoustics.

The staging of the Manx Grand Prix Presentations was one of the end-of-season events at the Palace. Here Deputy Mayor Alec Moore is presenting one of the 1964 awards. Keeping a watchful eye on the proceedings is popular Douglas schoolmaster the Rev. 'Bertie' Reid, Chairman of the Manx Motor Cycle Club.

continuity of live theatre but the company refused. There was more money in operating the place as a cinema. Only later when other places of live entertainment disappeared, notably the Crescent Pavilion (demolished between October 1962 and January 1963) and a wooden theatre at Onchan Head's White City Amusement Park which was destroyed by fire, did summer live entertainment return, mainly in the form of Stella Hartley's Summer Showtimes. Earlier, these audience participation shows had been a feature of the Pavilion, attracting many thousands each season. The Pavilion had been a 'temporary building' ever since its erection on the site in 1923; it had originally been used as a 'magnificent pavilion for dancing' in the popular Injebreck Pleasure Grounds. At the Crescent the Pavilion had acquired a semi-permanent status because of the economic conditions of the 1930s and post-war uncertainties. From 1948 onwards Douglas Corporation granted the Palace Company successive three-year extensions to its life but in December 1961, believing it to be an eyesore, had finally ordered the Palace Company to demolish it after the 1962 season. (Already, in 1958, the Corporation had ordered the removal of the dilapidated Pleasureland Crescent Cafe.) When this was done, and the site sold, the Pavilion was replaced by an amusement arcade, made possible by the phased closure of the White City Amusement Park on Onchan head. Stella Hartley was transferred to the Gaiety though there was a real threat the Gaiety might close permanently. Then in the early 1970s it was saved by Manx Government purchase after a brief hope in Government that the Corporation might acquire it instead. Since then, a phased restoration programme, part financed by Government and part from donations from the Island's expanding finance sector, has returned it to its old glory.

The Villa Marina suffered also. Once an important profit-maker for the town, it became a loss-maker. In search of a new role for it with the demise of ballroom dancing, Town Councillors vehemently denied rumours in 1973 that it was to be taken over by the leisure group, Trust House Forte. The following year there were proposals to convert the Royal Hall into a cabaret club (some called it a 'Theatre in the Round') but Councillors rejected this too. In July, 1971 a summer show started a planned seven-week run at the Villa. It featured comedian Charles Hawtrey of the 'Carry On' comedy film series. However, after one night the show was shut down on instructions from the Corporation's Parks Committee. It was the first and only time in the Villa's history that this happened. The committee's explanation was the show wasn't up to the Villa Marina standard.

The Royal Hall remained a public amenity during the winter and in the summer was used for multiple purposes: one-night shows, all-in wrestling and even displays of hypnotism by Ronrico. In the grounds, meanwhile, monuments to past glories disappeared. Now that afternoon open-air concerts and bathing beauty competitions for thousands of sun-drenched holidaymakers in deck-chairs were no longer viable the bandstand was demolished; so too the old wooden Pavilion at the back of the gardens which had been relegated as a store for the Corporation's thousands of deck-chairs. As large numbers were no longer needed because of a drop in the number of bucket and spade tourists, the Corporation privatised

the deck-chair service, demolished the Pavilion in 1988 and allocated the space to car parking. The only positive step to make better use of the Villa Marina was the building of a large room adjoining the Reading Room. Costing £133,000, the new addition used part of the glazed colonnade overlooking the gardens and required the removal of the fountain. Initially, when opened in 1973, it was called the Conference Hall but today is more commonly referred to as the Gardens Room having been used for a variety of events including small specialist cabarets, dances and exhibitions, with bar facilities available.

One social occasion started in 1977 by Gordon Connolly, Borough Entertainments Manager, was a 'Miss Isle of Man for Miss World' beauty competition. It was a reminder of the post-war years and up into the 1960s when, in keeping with many other holiday resorts, Douglas held Bathing Beauty Competitions. The Villa Marina Gardens made an ideal setting for these events and huge crowds attended the weekly heats leading up to the final and the crowning of 'Miss Queen of Man' or 'Miss Isle of Man' Popular overall winner one year was Joyce Lewis, daughter of Councillor T.D. Lewis. Success also went to Norma Hudson, another Douglas beauty. For the 'Miss Isle of Man for Miss World' contest fashion and personality were brought into the formula with the winner entering the 'Miss World' finals with the prospect of world-wide TV exposure. First winner was 20-year old typist Miss Helen Shimmin of Leigh Terrace, Douglas, and daughter of Fred Shimmin, Steam Packet foreman. Judges for the splendid occasion included Councillors, the reigning 'Miss World' and former 'Miss Isle of Man' Joyce Lewis, now Mrs Langridge of London. The glittering contests became annual events for which the Villa Marina was always packed. Getting local girls to enter proved difficult, however, and after 1988 the publicity achieved was not considered worth the effort and cash involved.

Subsequently a number of circuses were able to pitch their tents in the Villa grounds and attracted good business. Animal rights activists opposed to the exhibition of caged or performing animals picketed outside and eventually non-animal circuses were substituted. The Chinese State Circus, on tours in Britain in the 1990s, were particularly memorable occasions.

The imposing entrance to the Palace and Coliseum which was demolished in 1965.

In 1973 a major addition was made to the Villa Marina by the building of the Garden Room. This necessitated using part of the glazed colonnade while the fountain was moved to near the Broadway entrance. (Frank Cowin Library)

By now the Villa Marina was infected by dry rot. Remedial work was necessary. It meant the demolition of the old wood-panelled restaurant, privatised too in later years after failing to succeed under municipal control. Meanwhile, a rescue package for the rest of the building prompted a Government proposal that the Villa and the adjoining Gaiety Theatre should be jointly managed. This led to protracted and unsuccessful negotiations with the Corporation deciding to close the Villa Marina after the 1995 season. Tynwald responded by stating that Government should take over the Villa for a nominal fee if no agreement could be reached. Fresh talks and a more positive approach between the Corporation and the Department of Local Government and the Environment has resulted in mutual agreement for the Villa Marina's future. Refurbishment will commence in 1996, the Corporation funding £2.5 million of the estimated total cost of £7 million. The two parties will jointly manage the complex - which will include the nearby Gaiety Theatre - and the Department of Tourism will make a large contribution towards the Villa's running costs, removing a burden from the Douglas ratepayers. New features, including a function room, meeting rooms and a restaurant will be incorporated to provide a modern, flexible multi-use facility with the restoration and refurbishment of the Royal Hall. The main entrance will be relocated opposite the stage and access to the entrance will be from the promenade and from Broadway through the gardens. The announcement came as a relief to the great majority now that the Villa Marina is the only national indoor venue for the staging of major events from conferences to concerts.

In 1957 the Douglas Carnival Committee decided it couldn't continue. Its annual carnival wasn't getting enough entries, it said. Here was a sign of the deep depression that had settled on the Island and Douglas in particular after the immediate post-war boom. There was such mass unemployment in the winter men had to leave the Island to seek work. Hundreds paraded the town with banners appealing for work. Families were emigrating and the population was spiralling downwards. Subsequently, when the Carnival Committee reversed its decision and decided to carry on it was symptomatic of a change of mood within the community. The Island shrugged off its apathy and fought back. These might have been the twilight years of mass tourism but in a couple of years the chronic winter unemployment problems would be over and the population would be rising to new heights, promoted by a new low-tax policy which would bring in new residents and create a highly profitable finance industry.

The steady demise of mass tourism, however, had its consequences. Places like Port Soderick suffered. It was in decline. The Douglas Head Marine Drive Electric Tramway was a wartime casualty and never returned to service. The entire tramway fleet had remained untouched in the sheds at Little Ness but it was found that the six years of war had left the track in a bad condition and the bridges with dangerous defects. Restoration would be a costly business and the Tramway company sold its property to Government in 1946. Use for some of the traction poles was found on the MER and can be identified by their distinctive collars. The tramcars, trailers and track were sold as scrap. However, railway enthusiasts saved one of the tramcars for preservation and it can be seen today at the Tramway Museum at Crich, in Derbyshire. Pedestrians were occasionally allowed to use the Marine Drive up to 1956 when it was decided to convert it to a roadway for vehicular traffic through to Port Soderick. This major undertaking took seven years to complete and £250,000 was spent on the project, mainly as a winter work scheme. Quantities of loose rock had to be removed from the overhead rock face and the bridges were demolished to be replaced by the roadway which had to be blasted out of the cliff face. Later, well-known Douglas businessman Mr Harold Colebourn suggested another development. Having seen Disneyland in America he proposed a similar centre at Port Soderick. To link it with Douglas he proposed that Tynwald should fund a chairlift over Douglas harbour to Douglas Head and a novel transport system along the Marine Drive. Eventually Tynwald agreed to it despite warnings that it would be a waste of money. Then opposition led by West Douglas M.H.K. Victor Kneale led to the money being cut out of the budget. Thereafter, although the chairlift remained approved, the money for it was never forthcoming and the concept died. As regards the Marine Drive itself the tortuous and unstable nature of the Manx slates meant there were frequent rock falls and in 1976 it was decided to close the roadway in the interests of safety. But the magnificent coastal views can still be enjoyed by walkers and in 1994 the roadway from Keristal to

In 1956 Port Soderick was refurbished and developed by the Corporation and enjoyed a new lease of life. Access for visitors was by the steam railway, Corporation buses, by motor launches from Douglas or a stroll along the Marine Drive. (Frank Cowin Library)

Little Ness was opened again to vehicles.

Port Soderick was given a new lease of life when the Corporation first leased the beach, hotel and glen in 1955, followed by purchase the following year for £9,000. In an attempt to restore the popular creek over £95,000 was spent on improvements to the buildings and other developments. Regular bus services made it easily accessible to visitors who could also use the steam railway or the *Karina* operating from Douglas. But the numbers never reached anywhere near pre-war proportions. In 1975 the glen was transferred to the Forestry Mines and Lands Board and in 1984 the hotel, cafe and most of the land was sold for £70,000, the remaining lands being dedicated to Government Boards for public use.

The Douglas Head steam ferries had been moved to Castletown at the commencement of the war and could well have languished there for the duration. But a new role was found for them at Belfast Lough. Because of their shallow draught they were ideal for use as landing craft and in simulated beach landings. Thousands of American troops trained on them during a hectic spell of duty. The three ferries were just about worn out but were returned to Castletown after the war and beached on a bank overlooking the Silverburn river at Castletown. They were badly in

need of repair and the owners were negotiating for their sale. In August, 1948 they were craned back into the upper harbour, berthed near the Castletown Brewery and from there were eventually towed to Douglas. Moored at the Tongue the *Thistle* was the first to be reconditioned. She sailed to Ramsey in January, 1949 to undergo inspection on a Harbour Board grid there and resumed services across Douglas harbour in mid-June. The *Rose* acted as a landing barge at the Battery Pier until she could be restored for the following season. The third ferry, the *Shamrock* was retired and used as spares for the other two. In the autumn of 1950 the *Thistle* was sold to Pembrokeshire County Council to provide a ferry service planned by the Council. However, she never made it. Whilst being towed to Mildford Haven in October she was lost at sea. Two months later the original Douglas Steam Ferries Company (formed in 1898) was liquidated. The final pay-out was 38 shillings a share. The promoters were named as John A. Brown, the late G.S. Cain, Richard Cain, Chairman with J.M. Cain as Secretary. The new operators of the ferry service was the Cannell family of Royal Avenue, Onchan. This included marine engineer Douglas Cannell and a dental technician, Cyril Cannell. They replaced the steam engine of the *Rose* with a diesel for

The popular Douglas Head Steam Ferries 'Rose' and 'Thistle' were returned to service after the war. 'Shamrock,' also seen here, was used for spares.

These redundant amusement stalls on Douglas Head were finally demolished in the late 1960s. The photograph was taken from the foot of the incline railway which ceased to operate in August, 1954.

1951 and operated her across Douglas harbour with the support of a smaller motor vessel. In 1953 Vincent Quine Higgins of Wesley Terrace, Douglas took over the company and in 1956 a half-share had been acquired by engineer John Stanley Cooper of Richmond Grove, Douglas. The two ferries continued to operate until the late 1950s when the service faded away with the steady demise of tourism. The biggest blow was the Corporation's bus service from Victoria Pier to the top of Douglas Head with a specially built bus turning area by the Playdium. This was introduced in 1950 despite pleas from the ferry company to be allowed to maintain its traditional monopoly of ferrying passengers to Douglas Head. The Douglas Head Incline Railway was also badly affected by the bus service. Under new ownership the railway was returned to use late in 1949 but only survived until 1954 when it was dismantled.

Douglas Head with its stalls and funfairs never regained its pre-war atmosphere. The concert parties, its main attraction, were kept going but only because Douglas Corporation guaranteed artistes who appeared there a certain income which they could augment by appearing in pub concert halls at night. If wet, the Corporation allowed them to use the Villa Marina Royal Hall, mornings only. Towards the end a 70-year old came out of retirement to keep the shows going. But the Corporation regarded the cost as unjustified and the withdrawal of income guarantees for artistes as from 1972 meant the end of a tradition. The Playdium was sold by the Corporation in 1984 and converted into a restaurant. In 1991 a new Christian group hoped to revive the open-air theatre, with its stage still in place, for religious entertainment but nothing came off it. Last survivor of the Douglas Head attractions was the Grand Union Camera Obscura, now little used and in poor repair. Its rarity, however, ensured its survival. The Manx Government bought it with a view to its eventual restoration as a part of the Island's heritage - and a reminder of the 'good old days' on Douglas Head.

A scheme aimed at arresting tourism's decline which eventually got implemented was the licensing in Douglas of Britain's first public casino. Originally proposed in September, 1955 at a meeting of Douglas Corporation by Labour Councillor Alec Moore, it became a major political issue for years thereafter when Garff M.H.K. Charles Kerruish (later to be knighted as Speaker of the House of Keys) pursued the idea. Casinos were illegal in the rest of Britain so it was thought rich gamblers would be attracted and their yachts would line the bay. Supporters dreamed of a luxurious complex where high-class entertainment would be subsidised by gambling - but the arguing over it went on for so long that by the time the casino licence was granted to an American syndicate there were club-style casinos in Britain and much of its novelty had been lost.

The first Douglas casino, with concessionary drinking facilities until five in the morning, was housed in the Castle Mona Hotel regarded then as purely a temporary base until a purpose-built gaming centre and hotel could be built, probably on Onchan Head overlooking Douglas Bay. Opened by film star Diana Dors in May, 1963 its atmosphere was legendary. For a time there were hopes that a television drama series might be based around the gaming centre but other events intervened.

Whilst plans were being prepared for a permanent casino to be built in time for 1964 criminal practices imported from America threatened the casino's closure. Eventually the concessionaires returned to the U.S.A. and new concessionaires, Crockfords, who were associated with clubland casinos in the U.K. were named. They acquired a controlling interest in the Palace and Derby Castle with Sir Dudley Cunliffe-Owen as Chairman. The decision was then taken to demolish the Palace Coliseum which was suffering from poor audiences and build on its site the existing Palace Hotel and Casino. Val Doonican was the last of the stars to appear at the Coliseum in 1965. The Casino opened for May, 1966 on the termination of the Casino's lease of the Castle Mona and the hotel opened the following year.

Gaming officially ceased at the Castle Mona at 5am, 6th May. The official opening of the new casino was timed for that night so the concessionaires had approximately twelve hours to move the gaming tables and slot machines from the Castle Mona to the new purpose-built premises. Appropriately the official opening was conducted by film star Sean Connery, world-famous for his role as high-living and gambling British espionage agent OO7 James Bond. It had been hoped that he would come to the Island for a few days for a golfing holiday but he was

Hardly recognisable is the Palace Ballroom in its final guise as a cabaret theatre equipped for high-tech laser discos. (Noel Howarth)

The Palace Coliseum was demolished in 1965 to make way for the Casino and Palace Hotel. (R and L Kelly Collection)

needed in Venice the following day for filming so his visit was an overnight trip only. His official duty: one spin of a roulette wheel. To get to the Casino he travelled along the promenade from the new Sea Terminal. The man who originated the idea, Councillor Alec Moore, gave up his job as a postman and was trained by Crockfords (Isle of Man) Ltd. in gaming and administration. Eventually he became House Manager of the Palace Lido for Palace Entertainments Ltd., whose General Manager was Mr Bob Wilkinson.

Manx gaming legislation provided for a second casino once the first was completed. This was proposed as a basis around which the Crescent Cinema could be redeveloped but when this failed to find favour the ailing Palace Ballroom was licensed for gaming and became known as the Palace Lido with giant material 'mushrooms' hung from the ornate ceiling and gold drapes around the walls to further improve acoustics. More bars and a cafe were added with a late drinks facility. High-class cabarets were the main attraction during the season with

Sunday night appearances of such well-known artistes as Frank Ifield, David Frost, Andie Stewart and Vince Hill. In the 1980s sophisticated high-tech laser discos were introduced but even this venture wasn't enough to compensate for the steady loss of tourists. The place was too big for the number of customers available, even with the laser-projected videos on to giant screens either side of the stage. In 1992 the Lido closed and the building was demolished in 1994, but not before many of its decorative architectural features were removed for sale to international collectors. Today, only the Opera House, as a cinema studio, remains of this once great Palace entertainments complex created over a century ago.

Fashions change and for those seeking a night out on the town there are night clubs and discos found in such places as Jeffersons in the new Peveril building; Toffs in the Palace and Casino, now part of the Stakis Hotel group; Paramount City in the former Crescent Hotel, and the Cave Disco at Summerland.

A view of the newly-completed Casino (1966) and Palace Hotel (1967). (Frank Cowin Library)

SUMMERLAND

Summerland was a dream that became a nightmare: a seemingly bottomless pit for ratepayers' and Government money and the site of one of Britain's worst civil disasters. When first planned, though, it seemed exciting: a place where people could be entertained in an artificial environment that gave the impression of being out-of-doors. It seemed the perfect answer to British weather. Town Councillors thought they had a ready-made lessee too; the concessionaires of a proposed second casino for Douglas. Secret plans proposed that the place should be a gaming centre so it was a disappointment when Tynwald's Gaming Board of Control permitted the second casino to be established in the former Palace Ballroom immediately adjoining the Palace Hotel.

In October, 1964 Douglas Corporation bought the now ailing Derby Castle complex for £85,000 and earmarked the site for redevelopment. At first Councillors thought they would have a Manchester firm of developers, Shearer Estates Ltd., as partners. They had plans for a traditional entertainments structure topped by a fibreglass spike which would be lowered onto it by helicopter and be illuminated at night. However, negotiations fell through. Instead the Corporation pressed ahead with the promise of help from Tynwald. The old theatre, ballroom and adjoining castellated Strathallan Lodge which had been used as a pub, were demolished by the autumn of 1965 and to replace them local architects were commissioned to design a place where people would feel as if they were outdoors though protected from the weather.

One idea was that a swimming pool could be arranged like a natural seashore with sunbathers tanning themselves on golden sands from artificial ultra-violet light reflected off a false sky. Eventually this proved to be unworkable. The design for an artificial sea and the town's aspirations for a championship swim pool weren't compatible. A swim pool had to be built as a separate structure (part-financed from the sale of the old Noble's Baths). Artificial sunlight, meanwhile, presented legal questions like, would Summerland's operators be liable to damages if visitors bathed too long in ultra-violet light and were burned? To overcome that problem artificial sunbathing had to be confined to a sun dome where up to 50 people lay on beanbags for a controlled time limit. It was a lot less than the initial dream but even so the final result was impressive.

There were 3.5 acres of facilities, stacked in receding terraces overlooking a main hall and against a natural cliff down which a man-made waterfall cascaded. All was cocooned by a steel skeleton structure on a reinforced concrete base with a skin of plastic Oroglas. Tinted in bronze to give natural light the effect of golden sunrays, the Oroglas was fitted in pyramid-shaped six foot square panels. In the event of a fire these were designed to soften and shrink as they warmed then drop out of their fastenings before they could ignite - a belief which gave the operators of Summerland a false sense of security.

The interior heat was fixed at 80 degrees Fahrenheit. That meant that as the cliff face was planted out, the earth could dry out quickly. To overcome the problem Gardens Superintendant Eric Coward arranged for water mixed with plant foods to be piped to the top of the cliff and then be released through the soil. The Aquadrome was completed in July, 1969 and the adjoining entertainments complex by December, 1970. The latter was then leased for 21 years by the U.K.'s Trust House Forte Ltd. The total cost was £1,618,408 of which Tynwald contributed £645,000.

Summerland was an all-family centre. Its attractions included a modern disco in a basement, pubs, a cinema and a children's area incorporating their own theatre with Punch and Judy and conjuring by a resident 'uncle'. The idea was that youngsters could be left in one part of the building whilst parents had a drink or were entertained in another. This was to prove to be one of the worst horrors of the Summerland disaster - divided families trying to reunite in the midst of a fire that had been thought impossible. It happened on the night of 2nd August, 1973. Youths playing with matches on a crazy-golf course on a terrace outside

A view of the burnt-out shell of Summerland after the disastrous fire on the night of 2nd August, 1973. The adjoining Aquadrome escaped virtually unscathed. (R and L Kelly Collection)

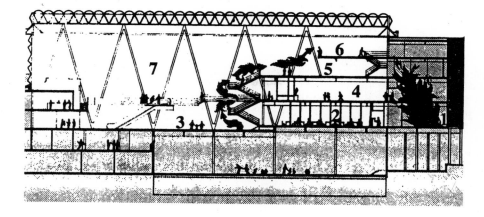

The fire started in a glass-fibre kiosk on the right (1) and spread through the cladding, bursting out into the amusement arcade next to the restaurant (2). Soon the flames spread upwards from the Solarium floor (3) to the Marquee Showbar (4), Leisure floor (5) and Cruise Deck (6). Within 20 minutes the Oroglas wall (7) was ablaze.

the main building lit the plastic thatching on a small hut. This fell against Summerland as attempts were made to extinguish the fire. It seemed such a small incident no one was particularly concerned and entertainment continued.

What no one realised was that the heat had spread and started another blaze in Summerland itself, hidden in a cavity wall overlooking the M.E.R. sheds. In that cavity there were substances which emitted inflammable gases. These accumulated then exploded devastatingly through an inner beauty-board lining into Summerland. There was a fiery flash-over and the heat rose so fast that the Oroglas panels had no chance to soften and fall from their fixings. They ignited and dripped molten plastic on to those below.

It was the worst land-based disaster in the town's history: one also of epic bravery and miraculous escapes; of children tossed from the upper levels to people below. Miraculously the vast majority of people in Summerland that night escaped the flames and toxic smoke. Afterwards one of the real trees planted inside gave the appearance of nothing untoward having happened. The adjoining Aquadrome escaped virtually unscathed. But in Summerland or afterwards in hospital 50 died and many others were scarred physically or mentally for the rest of their lives. That night and the following day as St. George's Church Hall was turned into an emergency mortuary with refrigeration equipment, the disaster plans at Noble's Hospital were tested to the limit. (Subsequently those involved lectured in Britain on how to cope so well in such an emergency.) Meanwhile, in an age of communication there was a strange sense of isolation. The news of the disaster was flashed by radio and television across Britain but so many wanted to 'phone their families and friends to let them know they were safe that the system was swamped. For many it was impossible to make a long-distance call.

Subsequently there were many who thought Summerland should not be rebuilt. An empty site should be left as a memorial. However, an agreement was reached eventually between Douglas Corporation, Tynwald's Local Government Board (who had provided an original cash grant) and Trust House Forte on the erection of a more traditional building minus the Oroglas. The new Summerland was opened on 22nd June, 1978 but proved unattractive to commercial operators. Trust House Forte disposed of their lease to a small concern. This did not achieve much so the responsibility for the centre was taken over by Tynwald's Department of Tourism.

The Lieut. Governor appointed a Commission of Inquiry which reported on the causes and circumstances of the fire. It also made 34 recommendations which had far-reaching results not only in the Isle of Man but throughout Britain. Theatre regulations and building bye-laws were tightened as were methods of fire prevention, detection, fire alarms and methods of escape. These were embodied in the Fire Precautions Act of 1975 which made Fire Certificates compulsory for public buildings, hotels, boarding houses and certain residential premises which would, henceforth, be regularly inspected.

A view of Summerland as rebuilt and opened in 1978. The concrete sloping walkway from the promenade has since been removed. (R and L Kelly Collection)

DOUGLAS CORPORATION TRANSPORT

The Corporation's bus fleet was fully occupied during the war period as a result of petrol rationing for private cars and in meeting the demands of the town's large population of service personnel. With many bus staff away with the armed forces it was necessary to recruit female staff to 'man' the buses, something unheard of in pre-war days. The heavy use through the six war years took its toll on the ageing Tilling Stevens and it was only with the considerable ingenuity on the part of the garage staff that they were kept in service. It was also an expensive business so when the end of the war was reached 13 of the 23 pre-war Tilling Stevens were withdrawn. In order to alleviate the situation the Transport Department had applied to the Ministry of Supply for replacements. They were a long time in coming - two utility Bedfords arriving in 1944. These were numbered 15-16 (FMN 899/900). The request for double-deckers resulted in three Daimlers arriving in 1945 - these being 51-53 and registered FMN 954/5 and GMN 242. Despite being of wartime utility finish and having wooden slatted seats they proved quite popular and remained in service until 1970. They were also the first Corporation buses to have diesel oil engines and it was soon noted they could average about nine miles to the gallon compared with the 4/5 of the petrol AEC Regents.

As Douglas returned to normal with every indication of pre-war levels of traffic being reached it was essential to modernise and even expand the fleet. By the end of 1949 some 18 of the latest AEC Regents had been acquired and numbered 54 to 71 (GMN 905/6; HMN 687-690; JMN 724-727; KMN 835-842). (It was one of these, No 62, which suffered collapsed suspension on the front nearside while travelling down Prospect Hill. In one of the very rare accidents involving Corporation buses, the double-decker crashed into King's cycle shop on the corner of Athol Street demolishing the front of the shop and sustaining major damage to itself requiring the chassis to be returned to AEC for repair). The following year, 1950, three rare Leyland Comets, 20-22 (KMN 518-520), arrived to add to the six pre-war Cubs. These were joined by two AEC Regals, also single-deckers - 30 and 31 (NMN 201 and 355). The 1926 Vulcan was retired in 1948 leaving two of these unique low-chassis Vulcans available for summer duty.

Mr Wolsey, the General Manager had been able in 1949 to introduce an extension of the promenade service to the White City (Onchan Head) with compensation being paid to the Manx Electric Railway Company who had objected most strongly. Another new service was to the end of the South Quay, though this was quickly changed to Douglas Head the following year and was supplemented by a summer service to Port Soderick. The early 1950s saw further demands from the new Spring Valley and Willaston estates. Also, a popular Circular Tour from Peveril Square for visitors was introduced which was advertised as covering nine miles for 2s 3d. Another innovation was the appearance of clock faces in glass cases at route stops, the fingers indicating the precise time of the next bus. This operation was carried out by the conductors but in the case of the one-man buses it meant quite an addition to the driver's workload.

Winter times saw many of the surviving pre-war Regents having their petrol engines removed and replaced with reconditioned and more economical diesel oil engines. The two Vulcans were also completely overhauled and given Bedford petrol engines. This provided plenty of winter work for the garage staff of six or seven mechanics at York Road. In 1957 four of the Regent Mk V double-deckers (with full width bonnets) were received, these being 72 to 75 (VMN 664-667). Also in 1957 five Guy Otters arrived and took the numbers 8 to 12 (WMN 484-488). These were specially designed for Douglas and had large humps front and rear to accommodate route indicators. They were nicknamed 'Wolsey's Camels' and soon afterwards the six pre-war Leyland Cubs (Wolsey's Midgets) were withdrawn, as were the two Vulcans and the wartime Bedfords. Further replacements for these were two AEC Reliances - 32 and 33 (XMN 290 and 289).

Years of difficult negotiations between Douglas Corporation, Isle of Man Road Services Ltd. and the Airports Board finally reached agreement in 1957 for a new Bus Station and Air Terminal to be built on the Lord Street Car Park. This would bring together the various termini around the Victoria Pier area and the 'out of town' services of Isle of Man Road Services. The years of negotiations were followed by long delays and it was not until 17th May, 1962 that the new Bus

One of the six Leyland Cubs which gave valuable service during the war years when they were operated by women driver/conductresses. Note the blackout shields on the headlights. (Michael Barry Collection)

One of the three 1945 wartime utility Daimlers which remained in service until 1970, complete with wooden slatted seats. (Michael Barry)

Terminus and Air Terminal came into operation. By this time the old Victoria Pier Buildings, a feature of the town since the turn of the century, had been demolished. Also, in 1961, Mr C.F. Wolsey retired as the Department's General Manager, a position he had held since 1932. He had the distinction of being the longest serving municipal transport manager in Britain and his period in charge of the 'yellow buses,' not forgetting the horse trams, is looked back upon as the Golden Years of Douglas Corporation Transport. Mr Wolsey was replaced by the appointment of the two senior heads of the Department as 'Joint Controllers'. These two well-known men in the town were Mr Dean Halsall and Mr Ambrose Hampton. When Mr Halsall retired in 1966, Mr Hampton was placed in sole charge as General Manager.

As the pre-war Regent double-deckers were withdrawn they were replaced by Regent Vs - five arriving in 1964/5, these being numbered 1 to 5 (8122-4 MN and 679 and 677 BMN). The two last Regents to be built were delivered to the Corporation in 1968 and numbered 14 and 15 (409/10 LMN). But the economics of the bus operations were dictating that more and more one-man buses be introduced. Already, in 1966, two Bedfords had been introduced, these being 6 and 7 (899 and 900 EMN). Costs of new equipment were increasing alarmingly and in 1970 the Transport Department were able to acquire eight second-hand Leyland Cubs, being surplus to the requirements of Lancashire United Transport. They took the numbers 34-41 (227 to 238 UMN). What were destined to be the last of the 'yellow buses' to be introduced were four Bedford saloons which could be used as buses or for charter work. These arrived in 1974 and were numbered 16 to 19 (MAN 51B, 52B, 138B and 139B).

While the Corporation bus operation, with the usual disparity between summer and winter traffic, continued to be run as effectively and efficiently as possible by Mr Hampton and a small administrative staff of three, and with only a small annual deficit, it was significant that the last four buses had been purchased as a result of a Government grant of £18,000, amounting to half the total cost. Holiday traffic was falling and more and more people were deserting the buses and travelling by car. This was also affecting in a much more serious way the workings of Isle of Man Road Services Ltd., whose general manager was now Mr W.T.

Lambden. The threat of reducing the 'out of town', and of even abandoning some of the quieter country routes, drew Government into increasing involvement. Since 1971 50% grants, totalling over £83,000, had been made in respect of 29 new and second-hand 'red' buses, with similar guarantees in place for those on order. Not for the first time, the whole question of the Island's bus services had been looked into by appointed consultants. In 1966 the Transport Commission's Report strongly advocated that both bus operations should be merged and that management should be in the hands of the larger Road Services. It was argued that merging the administrative and operating costs would be financially beneficial. The first meetings between the parties made little progress. Chairman of the Transport Committee was Alderman W.B. Kaneen with the members being Alderman R.F. Quayle and Councillors S.J. Cain, H. Cunningham, I.A. Fargher and W.Shimmin.

In 1971 Tynwald set up a Steering Committee with the avowed intent of a merger taking place. Corporation Transport Manager Mr Ambrose Hampton could not agree that the two different operations, with little in common as regards equipment and routes, could be run more effectively. Certainly this would not apply to the Corporation bus service. So strongly did he feel on the matter, and as he did not seem to have the full backing of the Transport Committee, he took the step of resigning. Mr Dean Halsall came out of retirement and was joined by the former Borough Treasurer Mr A.L. Costain as joint managers. At the end of the year Mr Wilson Gibb was confirmed as Manager.

Transport Committee members met with Road Services and Government representatives in the late summer of 1971 and it was agreed to work out details of a merger. This proved to be a long process and it was not until 1976 that the Steering Committee's recommendations were accepted by Tynwald. All Island bus services would be 'nationalised' and run by the Government-subsidised 'Isle of Man National Transport Ltd.' with Mr W.T. Lambden as its first General Manager. And so the proud history of the Corporation's bus undertaking came to an end. Their fleet of 38 buses was scrutinised and the older Regents withdrawn, the rest of the fleet gradually appearing in 'Road Service' red. The York Road Depot remained in use until 1983 when all maintenance work was transferred to the former Road Services garage at Homefield.

AEC Regent MkV No 72 being 'received' at the Town Hall in 1957. Among the four gentlemen standing on the left is General Manager C.F. Wolsey, in light raincoat, with Councillor Alec Moore in dark suit and Councillor 'Gussie' Craine with walking stick. On the right are Councillors Bert Stephens and Fletcher Quayle, D.C. Craine (Maintenance Engineer) and Alderman Frank M. Corkill.

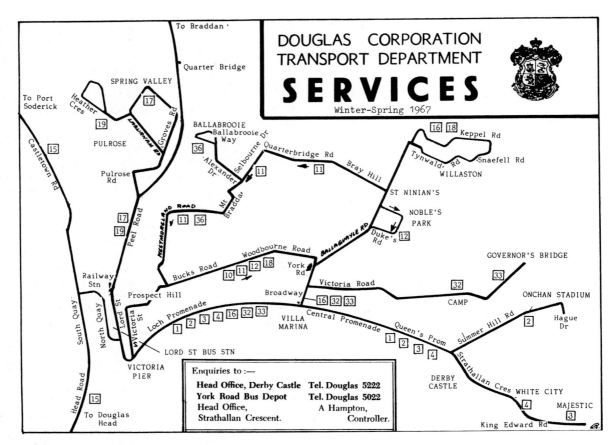

DOUGLAS CORPORATION
TRANSPORT DEPARTMENT
SERVICES
Winter-Spring 1967

Enquiries to :—

Head Office, Derby Castle	Tel. Douglas 5222
York Road Bus Depot	Tel. Douglas 5022
Head Office,	A Hampton,
Strathallan Crescent.	Controller.

One of the two Vulcans which arrived in 1935. They were unique in that the coachwork was designed for seasonal use by Corporation General Manager, C.F. Wolsey.

One of the five Guy Otter 'one-man' buses which arrived in 1957. They sported a Redskin chieftain radiator cap.

AEC Reliance of 1958 seen here in company with one of the AEC Regals which arrived in 1951.

Last buses to be purchased by the Transport Department were eight Leyland Tiger Cubs in 1970. No 34 is seen here on the Loch Promenade. (Photographs by the late Mr R.F. Mack)

THE DOUGLAS HORSE TRAMS

Despite the onset of war the horse trams were kept running until the end of September, 1939. Then 35 horses were sold off at an average price of £19.19s.6d followed by the remaining 40 in the spring of 1940 when it was realised that there would be no further 'seasons' until the end of the war. In any case the tram tracks were to be partly 'interned' behind the lines of barbed wire fencing of the camps along the promenades. The trams themselves lay idle in the depots at Derby Castle and York Road while the 49 acres of 'Corporation' fields used for winter grazing were cultivated as part of the wartime emergency measures.

The removal of the camp fencing at the end of 1945 meant that there was every chance of the horse trams returning to normal in 1946. In April 42 Irish horses arrived in the middle of the night and the clatter they made on the way to the stables caused quite a stir for those who heard them! After practice runs everything was in order for the official re-opening for the season, with the new Lieutenant Governor, Air Vice Marshall Sir Geoffrey Bromet as 'driver' of the first tram. In the circumstances it was a good season, but the 22 trams in use had only made a small profit and once again the future of the service came under scrutiny. Abolitionists talked about the cruelty aspect but the I.O.M.S.P.C.A. could find no fault in the treatment of the horses. The idea of replacing the horse trams with open-top buses was considered. Views of the travelling public were sought and an overwhelming number were in favour of retaining the trams. The Transport Committee agreed to give them a chance by keeping the same service for 1947 with a rise in the single fare from 2½d to 3d. Both 1947 and 1948 were boom years for tourism with over 600,000 seasonal visitors recorded, thus surpassing the pre-war years. The horse-trams soon proved to be as popular as ever, carrying over 2 million passengers during the 1947-49 seasons and producing healthy profits (£4,000 in 1947) which, in turn, meant a contribution to the rates. The future of the horse-trams was thus secured for the foreseeable future.

The eight remaining double-decker trams were withdrawn in 1949, seven being broken up and one, No 14, formerly 13, was transferred to the British Transport Commission for museum preservation. In 1952 the fleet was further reduced when seven of the small 'toastracks' and the two 'sunshade' cars were withdrawn. This left a variety of 31 trams which could be switched according to the weather. Equipped with roller bearings the trams could with ease carry 40 passengers. Weekends in early August remained the peak periods when as many as 26 cars could be in action carrying 30,000 passengers per day. A typical year was 1955 when the trams covered 100,000 miles with passengers over the 1,500,000 mark. For 1952 the fare from Derby Castle to Victoria Pier had been increased to 6d, the journey taking about 20 minutes at an average speed of 7-9 mph.

By 1955 the number of horses available settled around the 80 mark which meant that the working time of each horse was reduced to three hours a day during the four-month season. The rest of the year the horses were, and still are, put out to grazing on rented fields. In the stables at Summer Hill each of the horses had its own stall with the horse's name. For the mares, names varied from Bridget to Thelma while the horses had names such as Adam, Duke (after Geoff Duke) and Winston. The older horses soon got to know the routine and could tell when their tour of duty was coming to an end by stopping opposite the stables and waiting for its replacement to appear, something which still applies today. It was also established by this time that horses which had earned retirement should remain on the Island and be placed in the care of the voluntarily-run Isle of Man Home of Rest for Old Horses. Feeding the horses was one of the major items of expense with 100 tons of hay, 4,500 bushels of oats and 30 tons of straw being typical requirements for each year.

1956 was celebrated in grand style as the 80th Anniversary Year. Early in the morning of 7th August the stud of 80 horses was paraded to Victoria Pier where they were assembled rank upon rank. There they were watched by a huge gathering which included the Lieut. Governor and Lady Dundas, the Mayor Councillor W.B. Kaneen and Mrs Kaneen, Pat Smythe, the famous international horsewoman, and the grand-daughter of Thomas Lightfoot, founder of the Douglas Bay Tramway. Tram No 40, driven by Pat Smythe, was used by the official party for a trip to Derby Castle with the Promenade lined all the way three or four deep

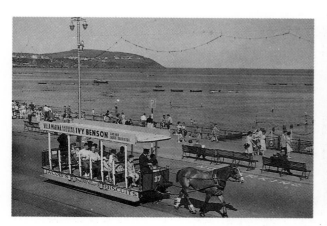

Tram No 37, dating from 1896, on the Harris Promenade in the early 1950s. (Bill Crisp)

Another early 1950s Promenade scene showing toastrack No 10 which was withdrawn in 1979. (Bill Crisp)

A busy scene from 1951 with plenty of transport interest. On the left is one of the Corporation's Leyland Comets while a Road Service Leyland double-decker emerges from the foot of Broadway. The traffic is under the control of the policeman standing in the box situated on the small traffic island seen on the left. Tram 35 is still in service as is No 44 and now known as the Royal Car. The third tram is one of the 'sunshade' toastracks.

With the Victoria Pier Arcade buildings in the background, 80 horses are assembled as part of the 80th anniversary celebrations of 1956.

Her Majesty Queen Elizabeth, Prince Philip, Princess Anne and Earl Mountbatten arriving opposite the Sefton Hotel on the occasion of the Royal Visit, 2nd August, 1972. Tram 44 is in use again as the Royal Car, having previously been used by the Queen Mother in 1964.

with waving and cheering people. It was a great day for the Transport Department under Chairman Councillor Bert Stephen and the tramway's staff of a hundred which included the stablehands, a saddler, and blacksmith and assistant. In charge of the proceedings were General Manager Mr C.F. Wolsey and Tramways Manager Mr Dean Halsall. Engineer was Mr J.D. Craine who had spent 30 years with the trams until he lost his life in the Winter Hill Air Disaster of February, 1958. During that year Mr J.C. Naylor was replaced by Mr G.B. Stubbs as the Corporation's part-time vet.

The late Fifties began to show a gradual decline in holiday traffic, which was reflected in a corresponding fall in passenger figures. By 1964 passengers had fallen to below the million mark for the first time followed by variations each summer, often determined by the weather conditions. The closure of the Fleetwood steamer service in 1962 added to the decline but by 1969 the million mark was once again nearly attained and figures remained fairly steady around that mark until well into the Seventies. By careful management the trams remained in profit and were able to continue subsidizing the buses. One of the decisive factors was the number of horses kept in the stud. For 1965 the total of horses stood at 58 after the arrival of 15 new horses chosen by Councillor E.G. Griffin, a riding enthusiast. By 1972 the horse total rose to 70 and the service was every ten minutes in early and late season and about one every one and a half minutes in the peak of the season. To meet rising costs the single fare for the full journey had by now been increased to 9d.

The horse trams have, and always will be, a great source of curiosity bringing valuable publicity to the town. They are in themselves a reminder of a bygone age, and are unique to the town. Whenever a Royal Visit is planned it is almost traditional to include a visit to the trams. This tradition started in 1964 when Her Majesty the Queen Mother visited the Island on 5th July. Tram No 44 was specially painted to serve as the Royal Car which was pulled by 'Winston', the Queen Mother travelling between Summer Hill and the Villa Marina. The following year Princess Margaret and Lord Snowdon were the Royal Guests. In 1970 The Duke of Edinburgh first made his acquaintance with the horse trams.

A red-letter day in the history of the horse trams was 2nd August, 1972. At ten o'clock that morning Her Majesty Queen Elizabeth, accompanied by HRH the Duke of Edinburgh, Princess Anne and Earl Mounbatten of Burma, came ashore at the Victoria Pier from the Royal Yacht Britannia. After the official greetings the Royal Party boarded tram No 44 which, with tram No 36 was bedecked with flowers and beautifully repainted for the occasion. The Douglas Corporation coat of arms was added above the canopies of both trams with a crown surmounting the emblems. The Royal Car was pulled by Pearl, an 11-year-old roan mare, magnificently turned out in polished harness and decorated with flowers. The pride of the stable staff, Pearl, did her work splendidly over the short journey as far as the Sefton Hotel, but when the Queen rewarded her with sugar lumps she promptly dropped them! Princess Anne stepped forward and rectified the situation. Driver for the occasion was Stables Foreman James Moughtin and Traffic Inspector Jack Corris was conductor. They had both completed long service with the trams and retired during that year.

The Transport Committee was now in the throes of the merger of its bus fleet with Isle of Man Road Services and, as already mentioned, Mr Hampton had resigned over the matter. He was succeeded by Mr Wilson Gibb who in 1973 took over as Manager of the horse tram undertaking, a position he would hold for the next 21 years. Passenger figures were remaining steady around the million mark, enabling the stud to be maintained at about 50. But a huge increase in the price of new horses led to a policy of local breeding and the first foal was born in August, 1974. The tram fleet stood at 31 made up of 5 Winter Saloons, 6 bulkhead Toastracks (with open sides and covered tops), 6 similar Sunshades, 11 fully open Toastracks and 3 All Weather Cars, affectionately known as 'tomato boxes'.

The Centenary of the Horse Trams was celebrated on 9th August, 1976. It was a magnificent occasion with many thousands lining the promenades for the Grand Parade. Here the trams are being mustered at the Victoria Pier with double-decker No 14 in the forefront filled with Corporation members and guests.

A timeless scene in the cobbled yard of the stables on Queen's Promenade. A horse is being prepared for another tour of duty.

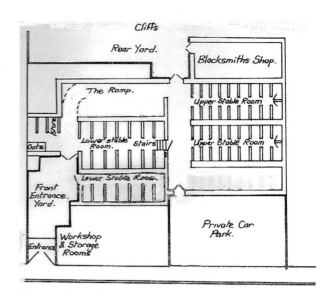

Plan of the stables as they are today, and basically the same as those used in 1887.

HORSE TRAM CENTENARY

There is no doubt that the celebrations of 9th August, 1976, arranged for the Centenary of the Horse Trams made it one of the greatest one-day events staged in the town for many years. A huge turn-out of 30,000 locals and visitors lined the seafront soon after breakfast to witness the spectacle. It began with the vintage tramcars being towed from the Derby Castle depot by a Corporation bus to the new terminus at the Sea Terminal. Then came the parade of 50 horses, including six foals - all resplendent in gleaming brasswork and bedecked with garlands and ribbons. The horses were then hitched to the tramcars in readiness for the grand procession back to Derby Castle. Guest of Honour for the occasion was Olympic Silver Medallist Anne Moore who held the reins as 'Sarah' led the way by pulling the double-decker No 14 and dating from 1883 It had been returned from the Transport Museum at Clapham specially for the occasion. Miss Moore was accompanied by the Mayor, Councillor F.J. Waterson J.P. and Chairman of the Transport Committee, Alderman Ernest Griffin. The rest of the tram was occupied by Councillors, Corporation officials and their guests. All along the Promenade the fleet of trams did a 'roll-past' for the delighted spectators and the overwhelming public response was a great reward for all those responsible for organising the grand parade.

One of the highlights in the parade was the re-appearance of one of the cable cars, not seen since the closure of the cable tramway in 1929. Two cars had been used as a habitation near the Killane river in Ballaugh. When discovered they were no longer in use, steps were taken to retrieve them and possibly recreate what would be the only example for posterity. It was an ambitious and costly enterprise but at the helm of the restoration was Mr Keith Pearson, the author of the definitive 'Isle of Man Tramways.' Work started in 1968 with

facilities made available in York Road bus garage. Work progressed slowly when both time (holidays) and funds (donations) became available. It was a mammoth task to rebuild a 'new' cable car from the relics of the original cars Nos 72 and 73 dating from 1896. Mr Pearson and his small team of engineering enthusiasts (The Douglas Cable Car Group) ensured that the reconstruction was authentic in every detail. Each year saw progress being made until 1976, and with car body repainted and the bogies completed the cable car was moved to Strathallan. In memory of the originals it was numbered 72 at one end and 73 at the other! For the Centenary Parade it was towed by a Land Rover. Today it can be inspected in the Tram Museum at Strathallan, together with memorabilia of the town's cable cars.

The Millennium of Tynwald, celebrated in 1979, gave a welcome boost to the visiting industry, but it was only a temporary halt to the almost annual decline in arrival figures. Throughout the 1980s the horse tram service suffered accordingly with passenger figures a mere shadow of what they used to be. No longer could it be relied upon to contribute to the Borough rate and, despite economies, the 1994 deficit reached £84,000. The number of passenger journeys that year was 187,131, though the previous year a total of over 205,000 was recorded during the celebrations for the Year of the Railways. Many locals have never ridden on the trams though to the great majority of visitors it is a popular attraction and there is still considerable interest in the tramway. The oldest tram remaining in continuous service is No 12, a toastrack dating from 1888 and built by G.F. Milnes and Co. of Birkenhead who supplied most of the tram fleet. The 'youngest' still in use is No 45, dating from 1908. Particularly interesting is the history of No 18. It was one of six double-deck cars purchased from the horse tramway company in South Shields which was dissolved in 1887. Built in 1883 they were the only second-hand trams ever brought to Douglas. They were numbered 13 to 18. Then in 1903 No 17 was converted to single-deck but was replaced by a new tram in 1914. No 18 was similarly treated but after a long period of service it was decided to restore it to its former double-deck configuration. Sponsored by Okell's Brewery the restoration took place during the winter of 1988/9 and was returned to service in immaculate condition. Passengers are limited to 20 on the top deck only. Another of this batch of double-deck trams is No 14 which is the only survivor of the eight withdrawn in 1949. It led the Centenary Parade of 1976 having been returned to Douglas from the Science Museum, London. It was afterwards stored at Derby Castle but today can be seen as an evocative exhibit in the Social History Gallery of the Manx Museum. Here it takes its place among the memorabilia which recalls life in Douglas during its heyday as a leading holiday resort.

Of the 51 tramcars which have been used since 1876, 21 are still maintained for regular service. These consist of 4 Winter Saloons (Nos 1 and 27-29); 6 open Toastracks (12,21,38,39,40 and 42); 9 covered toastracks with glazed protection, known as Bulkheads (32-37 and 43-45) and 1 Double-Decker (18). No 22 has been converted as the Tram Shop; it began life in 1890 as a toastrack. Additionally, trams 11 and 47 are stored in a shed at Douglas Railway Station, and 46 is currently preserved at Woodside Terminal, Birkenhead. Tramways Manager is Peter Cannon who took over from Wilson Gibb in 1993. Peter began his working life with the tramway as a conductor in 1975.

The number of horses for the 1995 season stood at 48 of which 38 are experienced in tram work. The remainder, locally bred, include foals and young horses which have to be four years old before their training begins. Winter grazing is on Corporation land at Anagh Cooar and Blackberry Lane in Onchan. Fields are also rented at Clypse and Honey Hill, Onchan, and in Maughold. For the summer season the working horses occupy four of the original stables which date from 1887 and are those acquired by Thomas Lightfoot, the founder, on what became the Queen's Promenade. The stables are largely unaltered and the cobbled entrance yard leads to the four stable rooms still in use. (The yard is a rose-grower's delight and the horse manure is put to good use on the Corporation's numerous flower beds and gardens). The horses are looked after by two permanent staff one of whom is a blacksmith, the horses having to be re-shod every four to six weeks. During the season three additional stablehands are employed and, the day's work over, a nightwatchman keeps guard over the horses. Nothing is spared in maintaining the horses in good health and the veterinary surgeons of Vanderplank, Davies and Cox pay weekly visits to the stables.

Only on the other side of the world, in Australia, can a similar horse tram service be found, thus making the Douglas Horse Trams unique in the Northern Hemisphere. It is a priceless piece of Victorian transport enterprise and a living museum which encaptures a slower and more leisurely way of life. The horse trams also take their place in the Island's rich transport heritage and will, no doubt, be clip-clopping their way into the twenty-first century. Douglas would never be the same without them.

Rolling into the future. Tram No 18 has a chequered history having been originally built in 1883. In 1903 it was converted to single-deck but in 1988/9 it was restored to double-decker configuration and is the only one of its kind still in service. (Ian Clark)

SOME NOTABLE EVENTS

In 1946 Douglas Corporation celebrated its Golden Jubilee. But these were hard times, the Island still recovering from the war. On Saturday, 2nd March a Civic Luncheon in the Villa Marina marked the occasion, strict rationing limiting what could be provided. Most people, meanwhile, had other things to celebrate like the arrival of the first consignment of bananas for five years. There were 700 bunches: enough for a banana for everyone under 18. Later, the arrival of lemons was worthy of public notice.

For others the great celebration that month was reserved for the return of the *Lady of Mann*. Here was the symbol of the Manx war effort and the return to peace. The 'Lady' had gone to war in 1939 under the command of the Steam Packet's Commodore, Captain T.C. Woods. Now, aged 66, he kept his vow to bring her back, the vessel bedecked in flags, people greeting her and her crew at Douglas harbour with emotional singings of Ellan Vannin and the National Anthem. Other vessels wouldn't return but the pride of the Steam Packet had made it. She'd braved the worst of Dunkirk. In one sailing alone she'd carried an incredible 5,000 troops: grounded at low tide and bombed by the Germans. Other Manx ships had gone down. The crew of the 'Lady' had seen them but had persevered ... then had gone on to help evacuate troops from Le Havre, Cherbourg, La Pallice and Brest. There she'd carried an even more amazing 7,000 passengers in one sailing. Come D-Day the 'Lady' had ferried troops to the landing beaches. In recognition of her achievements Captain Woods had been awarded the O.B.E. Now Councillor Tom Cowin, Mayor of Douglas, greeted him and his officers at the pier and took them by bus to the Town Hall for a Civic Reception. On Whit Saturday there was a Grand Victory Ball in the Villa Marina but this was the true moment of victory for most: a homecoming against all the odds.

It was a time also for farewells; the departure of the military, closure of the internment camps and a return to normality. Councillors were agitating already for the removal of air raid shelters from the promenade. At Douglas Head barbed wire entanglements which had sealed off the headland came down and its guards, locally recruited Admiralty civil police, disbanded. Thus was one of the war's big secrets revealed - the instruction in the use of radar, one of the great tools of victory. Douglas had such a familiarity with radar that it wasn't surprising that by 1948 its harbour was the first civilian one in the world to be controlled by it. The Douglas radar station was established at the end of Victoria Pier and attracted international interest. A 60 ft pylon was erected with a reflector which could scan to a distance of three miles and as close as 300 ft. Cabling fed the signal to a radar room 200 ft away. The equipment was installed by the Cossor Radar Company slightly ahead of the installation of similar equipment at Liverpool. To decide whether the height of the pylon was sufficient, harbour officials had a Douglas fire engine erect its turntable ladder at the edge of the pier. They then climbed to the top to check the view. The radar station became operational in March and was put into immediate use even before its official handing-over to Tynwald's Harbour Board because of thick persistent mist. Within months its range was increased from three to twelve miles.

One wartime item that was not removed was the siren above the Town Hall which was used as an emergency summons for fire crews. This was tested at 12 noon on Saturdays and people could set their watches to it. With the introduction of personal bleepers, however, the need for the siren passed some years ago. Other sirens, installed during the height of the Cold War in the 1950s and '60s by the Civil

This photograph, dating from about 1960, shows three of the Steam Packet's post-war passenger ships in company with the 'Lady of Mann' and the 'Ben my Chree,' berthed at the Victoria Pier. These two fine ships played their part at Dunkirk and in the Normandy D-Day landings. After being reconditioned they returned to passenger service and played a leading part in the post-war boom years. The 'Ben,' seen at the end of the pier, was withdrawn in 1965, and in 1971 the 'Lady of Mann' made her last departure from Douglas. She was held in great affection and huge crowds gathered on Douglas Head to bid her an emotional farewell.

Defence at the Court House, the Power Station, the Museum and St. Ninian's High School, remained operational until 1993 when the Cold War thawed. These were designed to provide a four-minute warning of an incoming atomic missile attack. They could be activated by either the police station or directly from the headquarters of the U.K. Warning and Monitoring Organisation in Preston. Once a year they were tested on Remembrance Sunday. The eerie wail which marked the 'All Clear' was sounded at 11am as a tribute to the war dead. However, the more menacing undulating tone known as 'Attack Warning Red' wasn't sounded. It was thought it would worry people too much. The sirens were removed in 1993 and sold for use as flood warnings in London.

Nothing more typified the return to normality for Douglas after the war than the switching on of its summer illuminations. They hadn't been used since 31st August, 1939. Now, on Saturday, 28th May, 1949, after four years of post-war austerity, the lights were switched on again by the Mayor, Councillor F.M. Corkill. Two electrically illuminated horse trams took Councillors on a leisurely ride of inspection.

June 2nd, 1953 was Coronation Day for Queen Elizabeth ll. To mark the occasion all public buildings in Douglas were floodlit. In Douglas also the celebrations included a novel re-enactment of the Coronation. Children in Chester Street, Frederick Street and Finch Road area who had their own private street party were dressed in appropriate costume for the re-enactment. Elsewhere in Douglas there was a Carnival Parade followed by a fancy dress ball at the Palace Ballroom. The elderly were entertained to afternoon tea at the Villa Marina. Then the following day it was the children's turn. After a procession to the Villa Marina from Lord Street they were given a tea party at Douglas Holiday Camp. The very young were given coach rides. It was a sunny but blustery time - the wind threatened to blow bunting away but most of it survived.

Two years later Her Majesty, accompanied by Prince Philip Duke of Edinburgh (who had visited the 1949 T.T.) paid the first of several visits to the Island. She arrived in Douglas Bay aboard the royal yacht *Britannia* with an escort of three Royal Navy vessels. A parade through a crowded Noble's Park was one of the highlights; another, an address to members of Tynwald assembled in their chamber at Douglas. A crowd of thousands outside the Legislative Buildings heard everything via loudspeakers and appreciated her conclusion: "And now, good morning and good luck," delivered in perfect Manx.

Probably the strangest event in the Corporation's 100-year history occurred in November, 1960. That was when Princess Alexandra, visiting the Island to open a 50-bed extension at Noble's Hospital which bore her name, met two different Mayors of Douglas within hours of each other. In the morning she met one; in the afternoon, another. It happened because her visit co-incided with the annual installation of the new Mayor. Visiting the Town Hall in the morning, she was greeted by the outgoing Mayor, Councillor T.D. Lewis, and as it was his wife's birthday the Princess shared with him and the Mayoress a celebratory drink. At 2.15pm the Princess was due to arrive at the hospital for the opening ceremony. Fifteen minutes earlier the Town Council met to instal the new Mayor, Alderman Tom Quirk, then promptly adjourned the meeting so they could attend the celebrations at Noble's Hospital. Alderman Quirk

During the summer of 1955 Her Majesty Queen Elizabeth, accompanied by Prince Philip, made the first of several visits to the Island. One of the highlights of her visit was a parade before thousands of schoolchildren assembled in Noble's Park.

was rushed by car to the Nurses' Home and was there at 2.10pm to be among the official welcoming party when the Princess arrived shortly afterwards!

In 1963 the Queen Mother paid a four-day visit to the Island aboard the royal yacht and became the first woman to preside over a sitting of Tynwald at St. John's. Her itinerary included a charity ball at the Villa Marina and a formal switching-on of Douglas illuminations. But probably the most novel feature of all was a horse tram ride along Douglas promenade on the afternoon of Tynwald Day from Summerhill to the Villa Marina where she was greeted by thousands of children and others in the gardens. Such was the success of it that when the Queen paid a return visit to the Island aboard the *Britannia* in August, 1972, accompanied by most members of the Royal Family, a tram ride was included in her itinerary. The specially decorated tram was designated the royal tram and retained for special events. Prince Philip took a keen interest in the controls, trying them himself. On this visit Her Majesty signed the town's visitor's book on a platform on Douglas promenade watched by a crowd of thousands. The floodlit *Britannia,* anchored in Douglas Bay, was used by Her Majesty on this occasion to host a reception for a large number of government and local authority guests. They were transferred to and from the royal yacht by a small fleet of harbour boats from the Victoria Pier supplemented by the royal barge. It was a bit choppy and spray flew over the decks on occasions - with the result that on arriving on board the yacht some guests had to be 'dried out' below decks before being presented to their royal hosts.

Probably one of the most significant events of 1957 for what it said of the changing character of Douglas was the loss of St. Barnabas Church which overlooked the Lord Street bus station. St. Barnabas was the oldest parish in the town, constituted in 1869. Now it was merged with St. George's. The church, whose spire had dominated the skyline of lower Douglas and the harbour area, was closed and eventually pulled down. It was a sign of the times. Fewer people were going to church. Also St. Barnabas had outlived its purpose. It was redundant, said the Church of England. Most of the homes that had once packed lower Douglas and provided St. Barnabas with its congregation had gone, cleared as slums.

Though the 1950s were recession years of mass unemployment, in which few new homes were built, a trend had been established already which would be accelerated later in the sixties, seventies and eighties in which the town's population shifted to the new homes on the town's periphery, leaving the old centre to decay and then be re-developed for commercial property. During the sixties and seventies visionaries anticipated the complete demolition of Loch Promenade, Strand Street, Castle Street and the property immediately behind it and the building of an entirely new lower Douglas. The cost would have been enormous so that never transpired.

One area that did succumb, however, was the crowded narrow terraces of homes in the Chester Street development area bounded by Finch Road, Well Road Hill, St. Thomas' Church and Wellington Square. The Corporation had acquired old properties and most of them were demolished in 1974 to make way for a multi-storey car park and supermarket. The last residents of the area was a colony of cats, abandoned by their owners but kept well fed by local cat lovers who visited the area sometimes as late as midnight. Members of the M.S.P.C.A. had begged Councillors to delay the demolition by two or three weeks so they could catch all the cats and provide them with good homes. Instead they got a week-end.

Athol Street, said to be the longest and straightest street in town, once had shops and private homes. Now it has become the Island's financial and legal centre. The final transformation was marked in the 1980s by the disappearance of the last of what had been a number of small cottages sandwiched between St George's Street and Athol Street. Modern offices and banking premises had been erected around it in the 1970s and early '80s - but there in what was known as St George's Walk was a reminder of the old town, with two residents in their mid-80s determined to stay until their dying days. Eighty-six year old Rhoda Bell had reached an agreement with developers. As long as she could stay in her home until she died they could have it for demolition afterwards, she'd said. It meant her enduring a lot of inconvenience: noise and interruptions in water and gas supplies especially. But there were memorable moments too, typifying a happy classless relationship that was emerging between the new financial sector and the Island's people. When a new banking office which overshadowed the cottage was opened the chairman of the company, Sir Roy Matthews, visited Mrs Bell and apologised for all the inconvenience that had been caused - then arranged for one of the waitresses serving distinguished guests at a reception in the bank to bring along some flowers, drink and a full spread for Mrs Bell and her companion so they could share in the celebrations.

In 1994-95 extensive demolition was undertaken between the Villiers Hotel and Athol Hotel sites on Loch Promenade; also at Drumgold Street and Back Strand Street. However, little of the proposed new development was tourist orientated. This reflected a trend which had become unstoppable in the '70s and '80s. Councillors had resisted, with Government support, suggestions that seafront hotels should be converted into offices or apartments. The seafront should be reserved for tourism, they believed.

However, it soon became clear that the declining tourist industry couldn't support the accommodation it once had.

Clouding everything in early 1958 was the Island's worst-ever air disaster. It happened on a cold, misty late February morning when a chartered Bristol Wayfarer of Silver City Airways took a plane load of local garage men, engineers and motor agents on a day's outing to see production of electric batteries at an Exide plant in England. Wrong tuning of a radio compass ended in the aircraft plunging into Winter Hill near a transmitter mast. It was a bleak, inhospitable end for a planned day of pleasure. The hill was covered with snow and approach roads were blocked. Out of 42 passengers aboard only seven survived. Thirty-three children lost their fathers.

In Douglas as the first news of what had happened filtered out crowds of anxious relatives packed Athol Street and waited for the latest news received by phone and wire from the Press Association to be released from the Isle of Man Times building. The following Sunday the BBC made broadcasting history by giving the Island briefly what was called its own 'Manx Home Service.' A National Memorial Service in St. George's Church was broadcast on VHF exclusively for the Island from a transmitter on Douglas Head. At the time few people had VHF receivers but it was a gesture that was appreciated nevertheless.

For taxi men October 1962 was historic in that it was when the Corporation ordered meters to be fitted for the first time.

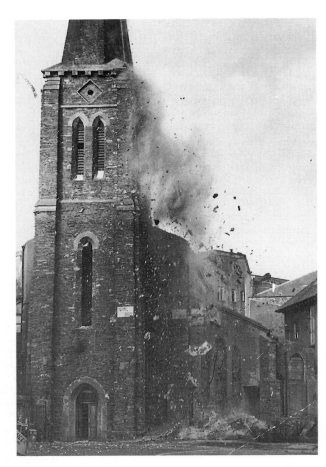

One of the most significant events of 1957 was the demolition of the redundant St. Barnabas Church. For over a century its tall spire had dominated the skyline of lower Douglas and the harbour area. (R and L Kelly Collection)

For All Saints Church the early sixties marked the end of the old 'Tin Tab' as it was known. The 19th century church built of corrugated metal was demolished in 1964 and a new church erected in its place the following year.

It was a time of embarrassment too for the crew of *HMS Manxman*. Arriving at Douglas in April, 1963 to pay a courtesy call on the Island after which the vessel had been named, the minesweeper went aground in thick fog on the Conister rock!

More than anything, however, this was a time of readjustment. Surtax had been abolished, capital gains tax removed and income tax lowered. New residents were beginning to flock to the Island and an embryo finance sector which would change the face of lower Douglas was beginning to develop. Tourism was still in decline; so badly now that whole streets of boarding houses would become transformed into apartments or 'bed-sits.' An historic turning point in the affairs of the Island, and of Douglas in particular, had been reached.

Socially one of the most significant post-war developments in the Isle of Man was the building by Douglas Corporation of a Crematorium in the Borough Cemetery. Until the 1960s burial was the traditional means of disposing of bodies but the increasing popularity elsewhere of cremation had begun to influence local opinion as early as the 1920s. There were suggestions even then at Council meetings that a Crematorium should be built but these weren't acted upon primarily because it was suspected that Manx people were conservative in their ways and a little-used Crematorium would cost ratepayers a substantial loss.

From the end of the Second World War onwards there were increasing calls for a Crematorium to be built. At first they represented only a small minority of the population and, conscious of the cost of building and operating such a place, Town Councillors still resisted them. As a Crematorium would meet an Island demand, they argued, it was a national responsibility to provide one rather than a municipal one. The result was that families who wanted to cremate their dead had to ship bodies to England and hold funerals there. In 1957 there were 35 off-Island funerals.

The following year Tynwald accepted the view that a Crematorium would be an all-Island facility and therefore its capital cost should be provided out of taxation if Councillors would accept responsibility for operating and maintaining the place. Some were reluctant for even that but by a majority of one vote the Council finally accepted the proposal. Many members were conscious of the fact that available land for traditional interments at the Borough Cemetery could be exhausted by the 1980s. In 1960, after a Public Inquiry had yielded not a single objection to converting the old chapel in the Borough Cemetery into a Crematorium, Tynwald voted the initial cost of £23,500.

When opened in 1961 much of the initial demand for its use originated from outside Douglas but soon town demand rose too - twice as fast, in fact, as Corporation advisers had expected. By the 1980s more than 50% of all funerals involved cremation, thereby easing pressure on cemetery space. At first most ashes were scattered in a Garden of Remembrance at the rear of the cemetery but in the mid 1980s the Corporation permitted the burial of ashes and the erection of mini headstones in space created from extra wide pathways between old graves. In this way people who wanted a place of remembrance could have one without adding to the pressure on space in the cemetery.

One of the most unusual post-war events occurred at the Villa Marina one April Sunday in 1963. That was when the Royal Hall became a synagogue for a day. Sandra Fingerhut, daughter of local businessman Benny Fingerhut, had established herself as a member of the nationally popular dance troupe 'The Toppers' who appeared regularly on television variety shows. Now she returned to the Island to be married to Dennis Levene. So many people wanted to see the traditional Jewish wedding ceremony that Mr Fingerhut hired the newly-decorated Villa Marina Royal Hall for the occasion. A queue of hundreds waited outside the Villa for the doors to open and eventually an estimated 2,000 attended. A traditional Jewish wedding canopy, last used at the Castle Mona 36 years earlier, was set up in the centre of the Royal Hall.

For Douglas the most traumatic post-war event was the national seamen's strike of 1966. From mid-May and throughout the whole of June it brought sea traffic to a halt, apart from some Union-sanctioned

The stately Fort Anne graced the entrance to Douglas harbour since the end of the eighteenth century and for some years had been the home of Sir William Hillary. It became a hotel at the beginning of the twentieth century but succumbed to the decline in tourism, being finally demolished in 1979. (Frank Cowin Library)

The new Douglas Sea Terminal for the Isle of Man Harbour Board was officially opened on 6th July, 1965 by Princess Margaret, Countess of Snowdon. (Frank Cowin Library)

emergency deliveries. The Island had attempted to be exempted from what was a UK-based dispute over pay but all approaches had been rebuffed. Now the tourist industry and local businessmen feared economic disaster. Air services boomed but they weren't enough to compensate for the loss of the steamers. The T.T. had to be postponed and that sent shockwaves through Douglas.

The relief was enormous when the strike ended at the beginning of July but by then it was feared that the rest of the season had been irreparably damaged by the uncertainties surrounding steamer services. Undaunted, everyone threw themselves into a concerted campaign to replace lost business with new late-season arrivals. The T.T. was salvaged for August and for September a 'Treasure Island' campaign was launched with all kinds of inducements for people to holiday on the Island then. There were specially reduced prices at shops and events. Hotels and guest houses offered free holidays for some members of parties and free sunshine 'insurance' was offered through the Tourist Board. If it rained on any day in September between 11am and 1pm or 2pm and 4pm, or if the weather was particularly poor, all cinemas in Douglas were opened free in the mornings and afternoons.

One of the most popular post-war slogans to promote the Isle of Man as a tourist resort as the Island became locked in a losing battle with Mediterranean sunshine resorts was 'Go Abroad to the Isle of Man.' To help project an image of sunshine and warmth Douglas Gardens Superintendent Eric Coward devised a plan to plant-out the seafront with tropical palms. These would be grown at the Corporation's nurseries then transferred to the promenade gardens when well grown. It involved trenching round part-grown palms at the nurseries, isolating their roots then leaving them for twelve months to recover before transferring them to the promenade. Mr Coward wasn't sure if it would succeed. His best estimate in 1964 when he prepared a pioneering experimental palm was that it had a 50-50 chance. In the event some palms survived, despite the winter battering from wind and waves. Notable survivors were in the sunken gardens immediately opposite the former Villiers Hotel site and in a roundabout opposite the Sea Terminal. A more successful venture in the mid-1980s was the offer free

of charge to hoteliers of 18-inch high palms for their gardens. It was a longer-term project but the smaller plants were easier to get established.

Briefly about now it seemed that at least one tradition would be saved. That was the century-old one of arriving steamers at Douglas being welcomed as they passed between the Battery and Victoria Piers by the firing of a small cannon. This lay in the grounds of the castellated and white-washed Fort Anne, once one of the premier hotels of Douglas. It was the duty of the hotel's gardener to fire the cannon and its loud report could be heard throughout much of Douglas. The tradition seemed safe when Fort Anne was extensively renovated and fitted out luxuriously. But sadly the hotel succumbed like many others to the decline in Manx tourism. It closed and was stripped of its valuable antique fireplaces and wooden panelling.

At first conservationists hoped that any future development would incorporate the castellated facade which had graced the harbour scene since the end of the eighteenth century. Initially this was a planning condition for any redevelopment of the site. But as the building fell into disuse and ruin it was finally demolished in 1979. Another loss to the town, but with a gain, was the demolition in the autumn of 1961 of the town's Victorian Sea Terminal topped by an ornamental clock tower. Architecturally it was pleasing but it offered few facilities for the travelling public. The new Sea Terminal which replaced it, built appropriately in the shape of three legs, was a much more satisfactory building for both arrivals and departures. It became known as the 'lemon squeezer' because of the circular restaurant on top with a spire in the centre.

A memorable event in more recent years was the Royal Visit of 1989 when Queen Elizabeth and Prince Philip returned in the royal yacht. During a hectic day the Queen officially opened the new extension to the Manx Museum, while the Duke of Edinburgh performed a similar duty at the new Pulrose Power Station for the Manx Electricity Authority. He then went on to join the Queen at the Royal Agricultural Show at King George V Park on the last occasion it was held there. That night the Queen hosted a reception on board *Britannia* while crowds along the promenades enjoyed a magnificent firework display.

SOME TOWN PERSONALITIES

One of the strangest stories from the Second World War involves Mr Charles Craine, a Douglas hairdresser. As secretary of the World Manx Association at a time of mass emigration from the Island because of shortage of work, he had become a key figure through whom Manx people throughout the world could maintain links with the home country. Now he found a new fulfilment during the war when Manx prisoners of war formed a Manx Society in their prison camps. Although told his mail would never get through he wrote to them and even sent Christmas cards. The mail got through too! His explanation? The WMA badge incorporated the Swastika. That, of course, had been chosen many years earlier when it was merely a good luck symbol and had no association with the Nazis. On seeing it Mr Craine reckoned that the Germans must have thought the WMA to be pro-Nazi!

Brothers Nigel and Bryan Kneale, sons of Tom Kneale (former editor of the *Mona's Herald* newspaper which was based in Ridgeway Street, Douglas and published on Tuesdays), made dramatic impacts on the literary and artistic world. Nigel, a former junior reporter with the *Herald*, became noted for writing about the macabre and supernatural; then in the mid-fifties he electrified Britain with gripping science fiction serials on BBC TV featuring the character Professor Quatermass. 'The Quatermass Experiment,' the first serial, 'Quatermass 11' and 'Quatermass and the Pit' were particularly memorable. London-based Nigel is still writing screenplays for television today.

Bryan Kneale became Professor of Drawing at the Drawing School in London's College of Art and became the first Manxman to be elected to London's Royal Academy in 1974. Noted especially for his sculpture work, a local monument to his talent, which was specially commissioned for Millennium Year, is the giant Three Legs of Man at Ronaldsway Airport.

In the Fifties and Sixties the 'Reverend Fred' was one of the town's most notable characters. In 1947 when a £500 a year Yorkshire rector the Rev Frederick Matthias Cubbon inherited a Manx fortune from his father and two bachelor uncles: one of them was Thomas Cubbon of Ballaquayle Road, Douglas, described by many as one of the Island's greatest financiers after 65 years' service with the Isle of Man Bank Ltd., in which he had held most of its senior positions. The other was J.M. Cubbon, chairman and managing director of Heron and Brearley Ltd, one of the Island's leading hotel owners and drinks supply firms. With the bequest there was an instruction: "Donate liberally to charity and complete the task we started." And so he did. Whilst the visible evidence of his wealth was a yacht in the harbour and a red sports car, the 'Reverend Fred' - a priest without a specific church who loved (and could afford) to attire himself in the finest vestments, spent the rest of his life helping the local Church of England and giving money to other charitable causes. A home for hard-up lady folk was one venture; the Cubbon wing at Noble's Hospital another. The 'Reverend Fred' became a canon in the church and was awarded the O.B.E. in 1977. New Mayoral robes were presented to the Corporation in 1955 and replaced in 1973. A Social Chain was also bequeathed to the Corporation.

A mysterious Douglas resident in the post-war years was Sir Alexander Cannon, a hypnotist and yogi, the holder of 30 orders, decorations and degrees, who required to be addressed as 'His Excellency.' For this he was condemned

Well known for his charitable works, the Rev. F.M. Cubbon, right, is seen here in conversation with Town Clerk Percy Shimmin.

by Lieut. Governor Granville. Only the Island's Governor could be addressed as 'His Excellency', he declared, but Sir Alexander maintained his posturing. At the entrance to his home at Laureston Mansion were two huge Tibetan idols: a warning of what lay inside. After a lifetime in the Orient Sir Alexander had brought a huge collection of idols and curios to Douglas giving his home the reputation of being 'the house of idols.' As an amateur magician he could go into trances, had been buried alive and in 1948 had lain for 30 minutes in an air-tight coffin in St. Andrew's Church Hall, emerging to claim he brought messages from 'the world beyond.' His interest led to his establishing a Hall of Enchantment at Laureston: a private theatre which could seat a hundred guests in a brooding atmosphere of eastern idols. Many famous magicians were invited to perform here for Sir Alexander and invited guests. When the main lights were extinguished coloured lights provided an ethereal effect. Elsewhere at Laureston Sir Alexander operated a private clinic for the treatment of nervous disorders. Visitors suggested that his principal treatments involved the use of gentle coloured lighting and the playing of soothing music. When Sir Alexander died international collectors and dealers descended on the Island for a major auction of his collection.

Another hypnotist who made an impact was Josef Karma. He came in the 1950s for summer shows at Onchan Head Pavilion and later settled in Victoria Road, Douglas. His private clinics for people who wanted to stop smoking or other bad habits led to his services being enlisted by the Health Services. Privately he also claimed to have hypnotised people into out-of-body experiences but he refused to regress people into previous lives.

One of the BBC's top radio personalities in the 1940s, Wilfred Pickles, nearly became a Douglas resident! Visiting the town with his wife Mabel in 1948 to record one of his popular quiz shows 'Have a Go!', he acted as a judge at one of the popular bathing beauty competitions in the Villa Marina Gardens which were attracting 5,000 spectators, then visited the Mayor at the Town Hall. He'd travelled a lot, he said, but this was where he wanted to settle down. Sadly, however, he never made it.

Two women made their mark in what had been until the 1960s an all-male preserve. In November, 1960 Mrs Alana Griffiths became the first woman Councillor, a post she held until 1969. In 1978 Mrs Mary Halsall of Woodbourne Road became the first woman Mayor....but chose to be referred to as 'Mr Mayor' rather than

'Madame Mayor.' She explained: "It isn't me personally that people are addressing." The Bradford-born widow of Councillor Wilf Halsall (elected in 1968 and died in 1972), she had been persuaded to seek election to the Town Council to fill the vacancy caused by her husband's death and had been elected. Now she was the 52nd Mayor when Tynwald celebrated its Millennium: one of the biggest social occasions of the century. Mrs Pat Talavera, also a widow and sister of another Councillor, the late Brian Delaney, was Mayoress.

In 1968 the death occurred at the age of 68 of William Collister, a well known character otherwise known as Billy Barrel. Thus ended a musical era in the town for he was the last of the town's licensed Hurdy Gurdy men. Towards the end of his life his pony and cart used to carry three organs of different types and a grinder as well to sharpen knives and garden shears. After his death the organs ended up in a London museum.

Two of Britain's greatest war leaders became Freemen of Douglas: former Prime Minister, Sir Winston Churchill, and Field Marshall the Viscount Montgomery of Alamein. Both were heroes. In the immediate post-war euphoria they were being honoured throughout Britain. Douglas, on behalf of the Isle of Man, wanted to show its appreciation so in July, 1946 Councillors agreed to confer the Freedom of the town on both Sir Winston and Monty. Sadly Sir Winston was so involved in other things and feeling his age that he never managed to get to the Island to receive his honour. After over ten years of waiting, Councillors had to take it to him in London so officially he never became a Freeman until much later than Monty.

What he missed was a welcome reserved usually for royalty. When Montgomery came to the Island on a three-day visit in mid-May, 1948 flags and bunting were out and children were given a full day's holiday. Arriving by boat, the route from the Pier to the Villa Marina was thronged with people and the Field Marshal experienced what in fact became a triumphal progress. The cheering was hushed when he approached the War Memorial and there, in complete and respectful silence, the victor at Alamein and of the Desert War, laid his wreath to the fallen. Monty toured the Island in his legendary Humber staff car 'Old Faithful' which he had used throughout the war and had become probably the most famous car in the world. One of his visits was to King William's College where his grandfather, Dean Farrar - author of 'Eric or Little by Little' - was educated between 1839 and 1847. Monty was given his silver casket and scroll in recognition of his services as a soldier and "indomitable leadership of men in the cause of human freedom." On receiving them from the Mayor, Councillor F.M. Corkill, Monty said he regarded the honour as "a mark of gratitude of the people of the Island for all the fighting men who served with me during the war."

When the Isle of Man decided to join in the 1951 Festival of Britain celebrations with special events of its own it was hoped that Winston Churchill would agree to attend that July's Tynwald Ceremony at St. John's and receive the Freedom of Douglas there. However, due to what he described as "the grave incertainty of the world situation," he couldn't leave London. Two years later, in May, 1953, as the Island prepared to celebrate the Coronation of Queen Elizabeth, Sir Winston confided in the Island's Lieut. Governor that he always regretted not being able to get to the Island. He was fully alive to the honour which Douglas had done him by offering him the Freedom of the town, he wrote, but "much as I hope to accept this when the opportunity offers and to pay a visit to the Isle of Man for the purpose I am sure you will realise that my inability to do so is solely due to the great weight of public affairs with which I am burdened."

Four years later, with Sir Winston now aged 83 and obviously not up to making the journey to the Island, Town Councillors decided to take the honour to him. They chartered a special plane to take the Mayor, Councillor Bill Kaneen, and eleven other Council members to Croydon. Not everyone approved of the cost, notably Labour members. Also the legality of conferring the Freedom of Douglas on someone at a meeting outside the town was questioned. The trip went ahead nevertheless and on 23rd July, 1957, seven and a half years before Sir Winston's death, the silver casket, scroll and a surprise gift of some sticks of traditional Manx rock (which brought smiles to many faces) were presented to him in a simple 15 minute ceremony at his home in Hyde Park Gate. Some hours later the Manx deputation was back on the Island. The whole affair had taken no more than twelve hours.

History was made in July, 1955 when the Freedom of Douglas was presented for the first and only time to an establishment. The Freedom to enter Douglas "band playing, bayonets fixed and colours flying" was conferred on the entire R.A.F. Station at Jurby in recognition of its long and happy association with the Island. On 7th July, with the town sweltering in a heat-wave which had sent temperatures in the shade to 73 degrees Fahrenheit, 20 officers and 400 officer cadets and airmen from the training station exercised their privilege, two of them fainting in the process because of the heat. They paraded from Harris Promenade where the Freedom was conferred on them, up Victoria Street to the Town Hall at Ridgeway Street where the Mayor, Councillor Fletcher Quayle (wearing for the first time the new sable-trimmed robes presented by the Rev Fred Cubbon), took the salute.

One of the more familiar characters of the town was the brave 'bobby' on point duty at the bottom of Prospect Hill until new traffic regulations were introduced. Drivers had to be proficient in giving hand signals for turning left, straight ahead or turning right. (Manx National Heritage)

Prior to the march the Scroll of Freedom was paraded in slow time among the assembled officers and cadets, watched by large crowds of holidaymakers and Islanders, many crowding the balcony of the Villa Marina Colonnade. Station Commander, Group Captain P. Burnett DSO, DFC, signed the town's Scroll of Honour on behalf of the station. Later, in appreciation of the Freedom, RAF Jurby presented the Corporation with a commemorative large stained-glass window for the Town Hall. This was erected and remains to this day overlooking the wide staircase which leads upstairs to the Council Chamber.

Deemster Sir Percy Cowley C.B.E., described once as 'the greatest living Manxman,' became the eighth Freeman of Douglas in 1956. His political life began as a young man in his twenties as a Commissioner in Ramsey, becoming its first citizen in 1934. In his legal progress he had been High Bailiff of both Ramsey and Peel, consequently rising to First Deemster in 1947. His conspicuous legal, judicial and political career was characterised by the award of the C.B.E. in 1945; during the war years he had been Chairman of the War Committee and the Island's chief administrator. In 1952 he was knighted. As Chairman of Tynwald's Public Works Committee for some 19 years Douglas Town Council felt particularly indebted to him for his interest and support.

One of four stamps issued by the I.O.M. Postal Authority to celebrate the birthday of Sir Winston Churchill. The stamp depicts the scroll and silver casket presented to Sir Winston when the Freedom of the Borough was conferred on him in London.

Douglas Buxton became a Freeman in 1989. Raised as a patriot by his father Fred who had a pierrot village on what is now the Crescent site, Mr Buxton became a leading choir conductor and music tutor in the town. His work with the Lon Dhoo Male Voice Choir, which he founded in 1938, and the Lon Vane Ladies Choir, founded in 1946, will long be remembered. He was a great

The occasion of the granting of the Freedom of the town to R.A.F. Jurby was the subject of a cartoon by well-known artist 'Dusty' Miller. His work appeared regularly in the 'Isle of Man Examiner' and 'Weekly Times. (R and L Kelly Collection)

Deemster Sir Percy Cowley C.B.E. addressing the court during the Tynwald Ceremony of 1956. It was during that year that 'the greatest living Manxman' was granted the Freedom of the Borough. Holding the Bishop's staff on the top of the Hill is the Rev F.M. Cubbon. (Manx National Heritage)

supporter of the Manx Music Festival and as Music Director of both the Douglas Choral Union (which celebrates its 100th anniversary at the same time as Douglas Corporation) and the Manx Operatic Society he helped shape the development of the amateur theatre of today. One of the many highlights of his musical career, which spanned over 70 years, was conducting the Lon Dhoo choir in 1948 when they recorded 'Ellan Vannin' and other songs for HMV on the steps of the Villa Marina with the Joe Loss orchestra. The recording session didn't start until midnight! It was appropriate that the Freedom ceremony in the Villa became a concert at which Mr Buxton's many pupils and friends graced the occasion in the way that Dougie would appreciate above all others.

In 1994 the well-loved film clown Norman Wisdom, a resident on the Island in his latter years, was made a Freeman too. Though not a resident of Douglas he is a frequent visitor; his love of the Island and his eager promotion of it had made him an excellent ambassador.

In 1973 there was a strange sequel to the granting of the Freedom of Douglas to Sir Hall Caine in 1924. Almost 50 years later his silver casket complete with hand-coloured parchment inside had embarked on a curious adventure. It had been kept at Greeba Castle whilst his estate had been wound up in a trust during the lifetime of his son, Derwent Hall Caine. On the latter's death, however, the contents were inherited by grandchildren in America. Mrs Ellin Gill, another grandchild who subsequently moved into and restored with her husband the long empty and now dilapidated Greeba Castle, believed the casket had been kept as a keepsake by one of the American heirs. So she was amazed one day in November, 1973 to be told by journalist Robert Kelly that the casket had been seen on an antique stall in London's Portobello Road. A search was instigated, the casket tracked down, purchased and brought back to Greeba Castle!

Mr 'Dougie' Buxton, well-known choir conductor and voice tutor, was granted the Freedom of Douglas in 1989 in recognition of his services to the musical life of the town.

The night of 28th January, 1994 was a great occasion at the Villa Marina when the much-loved comic and Manx resident Norman Wisdom was made an Honorary Freeman of the Borough. Here he is with Mayor, Councillor George Chatel.

POST WAR TOWN DEVELOPMENTS

Despite all the pre-war efforts of the Council to reduce the housing list, their stock of 803 houses was still far from adequate to meet the demands which were sure to be increased with the end of the war. Their land bank consisted of three fields at Spring Valley which they had purchased as long ago as 1932, and it was in May of 1944 that plans were made to build the first houses on that site.

The Town Fathers were not going to let the grass grow under their feet and peace was still a year away when they were studying a survey of other possible building sites around Douglas. In hindsight it is interesting to look at the areas they had under consideration. These were as follows: South Quay, the south side of the Old Castletown Road, Middle Farm, both sides of the new Castletown Road including Pulrose Farm, Ballabeg and Ballafletcher, land between Tromode and Ballanard Road, land adjoining Ballakermeen School i.e. the Gooseneck, Duke's Road below the Grandstand, Blackberry Lane, Somerset Road between St. Ninian's High School and Woodland Terrace, and Willaston. In the end the Council purchased 77 acres of the Willaston estate which, in 1944, they were able to acquire for £13,500 with Tynwald approval.

The Council's first post-war project was the development of Spring Valley and, for the first time women were included on the advisory committee in relation to the design of the houses. As had happened after the First World War, a shortage of materials delayed the scheme but in the meantime the Local Government Board were arranging for six experimental houses to be erected to the west of Groves Road. These were eventually passed over to the Council to form part of the Spring Valley Estate.

The contract for Spring Valley was awarded to R.E. Clucas but the work was far from complete when he asked to be released from his commitment. By April 1948 the first houses were ready for occupation, the first tenant being Constable Hector Duff. It was March 1950 when the keys to the last of the 116 houses were handed over, but by this time work was well under way on the Willaston Estate.

The land acquired at Willaston belonged to the ancient quarterlands of Tromode, Glencrutchery and Ballameanagh which were in the parish of Onchan. By the middle of last century part of these lands had come into the possession of John George Bennett who lived in Patrick and was married to a member of the Clague family from Lonan. Mr Bennett was a Magistrate and Gentleman who, it is thought, originated from Willaston in Cheshire, hence the non-Manx name. He built a mansion which was given the name Willaston and the farm on his land became known as Willaston Farm. Following the death of John Bennett and his widow the property had various owners until it came into the hands of a Liverpool businessman by the name of Cottle. To acquire all the land he had to wait until the death of the widow of Johnny Watterson who had a life-long interest in half the land. The land acquired by the Corporation in 1944 consisted of the Mansion House, outbuildings and 3.5 acres of garden; 63 acres of Willaston Farm with its dwelling house and farm buildings; and certain parcels of land totalling eleven acres of the Glencrutchery Estate bordering the Borough Cemetery, the nursery of Robert Hotchkiss, Norwood Drive and the road leading from Parkfield to Ballanard.

From the outset it was made clear that the land fronting Ballanard Road would be sold off in plots for private housing; it was also stated that 'a small portion of land adjoining the Borough Cemetery may be set aside for the building of a Crematorium.' Come the end of the war Willaston mansion was converted as temporary accommodation in the form of two flats for Council staff and officials. Willaston farm house was put to a similar use

Having purchased Glen Falcon House, its outbuildings and walled-garden from the Okell's Trustees, the Council demolished the properties in order to carry out road widening improvements during the winter of 1948/49. Broadway was widened from 26 feet to 50 feet and Derby Road and Glen Falcon Roads widened to 40 feet. The scheme was completed with the landscaping of Glen Falcon as a public amenity.

while the cart shed was used as the Scout Hut which was also used as the first meeting place for other groups who came to live at Willaston.

The roads and sewer lay-out for the estate was designed by the Borough Engineer and Surveyor, Mr Jack Bregazzi and the design for the housing by his brother, Mr Joe Bregazzi, the Borough Senior Architect. The contract for the building of the first phase of 154 houses was awarded to the local firm of McCormack and Davies Ltd. This was despite T. and H. Chapman Ltd. having submitted a lower tender. The Chapmans protested and the case went before Tynwald which referred the matter back to the Council. The members were prepared to compromise by offering the Chapmans a contract for 56 of the houses. This was declined by the brothers who felt they could not work for a client who had no confidence in them.

The semi-detached houses were finished to a high standard with built-in cupboards, dresser and sink. Outside, a coalhouse, wash-house and boxroom were provided. The selection of the first tenants was determined by those with a high number of priority points on the Corporation's Housing List - mainly married ex-servicemen with children. Ahead of schedule the first two houses in Barrule Road were ready to receive the first 'pioneers' on the estate and it was a happy day on Thursday, 17th August, 1950 when Councillor J.A. Cain, Chairman of the Corporation Estates Committee handed over the keys. The recipients were Mr and Mrs Alec Moore who had lived in two rooms in Albany Street and were delighted to realise their dream of having a house of their own. There were cheers as Mr Moore, a well known postman, swept his wife in his arms to cross the threshold, followed by six-year-old son David. His main worry was whether or not his tortoise would be considered a prohibited dangerous pet! No.3 Barrule Road went to lorry driver Mr Walter Hornsby and his wife and twelve-year-old son. They had previously lived in three rooms in Market Street, Douglas with a blank wall as their only outlook.

By this time it was noted that there were 1,397 names on the Housing List and the second phase at Willaston was approved with the Council having apparently learned their lesson and the contract being shared by McCormack and Davies and Maurice Clark. There were problems at Willaston when the Council offered a piece of land to the Education Authority for a school, which the Authority turned down on the grounds that it was too near the Cemetery. The Council were reluctant to change the site as it would lose places for 40 houses but the Local Government Board stepped in and threatened to withhold funding until the matter was resolved. The Council finally had to back down and the Education Authority got the site they wanted.

By mid-1952 the third phase was out for tender and this was again won by McCormack and Davies with 156 houses being built for £242,000. Progress continued until a total of 730 housing units were completed including a small number of bungalows and flats for the elderly. This made Willaston by far the largest municipal estate on the Island and much was achieved in reducing the Housing List, a list that time has shown will never be completely eliminated.

To begin with Willaston was 'out in the country' with few amenities - no shops, churches or a school or pub - which meant travelling into town. Few tenants had their own transport which meant either walking or relying on the No 18 bus service. But matters were slowly rectified. The first of the six shops was opened in July, 1954 and the houses for police and their families occupied. The following month saw the opening of St. Joseph's R.C. Church. The Mansion House was leased to Castletown Brewery Ltd. in August, 1954 and developed into the popular Manor Hotel. In 1955 Willaston Infants School was opened and 1960 saw the completion of Willaston Methodist Church. But right from the start there was engendered a strong community spirit as evidenced by the Willaston Sports and Social Club which did a lot to make up for the lack of entertainments. Foremost in encouraging

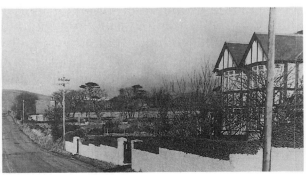

Views of Johnny Watterson's Lane, Willaston Farm and Ballanard Road before work began on developing the Willaston estate soon after the war. Plots along Ballanard Road were sold off for private housing; Johnny Watterson's Lane was widened and the derelict Willaston Farm house and buildings were eventually demolished. The site was used to build the Council's first Elderly Persons, Complex, Ballanard Court being opened in 1979.

the community spirit was Councillor Cyril Simpson, an early tenant in Keppel Road, while Councillors Edward Callister M.H.K. and Inkerman Faragher were all instrumental in supporting the fledgling estate. But it was Willaston's first tenant, Mr Alec Moore, who involved himself closely in the new community from which he launched himself on a long and distinguished political career, rising from Town Councillor to Member of the Legislative Council.

That part of Douglas upon which stands the Chester Street Car Park was originally known as the Big Garden. It was well out of the town when it was first developed in the early years of the last century and consisted of Wellington Square, Chester Street, Frederick Street, Edward Lane, part of Senna Road and the lower part of Finch Road which included a number of small terraces such as Edward and Callow Terraces.

It was from 1958 onwards that the Council initiated a policy of purchasing the existing properties with a view to their eventual demolition and redevelopment - something envisaged as long ago as the 1920s. By 1966 the Council was in a position to submit its development proposals but by the time they were ready to proceed, the unfavourable economic climate hindered any further progress and it was evident that a major scheme was quite beyond the resources of the town. It was agreed, therefore, in 1974 that the Local Government Board would purchase the whole area of three and one-third acres from the Council and would carry out an appropriate development at Government expense. The design work was by Ove Arup and Partners and the construction was by Myton Ltd. who commenced work in June, 1976. Just two years later, almost to the day, the Chester Street Car Park and the accompanying Shopping Complex was officially opened by His Excellency The Lieutenant Governor Sir John Paul. The multi-storey car park contains 663 car spaces above the shopping store and cafe which is now part of the Safeway Supermarket, though originally it was operated by Liptons (Allied Suppliers Ltd.).

The next major Council housing project was at Annacur, renamed via its root words Anagh Coar meaning 'the marsh of the heron.' Work began on developing the estate at the beginning of 1967 and some of the first occupants had formerly lived in the Chester Street area. By 1989 a total of 439 dwellings were completed making it the second largest municipal estate. Recent years have seen very little in the way of Council housing though the Donkeys Field

scheme has provided an additional 50 houses. Adjoining the upper part of Anagh Coar at Ballavargher 67 first-time buyers' houses have been built by a private developer on land provided by the Council.

The first steps taken by the Council to provide much needed sheltered housing for the elderly resulted in the building of Ballanard Court on the site of the former Willaston farm house. After being used as flats it was vacated in the mid-1950s and allowed to become derelict, provoking letters of complaint to the Press. Finally, the decision was made by the Council to demolish the house and farm buildings to make way for 21 independent units within the Elderly Persons' Complex which was opened in 1979. A much more ambitious and prestigious scheme for the elderly was embarked upon in 1989 when the entire York Road bus depot and garages were demolished. Work then began on building the Waverley Court complex, designed by Borough Architect Mr David Halsall. Waverley Court was completed in 1991 and contains 74 units completed to a very high standard. This brings the number of Corporation dwellings of various kinds to a total of 2,222 of which the Council can justifiably feel proud.

As with public sector housing, the private builders too had their problems after the war with shortages of materials and of experienced labour. The estate of Ballabrooie had been laid out and this was completed but subsequent developments took some time before being activated. There was considerable infilling in such places as Port-e-Chee Crescent, Victoria Road, Princes Road, Marathon Avenue, Thorny Road and Stoney Road before the builders cast their eyes onto 'greenfield' sites; modest size estates sprang up at Ballaughton, Woodlands, Cronk-y-Berry and Glen Park together with Laureston and on Hotchkiss's Mountain View Nurseries.

Not necessarily in chronological order came the start of the bigger estates of Tromode Park (1970) and Saddlestone Park, and the old 'Putts' at Falcon Cliff disappeared under apartment blocks. The Avenues on Glencrutchery Road were extended with the addition of Cronk Drean and with most of the available space within the Borough taken up, the builders thought up pretentious sounding names and moved out to the unlikely slopes that became Farm Hill and the popular sledging spot that became Hightonwood Hill. Johnny Watterson must be turning in his grave, what with having his Lane extended beyond Ballanard Road and doubled in width, his fields being built on and now his

Thursday, 17th August, 1950 was a happy day for Mr Alec Moore and his wife Ethel and son David. Here they are receiving the keys of No.1 Barrule Road, Willaston from Mr J.A. Cain, Chairman of the Estates Committee. Nos. 1 and 3 were the first houses to be occupied on the new estate. On the left is Borough Treasurer Mr Leonard Costain and on the right is Town Clerk Mr Percy Shimmin.

An aerial view of the Chester Street, Wellington Square, Well Road Hill area which was purchased by the Corporation for demolition but then sold to Government for re-development. Demolition was completed by 1976.

Chester Street prior to demolition. The street, dating from the early part of last century, was the centre of a close-knit community in this part of the town.

A final look at Well Road Hill, leading to Wellington Square. Behind the chimney of the old tannery can be seen the building of Well Road Hill Methodist Church.

A new look for Well Road Hill at the bottom of which further development has seen the construction of the Strand Shopping Centre.

Work on the supermarket and the car park above nears completion. The Chester Street Car Park was officially opened on 15th June, 1978 and can accommodate 633 cars.

paddock on the verge of being swallowed up to make room for more houses.

The proliferation of cars on the roads saw the private estates moving further away from the Town although which came first is anyone's guess. Ballaquark appeared adjacent to Anagh Coar and Cooil Drive later filled in the gap on the upper side, whilst only Ashley Park and a few fields have temporarily stopped Saddlestone and Farm Hill from joining up. Former Governors may well have taken their dogs for a stroll on Governors Hill, but it is unlikely that any of them would recognise the area with the spread of buildings that exists there today. The filling-in of the Gooseneck used up what was virtually the last piece of building land used within the town boundaries and one can only speculate where the next development will appear. Maybe the golf course, or Noble's Park; some have even cast covetous eyes on Douglas Head. Beware the speculative builder, for stranger things have happened!

On a brighter note we record that the normal evolution of any town has occurred in Douglas, and whereas we have seen many nostalgic buildings pulled down, we have seen many edifices replace them, not always for the better. We have seen the demise of such old buildings of Douglas as the Fort Anne, the Peveril, the Villiers and Athol Hotels, Clinch's Brewery and that of Heron and Brearley, all of Shaw's Brow to make way for another car park, and half of Albert Street to release space for the new Courthouse. The Holiday Camp became the site of Shoprite supermarket which led to a change in people's shopping habits and the demise of many a family grocer. The number of worshippers in the town must have been reduced dramatically when one considers the disappearance of so many churches - St. Barnabas, the Bethel on Circular Road,

Bucks Road, Finch Hill and St. Andrew's of which the spire has been retained as a monument to the past.

The new buildings that now grace our Town include the Police Station built, some would say, on part of our green belt along Glencrutchery Road; the Post Office Head Quarters in Circular Road and the Sorting Office on the Spring Valley Industrial Estate. The old sorting office had been situated in a building in Circular Road built soon after the war by Kelly Brothers as their joinery workshop and which then changed to making sweets under the Tres Bon Confectionery Company. Other new buildings which have appeared are the Fire Service Headquarters on Peel Road; the Palace Hotel and Casino on Central Promenade; the Dairy and Abattoir (or rather Meat Plant) at Tromode; the Brewery at Kewaigue which is, yes, in South Douglas; the new T.T. Grandstand; the new schools of St. Mary's and Ballaquayle with a rebuilt Murray's Road School as well, and the new Government Buildings on Prospect Hill which were overcrowded as soon as they were completed.

The Town has seen a large number of commercial/industrial developments during the fifty years since the war. Hills Meadow was something of a pioneer and now such developments are reaching out into the country as far as the Cooil, although the more recent developments here, generated by the proximity of Douglas, are technically outside the town boundaries.

Even at the time of writing many major schemes are in the course of construction and yet others are planned. It would appear that yet again the rate of change has increased and that development and redevelopment are rampant.

The sheltered accommodation of Waverley Court, with its main entrance from Laureston Avenue, was completed in 1991

The Waverley Court complex as seen from Waverley Road. The complex contains 74 units finished to a high standard.

FOR THE NATIONAL GOOD

The foresight of Douglas Corporation in building the Baldwin Reservoir in the early years of the century ensured that the town's water supply was more than sufficient to meet the demands of the post-war boom in holiday traffic and of the new housing estates. In fact, the town's Water Committee, under Tynwald's Water Act of 1955, were also supplying over 400,000 gallons a day to the Isle of Man Water Board which was responsible for supplying the needs of the Island outside Douglas and Onchan. The Water Board was having difficulty in supplying large areas of the south and west of their domain. Their answer, in the first instance, was to construct a new 150 million gallon reservoir in Glen Rushen at an estimated cost approaching £1 million. But before any decision was made it was decided to seek the advice of a senior engineering inspector from England with the Ministry of Local Government. His name was Mr C.H. Spens. He arrived in 1957 to make a survey of the Island's water supplies.

The subsequent Spens Report of 1958 submitted to the Isle of Man Local Government Board suggested that a major undertaking such as proposed at Glen Rushen was an unnecessary expense in view of the water already impounded by Douglas Corporation. He proposed that the Water Board should consult with the Corporation to determine to what extent 'town' water could be supplied to meet the needs of the rest of the Island. Additionally, amalgamation should be encouraged to establish one water authority. "In the Isle of Man, small by comparison with English counties, there should be no need for two water undertakings each with its own engineering and administrative staff."

The first step was to set up a Joint Water Advisory Committee to consider the matter and for that purpose members of the Water Board met with the Corporation's Water Committee. While the Council accepted that the Joint Committee could work towards improving the Island's water supplies, there were a number of members who pointed out that any take-over of the Corporation's water undertaking would be "over their dead bodies." The Council approved a recommendation that amalgamation be opposed as the Corporation 'would have little to gain from amalgamation and may suffer a sense of grievance at the loss of its undertaking.' There was also the current water rate to consider. The Douglas and Onchan water rates were half those paid by customers of the Water Board!

Douglas Corporation, quite understandably, were in no hurry to surrender one of their cherished utilities and, as matters stood, were required to supply the Water Board with up to 800,000 gallons a day. Water Board engineer, Mr Peacock, estimated that a series of pumping stations and connecting mains from the Glencrutchery service reservoirs to augment supplies to the south and west of the Island would cost £320,000 as opposed to the £880,000 for a new reservoir at Glen Rushen. With 1,600,000 gallons a day available Mr Peacock was of the opinion that such a quantity "is certainly large enough to meet all present deficiencies and to provide for future increases for a very considerable period." While Douglas Water Engineer Mr H. Cannell could not agree with all of the Peacock Report it gained the support of advisor Mr C.H. Spens. The latter expressed his disappointment that no steps had been taken towards amalgamation during the three years since his report.

The matter came before Tynwald when the Local Government Board presented the Water (Temporary Provisions) Bill in 1961. Out went the Glen Rushen scheme and its place was taken by the project to link up

Staff and members of the Water Committee at Injebreck during the annual water 'picnic' in the late 1940s. Standing on the back row, second from left, is Mr J.C. Bregazzi, Borough Engineer and Surveyor. Councillor W.C. Craine is on the top of steps. Standing on the left are Councillors T.W. Kneale, R.Q. Hampton, T.C. Cowin and, on steps, F.M. Corkill and T.D. Lewis Among those bottom right are Councillors Fletcher Quayle, W.B. Kaneen and Tom Radcliffe.

water supplies from Douglas with the rest of the Island. In the absence of agreement over amalgamation, then the Water Board would be empowered to receive 850,000 gallons a day leaving 750,000 available to Douglas Corporation. The Bill was duly passed and the matter of amalgamation was deferred for future consideration. However, it was accepted that amalgamation would involve a ten-year period in which the town water rate would be increased to a standard all-Island rate, and that the Corporation would have representation on the new authority.

Matters lay dormant until 1969 when Tynwald was confronted with a new Water Bill. It stipulated that there would be no Corporation representation on the new water authority and that the equalisation of rates would take place over a five-year period. (At that time the Douglas water rate stood at 1s. 3d. in the pound compared with 2s.6d. applied by the Water Board). Alderman Alec Moore, Chairman of the Water Committee, quickly called a Press Conference in the Town Hall and expressed his disappointment at being "sold down the river." In the Keys, Douglas members tried to have the first reading of the Bill deferred, but to no avail. The Bill had the backing of the Governor and Executive Council and, with country members heavily outvoting the Douglas members, the Bill became the Water Act, 1972. There was no compensation for what the Corporation considered a take-over of their investment valued at over £2 million. Thus the new Isle of Man Water Authority replaced the Corporation Water Committee and the I.O.M. Water Board with effect from 1st April, 1973.

Whereas the amalgamation of both water authorities had taken fifteen years to achieve, a much quicker operation was the merger of the Bus Section of the Corporation's Tramways Undertaking (including vehicles stock and spares) which was sold to Isle of Man National Transport in 1976 for £25,050.

But this was by no means the end of centralisation. A Joint Electricity Authority had been set up as early as 1965 for the mutual benefit of both the Electricity Department of the Corporation and the Isle of Man Electricity Board. The latter had been set up in 1933 and received a bulk supply from Pulrose Power Station for distribution via Harcroft to areas outside Douglas and Onchan. In 1950 the Board began to generate its own supply first at Peel and then at Ramsey. Occasionally the two authorities were able to help each other in times of breakdowns or storm damage. But any mention of a merger was quickly scotched by the Corporation representatives. With the loss of its water undertaking still rankling, the Corporation was in no mood to forego its successful enterprise which provided electricity for 13,800 consumers at rates a third less than being charged by the Electricity Board. It had also built up a reserve fund over the years of over £900,000 for new equipment. The Electricity Board, on the other hand, had no such reserves and was working at a considerable loss requiring annual subsidies from Government funds. With the generating plant of both authorities coming to the end of their working life, a Government Commission was set up to look into the matter.

While the Commission was not specifically asked to investigate the advisability of a merger, it was to 'consider all matters relating to amalgamation - with recommendations on the most effective and equitable means of achieving this object.' The principle seemed to have already been decided and it was not surprising that it was at the heart of the Douglas Corporation Electricity Bill which came before Tynwald in 1981. Once again it was the Douglas and Middle Keys members who were left to fight a rearguard action on behalf of the Corporation.

The Bill's passage through the Keys was one of the most protracted on record but much of the animosity was removed when one of the country members moved an amendment whereby the inevitable rise in tariffs should be spread over a guaranteed period of eight years instead of the five-year period written into the Bill during which differential tariffs could have been fixed without guarantee. The amendment was accepted without opposition and was regarded as 'a generous compromise.' It was also agreed that the Corporation would receive a total of £162,000 as being the value of the Corporation's assets. Details of the take-over took many more hours before the vital second reading of the Bill was passed by a margin of 15 votes to 8. The Act was formally promulgated and the Manx Electricity Authority was set up to take control of the Island's electricity supply with effect from 1st April, 1984.

Whilst the take-over of the town's water undertaking, the bus section of the Tramways Committee, and now the town's electrical undertaking was seen as benefiting the Island as a whole, there were many who lamented that these jewels had been removed from the municipal crown.

A view from the mid 1980s showing refurbished houses of Pulrose and the Corporation's Power Station taken over by the Manx Electricity Authority in 1984. The cooling tower is no longer in use, the much more efficient fan cooling being introduced when the new Power Station was built by the M.E.A. in 1989. Towering above the new power station is a 71 metre chimney surrounded by a concrete wind-break; the one shown here is still in use though it has been reduced in height. (Mr Combi/Manx National Heritage)

Yesterday (1973) . . . . and Today (1995)

Prospect Hill

Villiers Hotel

Peveril

Harbour

Photographs by Noel Howarth

YESTERDAY (1973) . . . . *and* TODAY (1995)

Central Promenade

Castle Mona and The Palace

Queen's Promenade

Summerland

Photographs by Noel Howarth

173

CHANGES IN 'THE STREET'

The fifty years since the Second World War have seen tremendous changes in the shopping thoroughfare of Strand Street and its neighbours. Such changes make it all the more remarkable that there are shops which were not only established before the war but continue to operate up until the present; some within the original family; some have changed hands, while others have found new locations. There aren't many, of course, but survivors include Maley's the Chemist, first established in 1895 but now in new ownership; Marks and Spencer and Woolworths, which was established in 1924 and rebuilt in 1951; Burtons the tailors, Ridgeway the jewellers, the Art Store and the Lexicon bookshop; Robinson's the fruiterers and Tinker the butchers. Stead and Simpson's shoe shop, formerly in Victoria Street, is now located in the Strand Shopping Centre. In Duke Street there is the Manx Co-operative stores; Dibbs for glassware and china, Cannell's cafe and Burtons the tailors. The name of Holmes and Davidson, opticians, is now found here after being many years in Strand Street. In 1926 Mr W.H. Chapman established the town's first travel agency at 23, Victoria Street; the name still survives across the street at Number 53. Moving into Castle Street four family shops have survived through three or four generations, these being Kermode and Bignell for shoes, Curphey's for leatherware, G.H. Corlett's the watchmakers and Brew's the butchers. Another name in Castle Street is that of Devereau the fishmongers first established in 1894.

A far greater number of shops, in name at least, have disappeared since the Second World War. To mention but a few, Strand Street no longer has Arthur Clague's and Fred Bridson's the men's outfitters; Madame Moore's for millinery; Peggy's Lounge, the toy centre; The Maypole, Lipton's and the Home and Colonial; Batesons's and Gray's for pork pies and sausage; Crellin's for Manx kippers and Shippam's for potted meat; Bon Marche the tailors; Quirk's and Elder's the bakers; Rowell's for sweets and confectionery; Lyons for high fashions and Purcell's the chemist at the foot of Well Road Hill.

Shops remembered in Duke Street are: R.C. Cain's which was an institution in itself; Emmet's Ladies Shop and Emmet's Menswear Shop; Plant's the newsagents, now part of the Pickwick group; Barron's the grocers; Clucas's the greengrocer and fishmonger; Todhunter and Elliot, general ironmongers; Witherspoons for sweets and Gilbert Harding's cycle shop. In Victoria Street Sayle's has long gone while the popular Boots the Chemist left in 1968; other shops which are no longer here include Miss Curphey and Vogue for fashions, Blakemore's for music and the nearby famous Wilson's restaurant which closed in 1972. In Castle Street one of the best known names was that of Higgins for fish and poultry along with Felice's cafes and Carter and Young for sports equipment.

A scheme which excited businessmen in the mid-1960s was the phased roofing-in of Strand Street, Castle Street and Victoria Street so all shopping could be undertaken without worrying

The popular Woolworth's store of 1924 was undergoing major reconstruction and extension when the building was gutted by fire in April, 1951. Temporary accommodation was found in the Palais de Danse.

The new Woolworth's store as it was in 1976.

Shops in Strand Street and Castle Street at the junction with Well Road Hill, prior to demolition to make way for the Strand Shopping Centre. On the corner can be seen Kermode and Bignell's shoe shop next to Gore's rock shop.

The popular Victoria Tavern in Drumgold Street survived until 1989. It was once a popular haunt for farmers on market days and Saturday nights. Their dogs were kept in kennels at the rear of the tavern, hence the more usual name of Dogs Home.

about the effects of the Manx weather. The idea was supported by the Tourist Board as part of their 'Go Abroad' campaign in an attempt to halt the fall in the number of tourists. It was suggested that a new fibreglass and nylon mix called Filon be used in order to create a rose-coloured atmosphere for shoppers. In the end the idea was a non-starter and too complicated for buildings of widely varying heights, a throwback to the days when the shops, mostly dating from the middle of last century, were built separately with living accommodation above them.

Strand Street can never be accused of being behind the times and it is always ready to reflect the latest trends. Shop frontages have seen the use of aluminium frames to make the maximum use of glazed fronts for displays, though more recent years have seen the return of traditional Victorian-styled fronts. Television, hi-fi and video shops are now present while there has been a proliferation of ladies' fashion shops with names such as Benetton, Cassis, Dash, Dorothy Perkins, Elle, Etam (in the former Palais de Danse and Holmes and Davidson's), Marianne's, Next, Smart Alex, Top Drawer and UZ. Menswear shops include Peter Luis, Burtons, Garrey Corneil, Esquire, Looney's and Next Man. Another notable feature is the presence of a growing number of travel agents which flourish on packet holidays and, at the same time, make it possible to purchase a ticket one day, and travel to most parts of the world the next day. Cannell's Cafe has now been joined by new names such as Route 66, the Buttery, Griddles and the Golden Grill. 1994 saw

the disappearance of the Picture House cinema, the site of its foyer becoming a shopping unit for the Superdrugs Store.

In 1978 the Corporation embarked on a major scheme to pedestrianise the main shopping thoroughfare from Duke Street, through Strand Street to Castle Street, the latter being completed in 1981. The scheme involved removing the old pavements, renewing drainage and the laying of thousands of uniblocks on a prepared base. Another new look to Strand Street was added in 1993 when the realistic figures of George Formby, complete with ukulele and lamppost, and a reclining Norman Wisdom were positioned by the raised gardens near the junction with Duke Street.

Busiest time of the year is Christmas time and when local traders suggested that 'the Street' should be given a more festive appearance by the use of decorative lighting the Corporation agreed to co-operate. The traders were to cover the cost of the lights and their installation after which the Technical Services Department would operate them and maintain them for future use. The first Christmas lights were officially commissioned at the beginning of December, 1984. So successful was the venture that subsequent years saw the inclusion of Duke Street, Castle Street, Market Hill and Ridgeway Street. Each year has seen the addition of special seasonal features. Not to be outdone, the traders of Prospect Terrace and the upper part of Windsor Road were also included in the scheme, beginning in 1991.

A new concept for Douglas has been the construction of the Strand Shopping Centre

November, 1978, showing Strand Street after pedestrianisation.

November, 1978, at the junction of Regent Street and Strand Street

November, 1978. Work begins in Duke Street.

February, 1988. Erecting the hoardings before the construction of the Strand Shopping Centre begins.

December, 1990. Christmas lighting in Duke Street.

Mayor Councillor Basil Callow and Norman Wisdom at the switching-on ceremony of the decorative lighting, Christmas 1992. (R and L Kelly Collection)

A preview of the entrance in Drumgold Street to the new Mark and Spencer Store as seen from Strand Street.

The entrance to the car park on the corner of Nelson Street and Wellington Street. (Isometric drawing, by kind permision of Bovis Construction Ltd.)

bringing with it the first escalator to the town. Demolition of the old properties began in 1987 resulting in the removal of shops on either side of the remaining part of Well Road Hill, in Strand Street and Castle Street. The long-established shoe shop of Kermode and Bignell and the adjoining Gore's confectionery shop, where its famous Manx rock was once made, both disappeared, with Kermode and Bignell relocating on the opposite side of Castle Street. The private development of the cleared area began at the beginning of 1988 with the new shopping centre being completed at the end of July, 1990.

Undoubtedly the shopping event of 1996 will be the opening of the new stores for Marks and Spencer. Demolition over the past few years on either side of Drumgold Street has made way for a joint venture between Government and M and S which will rejuvenate this area of down-town Douglas. Marks and Spencer (I.O.M) Ltd., one of the largest Manx companies, has been formed to take advantage of capital allowances and tax benefits. The shopping floor of 40,000 square feet more than doubles the space available in the present store and will allow for a much greater range of merchandise; staffing will be increased to between 85 and 90 full-time assistants. The main entrance will face Strand Street while another entrance in Nelson/Market Street will allow through passage replacing the traditional Drumgold access from the office area of the town into Strand Street. The second floor of the building will provide spaces for the parking of 296 cars. Access will be from the Wellington/Nelson Street corner and the car park will be Government-controlled and for the benefit of shoppers. The Marks and Spencer investment in the enterprise demonstrates the company's confidence in the prosperity of the town and the move will be exactly 60 years after Bovis, also the present contractors, completed the Strand Street store.

The old Drumgold Street and its adjacent buildings have virtually disappeared in a programme of development which will lead to the rejuvenation of this part of Douglas. Here will rise the Marks & Spencer store complete with public car park, to be opened in the Spring of 1996.

THE CHANGING FACE OF DOUGLAS

There are no more visitors staying at Mount Havelock. The nineteen of the splendid four-storeyed houses were built in the middle of last century, designed by local architect John Robinson, with Number 19 adjoining Christian Road. The latter was named after the Christian family who owned and developed the virgin land of this area as Douglas developed and spread above the older parts of the town. Mount Havelock was built as fine town houses for the merchant class; bell pulls in the upstairs rooms summoned the downstairs maids. No. 6 'Arden' boasted one of the first telephones in the town - Douglas 12. Built overlooking Finch Road, most had a garden across the road at the front to add to the elegance of these desirable residences in what became central Douglas. By the end of the century, however, Mount Havelock and the adjoining streets were participating in the great tourist boom. The lofty residences of Mount Havelock were ideal for the purpose with accommodation for up to 30 visitors each.

The twentieth century brought with it investment schemes of modernisation - gas lighting was replaced by electricity; pumped water was replaced by Corporation water piped to all bedrooms which would eventually boast 'hot and cold running water.' Each house could claim to be 'pleasantly situated and central for all parts' and, of course, were under the personal supervision of the proprietress who ensured her guests were well satisfied with their Tea, Bed and Breakfast accommodation.

Mount Havelock enjoyed the post Second World War boom which lasted into the 1950s. Then a gradual decline set in as holiday patterns changed. Package holidays to the sunshine of the

Mount Havelock in 1988 - the boarding houses have gone to make way for office developments.

Mediterranean rapidly expanded which offered clients brand new hotels with *en suite* accommodation, swimming pools and duty free goods. Mount Havelock couldn't compete, though the landladies did their best to keep tariffs as low as possible which meant there was little spare revenue for future investment. Some survived until the 1970s with the Millennium Year of 1979 giving a welcome boost to arrivals. But it was only a temporary reprieve, one of the 'special events' which would be relied upon increasingly now that the 'bucket and spade brigade' had largely departed. Only those in the town who had the resolve and enterprise to benefit from Government grants and loans to update their premises stood any chance of surviving in the diminishing market.

It was the end of the road for Mount Havelock; deterioration set in and the neglected buildings began to look their age. Several were converted to

Now under construction - the new General Registry on the left, Court House and Judicial Buildings.

'bed-sit' accommodation. But what fate would befall them? An inkling of their future was given in the early 1950s. Number 6 fell vacant and it was snapped up by Government, desperate for extra accommodation. The house found new life when its spacious rooms were turned into offices for the then small Local Government Board whose staff occupied Murray House, next to the General Registry. Reprographics occupied the ground floor; and the garden of No. 6 became an allotment for cabbages and brussel sprouts! The Island's administration continued to grow and the old properties in the neighbourhood of Government Office had plenty of room to house the growing army of civil servants. Among the first to be acquired were those above the original Government Offices in Bucks Road. Then the demolition experts moved in and razed them to the ground; the old Murray House and St. Mary's Roman Catholic School received similar treatment. Here would be built the new Central Government Offices taking the form of a plain quadrangular block whose floors were divided into simple boxes to house the office staff. The building was officially opened in July, 1975; there were many who bemoaned the loss of the lofty and airy rooms of the old Victorian buildings.

Then the two blocks of Mount Havelock, covering Nos 1 to 11, were earmarked for future development. The demolition gangs had a field day, first removing items of value such as roof slates, fire grates and ornate Victorian cast-iron baths which suddenly came back into fashion. Then the heavy machinery set to work as each house was dropped within its outer walls to which clung faded wallpaper and which exposed the outlines of stairways and fire places. The houses had been fashioned by skilled masons from the rough quarried slate from the cliffs along South Quay, and rendered in stucco with fine mouldings by local plasterers. But the work of the masons, carpenters and their fellow tradesmen was quickly reduced to dusty rubble for use as in-fill in some other development. The cleared area provided valuable spaces for car parking, the gardens being used for a similar purpose.

The centre block, between Albert Street and Mona Street, was built by a private developer and then bought by Government. It is now a large office complex in which can be found the headquarters of the Department of Agriculture, Fisheries and Forestry, the Department of Education and the Department of Local Government and the Environment. Within the foundations is a cavernous car park. As a reminder of the past, the new building has been named Murray House.

The site of the first block of Mount Havelock forms the base of a triangle completed by a side of Albert Street and Bucks Road. Within this triangle the old properties have been demolished to make way for the prestigious new General Registry, Judicial Buildings and Courthouse.

While the remainder of Mount Havelock has escaped demolition, it has been transformed almost beyond recognition. Many of the premises have been converted into modern offices to satisfy the almost insatiable appetite of the financial services sector of the Island's economy. Just as the visiting industry replaced the dependence on mining and fishing of last century, Douglas became the centre of this new form of business. Taking advantage of its right to determine its own rates of income tax on individuals and companies alike, the Isle of Man was presented as a tax haven. The foundations were laid in the 1960s and by the 1980s the financial sector had mushroomed and established itself as by far the most important part in the Island's economy. It lessened the fear of unemployment and, it is said, a thousand workers in the finance sector could be equal to four or five thousand average Manx workers. Amongst the first to benefit were the owners of the remaining Mount Havelock properties, as one by one they were bought up by these new finance companies and renovated to provide smart offices equipped with the latest in world-wide telephonic communications, fax machines, electronic copiers and the latest in computer technology. To passers-by shiny brass plates indicate company names which give little idea of what goes on behind the

A view of Victoria Street in 1976 (Manx National Heritage)

Victoria Street Church and its accompanying schoolrooms in Thomas Street were demolished in 1977 to make way for the first Celtic Bank which is now occupied by Barclays Bank.

uPVC doors and windows; but it is all to do with finance in one form or another - banking, insurance, and investment, property and company management. No. 19 Mount Havelock is the base for the Europlan Trust Company (I.O.M.) Ltd. while opposite, at the bottom of Christian Road, stands the imposing building of the Bank of Ireland (I.O.M.) Ltd.

There are no more visitors staying in many other parts of Douglas. The changes that have taken place at Mount Havelock have been repeated many times over in both the central and lower parts of the town. No one envisaged the impact that the demands of this new 'industry' would have upon the appearance of the town. Office space was at a premium and developers sank many millions of pounds into prestigious office developments which have given the town a new look, with architects vying with each other to produce distinctive designs for their clients. The town has been transformed in a manner which has not found favour in all quarters. What has happened at Mount Havelock can be seen in such roads as Finch Road, Circular Road, Hill Street, Athol Street, Church Street, Ridgeway Street, Victoria Street, Prospect Hill and now Peel Road. Many landmarks and well-known buildings of the town have been demolished to make way for these new developments. One of the wealthiest developers has been Mr Albert Gubay whose Clinch's Brewery site on the North Quay has found general favour while the former Regal Cinema in Victoria Street was demolished to make way for Mr Gubay's Celtic Bank. Some of the original buildings of 1878 in Victoria Street have also succumbed to demolition, not least the edifice of Victoria Street Methodist Church. Its modern replacement first housed the independent Celtic Bank and is now the centre for the varied activities of Barclays Bank Plc. Opposite, stands the newly-built Queen Victoria House now housing the headquarters of Manx Telecom which has flourished from providing its vital services to the office fraternity. To many the site will be remembered as the ironmongery and hardware showroom of Gellings whose actual iron foundry was on the South Quay.

Demolition has seen the demise of the historic Fort Anne, the prime site awaiting some future development; the Peveril Hotel has been replaced with another block of offices while the fate of the Villiers site has at last been decided. The Villiers Hotel has been demolished along with its neighbours including the Belvedere and Athol Hotels leaving a yawning gap to be filled by an

Victoria Street after conversion to one-way traffic

Queen Victoria House, complete with Her Majesty.

office complex employing the latest building technology. Indications are that the new complex, incorporating bay windows and dormers, will harmonise with the traditional Victorian appearance of the Loch Promenade. And so the pattern of change has been set, a pattern which will continue well into the twenty-first century.

DOUGLAS 2000 was launched in 1992 to plan for the next century; to maintain the impetus of modern developments while preserving the best of the old Victorian town. To achieve this DOUGLAS 2000 has been formed from a partnership of Douglas Corporation, three Government Departments, the Isle of Man Chamber of Commerce and numerous supportive local business concerns. One of the first aims has been to improve the general appearance of the town, especially the main shopping areas, by the cosmetic use of floral initiatives (600 features), new pedestrian signs, civic painting with the new colours of blue and gold, new litter bins and other street furniture, distinctive statues and improved shop fronts. Perhaps the most successful and pleasing project so far has been the glazing along the Villa Marina Colonnade making it possible for the passer-by to enjoy the Villa Gardens.

Douglas undoubtedly is a flourishing town; its population has reached almost saturation point at 22,200, its native population now outnumbered by those who have arrived to join in the booming finance sector or to work on the office construction. Beyond the town boundaries private housing developments have kept pace with the office developments. Businesses have flourished to service the finance industry, just as they did a century ago to service the visiting industry. The money circulates to the benefit of stores, shops, hotels and restaurants. Taxes enable Central Government to employ more and more staff in modern offices; rates are paid to the Town Hall so that the dignity of the town can be maintained. But the town is not without its stresses and strains, a major problem being caused by the daily influx of cars bringing their owners to their places of employment. With 40,000 cars, apart from other registered vehicles, the Isle of Man has more cars per head of population than any other country in Western Europe, if not in the world. So Douglas is confronted with a problem still to be solved; there should be either more parking spaces or fewer cars. A visitor returning after twenty years would notice with a certain amount of horror the proliferation of traffic signs and the heavy use of painted yellow lines. Traffic wardens have been introduced, while traffic lights abound along with one-way streets and restrictive parking signs which have even crept into the upper parts of the town.

In 1878 a statue was placed in the newly-completed Victoria Street. Appropriately it was a statue of the monarch the street was named after - Queen Victoria, in her coronation robes. It was positioned on the facade of Doyle's Victorian Bazaar, later occupied by Gelling's hardware store. Before the premises were demolished in 1987, the 7' 6" statue, weighing almost a ton, was gently removed to undergo a thorough restoration. The pearwood from which it was fashioned was found to be in remarkably good condition, after the many layers of paint had been removed. By 1990 the £2 million Queen Victoria House had been completed. And Her Majesty was not forgotten. In pristine condition she was placed in a corner niche at second floor level, ready to observe another century or more. Her face remains immutable, perhaps the best way to cope with the many changes that she has witnessed; though it would be interesting to know what she thinks about the traffic calming geometry inflicted on the once stately Victoria Street! More importantly, has she been amused by the changing face of Douglas?

This computerised drawing gives an indication of the development of the old Villiers Hotel block as projected for the international headquarters of AXA Equity and Law, investment managers. It will provide a new gateway to Douglas in the twenty-first century while retaining the essential characteristics of the old Victorian seafront as typified by the bay windows and dormers. The new complex will front Victoria Street, Loch Promenade and Regent Street while to the rear, in the old Villiers yard, a Town Square is envisaged with deciduous trees, outdoor seating, a cafe, and space for outdoor markets and public concerts. (By kind permission of AXA Equity and Law)

Clinch's, North Quay

Meghraj Centre, Upper Church Street

Belgravia House, Circular Road

Post Office Headquarters, Circular Road

AIB Bank, Finch Road

Standard Bank, Athol Street

St. Andrew's spire, Skandia House, Finch Road

THE TOWN HALL TODAY

The present Douglas Corporation comprises the worshipful the Mayor of Douglas and seventeen other elected members, three each being appointed to serve the six wards in the Borough - St. George's Ward, Victoria Ward, Hill's Ward, Derby Ward, Murray's Ward and Athol Ward. Until 1989 there were twenty-four members, six being elected as Aldermen by the Councillors and the remaining eighteen being elected members.

The Council meets once a month but most of its business is delegated to four standing committees, these being:-

The Policy and Resources Committee
The Public Health and Housing Committee
The Leisure Services Committee
The Public Works Committee

There are other special committees that meet for specific ancillary or time-limited purposes.

The number of Chief Officers serving the Council and Committees has been reduced to three, each of whom is responsible for the provision of a part of the Council's services currently grouped in the following way:-

1. TOWN CLERK AND CHIEF EXECUTIVE'S DEPARTMENT:

Common corporate services (legal, personnel, management, information, common services and performance review).

The formation of recommended policy for consideration by members through Chief Officers' Management Team.

Common secretarial and administrative services to Members, the Council, Committees and Departments. Support for the Mayoralty, ceremonial and civic activities.

The provision and management of:

Byelaws and statute revision;
Car parks;
Cemetery and Crematorium;
Douglas 2000 and other co-ordination with Government and outside bodies;
Entertainments and leisure functions;
Environmental health;
Housing administration;
Letting of Council properties;
Parks and Gardens;
Theatre, street trading and other licensing functions;
Town Hall buildings and telephones;
Taxi-cab licensing;
Tramways.

The above services are currently operated by a full-time equivalent work force of 74 employees.

2. BOROUGH TREASURER'S DEPARTMENT:

SUPERVISION AND CONTROL OF COUNCIL'S MONETARY ACTIVITIES

Income Section
The levy and collection of the general rate;
The collection of rents and charges (e.g. housing and commercial tenants);
The receipt of miscellaneous income (e.g. car park revenues and charges for refuse collection bins);
The issue of capital bonds;
The investment of surplus funds.

Expenditure Section
Payments to creditors and payroll services;
Budgetary advice and control;
Provision of financial information and advice;
Computer services;
Local Government Superannuation Services for the Island, internal audit services and insurance - see contracted-out services (4).
The Borough Library

The above services are currently operated by a full-time equivalent work force of 22 employees under the Borough Treasurer, Mr R.P. Lynch, IPFA.

3. BOROUGH TECHNICAL OFFICER'S DEPARTMENT

Refuse collection and street cleaning;
Building Control (building work, dilapidations etc.);
Street and decorative lighting;
Design and provision of new local authority housing;
Maintenance of all property under the ownership of Douglas Corporation;
Drainage and surface water maintenance;
Maintenance and purchase of Corporation-owned vehicles;
Consultation with Department of Transport on highway and drainage matters in Douglas;
Consultation with the Department of Local Government and the Environment on planning, environmental health and housing matters in Douglas;
Consultation with Department of Tourism on major tourist events in Douglas.

The above services are currently operated by a full-time equivalent of 106 employees under the Acting Borough Technical Officer, Mr B.D. Halsall MCIOD, MSST, pending the appointment of a permanent Chief Officer.

4. CONTRACTED-OUT SERVICES

A number of the Council's services are operated on a contractual basis, either in whole or part, in order to provide maximum cost-effectiveness. Examples are some refuse collection services, painting, superannuation, insurance and internal audit. Together with the provision of other direct Council-provided services, they illustrate the Council's desire for ongoing improvements to its services. Like any business, the Corporation is increasingly looking at ways in which it can more effectively deliver value for money services geared to the needs of its customers.

The Town Clerk and Chief Executive is the Council's principal paid official who, together with the other two Chief Officers, makes appropriate recommendations to Committees of the Council and provides services in accordance with such levels and other requirements as are set by the Council's eighteen elected representatives. Some of the services provided by the Council are provided on an agency basis for Central Government. The present revenue expenditure of the Corporation on both its own and agency services amounts to a figure of £12.1 million for 1995/96. A further £4.4 million will be expended during the current year on capital schemes.

The Council is facing particular challenges at the time of its own Centenary and the approaching year 2000. It has strongly supported all realistic developments designed to equip Douglas for the needs and challenges of the next decade and beyond. Examples are to be found in increasing joint working with Government Departments and the private sector, first through the medium of Douglas 2000 but also through joint proposals with Government Departments for the restoration of the capital's sewerage infrastructure; the provision of large scale leisure facilities in providing land for the National Sports Centre's first and second phase; and the refurbishment of the Villa Marina site and its proposed operation in partnership with the Gaiety Theatre. The Council looks forward to further joint initiatives of this kind with the object of satisfying those who live and work in Douglas and to promote the Town of Douglas as the Island's capital, both in growing and in developing to meet current and future needs.

The Corporation is the only public body on the Isle of Man that is empowered to bestow the honour of Freeman of the Borough on persons who have been selected for the services that they may have given to the Borough and/or the Island as a whole. Names of those on the Roll of Honour are set out under Appendix I.

As we come full circle at the end of one hundred years, we are reminded of those predecessor Mayors, members and officers who have given so much to Douglas in the past - it provides us with a reminder of all that they have achieved and of the responsibility now placed upon the shoulders of all those who serve the Council today both as members and officers to live up to their achievements. As a mark of that respect the Town Hall has recently been refurbished externally to reveal for the first time in many years the civic centre that was built almost one hundred years ago.

The Corporation has played a significant role in the development of the Island through its initiation of a public water supply, environmental health and fire services, public transport and the generating of electricity.

The Corporation is proud in having played such a significant role in the development of the Island and looks forward to working closely in partnership with Government to provide services of the highest standard to meet the needs of this important capital town and seat of Government.

David R. King Ll.B.

Town Clerk and Chief Executive.

Co-operation between Corporation and Government has seen the creation of the National Sports Centre on the site of the former King George V Park. (Island Photographics)

APPENDIX I

THE BOROUGH'S CIVIC INSIGNIA

The **Mayoral Mace** was presented to the Council by Alderman Samuel Webb as a memento of his Mayoralty, 1898-1900. It is of silver-gilt throughout, nearly four feet in height and has a finial in the form of a Maltese Cross. On the Head is emblazoned in enamel the Arms of the Borough of Douglas, with the motto on the scroll beneath.

The Head, which is also liberally relieved with large and well-cut carbuncles and amethysts, is supported by three brackets, ornamented with the letter 'D', indicating Douglas. The town being a fishing port, beneath the Head are engraved figures representing dolphins. The staff is beautifully wrought and is chastely engraved with entwining garlands.

The larger boss of the staff is decorated with the Three Legs and the Royal Crown is engraved near the foot of the staff. The Donor's monogram, S.W., is also shown, it being tastefully executed in gold on a blue enamel ground. Surrounding the boss the words 'Borough of Douglas' appear in bold relief.

The **Mayoral Chain** was presented by Major Robert S. Stephen, Mayor of the Borough from 1896-1898.

The **Mayoral Social Chain** was provided by bequest of the late Rev. Canon F.M. Cubbon, Hon. C.F., D.C.

The **Mayoress's Chain** was the gift of Miss E.E. Oates and Mrs M.M. Quayle in memory of their brother, Councillor James N. Oates, who was a Member of the Council from 1923-1931.

The **Mayoress's Brooch** was presented by Mrs E. Quayle in memory of her husband, Alderman R.F. Quayle J.P., former Mayor and Member of the Council from 1940 to 1975.

The **Deputy Mayor's Badge** was presented by Alderman F.M. Corkill in commemoration of his term of office as Mayor, 1947 to 1949.

The **Deputy Mayoress's Badge** was the gift of the late Rev. Canon F.M. Cubbon, Hon. C.F., D.C.

The **Mayoral Robes** were presented to the Council in 1955 and replaced in November, 1973, by the late Rev. Canon F.M. Cubbon, Hon. C.F., D.C.

The **Oak and Teak Case** in which to carry the Chains of Office of the Mayor and Mayoress was presented by Alderman J.E. Collister in commemoration of his term of office as Mayor, 1966 to 1968.

FREEMEN OF THE BOROUGH : ROLL OF HONOUR

1924: The Right Honourable the Earl of Derby, K.G., P.C., G.C.V.O., C.B.

1926: Mr Alderman J.T. Faragher, J.P.

1929: Sir Hall Caine, K.B.E., C.H., J.P., O.O.L.

1930: Mr Alexander Robertson, O.B.E., J.P., ex-Town Clerk.

1932: Mr Alderman R. Corlett, J.P.

1948: Field Marshall the Viscount Montgomery of Alamein, K.G., G.C.B. D.S.O.

1950: Mr Alderman J.H. Skillicorn.

1955: Freedom of entry into Douglas granted to Royal Air Force Station, Jurby.

1956: His Honour Deemster Sir Percy Cowley, C.B.E.

1957: The Right Honourable Sir Winston Churchill, K.G., O.M., C.H., F.R.S., M.P.

1964: Mr Alderman J.C. Fargher.
 : Mr Alderman A.J. Teare, M.B.E., J.P.

1975: Mr Alderman R.F. Quayle, J.P.
 : Mr Alderman W.B. Kaneen.
 : Mr Alderman T.D. Lewis, O. St. J., J.P.
 : Mr Alderman T.A. Corkish.

1985: Mr Alderman W.A. Moore.

1986: Mr Alderman C. Simpson.
 : Mr Alderman F.E. Griffin.

1989: Mr F.D. Buxton.

1994: Mr Norman Wisdom.

APPENDIX II

CHURCHES AND SCHOOLS OF DOUGLAS

Douglas fell outside the normal arrangement so far as Church organisation was concerned because, although it lay in the civil parish of Onchan, ecclesiastically it was joined to Braddan. This still gives the townspeople certain rights with regards to Braddan Church. The parish system was probably set up in the second quarter of the twelfth century when the parish churches superceded the treen chapels which had previously existed. The treen of Douglas extended along the river to a point close to the present Tromode Park Estate and then the boundary returned via St. Ninian's and Glencrutchery Road to the seashore near Castle Mona. We do not know where the treen chapel was situated but probably it was near the harbour on the site later occupied by the town chapel but which had various dedications ascribed to it - St. Mary, St. Martin and St. Peter. All we know about this chapel is that it was there when Daniel King prepared his view of Douglas in 1651 (see page 5) and that it was in disrepair by the end of that century. The site was sold off about the time that **St. Matthew's** was consecrated by Bishop Wilson in 1708. St. Matthew's stood on a site which is now the rear part of the Old Cast Iron Market, now the British Legion Club, and was erected as a chaplaincy under Kirk Braddan. However, despite the building of the new chapel Kirk Braddan needed to create a gallery in 1737 and to undergo alterations in 1774.

The first three quarters of the eighteenth century had seen a dramatic increase in the population of Douglas and in 1761 work started on a totally new church on a 'green field site' outside the town - **St. George's**. A committee was sent to Whitehaven to copy the design from a church there which led to problems which were only rectified in later extensions and alterations. However, before the work

was completed Revestment had occurred, finance dried up and work ceased for a long period. The church was only completed in 1780. St. George's had one of the first organs fitted in Manx churches, this having being brought from Dublin though apparently not, as commonly thought, the organ used for the first performance of Handel's 'Messiah.'

1758 had seen the first of the Methodist Preachers visiting the Island but it was not until 1775, with the arrival of John Crook and the visits of John Wesley himself in 1777 and 1781, that Methodism became a major force. Whilst the first Methodist Chapel on the Island was built at Peel, Douglas was not far behind with **Thomas Street** opening in 1787. This chapel was rebuilt with a much increased capacity in 1819.

By 1837 numbers had risen to a point where a new chapel - **Well Road Hill** - was required.

In the meantime there were those who felt that Methodism had moved far from its evangelistic origins and in particular had given up its open-air meetings. Those who tried to redress this were removed from membership and so Primitive Methodism was born. John Butcher missioned the Isle of Man for the 'Prims' in 1822 and by 1824 there were eighteen preaching places including one in Preaching House Lane (now Wellington Street) almost opposite to the Wesleyan Thomas Street Chapel. **Wellington Street Primitive Methodist Chapel** (as it became) was rebuilt in the 1830s and extended and a hall added (the Bourne Hall in Drumgold Street) following a visit by the Rev. Hugh Bourne in 1839.

The episcopacy of Rev. William Ward in the 1830s led to a big building campaign by the Church of England throughout the Island but marked in Douglas by the building of **St. Barnabas** in 1832 and the arrival of the Floating Chapel - an ex-Royal Navy

frigate supplied through the good offices of Earl Grey (of tea fame) and known as the de Grey or **Mariners Church**. It was ultimately broken up in 1846.

All but one of the Bishop Ward churches were designed by Hansom and Welch, Messrs. Welch or John Welch, and this included St. Barnabas. John Welch also designed the Scotch Kirk - **St. Andrew's** - which opened in 1832 although founded seven years earlier. It was rebuilt in 1867 and the Sunday School buildings added in 1909.

Roman Catholic numbers, which had been minimal since the Reformation, had started to increase during the hectic trading days prior to Revestment (1765) but it was not until 1814 that they opened their first church at Park View on the Old Castletown Road and dedicated to St. Bridget. Numbers continued to grow and after using a number of 'temporary' premises, including No 1 Athol Street, they opened the present St. Mary's in 1859 to some unseemly opposition from the other denominations.

The Anglicans were also having problems, but internal ones, regarding the appointment of Vicars at **St. Thomas's Church** following its completion in 1849. These problems rumbled on until it was created a separate parish in 1872. St. Barnabas had become a separate parish three years earlier.

An **Independent Chapel (Congregational)** had been built in Athol Street in 1811 but they moved from this to new buildings in Finch Road in 1866 and also to another in Circular Road but this was disbanded in 1883; the building was used as the first meeting place of the Douglas Corps of the Salvation Army.

As the town spread and its population grew so new churches were built and old ones expanded. These included:

St. George's Church, completed 1780.

St. Barnabas Church, opened 1832.

St. Thomas's Church, built 1849.

Thomas Street Methodist Chapel, rebuilt 1819.

Well Road Hill Methodist Chapel, 1837.

Wellington Street Primitive Methodist Chapel of the 1830s.

ANGLICAN

1897 - **St. Matthew's** rebuilt on a new site on the North Quay as a result of town development.

1898 - **All Saints** - the 'Tin Tabernacle' opened.

1913 - **St. Ninian's** opened.

1933 - St. George's Hall built.

1965 - The 'Tin Tabernacle' demolished and the new All Saints built, being consecrated in 1967.

METHODIST

1878 - **Loch Parade (Primitive) Church** opened.

1886 - **Rosemount (Wesleyan) Church** opened. Spire completed in 1911.

1893 - **Salisbury Street Church** opened.

1931 - sees the uniting of Wesleyans, Primitives and New Connection Methodists.

1935 - **Pulrose Church/Hall** opened.

1960 - **Willaston Church** opened and incorporated the organ from the Circular Road **Seamen's Bethel** (ex Congregational) which had closed three years earlier.

Other short-lived ventures were the **Esplanade Chapel** and the **Redferns Mission.**

ROMAN CATHOLIC

1939 - **Church of the Sacred Heart** opened in Pulrose.

1954 - **St. Joseph's, Willaston** opened.

SALVATION ARMY

1932 - Foundation stone laid for their Citadel in Lord Street following the redevelopment of this area. The Salvation Army had been present in strength holding meetings in various locations in the old part of the town since 1883.

BAPTIST

The Broadway **Baptist Church** first opened in 1893 but has been rebuilt and extensively altered in recent years.

The movement of people away from the town centre and the fall in church attendance have more recently compounded to effect more changes. In 1957 St Barnabas Church closed and the parish merged with St. George's which also included All Saints. More recently still All Saints has 'moved' to join forces with St. Thomas's. St. Barnabas Church was demolished in 1969 and its Sunday School buildings in Market Street in 1981.

Rosemount and Bucks Road Methodist Churches united in 1967 to form **Trinity Church** at Rosemount. The Bucks Road premises were sold to become offices. Well Road Hill Church closed in 1950, effectively merging with Victoria Street which, in 1972 then joined with Loch Parade. The latter was bebuilt as the **Promenade Methodist Church** which opened in 1976. In 1977 Victoria Street Church was demolished to be replaced with the Celtic Bank building, now Barclays Bank.

Marathon Road Chapel was closed in 1978 and was sold to The Quakers although they have since resold it.

Nationally, the Congregational Church and the **Presbyterian Church** joined forces to become the **United Reform Church**. Locally, however, Finch Hill and St. Andrew's retained their own identities although under a single combined ministry. Ultimately both buildings closed and St. Andrew's relocated to the former Scout Headquarters adjoining the grounds of St. Ninian's Church.

Other places of worship present in the town now include the following:

Christadelphian Ecclesia.

Christian Brethren Assembly, Little Switzerland Road.

First Church of Christ Scientist, Woodbourne Road.

The Greater World Christian Spiritualist Church, Lower Duke's Road.

The Elim Pentecostal Church, Park Road.

Jehovah's Witnesses, Albany Road.

The Church of Jesus Christ and Latter Day Saints, Woodbourne Road.

SCHOOLS

In 1700 Bishop Wilson established the Douglas Grammar School in Bond Street to complement those of Castletown, Ramsey and Peel. Following the building of St. Matthew's Church, overlooking the open market place on the North Quay, the Grammar School was placed in charge of the chaplain. Instruction took place within the church until 1714 when the school moved to a new

St. Mary's R.C. Church, built 1859.

St. Andrew's Presbyterian Church, rebuilt 1867.

St. Matthew's Church, rebuilt 1897.

Victoria Street Methodist Church of 1878 showing on the left the Thomas Street building used as a school.

Interior of Victoria Street Church with seating for a congregation of two thousand.

building - Dickson's House. The purpose of the Grammar School was to provide boys aged ten and over with a classical education based on Greek and Latin. This would form the basis for those seeking to qualify for taking holy orders. Throughout the century there were some eminent schoolmasters in charge of the school, but it came to an end following the departure in 1832 of the Rev Robert Brown (father of Thomas Edward) to take up his appointment to Braddan Church. In 1858 a New Grammar School was opened in Dalton Street, again for fee-paying boys, but who were now taught a much wider curriculum.

The eighteenth century saw the growing need for education met by the opening of denominational schools. By far the largest of these was the National (Church of England) School opened in Athol Street in 1810. In 1824 the first St. Mary's R.C. School was opened in two cottages, still standing, opposite the Nunnery Grounds on the Old Castletown Road. An influx of Irish fleeing from the famine in 1848 saw the school moving to larger premises in Fort Street, and a new school was built in Finch Hill in 1862. With the National School in Athol Street overflowing the Barrack Street School was opened in 1839 for children connected with St. George's

Church. St. Barnabas had its own school since being built in 1832. St. **Thomas's C.of E. School** was opened in 1879. The Methodist Church held their day schools in Thomas Street from 1841 to which was added the school belonging to Well Road Hill.

Besides the denominational schools there were many private schools which flourished for the better-off though they varied considerably in the standards they offered their pupils. At the same time there were many children in the poorer part of the town - the 'waifs and strays' - to whom the idea of sitting in a classroom was entirely foreign.

In 1872 Tynwald passed the Education Act which for the first time established a national system of education and placed a large share of the cost on the revenue of the Island. It had to overcome strong opposition from the churches who were reluctant to lose their influence over the young of their congregations. The far-sighted Act provided for the establishment of School Boards in every town and parish; attendance was to be compulsory for all children between the ages of 7 and 13; non-denominational education was to be given in all but Roman Catholic Schools. Subsequently children of 5 years came within the scope of the Act.

In Douglas, elections for the School

Board were fiercely contested with many opponents of the Act gaining seats. But it was one such member who courageously changed from opposition to become the leading protagonist on behalf of the new Board Schools. He was William Isdale, Postmaster of the Isle of Man. As a boy he had attended St. Barnabas School free of charge, his widowed mother being unable to pay the weekly pence. It was largely through his efforts, and the respect he gained from others, that the Board's first purpose-built school was opened in **Tynwald Street** in 1882. Within the same building an Infants School for 5-year olds was opened in 1884 under a separate Headmistress. Subsequent schools within the town are detailed as follows:

1889 - **Hanover Street School** opened with separate Infants department for boys and girls.
1894 - **Higher Grade Board School** (The Douglas School of Science) opened in Park Road for boys and girls, many of the boys transferring from Dalton Street Grammar School.
1894 - **St Mary's (R.C.) School** opened at Mount Havelock.
1899 - **Murray's Road School** opened with separate Infants School.
1907 - **Demesne Road Boys School** opened, boys drawn from Athol Street School which was closed, and

Loch Parade Primitive Methodist Church, 1878.

Rosemount Methodist Church opened in 1886. Spire completed in 1911.

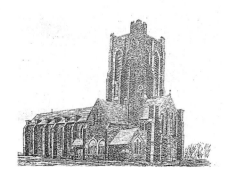

St. Ninian's Church opened in 1913.

The Higher Grade Board School in Park Road. Opened in 1894 it was renamed the Eastern District Secondary School in 1924 and the Douglas High School for Girls in 1927.

Tynwald Street which became **Tynwald Street Girls School**.

1922 - Isle of Man Education Authority formed bringing together all Board Schools.

1922 - Park Road School renamed **Eastern District Secondary School**.

1927 - **Douglas High School for Boys** opened at St. Ninian's.

1927 - **Douglas High School for Girls** at Park Road.

1937 - **Pulrose Infants School** opened, known locally as 'The Sunshine School' because of its modern design.

1946 - Multilateral education, the forerunner of Comprehensive education, was introduced for all children of secondary school age with the opening of the **Ballakermeen Schools** where the first three years were spent before proceeding to the Douglas High Schools at Park Road (Girls) and St. Ninian's (Boys).

Hanover Street School and senior departments of other schools closed.

1948 - Education Act brought Manx educational system into complete line with the English 1944 Act with provision for Primary, Secondary and Further Education.

Private schools which continued to function until comparatively recent times included the Collegiate, Ingleby School, Convent R.C. School and St. Francis High School.

1955 - **Willaston Infants School** opened.

1964 - Willaston school extended to become **Willaston Primary School**.

1964 - New St. Mary's R.C. Primary School opened.

1967 - Murray's Road Junior and Infants Schools were closed and a new combined school opened - **Murray's Road Junior Mixed and Infants School** - it being built on the playground of the old building which was demolished.

1968 - Education Authority amalgamated with Isle of Man Board of Education.

1970 - **Ballaquayle Infants School** opened, leaving Murray's Road to become a Junior Mixed school.

By 1972 the **Isle of Man College of Further Education** was formed combining the Kensington Road Art School, the Domestic Science College in Kingswood Grove, engineering classes in Hanover Street and all Evening Classes. The College building in Homefield Road was officially opened 9th May, 1975 since when there have been extensions built to accommodate the growing number of courses provided.

1973 - Demesne Road Boys School closed and modified to become **Ballacloan Infants School**, taking in the infants from Tynwald Street Infants School. Tynwald Street school was renamed **Fairfield Junior Mixed School**.

1973 - **Manor Park Junior School** opened.

1974 - Ballakermeen became a co-educational school as **Ballakermeen Junior High School**. Children advanced to Douglas High School at St. Ninian's with use being made of accommodation and facilities at Park Road.

1974 - **Glencrutchery Special School** was officially opened.

1976 - **Anagh Coar Primary School** opened.

1985 - Secondary Schools re-organised into two all-through and separate schools - **Ballakermeen High School** and **St. Ninian's High School**, the latter having its Lower School at Park Road.

1986 - Pulrose Infants School closed, children transferring to **Manor Park Primary School**.

1990 - College of Further Education renamed **Isle of Man College** following the introduction of degree-level courses.

Murray's Road School, with separate Infants School, was opened in 1899.

The new Murray's Road School opened in 1967.

MEMBERS OF THE TOWN COUNCIL 1896-1996

(including those who were former Town Commissioners)

Thomas Keig	1874-1896
John Curphey	1874-1881
	1884-1902
Samuel Webb	1881-1903
Alexander Lewthwaite	1882-1889
	1892-1904
William Proctor	1883-1886
	1887-1892
	1895-1904
Joseph Hall	1887-1904
William Goldsmith	1887-1907
	1917-1923
Edmund Chadwick	1888-1904
John T. Faragher, J.P.	1890-1931
Andrew Caley	1887-1892
	1896-1915
Henry Brearley	1891-1920
John Barron	1893-1897
Robert Clucas	1894-1907
Robert Corlett, J.P.	1894-1940
Joseph Kaye	1894-1910
Robert Knox	1896-1898
Alfred Fleming	1896-1897
Robert G. Cottier	1896-1906
John Williams Clinch	1872-1874
	1896-1899
Robert H. Cubbon	1896-1904
Robert Moore	1896-1917
James Kewley	1896-1904
Joseph Carr	1896-1906
James Craine, J.P.	1896-1930
Robert S. Stephen	1896-1898
John Skillicorn	1896-1904
Robert Moughtin	1897-1900
	1906-1912
William Joughin	1897-1913
Arthur H. Marsden	1898-1911
George Thornley	1899-1908
Herbert Hambleton	1900-1904
Joseph Sharpe	1902-1910
Albert H. Fayle	1903-1910
William Radcliffe	1904-1906
Robert L. Cain	1904-1907
Alexander Gill	1904-1909
Robert J. Kelly	1904-1908
	1909-1916
John J. Gell	1904-1905
William Knox	1904-1905
	1911-1919
	1931-1934
Robert D. Cowin	1887-1896
	1904-1917
David Gray	1904-1925
Daniel Flinn	1905-1911
	1912-1919
William J. Corlett	1905-1911
Thomas M. L. Quayle	1906-1928
Robert Curphey	1906-1909
Alexander Hough	1892-1896
	1907-1910
Henry C. G. Clague	1907-1915
John Kelly	1907-1921
William F. Cowell	1908-1913
Francis Gale	1908-1948
John J. Corlett	1909-1944
Thomas G. Kelly	1910-1934
William Quirk, J.P.	1910-1932
William Ashburner	1910-1913
David Collister	1910-1928
Robert C. Cain, M.L.C.	1910-1923
Edward Corrin	1911-1921
John H. Kelly	1911-1911
Arthur B. Crookall, J.P., M.H.K.	1911-1932

George Gilmore	1913-1927
John Kelly (Christian Rd)	1913-1919
John J. Quine, J.P.	1913-1934
John William Parkes	1915-1923
John A. Gelling	1915-1917
Peter Milne	1916-1919
W.G.T. Hargrave	1917-1927
Thomas H. Cowin	1917-1923
	1925-1928
Sydney T. Shippam	1918-1922
Edwin Creer	1919-1925
William J. Corkill	1919-1932
Ramsey G. Johnson	1921-1931
James Hy. Skillicorn	1921-1954
Morris J. Forrester	1922-1926
James T. Clague	1923-1931
Robt. Hartwell Collister, J.P.	1888-1891
	1923-1934
James Nelson Oates	1923-1931
Edward. C. Hudson	1923-1949
Thomas W. Cain	1925-1942
John Holmes	1925-1936
Walter C. Craine, J.P., M.H.K.	1926-1959
D. Claude Shimmin	1927-1938
Robert Cowell	1927-1958
Thomas W. Shimmin	1928-1931
John C. Fargher	1928-1967
William R. Drennan	1928-1931
Thomas Cowell	1931-1951
James Ducker	1931-1943
Thomas. C. Cowin, M.H.K.	1931-1950
E. Herbert Faragher	1931-1940
George S. Johnson	1931-1935
Stephen A. Quirk, J.P.	1931-1954
William Henry Clucas	1932-1936
	1938-1946
Frederick H. Callow	1932-1939
Alfred J. Teare, M.B. E., M.L.C., J.P.	1933-1965
William D. Radcliffe	1934-1960
George P. Quine, M.H.K.	1934-1947
William Hough	1934-1940
Frank M. Corkill	1934-1963
Thomas Radcliffe, J.P.	1935-1954
Joseph A. Cain	1936-1955
Thomas H. Dunbar	1936-1944
Thomas Clucas	1939-1950
William S. Shimmin	1940-1946
John B. Bolton, M.L.C.	1940-1946
R. Fletcher Quayle	1940-1975
William D. Moore	1943-1947
Joseph Ashton	1943-1946
Frank H. Gore	1945-1953
Thomas H. Shimmin	1945-1954
Robert. C. Collister	1946-1966
George E. Craine	1946-1956
Thomas A. Quirk, J.P.	1946-1955
	1957-1963
William B. Kaneen	1946-1957
	1958-1980
John J. Quaye	1947-1949
	1950-1952
Thomas William Kneale, M.Eng.	1947-1956
T. Douglas Lewis, J.P.	1949-1957
	1958-1978
Evan Gill	1949-1961
John R. Killip	1949-1958
Percy Coupe	1950-1953
	1954-1957
R. C. Stephen, M.H.K.	1951-1959
Henry W. Callow	1952-1955

T. Albert Corkish	1953-1978
Harold M. Rowell	1953-1958
Fred Faragher	1954-1959
Joseph H. Moore	1954-1965
W. Alexander Moore	1954-1971
Stanley J. Cain	1955-1957
	1968-1973
Fred Royle	1955-1965
James E. Callister	1955-1974
Charles E. Burke, M.H.K.	1956-1971
Edgar C. Hamill	1956-1971
Ramsey L. Quayle	1957-1966
Crawford A. Kinley	1957-1966
Edward Callister, M.H.K.	1957-1963
Morris S. A. Forrester	1958-1961
Harold H. Furlong	1959-1964
Laurence W. Astin	1959-1963
Robert Harold Teare	1959-1972
Mrs. M. Alana Griffiths	1960-1969
Robert G. Lees	1961-1967
Cyril Simpson	1961-1989
James Haydn T. Wood	1963-1969
Steven G. Quirk	1963-1971
John J. Bell	1963-1968
	1969-1971
Mrs. Gwen Cannell	1963-1965
Frederick E. Griffin	1964-1988
G. Alfred Devereau, M.H.K.	1965-1968
John Parkinson	1965-1974
Kenneth K. Teare	1965-1966
Ernest Ackary	1966-1989
Wilfred Ward	1966-1989
Inkerman A. Faragher	1966-1969
	1970-1976
	1979-1982
	1983-1983
	1985-1987
	1990-1993
William Shimmin	1966-1980
Frederick J. Waterson	1966-1989
	1990-1992
Harold Richmond	1967-1970
Wilfred C. Halsall	1968-1972
E. Matthew Ward	1968-1974
Harold Cunningham	1969-1983
Frederick Griffin	1969-1972
Brian Delaney	1971-1973
Douglas W. Kerruish	1971-1973
Dennis A. Cowley	1971-1975
Roy N. Birch	1972-1975
	1977-1985
Paul Hardinge	1972-1976
	1977-1978
Mrs. K. Mary Halsall	1972-1982
Miss L. May Teare	1972-1982
	1988-1989
Dominic F. K. Delaney	1972-1975
	1976-1976
Norman Chatel	1973-1977
A. Leonard Costain	1973-1977
David Martin	1973-1976
	1977-1981
Thomas F. Cain	1974-1979
Mrs. Joan M. Cowin	1974-1977
Daniel T. Cannon	1974-1986
Alfred Duggan	1975-1987
	1988-1992
Brian Gelling	1975-1981
T. Douglas Jones	1976-1977
Adrian C. Duggan	1976-1981
Norman E. Mills	1976-1982
Michael J. Shimmin	1976-1985
	1986-1989

Arthur T. Quilliam	1976-1983	Roy F. Hall	1982-1985	David W. Christian	1987-1994	
	1984-1989	John A. S. Christian	1982-1995		1995-	
Mrs. Audrey A. Ainsworth	1977-1986	Roy D. Cain	1982-	Charles A. K. Dougherty	1987-1994	
George Jolley	1978-1980	David C. Cretney	1983-1985	R. Abba Oates	1987-	
George S. Shimmin	1979-1984	Mrs. Julia Delaney	1983-1986	John Morley	1990-1994	
Reginald Owen	1979-1980	J. Basil Callow	1984-		1995-	
Bernard May	1980-1985	Albert Kelly	1985-1987	Peter B. Warriner	1992-1995	
Edward C. Hill	1980-1990	Patrick T. Bell	1985-	Mrs. Brenda J. Cannell	1992-1995	
Norman G. Cadwallader	1980-1987	Peter A. Craine	1985-1992	Mrs. Doreen M. Kinrade	1993-	
Philip W. Kermode	1981-1986	Mrs. Raina Chatel	1985-1995	Richard H. McNicholl	1993-	
Ernest Humphrey	1981-1984	Kevin C. Kelly	1985-1988	Mrs. June T. Craine	1994-	
George R. Chatel	1982-1990	William J. Corkish	1985-1992	Kenneth J. Whipp	1994-	
	1991-		1993-	William R. Jones	1994-	
Frederick A. Kennish	1982-1985	Miss Barbara J. Quine	1986-1993	Miss F. Margaret Joughin	1944-	
	1986-	Alexander F. Downie	1987-1991	Mrs Elizabeth C. Quirk	1995-	
Stephen R. Pitts	1982-1985	James R. Mitchell	1987-1991			
	1992-		1992-1994			
			1995-			

TOWN CLERKS OF THE BOROUGH

Thomas Nesbitt	1896-1898	Walter Mylrea	1978-1982
Alexander Robertson	1898-1930	Donald R. Peers, Ll.B.	1983-1992
Percy Shimmin	1931-1955	David R. King, Ll.B.	1992-
Douglas N. Blakey	1955-1978		

THE TOWN COUNCIL 1995-96

Back Row, left to right: Councillor R. H. McNicholl; B. D. Halsall (Acting Borough Technical Officer); R. P. Lynch (Borough Treasurer); The Mayor, Councillor W. J. Corkish; D. R. King (Town Clerk); Councillors F. A. Kennish; J. B. Callow and J. R. Mitchell. Middle Row: Councillors D. W. Christian; S. R. Pitts; P. T. Bell; K. J. Whipp; R. A. Oates and R. D. Cain. Front Row: Councillors G. R. Chatel; Mrs J. T. Craine; Mrs D. M. Kissack; Mrs E. C. Quirk; Miss E. M. Joughin and J. Morley. (Councillor W. R. Jones - absent.)

MAYORS OF THE BOROUGH : 1896 - 1996

1896	- Alderman Thomas Keig
1896	- Major R. S. Stephen
1898	- Alderman Samuel Webb
1900/01	- Alderman Joseph Hall
1901/02	- Alderman Samuel Webb
1902/03	- Alderman William Proctor
1903/04	- Alderman Robert H. Cubbon
1904	- Alderman Edmund Chadwick
1904/05	- Alderman Joseph Kaye
1905/06	- Alderman John T. Faragher J.P.
1906/08	- Councillor Joseph Sharpe
1908/10	- Councillor Arthur H. Marsden
1910/12	- Alderman William Joughin
1912/14	- Alderman Robert Corlett J.P.
1914/16	- Councillor Daniel Flinn
1916/18	- Alderman John T. Faragher J.P.
1918/20	- Alderman John Kelly
1920/22	- Alderman Thomas G. Kelly
1922/27	- Alderman Arthur B. Crookall J.P., M.H.K.
1927/30	- Alderman William Quirk J.P.
1930/32	- Alderman William J. Corkill
1932/33	- Alderman Edward C. Hudson
1933/35	- Alderman James H. Skillicorn
1935/37	- Alderman Thomas W. Cain
1937/39	- Councillor Walter C. Craine J.P., M.H.K.
1939/41	- Councillor John C. Fargher
1941/43	- Alderman Francis Gale
1943/45	- Alderman Stephen A. Quirk J.P.
1945/47	- Councillor Thomas C. Cowin M.H.K.
1947/49	- Councillor Frank M. Corkill
1949/51	- Councillor Thomas Radcliffe J.P.
1951/53	- Councillor Joseph A. Cain
1953/55	- Councillor R. Fletcher Quayle J.P.
1955/57	- Councillor William B. Kaneen
1957/58	- Councillor John R. Killip
1958/60	- Councillor T. Douglas Lewis J.P.
1960/62	- Alderman Thomas A Quirk J.P.
1962/64	- Councillor T. Albert Corkish
1964/65	- Alderman Joseph H. Moore
1965/66	- Alderman W. Alexander Moore
1966/68	- Alderman James E. Callister
1968/69	- Councillor Charles E. Burke M.H.K.
1969/70	- Councillor Edgar C. Hamill
1970/71	- Councillor Cyril Simpson
1971/72	- Councillor Frederick E. Griffin
1972/73	- Councillor John Parkinson
1973/74	- Councillor Ernest Ackary
1974/75	- Councillor William Shimmin
1975/76	- Councillor Frederick J. Waterson
1976/77	- Councillor Wilfred Ward
1977/78	- Councillor Harold Cunningham
1978/79	- Councillor Mrs K. Mary Halsall
1979/80	- Councillor Miss L. May Teare
1980/81	- Councillor Inkerman A. Faragher
1981/82	- Alderman Frederick E. Griffin
1982/83	- Councillor Daniel T. Cannon
1983/84	- Alderman Roy N. Birch
1984/85	- Councillor Alfred Duggan
1985/86	- Councillor Mrs Audrey A. Ainsworth
1986/87	- Councillor Edward C. Hill
1987/89	- Councillor Michael J. Shimmin
1989/90	- Councillor Frederick A. Kennish
1990/91	- Councillor Roy D. Cain
1991/92	- Councillor John A.S. Christian
1992/93	- Councillor J. Basil Callow
1993/94	- Councillor George R. Chatel
1994/95	- Councillor Mrs Raina Chatel
1995/96	- Councillor William J. Corkish

ACKNOWLEDGMENTS

The editor wishes to acknowledge the valuable co-operation received from the Town Clerk and various members of his staff; Manx National Heritage including Mr Roger Simms, Archivist, and staff of the Museum Library; and the many others who have assisted in the preparation of this Centenary publication.

Photographs and illustrations are from Town Hall sources and from The Manx Experience unless otherwise acknowledged.

Cover photography by Susan Jones

The Manx Experience

Edited and designed by
GORDON N. KNIVETON

Published by
The Manx Experience, 45 Slieau Dhoo, Tromode Park, Douglas
in conjunction with
The Centenary Committee of Douglas Corporation.

Typesetting and preparation for printing by The Manx Experience.

Photographic scanning by Mannin Repro, Spring Valley, Douglas.

Printed and bound by The Alden Press, Oxford.